INTRODUCTION TO
ALCOHOL RESEARCH

INTRODUCTION TO ALCOHOL RESEARCH

Implications for Treatment, Prevention, and Policy

DANIEL YALISOVE

John Jay College of Criminal Justice

Boston ■ New York ■ San Francisco
Mexico City ■ Montreal ■ Toronto ■ London ■ Madrid ■ Munich ■ Paris
Hong Kong ■ Singapore ■ Tokyo ■ Cape Town ■ Sydney

Series Editor: *Kelly May*
Editorial Assistant: *Marlana Voerster*
Marketing Manager: *Wendy Gordon*
Editorial-Production Service: *Omegatype Typography, Inc.*
Manufacturing Buyer: *JoAnne Sweeney*
Composition and Prepress Buyer: *Linda Cox*
Cover Administrator: *Kristina Mose-Libon*
Electronic Composition: *Omegatype Typography, Inc.*

Library of Congress Cataloging-in-Publication Data

Yalisove, Daniel L.
    Introduction to alcohol research : implications for treatment, prevention, and policy /
Daniel Yalisove.
        p. cm.
    Includes bibliographical references and index.
    ISBN 0-205-33129-7 (alk. paper)
        1. Alcoholism—Research.   2. Alcoholism—Treatment.   3. Alcoholism—Prevention.   4.
Alcoholics—Psychology.   5. Alcoholics—Mental health.   I. Title.
HV5047.Y34 2004
362.292—dc21

                                                                                                2002043763

Printed in the United States of America

10   9   8   7   6   5   4   3   2   1   08   07   06   05   04   03

This book is dedicated to the loving memory of my dear sister Barbara.

CONTENTS

CHAPTER FIVE

Statistics on Alcohol Use: Epidemiologic Research on Alcohol   87

CHAPTER SIX

Longitudinal Studies on Alcohol: Alcohol and the Life Span 111

CHAPTER SEVEN

Environmental Factors Affecting Alcohol Use: Cultural and Social Research Findings   137

CHAPTER EIGHT

Alcohol, Emotion, Sex, and Aggression 157

CHAPTER ELEVEN

**Outcome Studies on Alcohol and Drug Abuse Treatment:
From the Rand Report to the MATCH Study**   **221**

CHAPTER TWELVE
Summary and Recommendations   255

LIST OF FIGURES

LIST OF TABLES

PREFACE

The primary aim of this book is to introduce the reader to the large body of alcohol research that is relevant to the understanding and treatment of alcohol disorders. It is hoped that clinicians and other professionals, by becoming more knowledgeable about alcohol research and its methods, will be more open to its findings and make use of them in their clinical, prevention, or policy work.

In most disciplines and professions there is a substantial body of knowledge that provides the foundation for education and training. In medicine, for example, anatomy and physiology provide the foundation for medical education. In the field of alcohol studies, however, there is no commonly agreed on fundamental knowledge. Rather, alcoholism counselors typically depend on their personal experiences in recovery and mental health professionals depend largely on various clinical theories and clinical experiences to shape their views on alcoholism. I believe that there is now a substantial body of research knowledge that provides a foundation for understanding alcohol use disorders. This book summarizes alcohol research in one volume for the first time.

Research, of course, is constantly evolving. Hence, a basic understanding of research methods is needed for clinicians to evaluate and make use of new findings. To introduce the reader to research methods and issues, I have provided a discussion of basic research methods in Chapter 1. Subsequent chapters include a methodology section, which focuses on specific methodological issues that arise in the research of the specific area discussed in the chapter.

Although I make some suggestions about implications for treatment, prevention, and policy, this book does not propose an overall model for any of them. Such a project involves making a number of inferences, and its validity would be only provisional. I prefer to encourage readers to begin to think about the implications of the research for themselves. Although most readers will be interested in the implications for treatment, the implications of the research for prevention and policy are important, too. Treatment of alcohol disorders is only one aspect of alleviating alcohol problems. Hazardous use by drinkers without alcohol disorders, which causes accidents and other problems, is responsible for more of the social costs of alcohol misuse than the costs incurred by those with alcohol disorders. The book cites considerable research evidence that shows there are effective policies that can reduce problems caused by this hazardous use.

I have been an alcohol educator in the Addictions Studies Program at John Jay College of Criminal Justice since 1987. Teaching in a program that is a part of a liberal arts college, I believe it is important to provide an objective view of our current understanding of alcoholism. I provide this information in a course called Psychology of Alcoholism. I have had difficulty finding an appropriate text. There are books that provide relevant information, but they are often written from an Alcoholics Anonymous (AA) or cognitive behavioral approach. To the extent that research is discussed, it is used to bolster either the views of AA or cognitive behavioral theory. I wrote this book with the goal of presenting alcohol research in a neutral and objective manner rather than to advocate for any theory.

I have not laid out the differences between the AA view of alcoholism and the cognitive behavioral approach, nor have I made any effort to indicate my opinions regarding them. I did this for two reasons. First, I do not think the resulting controversies have been useful for the advancement of our understanding of alcoholism. Second, the usefulness of the research knowledge is, in my view, sometimes trivialized by using it to bolster one theoretical position or another. For a good summary of the theories, see Thombs (1999) or Rotgers et al. (1996). Both books present the popular theoretical convictions about alcoholism, its origin, and its course. Those readers who are familiar with these convictions can use this book to find out what the research has shown about their validity.

In my classes there are often two large subgroups of students: those who are recovering from alcohol or substance abuse and those who have had some personal experience with an actively addicted person. When I have used a text that is derived from the experiences of recovering addicts, the AA-derived approach, students in that community strongly endorse these views, while those with personal experiences with addicted people tend to feel alienated. When I have used a cognitive behavioral text, on the other hand, those in recovery tend to feel alienated. Whichever type of text I have used, there has been a tendency for these two groups to "pair off" against each other. The class is diverted from examining what is known about alcoholism to defending theoretical positions about the nature of alcoholism. Using this book, which presents empirical research in a neutral way, should alleviate this problem.

Recently there have been efforts to bridge the gap between the views of clinicians who treat addicted populations and researchers who conduct alcohol and substance abuse studies. For too long, researchers and clinicians have gone their separate ways and have not integrated the perspectives of research and clinical practice. This book is a pedagogical step to help clinicians and future clinicians learn the benefits of understanding and utilizing alcohol and substance abuse research in their clinical practice. Researchers can benefit from recommendations I make for help in determining what additional research is important for improved clinical practice and developing methods for making research articles more relevant and accessible to clinicians. Researchers may also find it interesting to see my approach to applying their work to clinical practice.

For students of alcoholism counseling, who often have not had any formal training in research methods, the book provides a basic introduction to empirical research as well as summarizing important findings. For students in the mental health professions, the book supplements the theoretical texts that are available.

For the most part, the book focuses on *alcohol* research. I chose to do this for two reasons. First, a large number of books summarize important aspects of the research on psychoactive drugs other than alcohol (see Julein, 2000; Ray and Ksir, 2002; and Levinthal, 2002, for example). Usually these books devote only one chapter to alcohol. Considering the great cost of alcohol problems to society and the enormous research on alcohol that has been conducted, I feel that a more extensive discussion is warranted. The second reason is that to include other psychoactive drugs would have lengthened the book considerably. In some areas, however, I felt it was essential to include a discussion of substance abuse. It is discussed in the following chapters:

1. Chapter 9 focuses on substance use disorders as well as alcohol use disorders in the criminal justice system.
2. Chapter 10 includes substance abuse as well as alcohol abuse in the treatment of co-occurring psychiatric disorders.
3. Chapter 11 includes outcome studies that consider substance abuse as well as alcohol abuse.

In the recommendations section of the topical chapters, I have provided some implications for treatment, prevention, and policy. Intelligent readers can trace back my inferences and decide whether these implications are warranted. They can also derive additional implications by drawing on research presented in these chapters. Some preliminary methods for doing this are discussed in Chapter 1. For classes that use this book as a text, it is my fervent hope that class discussions move in this direction rather than to the theoretical debates.

I hope that current and future substance abuse counselors and mental health professionals who read this book will begin to appreciate and understand how research can be relevant in their work. I hope that researchers will begin to appreciate the perspective of clinicians and help make research more relevant and accessible to them.

ACKNOWLEDGMENTS

I am grateful for the help I received from Keith Markus, a colleague with great insight and generosity, Lawrence Gould, who made suggestions on revising Chapter 7, and the librarians of the Lloyd Seal Library of John Jay College, whose dedication and helpfulness are matchless. The spirit of the book comes from the wisdom of AA imparted to me by Charles Peckham and Pedro Zapata and the objectivity of alcohol research imparted to me by the alcohol researchers I met in the Society of Psychologists in Addictive Behaviors (SPAB), now the Division of Addictions in the American Psychological Association. I would like to thank Shannon Foreman of Omegatype Typography for her assistance with this project. I would also like to thank the following reviewers: Joanne Fishman, Ph.D., John Jay College, and Joan E. Zweben, Ph.D., University of California at San Francisco.

REFERENCES

Julien, R. M. (2001). *A primer of drug action* (9th ed.). New York: Worth.
Levinthal, C. F. (2002). *Drugs, behavior, and modern society.* Boston: Allyn & Bacon.
Ray, O., & Ksir, C. (2002). *Drugs, society, and human behavior* (9th ed.). New York: McGraw-Hill.
Rotgers, F., Keller, D. S., & Morgenstern, J. (Eds.). (1996). *Treating substance abuse: Theory and technique.* New York: Guilford Press.
Thombs, D. L. (1999). *Introduction to addictive behaviors* (2nd ed.). New York: Guilford Press.

CHAPTER ONE

HOW DO WE KNOW ABOUT ALCOHOL AND ALCOHOLISM?

Knowledge about Alcohol, Alcohol Problems, and Alcoholism

A congressman was once asked by a constituent to explain his attitude toward whiskey. "If you mean the demon drink that poisons the mind, pollutes the body, desecrates family life, and inflames sinners, then I'm against it," the congressman said. "But if you mean the elixir of Christmas cheer, the shield against winter chill, the taxable potion that puts needed funds into public coffers to comfort little crippled children, then I'm for it. This is my position, and I will not compromise."

—Popular anecdote, cited in Lender & Martin[1]

Ask anyone about alcohol and chances are you will discover strong convictions. In the above quotation the politician argues forcefully for both the benefits and evils of alcohol, befitting the stereotype of a politician. Of course most people take one side or the other regarding the benefits or ills of the substance alcohol. Beyond its complete acceptance or rejection, there are many strongly held convictions about alcohol, alcohol use disorders, and the manner in which to address alcohol-related problems. How can we can determine the validity of these convictions about alcohol-related phenomena? We can draw on three sources of information:

1. *Experiential knowledge:* We can evaluate our personal experience or personal experiences of others.
2. *Professional knowledge:* We can rely on the knowledge of trained professionals.
3. *Research knowledge:* We can use research data relevant to specific issues.

[1]Reprinted with the permission of The Free Press, an imprint of Simon & Schuster Adult Publishing Group, from *Drinking in America: A History* by Mark Edward Lender and James Kirby Martin. Copyright © 1982 by The Free Press.

Each of these types of knowledge has advantages and drawbacks.

Most of us have personal experience regarding alcohol. Most of us drink at least occasionally, and we certainly observe others drink. Some develop alcohol problems, and many are able to overcome them. In the United States, membership in Alcoholics Anonymous (AA), a self-help group, is the most common pathway used to arrest alcohol disorders. The personal experiences of AA members about drinking and their recovery in AA understandably affect their convictions about the nature of alcohol problems. Others draw on different personal experiences when they watch a significant figure in their lives be consumed by an alcohol disorder with devastating consequences. Such experiences also influence the beliefs about the nature of alcohol disorders. Both are examples of what is called **experiential knowledge.**

Mental health professionals, including psychologists, social workers, and psychiatrists, receive professional education, which results in the acquisition of a knowledge base that is commonly called, logically enough, professional knowledge. Professional knowledge acquired in professional schools consists of:

1. Courses in understanding mental disorders and their treatment
2. Courses that teach research methods and evaluation of research findings regarding mental disorders and their treatment
3. Supervised fieldwork and/or internship experiences (Polkinghorne, 1999, p. 1433; Trierweiler & Stricker, 1998, pp. 219, 226).

Thirdly, research knowledge may be used to obtain data about alcohol use and abuse. An important advantage of this knowledge is that there are special safeguards in its methodology that ensure a higher degree of objectivity than the other two types of knowledge. This book focuses primarily on research relevant to alcohol, its use, and, abuse. The reason is not that research is superior to the other two methods in all respects, but that it is seriously underrepresented in current literature on treatment, prevention, and policy of alcohol problems. Table 1.1 compares these three forms of knowledge.

EXPERIENTIAL KNOWLEDGE

Most of the counselors in drug and alcohol treatment programs are individuals who have suffered from the disorder they are treating (Brown, 1997; Saxe et al., 1983). Since a large number of these counselors are also members of AA, the experiential knowledge of AA is a large part of their understanding about alcoholism.

Borkman (1976) has outlined the elements of the specific experiential knowledge of self-help groups such as AA. The knowledge is

1. Concrete, specific, and commonsensical
2. Felt with a great deal of conviction
3. Holistic and total

TABLE 1.1 Comparing and Contrasting the Three Knowledge Bases

	EXPERIENTIAL KNOWLEDGE	PROFESSIONAL KNOWLEDGE	RESEARCH KNOWLEDGE
Data are	private	private	public
Based on	personal experience	clinical observation	measurable observation
Collected	unsystematically	systematically	systematically
Presented	unsystematically	unsystematically	systematically
Nature of knowledge	concrete	abstract	abstract
Acceptance based on	personal conviction	professional conviction	hypothesis testing
Replicable	through experience	with repeated clinical observation	by repeating controlled observation

The second row of the table should be read "In experiential knowledge data are private. In professional knowledge, data are private. In research, data are public." And so on.

The Twelve Steps and Twelve Traditions are the codification of the collective experiential knowledge of AA members (Alcoholics Anonymous World Services, 1976), shown in Table 1.2. Borkman suggests that members of self-help groups also develop **experiential expertise** which refers to competence in solving problems through the use of one's own experience. AA members often learn through participation in AA ways to help others overcome their drinking problems. It is not surprising that counselors who have utilized AA would develop counseling techniques heavily influenced by their personal experiences and experiential expertise in AA. The principles of AA have also been more formally adapted for professional treatment, called Twelve-Step facilitation. This treatment will be discussed in Chapter 11.

Counselors with personal experience of alcoholism have potential advantages and disadvantages as therapists. On the positive side, such counselors have a deep commitment to help similarly afflicted individuals and can draw on their personal experiences to express empathy and hope and to serve as positive role models for active alcoholics. They often know the world and language of the alcoholic, can see through the denials and manipulations that are common among alcoholics, and can confront them in an open and respectful manner. On the other hand, such individuals can lose sight of objectivity because of deeply held convictions based on their personal experiences in AA or other type of recovery (Freudenberger, 1976). Because they are not educated in other knowledge bases, these personal convictions may prevent some counselors from being open to knowledge that would enhance their ability to treat clients successfully. Similarly, those individuals who have been affected by the alcoholism of a significant other bring a point of view that has both advantages and drawbacks. The needs of the significant others of the alcoholic are seen clearly, but empathy for the alcoholic may be lacking. Although most mental health professionals have some training in research, the counselor who is in recovery typically does not. A major objective of this book is to provide these counselors with a good introduction to the research perspective on alcoholism.

TABLE 1.2   The Twelve Steps and Twelve Traditions of Alcoholics Anonymous

THE TWELVE STEPS OF ALCOHOLICS ANONYMOUS	THE TWELVE TRADITIONS OF ALCOHOLICS ANONYMOUS
1. We admitted we were powerless over alcohol—that our lives had become unmanageable.	1. Our common welfare should come first; personal recovery depends upon A.A. unity.
2. Came to believe that a Power greater than ourselves could restore us to sanity.	2. For our group purpose, there is but one ultimate authority—a loving God as He may express Himself in our group conscience. Our leaders are our trusted servants; they do not govern.
3. Made a decision to turn our will and our lives over to the care of God as *we understood him.*	3. The only requirement for A.A. membership is a desire to stop drinking.
4. Made a searching and fearless moral inventory of ourselves.	4. Each group should be autonomous except in matters affecting other groups or A.A. as a whole.
5. Admitted to God, to ourselves and to another human being the exact nature of our wrongs.	5. Each group has but one primary purpose—to carry its message to the alcoholic who still suffers.
6. Were entirely ready to have God remove all these defects of character.	6. An A.A. group ought never to endorse, finance, or lend the A.A. name to any related facility or outside enterprise, lest problems of money, property, and prestige divert us from our primary purpose.
7. Humbly asked Him to remove our shortcomings.	7. Every A.A. group ought to be fully self-supporting, declining outside contributions.
8. Made a list of all persons we had harmed, and became willing to make amends to them all.	8. Alcoholics Anonymous should remain forever non-professional, but our service centers may employ special workers.
9. Made direct amends to such people wherever possible, except when to do so would injure them or others.	9. A.A., as such, ought never be organized; but we may create service boards or committees directly responsible to those they serve.
10. Continued to take personal inventory and when we were wrong promptly admitted it.	10. Alcoholics Anonymous has no opinion on outside issues; hence the A.A. name ought never be drawn into public controversy.
11. Sought through prayer and meditation to improve our conscious contact with God, *as we understood Him,* praying only for knowledge of His will for us and the power to carry that out.	11. Our public relations policy is based on attraction rather than promotion; we need always maintain personally anonymity at the level of press, radio, and films.
12. Having had a spiritual awakening as a result of these steps, we tried to carry this message to alcoholics, and to practice these principles in all our affairs.	12. Anonymity is the spiritual foundation of all our traditions, ever reminding us to place principles before personalities.

PROFESSIONAL KNOWLEDGE

Graduate schools in the mental health professions provide students with a combination of courses on theory, research findings, and commonly accepted clinical principles in the understanding and treatment of psychiatric disorders. This knowledge is then applied by the students in closely supervised clinical situations. In these internships and fieldwork placements, trainees are supervised by experienced professionals as they learn to perform professional tasks. This aspect of training is not typically research based (Beutler et al., 1995, p. 985; Crits-Cristoph, 1995). Rather, it is based on the clinical experience of the supervisor, which is passed on to his supervisee (Barlow et al., 1984; Trierweiler & Stricker, 1998, p. 226).

An important but unexamined consideration is how students choose among research knowledge, clinical theories, and knowledge obtained in a variety of supervisory settings in developing their professional knowledge. There is no research indicating whether students in professional schools are able to develop and maintain objectivity in evaluating the many sources of knowledge offered them in applying it to their own work. This concern extends to experienced clinicians. Throughout their careers, clinicians increase their professional knowledge by reading professional journals and books and by attending professional meetings with colleagues. Clinicians selectively apply these concepts to their own work, and assess the usefulness of the clinical idea based on the outcome of their work with patients (Trierweiler & Stricker, 1998; Polkinghorne, 1999). Hence every clinician has a unique, informal system of enhancing his or her clinical knowledge.

There is no research indicating how clinicians make decisions in developing and modifying their treatment techniques. Ideally, clinicians would be objective in undertaking this important process by using, for example, self-reflection or the local scientist model discussed in Box 1.1. Surveys of clinicians regarding their practices for ensuring objectivity would be an initial step in researching this important area.

Evaluating Clinical Texts

Several clinicians have written books or papers on alcohol disorders. Typically, the basis for their generalizations about alcoholics and their treatment is their clinical experience. For example, Zimberg (1982, p. ix), in his book on alcoholism, states: "The information in this book is based on the author's clinical experience in the treatment of alcoholics in a private psychiatric practice, in an urban general hospital alcoholism treatment program, in a suburban community mental health center alcoholism treatment program, and in the public health and public policy aspects of alcoholism."

These books characterize the nature of alcohol disorders and those who develop them, and offer techniques that work in treating the disorder. The question arises how to assess the validity of these observations. Usually, the author has had extensive experience treating alcoholics. The knowledge is useful to the degree that the clinician is an objective observer and distinguishes between those techniques that work and those that do not work with alcoholics. Regrettably, there has been no effort to evaluate authors in this regard.

Typically, writers use clinical material, often presented in the form of case studies, to illustrate the principles they are advocating. The material usually includes some discussion

BOX 1.1

SELF-REFLECTION AND THE LOCAL CLINICAL SCIENTIST

One method to help instill clinical objectivity is to train students to become "self-reflective" (Schon, 1983) and thus, ideally, they can learn to be objective, determining what works and what does not in clinical situations (Hoshmand & Polkinghorne, 1992).

Trierweiler and Stricker (1998) have developed the local scientist model, which details a specific method of self-reflection. In this model, clinicians can review their work with clients to find areas of strength and weakness. They can examine which clients have dropped out of treatment and seek to understand why. A good example relevant to alcoholism treatment is in a paper by Brickman (1988). He states, "A systematic review that I have recently conducted of the success and failures in the 20 years of my own psychotherapeutic and psychoanalytic practice has demonstrated that alcohol and drug dependence (alcohol, cannabis, cocaine, opiates, and various prescription drugs such as benzodiazepine) were significantly implicated in over 60% of cases that either unilaterally interrupted treatment because of little or no improvement or in which stalemated treatment was terminated by mutual consent (p. 355)." This led him to reassess his approach to treating addictions. He switched from the traditional analytic neutrality regarding substance use (i.e., interpret the meaning of drinking, but not take a stance regarding abstinence) to a much more abstinence–AA-oriented approach.

Brickman quotation © American Academy of Psychoanalysis. Reprinted with permission.

of family background, current status of the patient and his or her symptoms, the treatment for the alcohol disorder, and the outcome. There is no formal way of making these presentations, and writers vary greatly in their manner of doing so. Edelson (1985) and Elliot (1983) made some suggestions regarding guidelines for case studies, but none of them has been widely adopted. The reader must rely on his or her judgment as to whether the clinical data warrant the conclusions drawn.

Authors of clinical writing vary in the manner of presentation. Some rely heavily on theoretical assumptions. Other develop persuasive, closely reasoned arguments that support their assertions. How can we evaluate the accuracy of a clinician's conclusions? The only current method is by book review, which of course is also influenced by the views of the reviewer. Although there is no simple way to evaluate the claims made in clinical writings, I have listed some questions that may help you reach your own conclusions about the validity of clinical texts:

1. Is the approach sensible to you?
2. Are the clinical detail and explanation convincing to you? (Compare the case studies in Boxes 1.2 and 1.3.)
3. Does it correspond to your own professional experience?
4. Is the writing logical, coherent, and well reasoned?
5. What is the population treated? Is it sufficiently representative of all suffering from alcohol use disorders, or is it restricted to a particular segment?
6. How much do the conclusions depend on theoretical concepts versus clinical data?

BOX 1.2
CASE STUDY OF AN ALCOHOLIC

"The patient was the youngest son of hard-working, rigid, German immigrant parents, and recalled but little pleasure in his childhood and youth. Although his family was of moderate means he was forced to work hard on the farm, receiving no praise for a job well done, and much censure for one poorly done. As a child he was 'the runt,' and the butt of his older brother's jibes. As he grew older he sought attention through athletic feats, but these evoked only scoffing from his parents. He soon turned to committing minor misdemeanors, and instead of receiving notice for socially acceptable acts, he obtained notoriety. After graduating from high school he worked as a clerk and occasionally did bookkeeping. Although he was intelligent and diligent, his jobs were always short-lived because of his irascibility; the pattern that he was establishing was one of a brief satisfactory progress, ended abruptly by an inappropriate outburst of anger directed at his employer for some real or fancied minor injustice. In the Air Corps, in World War II, his adjustment seemed satisfactory until he 'washed out' of cadet training for reasons which were unknown to him. Shortly thereafter he was in a jeep accident, in which he sustained lacerations of the face. His drinking, which previously had been within socially acceptable limits, now became more pronounced. He also became more irascible, felt that his Commanding Officer was treating him unjustly, and developed headaches, backaches, insomnia, restlessness, anorexia, and a general feeling of dissatisfaction. Eventually he was hospitalized and given a medical discharge with the diagnosis of anxiety reaction.

For the next three years this embittered, complaining man was unable to work except for short periods of time; drank excessively, with few days of sobriety; sometimes wrote worthless checks; and was sustained principally by the financial support and care given by his wife. He had entered this hospital twice before the last admission; during his two earlier hospitalizations he had become dissatisfied with the treatment received and left against medical advice after short stays. During his last hospital stay he was transferred to the alcoholic ward after several episodes of intoxication on another ward.

Physically he was of medium size, appearing to be about his stated age of 36 years. He complained often and at length of headaches, backaches, irritability and insomnia, and thought that these symptoms were referable to some obscure but grave organic disorder. His drinking he explained as a necessary evil to relieve these symptoms. For about 10 days he continued to complain at every opportunity, was invariably sullen and sarcastic, demanded medical or surgical attention, and alienated several of the other patients by his irascibility. During the third office interview he delivered himself of a long tirade of hostility and ended by saying, 'I guess you think I'm just a chronic complainer.' He was then told that since physical and laboratory examinations had failed to disclose any basis for his complaints, the examiner felt that his symptoms were probably mainly due to emotional factors. A brief explanation assured that the reality of such symptoms was not in question. He was told, further, that although the examiner was willing to take cognizance of his symptoms as such, he was nevertheless rather weary of functioning as a sounding board and could perhaps be of greater service to the patient by investigating the cause of the symptoms.

The description of what followed is necessarily inadequate, but the therapist had a vivid impression that the patient's attitude underwent a transformation within a few minutes—this was certainly not an anticipated reaction. He smiled sheepishly, appeared a bit uncertain of just what he was trying to express, and then, with no trace of his former hostility, began to speak of his earlier frustrations with his parents, employers and Commanding Officer. From then on a change was apparent; he became more sociable, his somatic complaints disappeared in 2 weeks, and he became a willing participant in Ward activities. Simultaneously, a genuinely warm relationship with the examiner became evident. Later interviews, totaling about 12 hours, were filled with an elaboration of his excessive hostility toward his parents and brother, and some attempt was made to enable him to understand that he was repeating these patterns with his

(continued)

BOX 1.2   CONTINUED

employers and associates. Still later he was given passes to seek employment, and was proud of himself when he succeeded in obtaining a good job. During the 9 months which have elapsed since his discharge he has not had a single drink, he has been promoted several times at his job, and both he and his wife are happier than they have been in years. He maintains regular contact with the examiner, calling him about once a month merely to say 'Hello' or to report concerning his job, his proposed new car, or his wife's health" (Brown, 1950, pp. 407–409). Although it appears that Brown's intervention at the beginning of treatment was crucial, the larger point he makes is that the relationship with the therapist is more important than the specific type of therapy.

Quotation reprinted with permission from *Quarterly Journal of Studies on Alcohol*, vol. 11, pp. 403–409, 1950 (presently *Journal of Studies on Alcohol*). Copyright Journal of Studies on Alcohol, Inc., Rutgers Center of Alcohol Studies, Piscataway, NJ 08854.

BOX 1.3

CASE STUDY OF AN ALCOHOLIC

"A.. a 37-year-old alcoholic salesman, was admitted to the psychiatric services of a University Hospital directly from jail where he was serving a sentence for driving while intoxicated. Before admission, he discussed his severe alcohol problem frankly and intelligently, acknowledging that his illness had made a shambles of his social and economic life. He was genuinely interested in arranging for his admission. After several days, it became apparent to the patient that his psychotherapist expected him to play an active role in his rehabilitation. The patient, who had started complaining of mild pain in his left wrist during his third hospital day, thereupon began to complain much more vehemently about the pain and was referred to the orthopedic clinic. A diagnosis of mild arthritic condition was made, the wrist was placed in a cast and analgesic medication was prescribed.

Despite this, the patient's demands that something more be done about his wrist pain became increasingly strident and manipulative. He felt he was being medically neglected and it was impossible to satisfy his demands for more than a few hours at a time. He loudly informed anyone who would listen that the ward was run by a bunch of quacks, and that if his doctor weren't careful, he would find himself involved in a malpractice suit. To make matters worse, the patient's pain seemed of dubious authenticity because it appeared to fluctuate with the different situations in which the patient found himself. The resident psychotherapist attempted to remain objective but it was apparent that he was becoming increasingly angry about the patient's slanderous statements and unprovoked attacks upon him. Ultimately, the therapist, perhaps too guilty about his resentment of the patient, decathected [emotionally withdrew from] the treatment situation and became increasingly indifferent toward the patient and his demands" (Selzer, 1967).

Selzer's point is that many alcoholics have dependency traits and that these traits can cause an emotional reaction in the therapist, which is not therapeutic.

Quotation from Selzer, M. L. (1967). The personality of the alcoholic as an impediment to psychotherapy. *Psychiatric Quarterly* 41, 38–45. Reprinted by permission of Kluwer Academic/Plenum Publishers and the author.

Great responsibility is placed on readers to evaluate the validity of the approach. Not only must they read the book and understand it, which in some cases is not easy, they must make an evaluation—hopefully more complex than "Since it agrees with my ideas, he's on target." Regrettably, there is no research to indicate how clinicians evaluate clinical texts.

When there is a consensus among clinicians regarding a specific disorder such as alcohol dependence, it means that a great deal of clinical knowledge is commonly shared and agreed on. For example, Craig's (1993) article on addiction summarizes the accepted clinical knowledge about alcohol use disorders and their treatment. Still, this is not the same as an objective research process of establishing the validity of a concept or principle.

There are many issues relating to the treatment of alcohol disorders, however, where there is not a clinical consensus. Controversies that have not and probably cannot be resolved with clinical knowledge include the nature of alcohol use disorders and those who have them, abstinence versus controlled drinking as a goal in treatment of alcohol use disorders, and the usefulness of self-help groups in recovery. Clearly there is a need for objective, empirical data that can more definitively answer these and other similar questions, which is another important rationale for this book.

Case Studies and Their Usefulness

Case studies are presented to illustrate a clinical principle. Brown's case study (Box 1.2) demonstrates the importance of the therapeutic relationship. Brown indicates that the alcoholic patient was being provocative, and when retaliation was not forthcoming, the patient was surprised and gained some insight into his behavior. This permitted the patient to develop a good relationship with the therapist. Although this is a plausible explanation for the success in this case, we cannot be sure the explanation is accurate and we cannot determine to what degree an example can be generalized to other alcoholics.

Selzer's vignette (Box 1.3) was written to indicate how an alcoholic's dependency in the treatment situation can elicit strong emotional reactions on the part of the therapist, in this case emotional withdrawal. Similarly, this case study cannot suggest how often alcoholics are dependent and how often therapists react as did the resident in the example. The reader should note that these case studies are highly edited and do not include all the information that may having a bearing on the outcome. On the basis of their presentations there is no way to determine how accurate and generalizable their observations are. Thus, the appropriate use of case studies is to demonstrate a clinical principle or technique. Case studies do not provide sufficient information to confirm or reject the validity of clinical assertions.

By the same token, we cannot determine what factors account for the successful outcome in Brown's example and the negative one in Selzer's. For example,

1. Brown's intervention may have been more skillful than the resident's.
2. Brown's greater professional experience may have allowed him to relate more therapeutically to the patient. (A psychiatric resident is still in training.)
3. There may have been differences in the patient or setting, not reported in the case studies, which may account for the difference in outcome.
4. Some or all of the above factors may be acting in combination.

Because case studies differ on many dimensions, comparisons between them are difficult to make. Further, the information reported is often very selective. The reader can see that many potentially relevant factors were not reported in these case studies. Thus, it is impossible to be sure what factors were responsible for the patient's improvement in Brown's case study and lack of improvement in Selzer's.

Clinical versus Experiential Knowledge

If we compare experiential knowledge with clinical knowledge, we see similarities and differences. (See Table 1.1.) The primary difference is that professionals have developed a structured, systematic, and theoretical knowledge (Borkman, 1976), which sets out to understand the factors that contribute to alcohol disorders; whereas the experiential knowledge of AA is focused mainly on practical advice to help the alcoholic. Theoretically, there are two other differences. Proof is evidenced by personal conviction in experiential knowledge, whereas it is based on professional conviction in professional knowledge. The knowledge is replicable through personal experience in experiential knowledge and through repeated clinical observation in professional knowledge. It is not clear that the replication in clinical observation is more objective than personal experience. Similar to personal experience, clinical data are neither uniform nor uniformly organized. Clinical material, which includes the participants' comments and thinking processes, is private and only retrospectively reconstructed like experiential knowledge. This makes it impossible to assess professionals' accuracy in reporting the material. For these and other reasons, Lowman (1985) suggests that biases are more likely to occur in clinical studies than in scientific research studies.

Conflict between Professional Knowledge and Experiential Knowledge

In the 1980s, recovering alcoholics in AA were recruited in large numbers to staff alcoholism clinics. There was friction between the counselors, who relied on their personal experiences with AA, and the mental health professionals, who relied on professional knowledge (Yalisove, 1998). At that time, mental health professionals received little or no education on alcoholism and thus had very little professional knowledge on which to draw. To make matters worse, a clinical theory popular at that time was that alcoholism was a symptom of an underlying problem and that if this underlying problem was treated, the alcoholism would ameliorate. Thus, the professionals believed that insight-oriented psychotherapy would lead to understanding the symptom and thereby lead to a cure. By contrast, the recovering alcoholics favored treatment based on AA principles. It became clear that alcoholic patients responded better to the latter approach than to the former. This is one reason that the experiential knowledge of AA became the basis of most U.S. alcoholism treatment. Regrettably, professionals still do not receive sufficient education in alcohol and substance use disorders, and many professionals still hold the view that alcoholism is a symptom treatable by insight therapy—despite there being no research evidence that such therapy has been helpful in treating these disorders.

RESEARCH KNOWLEDGE: BASIC CONCEPTS IN RESEARCH

Good research is objective and verifiable. The findings of a good research study are transparent: the method of collecting information is clear, the information itself is measurable and objective, and thus verifiable. This allows other investigators to replicate the study and determine if the new findings match those of the original one. The following research methods help ensure objective and valid findings about alcohol use and alcohol problems.

Sampling Methods to Obtain Representative Populations

If we want to know the drinking practices of Americans, we can interview them all. Obviously this would be an enormous task, not unlike the undertaking of the Census. The cost would be prohibitive, and it would be exceedingly time consuming. Fortunately, statistical theory provides a means of interviewing a small fraction of the population to make a very good estimate of the entire population, provided that the individuals chosen are an accurate reflection of the entire population. Similarly, statistical theory allows us to sample a fraction of alcohol abusers, or any other special group, and be reasonably certain that the results reflect all alcohol abusers. There are a number of selection methods to ensure that the sample selected fairly reflects the group of interest. Choosing participants randomly is one means to accomplish this. Another is to include all significant subgroups of the larger population. (See Utts [1999] for details on sampling methods.)

Observation versus Experimentation

In the social sciences, there are two primary ways to collect data: by observing relationships among events, or by experiment. In observational studies, researchers tabulate instances of naturally occurring events, such as alcohol consumption patterns of different age groups. Experiments involve systematically controlling the situation in order to determine if a chosen factor affects the outcome. Observational data can be used to determine drinking patterns and estimate alcohol abuse and dependence among different groups; associations between alcohol intoxication and negative events such as automobile accidents, violence, and suicide can be noted. Observational data are useful in suggesting the extent of various problems, but do not explain the causes of the problem. For example, there is an observed association between violent behavior and intoxication. From this type of research we cannot determine whether or to what extent alcohol consumption causes the violent behavior. We only know that they co-occur. The degree of co-occurrence of two variables is typically expressed as a **correlation coefficient.** This number ranges from −1 to +1. Typically, it is a decimal. The closer the decimal is to +1, the more often the two events co-occur, called a *positive correlation.* The closer the decimal is to −1, the more likely one event will not be present with the other (commonly expressed as an *inverse* or *negative correlation*). If the decimal is close to 0, there is relatively little relationship between the two events. To illustrate with some everyday examples, we would find a positive correlation between number of hours spent shopping and money spent. We would find a negative correlation between weight of total clothing worn and temperature. We would expect to find no correlation between shoe size and IQ.

In addition to the correlation, observational studies report the significance level of the association. This is a statement of how confidently we can say that the result is not a coincidence or a chance occurrence. In the social sciences, researchers typically use a method called **null hypothesis** statistics testing. The experimenter has a hypothesis, which generates one or more predictions. This is called the *research hypothesis*. The null hypothesis is that there is no relationship and that only chance is operating. The null hypothesis statistical test determines how unlikely the results obtained are if the null hypothesis is true. If the null hypothesis can be rejected, the investigator reasons that the research hypothesis is supported. The resulting statistic is called the p value. Typically, researchers use the p value of .05 as indicating significance. That is, this outcome could be expected to occur 5 times out of 100 if the null hypothesis were true. (See Box 1.4.) In observational studies, results are reported both with a correlation and with a significance level. More detail about statistics can be found in Utts (1999) or any statistics text.

Getting back to the topic of aggression and alcohol, since they co-occur at high rates, and thus have a high correlation, one possible explanation is that alcohol facilities aggression. On the other hand, it may be that violent people happen to drink more than average. Or aggression facilitates alcohol consumption. No matter how high the correlation, or how significant it is, we cannot conclude that alcohol facilitates aggression. Observational research, then, suggests a **hypothesis** that can be tested in an experiment, in which possible causes (**variables**) can be systematically controlled. The considerable laboratory research on alcohol and aggression complements the findings of the correlational studies and provides a better test of the effect of alcohol on aggression. To consider another example, there is a strong relationship between participation in AA and abstinence from alcohol. Although it is tempting to conclude that AA attendance is causing the improved outcome, an alternative hypothesis is that there is some special characteristic of those who abstain and attend AA, such as higher motivation, greater cognitive capacity, greater ability to socialize, or something else within the person (a personality trait, for example) that accounts for both results. Such a factor is called a **confounding variable.** We cannot know how much it is AA or some special characteristic of the person that accounts for the improved outcome based on the observed relationship. Similarly, length of time in alcohol treatment is correlated with good outcome. The same confound applies.

BOX 1.4

AN EXAMPLE OF HOW A CORRELATION IS REPORTED

$$r = 0.41, p < 0.05,$$

where r is a symbol for correlation, p stands for probability the null hypothesis is correct, and $<$ means less than. The above example is read: "There is a correlation of 0.41 between the two events, the correlation is statistically significant at the 0.05 level," that is, we would expect this correlation to occur 5 times in 100 if there were no relationship.

Experimental Design and Statistical Tests

Even though events may co-vary significantly (have a high positive or high negative correlation), we do not know if one event causes the other. We need to control the possible influences systematically, to assess what is causing what. The most common way of testing this in human subjects is to assign subjects randomly to the **experimental group,** with the hypothetical "cause," the *independent variable,* and another group, called the **control group,** with something inert (a **placebo,** no treatment, etc.), and then compare the *outcome variable* or (*dependent variable*) of the two groups. Only if the the performance of experimental group is significantly different from that of the control group can we infer that the independent variable is implicated in causing the result. To test the effect of alcohol on aggression, for example, investigators can give an experimental group alcohol and a control group a placebo (simulated alcohol) and see if the experimental group exhibits more aggression. If in fact the experimental group demonstrates significantly more aggression, we can say that the research supports the hypothesis that alcohol facilitates aggression. Experimental designs are usually more complicated than this; some common research designs are discussed in Chapter 8.

There is one additional statistical term to be introduced: **effect size.** Significance tells us how probable the results would occur given that the null hypothesis is true; effect size indicates an estimate of how important or powerful the independent variable is in the experiment. For example, in the alcohol and aggression experiment, alcohol is the independent variable. Even if the group that receives alcohol has significantly higher aggression, if there is a small difference between the mean scores of aggressive responses between the two groups, the effect size is small. On the other hand, if there is a great difference between the mean aggressive responses in the alcohol and placebo groups, this suggests a larger effect size. There are statistical tests to estimate the effect size. The interested reader can find a more detailed discussion of effect size in Kirk (1999).

Certainty and Social Science Research

In the social sciences, results from one or two research studies are not definitive. For example, acupuncture was shown to be effective in treating alcoholism in two early studies (Bullock et al., 1987, 1989). However, two later studies failed to replicate the finding (Worner et al., 1992; Sapir-Weise, 1999). More research will be required to determine whether acupuncture is effective in treating alcoholism. Such mixed findings are common in the social sciences. Generally, in the social sciences, any single study can be said to support a hypothesis rather than to prove one.

When they are available, we must consider the aggregate of studies in an area of interest. For example, there are hundreds of outcome studies on the treatment of alcoholism. The results of these studies have both similarities and differences. How are we to assess them? In general, there are two approaches.

1. The traditional approach is called a narrative literature review. Here the author reviews the current research in a particular area and summarizes the findings. For example, several authors, including this one, have made an effort to summarize the research on the relationship between alcohol and aggression (Yalisove, 1998). One can see if consistent findings relating to a specific phenomenon occur across different populations, situations, and procedures. If the finding persists across several domains, the finding may be considered robust, that is, powerful. This is a judgment that reviewers make. Because reviewers cite the articles they consider, readers can analyze the research articles themselves and determine if the reviewers have drawn appropriate conclusions.

2. A methodology called **meta-analysis** uses statistical approaches to combine the data of similar types of studies to generate an overall finding. These analyses control for the statistical designs of the studies and use statistical methods to estimate the aggregate effect size of the combined results. This book will make use of relevant meta-analysis studies.

Format of Research Articles

Research articles begin with an *abstract,* summarizing the procedure and the results. This is useful to help determine whether this research is really of interest to the reader. Then there is an *introduction.* This should set the context for the current research project, citing the relevant research that has preceded the study. The authors state their focus, their hypotheses, and how they will test them in this section. The *procedure* indicates how the researchers collect their data. Instructions to the subjects are noted, and special materials and environments are detailed. (A common procedure used in the experimental studies of aggression is described in Chapter 8). The *results* present the data that were collected. The results are displayed in graphs and tables, and statistical results are reported that indicate support or lack of support for the hypotheses. The *conclusions* section interprets the results, makes suggestions for further research, and suggests implications of the results of the study. In more recent studies, articles include a *limitations* section, which indicates the factors that restrict the application of the findings of the study.

Basic Guide for Understanding and Evaluating a Research Article

The following can be used as a basic outline for evaluating a research article.

1. The research article should state clearly what is being investigated.

2a. The data should be a good measure of the phenomenon under investigation. If the research is about aggression, for example, is the measure of aggression valid? In Chapter 8, studies are summarized that measure aggression by use of a simulated game in which the subject believes he is delivering shocks to an opponent. The intensity and the amount of these shocks are used as measures of aggression. Is this a valid measure of aggression?

2b. The data should be collected in an objective and unbiased manner. In the above example, the shock level and number of shocks can be automatically tallied by the computer that operates the simulator.

2c. The subjects of the experiment should be clearly identified, and the method of choosing them specified (see discussion of sampling methods). Often, aggression experiments use male college students as subjects. It is necessary to replicate the study with females and other age groups to test whether the results of the male college students are similar to those for other groups.

2d. The experiment should make efforts to overcome the artificiality of the laboratory setting. That is, it may be that the experimental procedure accurately measures a phenomenon in the laboratory but has no generalizability to normal interactions. When reading an experimental research report, you must consider whether the study has taken sufficient precautions to make this generalization feasible. In laboratory experiments on alcohol, experimenters have created simulated bars and social situations to make the situations in which alcohol is consumed more realistic. (This is discussed in Chapter 8.)

3. Although it is beyond the scope of this text to provide guidelines on evaluating statistical procedures in a research report, the reader can examine how researchers have tabulated their results and commented on them. Have they included all of the measurements they said they would in the introduction? Are all the subjects accounted for in the results? Have they commented on interesting findings that may or may not support their hypotheses? Do all of the numbers add up appropriately? For example, in tables, do the percentages add up to 100 percent?

4. In drawing conclusions, the researchers should be concerned primarily with the results of the current investigation. They should present the results in a manner that shows fairly both where their predictions were supported and where they were not. It is expected that research studies on the same phenomenon will have similar results. If the results are far out of line with other research in the area, the investigators should provide a reasonable explanation. Sometimes conclusions are drawn based on inferences. Such explanations may be plausible but probably need to be tested themselves in additional research. The larger the number of inferences used in a research report, the less the actual results can be said to support conclusions. This guide is summarized in question form in Table 1.3.

TABLE 1.3   Guide to Evaluating Research Articles

1. What are the researchers trying to find out?
2. What is the procedure?
   a. What data are they using? Is it a good measure of the phenomenon? (i.e., If the study is on aggression, are they really measuring aggression?)
   b. How are they collecting the data?
   c. What sample of the population are they using? Is it representative and/or random?
   d. Is it reflective of real-life situations?
3. Are the results accurate? What statistical tests were used, and what were the results? Do they support the hypotheses? Are there other interesting findings?
4. Are conclusions fairly drawn? Are they based on the results of the study? How many inferences are used to justify the conclusions?
5. Are results in line with similar research?

A more detailed evaluation of a research article would include consideration of how the research safeguarded against threats to validity, factors that would compromise the results. For example, Shadish et al. (2002) detail four general categories of pitfalls that would make research results potentially invalid.

Comparison of Research and Professional Knowledge

The differences between professional and research knowledge are substantial. Research is objective and transparent; professional knowledge derived from clinical experience is expected to be objective, but there is no transparency to ensure this. Clinical knowledge is derived from private situations, collected and reported in a relatively unsystematic fashion. Research is public, collected, and reported systematically. In clinical writing, plausible explanations are offered but cannot be proved. In research, plausible explanations can be tested systematically for their accuracy through hypothesis testing (see Table 1.1).

Another way to see the differences between these two approaches is to understand the use of theory by clinicians and researchers. Clinicians use theory to understand human behavior. Since clinicians' expertise lies in understanding behavior, they are reluctant to view behavior as mystifying. Their first impulse is to expect that the patient's behavior conforms to the theory of human behavior they have learned in professional school. If the patient's behavior does not fit the theory, they expand the theory to conform to the new information. Thus, at the end of the day, clinicians feels they have understood their patients and have expanded their theories to incorporate any new data. Clinical theory, then, is a structure on which to build an understanding of human nature. Scientific theory, by contrast, has as its primary purpose to promote useful research. The purpose of theory is to generate testable hypotheses that will advance our knowledge of alcohol consumption and its effects.

A second major difference is that, as Popper argues in Box 1.5, scientific theories can be tested by generating refutable hypotheses, whereas clinical theories cannot.

Limitations of Research

Obviously, the author believes that research is quite important in understanding and treating alcoholism. Still, there are important limitations to applying research in this area. First, there simply may not be valid research available on important clinical concerns. One reason for this is that many clinical problems are difficult to study using research designs. For example, group therapy is difficult to study because there are so many possible factors that may be operating, which the researcher cannot control. Another problem is that research is dependent on funding. Those providing the funding can influence the focus and types of studies that are conducted. Results of studies funded by the liquor industry or drug companies may be influenced by their vested interests. Thus, the good clinician must evaluate research information judiciously, just as he or she evaluates experiential and professional knowledge.

How Research Can Be Used in Expanding Our Knowledge of Alcohol Use and Disorders

1. Research methods can be used to survey current drinking practices and consumption. This enables us to see what the current typical drinking practices are, estimate how many alcohol dependents and abusers there are, and estimate the extent of alcohol-related prob-

BOX 1.5
NONREFUTABILITY OF CLINICAL THEORIES

Monte (1999) cites Popper's argument that clinical theories are not refutable. "Some personality [clinical] theories are stated in terms . . . [such that] no conceivable observable outcome would count as evidence against the theory. A personality theory that postulates unobservable, unmeasurable processes easily falls into the trap of non-refutability. Such a theory is so general and inclusive that the validity of its explanations must always be suspect. To be compatible with any and all outcomes is to be an explanation of none" (p. 35). To illustrate the point, he recounts the following conversation between Popper, a philosopher, and Alfred Adler, a psychotherapist. "[Popper] discussed a case with Adler and found that Adler could account for a child's behavior easily with his theory of inferiority feelings. Popper asked Adler how he could be so sure of his interpretation, and Adler replied, 'Because of my thousand fold experience.' Popper responded wryly, 'And with this new case, I suppose your experience has become thousand-and-one-fold' " (p. 488).

To put it simply, Adler argued that all behavior can be explained by an inferred sense of inferiority. A well-functioning person has successfully overcome his sense of inferiority. A person with psychological symptoms has not successfully overcome his sense of inferiority. Thus, all outcomes can be explained by the theory, and by extension, no possible outcome can refute it.

lems. This is the **epidemiology** of alcohol use, and it will be covered in Chapter 5. Such information is very useful, but it does not indicate causes because the data are observational and do not allow for the testing of hypotheses.

   2. Hypotheses can be tested by special types of research. For example, research can help determine whether genetic and/or childhood experiences increase the risk of developing an alcohol use disorder. Another important area of research provides information about the effects of alcohol on behavior. Researchers can determine how much alcohol treatment benefits patients, whether specific treatments for alcohol use disorders are more helpful than others, and what aspects of treatment are most important.

In the succeeding chapters, important research studies of both types will be reviewed.

How to Infer Practice Improvements from Research Findings

This is, surprisingly, a relatively new and undefined process in the alcoholism and substance abuse treatment community. First, and most obvious, outcome research can inform us what treatments are helpful. This is discussed in Chapter 11. Many findings that affect treatment outcome do not bear on specific treatments. For example, the common co-occurrence of other disorders with alcoholism suggests that screening for these disorders is important. In addition, important and relevant research findings can be imparted directly to the client. This is commonly called psycho education. For example, clients can be informed about the causes of relapse, the association between use of any drug and relapse, and the association between violence and crime. Chapter 12 summarizes the recommendations I have made for treatment, prevention, and policy.

RECOMMENDATIONS

Research

Although there is much to recommend the use of research in understanding and treating alcoholism, there are ways in which researchers could improve its usefulness. Research articles rarely provide a useful discussion of the clinical implications for their work. This places a burden on clinicians, who have limited time to spend reading the research literature. One solution would be for journal editors to enlist clinicians to review important research articles and provide commentary on possible clinical applications. The National Institute on Drug Abuse has just announced a new publication that will provide a dialogue between researchers and providers, called *NIDA Science and Practice Perspectives.* A reliable method of applying research to clinical practice needs to be articulated and developed.

SUMMARY

Experiential knowledge is based on personal experience. The collective knowledge and wisdom of AA is based on experiential knowledge. This knowledge is spelled out in *Alcoholics Anonymous* (Alcoholics Anonymous World Services, 1976), and summarized in the Twelve Steps and Twelve Traditions. Most counselors in the field of alcoholism are recovering alcoholics themselves and can be expected to use the principles of AA in their counseling approach.

Professional knowledge taught in graduate schools in the mental health professions includes courses on theory, research findings, and commonly accepted clinical principles in the understanding and treatment of psychiatric disorders. Professional knowledge makes extensive use of clinical experience. Such knowledge is neither systematic nor public (the interventions of the clinician and the responses of the client are not available to the public). Many books have been written based on the clinical experience of professionals. Authors of these books provide a variety of persuasive arguments to bolster their views, the most important being the use of clinical case studies. Unfortunately, there is no uniform or formal means to evaluate the reliability or validity of these claims. Hence, the reader must make his or her own determination. I have suggested some guidelines to help the reader evaluate such texts. These clinically derived texts are useful to clinicians in providing ideas about refining clinical technique for treating alcohol use disorders in a variety of ways. Clinicians can apply these insights in their own practices, and if useful, incorporate them.

Research on alcohol is extensive, sophisticated, and potentially useful to clinicians. Professionals treating those with alcohol use disorders need to learn to read, understand, evaluate, and apply relevant findings of research into their practice. Regrettably, neither mental health professionals nor alcoholism counselors have a tradition of examining this research. The primary goal of this book is to introduce clinicians to alcohol research. The two vital elements of research are its objectivity and verifiability, which are safeguarded by a number of research methodological considerations. I have outlined the format of a research article and suggested a basic outline for evaluating research. Finally, having determined there is a useful finding, there must be a method to determining how to apply it to practice. This will be discussed in each of the topical chapters.

READINGS

Kirk, R. E. (1999). *Statistics: An introduction* (4th ed.). Orlando, FL: Harcourt Brace.
Good discussion of effect size.

Pyrczak, F. (1999). *Evaluating research in academic journals: A practical guide to realistic evaluation.* Los Angeles: Pyrczak.
Provides an introductory method of evaluating research articles.

Rotgers, F., Keller, D. S., & Morgenstern, J. (Eds.) (1996). *Treating substance abuse: Theory and technique.* New York: Guilford Press.
A good introduction to clinical theories of addiction.

Shadish, W. R., Cook, T. D., & Campbell, D. T. (2002). *Experimental and quasi-experimental designs for generalized causal inference.* Boston: Houghton Mifflin.
A good introduction to social science research design.

Stricker, G., & Trierweiler, S. J. (1995). The local clinical scientist: A bridge between science and practice. *American Psychologist 50*, 995–1002.
This article suggests a model that aids the clinician in maintaining objectivity.

Utts, J. M. (1999). *Seeing through statistics* (2nd ed.). Pacific Grove, CA: Duxbury Press. Basic introduction to statistics.
Provides basic information on evaluating empirical research.

Yalisove, D. L. (Ed.) (1997). *The essential papers on addiction.* New York: New York University Press.
A compilation of clinical papers on addiction. Several clinical case examples can be reviewed and analyzed.

REFERENCES

Alcoholics Anonymous World Services (1976). *Alcoholics Anonymous.* New York Alcoholics Anonymous World Services.

Barlow, D. H., Hayes, S. C., & Nelson, R. O. (1984). *The scientist practitioner: Research and accountability in clinical and educational settings.* New York: Pergamon Press.

Beutler, L. E., Williams, R. E. Wakefield, P. J., & Entwistle, S. R. (1995). Bridging scientist and practitioner perspectives in clinical psychology. *American Psychologist 50*, 984–994.

Borkman, T. (1976). Experiential knowledge: A new concept for the analysis of self-help groups. *Social Service Review 50*, 445–456.

Brickman, B. (1988). Psychoanalysis and substance abuse: Toward a more effective approach. *Journal of the American Academy of Psychoanalysis 16*, 359–379.

Brown, B. S. (1997). Staffing patterns and services for the war on drugs. In D. M. Fox, J. Egertson, and A. I. Leshner (Eds.), *Treating drug abusers effectively.* Malden, MA: Blackwell.

Brown, C. L. (1950). A transference phenomenon in alcoholics. *Quarterly Journal of Studies on Alcohol 11*, 403–409.

Bullock, M. L., Culliton, P. D., & Olander, R. T. (1987). Controlled trial of acupuncture for severe recidivist alcoholism. *Lancet 1*, 1435–1439.

Bullock, M. L., Umen, A. J., Culliton, P. D., & Olander, R. T. (1989). Acupuncture treatment of alcoholic recidivism. A pilot study. *Alcoholism: Clinical and Experimental Research 11*, 292–295.

Craig, R. J. (1993). Contemporary trends in substance abuse. *Professional Psychology: Research and Practice 24*, 182–189.

Crits-Cristoph, P., Frank, E., Chambless, D. L., Brody, C., & Karp, J. F. (1995). Training in empirically validated treatments; What are clinical psychology students learning? *Professional Psychology: Research and Practice 26*, 514–522.

Edelson, M. (1985). The hermeneutic turn and the single case study in psychoanalysis. In D. N. Berg and K. K. Smith (Eds.), *Exploring clinical methods for social research* (pp. 71–104). London: Sage.

Elliot, R. (1983). Fitting process research to the practicing psychotherapist. *Psychotherapy: Theory, Research and Practice* 20, 47–55.

Freudenberger, J. J. (1976). The professional and the human services worker: Some solutions to the problems they face in working together. *Journal of Drug Issues* 6, 273–282.

Hoshmand, L. T., & Polkinghorne, D. E. (1992). Redefining the science-practice relationship and professional training. *American Psychologist* 47, 55–66.

Kirk, R. E. (1999). *Statistics: An introduction* (4th ed.). Orlando, FL: Harcourt Brace.

Lender, M. E., & Martin, J. K. (1987). *Drinking in America*. New York: The Free Press.

Lowman, R. L. (1985). What is clinical method? In D. N. Berg and K. K. Smith (Eds.), *Exploring clinical methods for social research* (pp. 173–187). London: Sage.

Monte, C. F. (1999). *Beneath the mask* (6th ed.). Fort Worth, TX: Harcourt Brace.

Polkinghorne, D. E. (1999). Traditional research and psychotherapy practice. *Journal of Clinical Psychology* 55, 1429–1440.

Rotgers, F., Keller, D. S., & Morgenstern, J. (Eds.) (1996). *Treating substance abuse: Theory and technique.* New York: Guilford Press.

Sapir-Weise, R., Berglund, M., Frank, A., & Kritenson, H. (1999). Acupuncture in alcoholism treatment: A randomized outpatient study. *Alcohol and Alcoholism* 34, 629–635.

Saxe, L., Dougherty, D., Esty, K., & Fine, M. (1983). The effectiveness and costs of alcoholism treatment. *Health Technology Case Study 22,* Office of Technology Assessment. Washington, DC: U.S. Government Printing Office.

Selzer, M. L. (1967). The personality of the alcoholic as an impediment to psychotherapy. *Psychiatric Quarterly* 41, 38–45.

Schon, D. (1983). *The reflective practitioner: How professionals think in action.* New York: Basic Books.

Shadish, W. R., Cook, T. D., & Campbell, D. T. (2002). *Experimental and quasi-experimental designs for generalized causal inference.* Boston: Houghton Mifflin.

Trierweiler, S. J., & Stricker, G. (1998). *The scientific practice of professional psychology.* New York: Plenum Press.

Utts, J. M. (1999). *Seeing through statistics* (2nd ed.). Pacific Grove, CA: Duxbury Press.

Worner, T. M., Zeller, B., Schwarz, H., Zwas, F., & Lyon, D. (1992). A failure to improve treatment outcome in alcoholism. *Drug and Alcohol Dependence* 30, 169–173.

Yalisove, D. L. (1998). A review of the research on the relationship between alcohol consumption and aggressive behavior and its implications for education, prevention, treatment, and criminal justice policy. *Security Journal* 11, 237–241.

Zimberg, S. (1982). *The clinical management of alcoholism.* New York: Brunner/Mazel.

CHAPTER TWO

MEASUREMENT AND BASIC CONCEPTS OF ALCOHOLISM RESEARCH

Before we can examine the research on alcohol and alcoholism, it is important to define essential terms, including basic measuring units and common classifications. We need these agreed-upon definitions to compare results of different research studies. These basic terms include:

1. A standard measure of alcohol content
2. A measure of how much alcohol a person has in his or her body
3. Measures of alcohol problems
4. Diagnoses of alcohol use disorders
5. Outcome criteria—ways to measure improvement for those suffering from alcohol use disorders

KEY MEASUREMENTS IN ALCOHOL RESEARCH

Standard Drink Measurement for Alcoholic Beverages

Moe: "How many drinks did you have last night?"
Joe: "One or two."

Joe's response is ambiguous because we do not know how much a drink represents to him. Some people exaggerate their consumption by stretching two sips to two drinks, others minimize their consumption by calling two half-pints of hard liquor "one or two drinks." In order to measure alcohol consumption accurately, it is obviously important to have a standard measure of it.

The most common measure of alcohol is called a **standard drink.** A standard drink contains one-half ounce (0.5 oz) of absolute or pure alcohol. One 12-oz can of beer, one 5-oz glass of wine, or 1.5 oz of hard liquor each comprise one standard drink, corresponding to the everyday notion of a drink (see Table 2.1). Because all alcoholic beverages are diluted with water or other liquids, alcohol is only a percentage of the total volume of the beverage.

TABLE 2.1   Number of Ounces of Common Alcoholic Beverages That Approximate a Standard Drink[a]

BEVERAGE	ABSOLUTE ALCOHOL	STANDARD DRINKS
1 12-oz bottle of 4.5% beer	0.54 oz	1.08
5 oz of 12% wine	0.60 oz	1.2
1.5 oz of 80-proof liquor	0.60 oz	1.2

[a]Rounded off, each of these are one drink. In fact, each is a bit more than a standard drink.

Wine is approximately 12–13 percent alcohol; beer, 4.5 percent, hard liquor, 40–45 percent. The percent alcohol is noted on the back label of wine bottles. For hard (distilled) liquor, the amount of alcohol is expressed in proof, which is double the percentage. Oddly, beer containers do not report the percentage of alcohol.

Calculation of Standard Drinks.   In order to calculate the number of standard drinks in any alcoholic beverage, we first calculate the number of ounces of absolute alcohol in the drink and then multiply by 2, since each standard drink contains 0.5 oz of absolute alcohol. To do this, we multiply the number of ounces times the decimal equivalent of the percentage alcohol. The decimal equivalent of percentage is calculated by dividing the percent by 100 (or by moving the decimal place two places to the left). Thus, converting 12 percent alcohol to a decimal is $12/100 = 0.12$. We multiply this number by the number of ounces of the beverage. This gives the number of ounces of absolute alcohol in the beverage. We multiply this total by 2 because each 0.5 oz equals one drink. For example, to determine the number of standard drinks in 12 oz of 4.5 percent beer:

Convert 4.5 percent to a decimal: $4.5\% = 0.045$.

Multiply the number of ounces by the decimal equivalent: $12 \times 0.045 = 0.54$ oz absolute alcohol.

Multiply by 2 to get the number of drinks: $2 \times 0.54 = 1.08$ drinks

Calculating the number of standard drinks when alcohol content is noted in proof requires a conversion from proof to percentage. Proof is easily converted to percentage by dividing by 2. Thus, if brandy is 80 proof, its percentage of absolute alcohol is 40 percent. For example, to determine the number of drinks in 1.5 oz of 80-proof brandy:

Convert 80 proof to percentage: $80/2 = 40\%$.
Convert 40 percent to decimal form: 0.40.
Then 1.5 oz $\times 0.40 = 0.6$ oz absolute alcohol.
$2 \times 0.6 = 1.2$ drinks.

It is a useful skill to be able to calculate how many standard drinks are in any alcoholic beverage. Drinkers can keep track of the number of standard drinks they have had and know when they are exceeding their normal doses and slow down or stop. Clinicians can compare the individual's consumption pattern with established norms and levels of safe drinking guidelines. When researchers use a standard measure of alcohol consumption, it is possible to compare results across studies.

Blood Alcohol Concentration Measurement

Now that we have a standard measure of alcohol content, we need a measure of its relative dose level for each individual. The same amount of alcohol will be more or less potent to an individual, depending on body weight, sex, and length of drinking episode. When alcohol is consumed, it is diluted by the fluids in the body. One standard drink is diluted more in the body of a 250 lb man than in one who weighs 125 lb. Thus, one standard drink is more potent for a small person than a large one. Additionally, we must consider the time period of consumption. The body metabolizes about a standard drink per hour. Thus, an hour after consuming one drink, the alcohol percentage in the blood will return to 0.00 percent. If more than one drink is consumed per hour, the residual from the first hour adds cumulatively to that which is consumed in the second (see Figure 2.1). The measure commonly used to estimate this dose level is called the blood alcohol concentration (BAC), that is, what percentage of the blood's liquid is alcohol.

Blood can be drawn from an individual and the alcohol content measured directly, but it has been found that measuring the alcohol content in the air of the lungs is a good estimate of the alcohol in the blood. The Breathalyzer measures the alcohol in the lungs

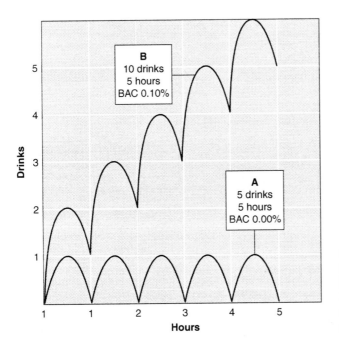

FIGURE 2.1 Cumulative Effects of Drinking Overlapping Doses Hypothetical BAC for a 160 lb man who drinks (A) one drink per hour and (B) two drinks per hour.

and is used by law enforcement and some alcohol treatment centers to measure BAC. Tables 2.2 and 2.3 provide estimate of BACs based on body weight and numbers of standard drinks consumed in a given time period for men and women. It can be seen from comparing these tables that women, even at the same body weight as men, have higher concentrations of alcohol in their bodies than men who have had the same number of drinks. The reasons are as yet not entirely clear. One factor may be that women have proportionately less body water and more body fat than men and so the alcohol is diluted less (Dufour, 1999, p. 13).

BAC levels are associated with typical effects of alcohol on the drinker. As the BAC level increases, the imbiber becomes more and more impaired. Table 2.4 indicates typical effects for several BACs and the number of drinks needed to reach these BACs for average 160 lb males and 125 lb females. For 160 lb males, one drink increases the BAC by approximately 0.02%. For 125 lb women, each drink raises the BAC by 0.04%. A disturbing error that appears regularly in the literature is the reporting of BACs at 100 times their actual value. That is, the author reports the BAC as a decimal rather than a decimal of a percentage. For example, the author may report the BAC as 0.05 when he actually means 0.05%. Five hundredths of a percent (0.05%) expressed as a decimal is 0.0005.

Habitual drinking patterns and other factors may alter the effects shown in Table 2.4. For instance, a heavy drinker may have developed a tolerance for alcohol (**acquired tolerance**) and thus at a relatively high BAC show minimal effects of the drinking. This is an indicator of potential alcohol problems. We will discuss this more fully in the diagnostic section of the chapter. A useful application of Table 2.4 is that counselors can translate drinking patterns into approximate BAC levels for their clients, informing them of their

TABLE 2.2   Estimated BAC Levels Based on Number of Drinks Consumed and Body Weight for Men

Drinks	BODY WEIGHT (LB)							
	100	120	140	160	180	200	220	240
0	0.00	0.00	0.00	0.00	0.00	0.00	0.00	0.00
1	0.04	0.03	0.03	0.02	0.02	0.02	0.02	0.02
2	0.08	0.06	0.05	0.05	0.04	0.04	0.03	0.03
3	0.11	0.09	0.08	0.07	0.06	0.06	0.05	0.05
4	0.15	0.12	0.11	0.09	0.08	0.08	0.07	0.06
5	0.19	0.16	0.13	0.12	0.11	0.09	0.09	0.08
6	0.23	0.19	0.16	0.14	0.13	0.11	0.10	0.09
7	0.26	0.22	0.19	0.16	0.15	0.13	0.12	0.11
8	0.30	0.25	0.21	0.19	0.17	0.15	0.14	0.13
9	0.34	0.28	0.24	0.21	0.19	0.17	0.15	0.14
10	0.38	0.31	0.27	0.23	0.21	0.19	0.17	0.16

Subtract 0.01% for each 40 min of drinking.

One drink is 1.25 oz of 80-proof liquor, 12 oz of beer, or 5 oz of table wine.

Source: NCADI, Alcohol impairment chart: BAC chart, www.health.org/nongovpubs/bac-chart/index.htm.

TABLE 2.3   Estimated BAC Levels Based on Number of Drinks Consumed and Body Weight for Women

Drinks	BODY WEIGHT (LB)								
	90	100	120	140	160	180	200	220	240
0	0.00	0.00	0.00	0.00	0.00	0.00	0.00	0.00	0.00
1	0.05	0.05	0.04	0.03	0.03	0.03	0.02	0.02	0.02
2	0.10	0.09	0.08	0.07	0.06	0.05	0.05	0.04	0.04
3	0.15	0.14	0.11	0.10	0.09	0.08	0.07	0.06	0.06
4	0.20	0.18	0.15	0.13	0.11	0.10	0.09	0.08	0.08
5	0.25	0.23	0.19	0.16	0.14	0.13	0.11	0.10	0.09
6	0.30	0.27	0.23	0.19	0.17	0.15	0.14	0.12	0.11
7	0.35	0.32	0.27	0.23	0.20	0.18	0.16	0.14	0.13
8	0.40	0.36	0.30	0.26	0.23	0.20	0.18	0.17	0.15
9	0.45	0.41	0.34	0.29	0.26	0.23	0.20	0.19	0.17
10	0.51	0.45	0.38	0.32	0.28	0.25	0.23	0.21	0.19

Subtract 0.01% for each 40 min of drinking.

One drink is 1.25 oz of 80-proof liquor, 12 oz of beer, or 5 oz of table wine.

Source: NCADI, Alcohol impairment chart: BAC chart, www.health.org/nongovpubs/bac-chart/index.htm.

TABLE 2.4   BACs, Number of Drinks Typically Required for the Average Man of 160 lb and Woman of 125 lb to Achieve the BAC, and Typical Effects

BAC	STANDARD DRINKS FOR		EFFECTS
	Men	*Women*	
0.50%	25	13	Death; varies from 0.30% to 0.80%, for alcoholics with very high tolerance
0.40%	20	10	Stuporous
0.20%	10	5	Erratic emotions; lack of coordination; legally drunk for 6 h
0.10%	5	2.5	BAC for DWI in most states
0.05%	2.5	1	Impaired judgment
0.02%	1	.5	Relaxed

It is assumed that these amounts are consumed within an hour. Calculations are necessarily approximate because of individual variation and effects of prior food consumption and other factors.

Sources: NCADI, Alcohol and BAC facts, www.clearinghouse.com/factsheets/AlcoholBACTFacts.htm; Charness et al., 1989, Cohen, 1983; Kinney, 2000.

probable BAC, and the degree to which they are probably impaired (Miller & Rollnick, 1991).

Alcohol intoxication is a relative phenomenon, as shown in Table 2.4. An example of someone with a diagnosis of alcohol intoxication is listed in Box 2.1.

BOX 2.1

INTOXICATION: "JOE COLLEGE"

A 19-year-old college freshman spends an afternoon drinking beer in a bar with fraternity brothers. After 8 or 10 glasses, he becomes argumentative with one of his larger companions and suggests that they step outside and fight. Normally a quiet, unaggressive person, he now speaks in a loud voice and challenges the larger man to fight with him, apparently for no good reason. When the fight does not develop, he becomes morose and spends long periods looking into his beer glass. He seems about to cry. After more beers, he begins telling long, indiscreet stories about former girlfriends. His attention drifts when others talk.

He tips over a beer glass, which he finds humorous, laughing loudly until the bartender gives him a warning look. He starts to get up and say something to the bartender, but trips and falls to the floor. His friends help him to the car. Back at the fraternity house, he falls into a deep sleep, waking with a headache and a bad taste in his mouth. He is again the quiet, shy person his friends know him to be.

DISCUSSION OF "JOE COLLEGE"

Although intoxication in the physiologic sense occurs in social drinking, maladaptive behavior is required for the mental disorder diagnosis of a substance-induced intoxication. In this case there is evidence of disinhibition of aggressive impulses (picking a fight), impaired judgment (telling indiscreet stories), mood lability (argumentative, then crying and morose), and physiologic signs of intoxication (incoordination and unsteady gait). This is therefore alcohol intoxication, as obviously alcohol is the offending substance.

We are not told if this kind of behavior occurs repeatedly. If it does, the diagnosis of alcohol abuse, or even alcohol dependence, should be considered.

Source: Spitzer, R. L., Gibbon, M., Skodol, A.E., Williams, J. B., and First, M. B. (1994). *DSM-IV casebook.* Washington, DC: American Psychiatric Association. Reprinted by permission of American Psychiatric Publishing.

Measurement of Alcohol Consumption

There are a number of ways of measuring drinking patterns. Typically, individuals are asked a series of questions about their consumption. Table 2.5 shows the range of drinking patterns.

The quantity/frequency index is a common way of measuring alcohol consumption. It determines the average quantity a person drinks per occasion and how often he or she drinks. A problem with this measure is that there can be a large range of different styles of drinking which would measure the same on this scale. A more complicated measure, but more precise, is the graduated frequency measure. A series of questions begins with asking about the greatest number of drinks consumed on any one drinking occasion during the past year. Subsequent questions then ask about the number of occasions on which progressively lower alcohol quantities were consumed (Dufour, 1999, p. 11).

Another method of gaining a picture of alcohol consumption is called the "Time-Line Follow-Back" interview, developed by Sobell et al. (1980). The interviewer asks the client to reconstruct the past year's drinking activity. Results indicate that most individuals are able to do this when offered various prompts. This approach has the advantage of providing a picture of drinking practices for a full year.

TABLE 2.5   Common Drinking Patterns

1. Abstinence.
2. Occasional or ceremonial drinking. One or two drinks on special occasions.
3. Light drinking. One or two drinks per week.
4. Moderate drinking. One drink per day for women. Two drinks per day for men. (More on moderate or safe drinking in Chapter 3).
5. Heavy drinking. More than 2 drinks per day for women. More than three drinks per day for men; daily drinking.
6. Binge drinking: Women: more than three drinks per occasion. Men: more than four drinks per occasion. Binge drinking refers to the practice of drinking to seek intoxication.
7. Chronic, excessive drinking. Men: more than seven drinks per day several times a week. Women: more than four drinks per day several times a week.

Source: Adapted from Dufour, 1999.

Self-monitoring procedures ask the client to keep an accurate record of drinking practices for a period of time. These procedures eliminate possible distortions that may be caused by faulty memory. The importance of having a standard measure for a drink is evident for each of these procedures.

Self-monitoring methods produce higher estimates of alcohol consumption than recall methods. In survey methods, it has been found that the more detailed and specific the questions are about alcohol consumption, the higher the estimates of alcohol consumption reported (Dufour, 1999, p. 10).

Measurement of Alcohol Problems

Measurement of alcohol problems is done by surveying the different types of negative consequences that a person has as a result of drinking. The total number of problems is sometimes used as a score, which provides a quantitative measure of alcohol problems. Some people have no negative consequences, including, obviously, abstainers. Some have one or two problems. And at the far end of the spectrum, some individuals have multiple problems. The first problem scale was Cahalan's problem drinking scale (1970). The Diagnostic Interview Schedule alcohol symptom list, shown in Table 2.6, has been used in more recent research. The score on the scale ranges from 0 to 17. The advantage of such a scale is that it measures the range of alcohol problems individuals encounter and can be expressed quantitatively. This gives more statistical power to testing the association between alcohol problems and other variables than if alcohol use diagnoses were used, which are restricted to categorical determinations.

DIAGNOSIS OF ALCOHOL USE DISORDERS

There are two alcohol use diagnoses used by contemporary clinicians and researchers: alcohol abuse and alcohol dependence. The common use of these terms began with the *Diagnostic and Statistical Manual of Mental Disorders,* Third Edition (DSM-III) (American

TABLE 2.6 Symptom List of Alcohol-Related Problems Derived from the Diagnostic Interview Schedule

1. Family objected to drinking
2. Heavy use for one day
3. Heavy use for one week
4. Professional warning about drinking
5. Desire to stop drinking
6. Tried to control drinking
7. Drinking in the morning
8. Alcohol-related job/school problems
9. Lost a job because of drinking
10. Problems with driving related to alcohol use
11. Arrested while drinking
12. Fights when drinking
13. Two or more binges
14. Experiences blackouts
15. Physical symptoms related to alcohol use
16. Use despite worsening condition
17. Alcohol necessary to function

Source: Robbins et al., 1981; cited by Pickens, 1991.

Psychiatric Association, 1980), and its subsequent revisions, DSM-III-R (1987), DSM-IV (1994), and DSM-IV-TR (2000). Although there are differences in these diagnoses among the various editions, all have in common a well-defined set of criteria. Prior to DSM-III, a variety of different terms and criteria for alcohol disorders were used, including many different definitions of alcohol abuse and alcoholism. Where possible, this book uses the criteria of alcohol abuse and dependence as delineated by DSM-IV-TR.

Orientation to DSM-IV-TR

The American Psychiatric Association's *Diagnostic and Statistical Manual of Mental Disorders* (Fourth Edition, Text Revision, 2000), commonly abbreviated DSM-IV-TR, is the manual that lists the current diagnoses for mental disorders and the diagnostic criteria for making these diagnoses. Beginning with DSM-III, an important goal of the manual's collaborators has been to create objective and reliable diagnostic criteria, based on available research data whenever possible (Nathan, 1991). That is, the criteria were constructed so that appropriately trained professionals would make the same diagnosis most of the time given the same symptom and history picture. By making diagnostic criteria standardized and reliable, it is easier to compare studies that focus on specific psychiatric disorders. In alcohol research, for example, when a study uses alcohol-dependent subjects as defined by DSM-IV-TR, we know what diagnostic criteria have been used and can compare its results with another study that uses alcohol-dependent subjects. Nonetheless, it is important to keep in mind that the diagnoses are a categorical classification (American Psychiatric Association, 1994, p. xxii) and are not the same as physical "diseases" (Beresford, 1991). When you look at the criteria for alcohol abuse (Box 2.3), for example, you can see that many different drinking patterns can result in this diagnosis. The criteria for alcohol abuse and alcohol dependence have been revised twice since DSM-III and will probably be revised when DSM-V appears. A brief description of the revision process is given in Box 2.2. In the end, it is the collective opinion of the experts in each area of disorders that decides what diagnoses to include and how to diagnose them.

Alcohol Use Disorders in DSM-IV-TR

In DSM-IV-TR, alcohol use disorders are included in the general category of substance use disorders, which are either substance abuse or dependence. All of the substance use disorders use the same criteria to determine substance abuse or dependence. If the criteria are met for a specific substance, then the substance is named in the diagnosis: that is, someone meeting the criteria for substance abuse by drinking alcohol receives the diagnosis alcohol abuse. Substance abuse or dependence are not accepted diagnoses.

Alcohol Abuse.   The diagnostic criteria for substance abuse are listed in Box 2.3. If a person's alcohol use meets these criteria, the correct diagnosis is alcohol abuse.

All of the criteria for this diagnosis refer to the functional impact of the alcohol on the subject. If alcohol causes significant problems in the person's life, the diagnosis can be made. There is no reference to amounts of alcohol consumed, pattern of drinking, tolerance, or withdrawal. Only one of the four diagnostic criteria must be met to make the diagnosis of alcohol abuse.

Criterion 1.   The first criterion relates to use of alcohol that is persistently implicated in impairing a person's important life responsibilities. A parent who repeatedly drinks heavily late at night and fails to wake up and prepare his or her children for school is an example.

BOX 2.2
HOW DSM-III WAS REVISED TO BECOME DSM-IV

The revision of the DSM-III culminated in the DSM-IV. Specialty work groups were formed to review diagnoses relevant to their expertise. These groups conducted extensive literature reviews, did selected data reanalysis (applied differing types of diagnostic criteria to see if more or less reliable and more or less diagnoses were made), and field-tested the provisional diagnostic criteria. The process of revision is transparent because there is a five-volume *DSM-IV Source Book* (Widiger et al., 1994), which details the evidence that was used to make the revisions in the new manual, including condensed versions of the literature reviews for each of the diagnostic areas. Hence, the interested reader (with lots of time) can examine these volumes and see how various decisions were made. Alcohol use disorders were studied by the Substance-Related Disorders Advisors (American Psychiatric Association, 1994, p. 860). The chair of the committee was Marc Schuckit, a well-respected and prolific alcohol researcher. Details about the issues in revising the alcohol use diagnoses are discussed by Nathan (1991). Schuckit et al. (1994) found that substance dependence was highly correlated between DSM-III-R and DSM-IV, but substance abuse was not.

BOX 2.3

DIAGNOSTIC CRITERIA FOR SUBSTANCE ABUSE

A. A maladaptive pattern of substance use leading to clinically significant impairment or distress, as manifested by one (or more) of the following, occurring within a 12-month period.

(1) Recurrent substance use resulting in a failure to fulfill major role obligations at work, school, or home (e.g., repeated absences or poor work performance related to substance use; substance-related absences, suspension, or expulsions from school; neglect of children or household)

(2) Recurrent substance use in situations in which it is physically hazardous (e.g., driving an automobile or operating a machine when impaired by substance use)

(3) Recurrent substance-related legal problems (e.g., arrests for substance-related disorderly conduct)

(4) Continued substance use despite having persistent or recurrent social or interpersonal problems caused or exacerbated by the effects of the substance (e.g., arguments with spouse about consequence of intoxication, physical fights)

B. The symptoms have never met the criteria for substance dependence for this class of substance.

Source: Diagnostic and Statistical Manual of Mental Disorders. Fourth Edition, Text Revision. Washington, DC, American Psychiatric Association, 2000. Reprinted with permission from the *Diagnostic and Statistical Manual of Mental Disorders,* Fourth Edition, Text Revision. Copyright 2000 American Psychiatric Association.

Criterion 2. This criterion is met when the person drinks sufficient amounts of alcohol to impair attention, concentration, or coordination before or during an activity in which these skills are required to perform them safely. The most obvious example is driving an automobile when intoxicated. Even if a person has not been arrested, if he has driven intoxicated several times in the past year, he fulfills this criterion. The number of drinks needed to create impairment depends on the person's weight, sex, and, tolerance. Hence, for a small woman, two or three standard drinks may be sufficient to cause impairment. The reader may refer to the earlier discussion of BAC to examine this more closely.

Criterion 3. This criterion is met when an individual has persistent legal problems related to substance abuse. If someone has been arrested several times for assault as a result of fights when intoxicated, the criterion would be met. The criterion is not couched in legalese. The individual is not required to have been convicted of a crime. He may be "innocent." The point is not his legal guilt or innocence but simply whether his drinking patterns have led him to get into trouble with the law.

Criterion 4. If a significant other is concerned about the impact of drinking on the individual's life and conflict ensues, this criterion is met. It is possible that the significant other is "overreacting," and disputes over very modest amounts of alcohol or substance use may cause conflict. This possibility must be counterbalanced with the drinker's tendency to minimize his consumption. This is an area where the clinical judgment of the interviewer is important.

The reader may wonder why there is a category, "B. The symptoms have never met the criteria for substance dependence for this class of substances" in Box 2.3. The idea is that someone who was previously diagnosed with alcohol dependence and who is currently drinking symptomatically has **relapsed** to his former state. Thus, someone who meets the criteria for alcohol abuse and has been diagnosed as alcohol-dependent in the past is typically diagnosed as alcohol-dependent, even if he does not meet the alcohol dependence criteria yet. Box 2.4 gives an example of someone with alcohol abuse.

Alcohol Dependence. The diagnostic criteria for substance dependence are listed in Box 2.5. If alcohol use meets these criteria, the correct diagnosis is alcohol dependence. When three of the seven criteria are met, the diagnosis of alcohol dependence is applied.

Criterion 1. Tolerance refers to an increased capacity to drink. The body has adapted to heavy drinking in order to minimize its impact. Thus alcohol-dependent people can appear less intoxicated than average drinkers even though they may have consumed large quantities of alcohol. This is referred to as **acquired tolerance.** Stated differently, the drinker requires more alcohol to get the desired effect and, stated in yet another way, quantities of alcohol that used to be sufficient for intoxication are no longer so. Acquired tolerance will be discussed further in Chapter 3.

Acquired tolerance can be inferred when an individual appears relatively unimpaired with a high BAC; that is, anyone who appears normal with a BAC of 0.15 percent or above probably has acquired tolerance; someone with a BAC of over 0.30 percent who is conscious, or at least not stuporous, probably has acquired tolerance; someone who consumes quantities of alcohol that would render a normal drinker unconscious (a gallon of wine, a quart of hard liquor, or a case of beer a day) probably has acquired tolerance.

Criterion 2. Withdrawal refers to the alcohol withdrawal syndrome, listed in Box 2.6. The person meets this criterion if he or she manifests the syndrome as described in Box 2.6 or if an individual has a pattern of drinking or taking a similar-acting drug to stave off the effects of withdrawal. Persistent morning drinking fulfills this criterion.

Withdrawal symptoms appear most often in restricted environments such as prisons and hospitals, where access to the alcohol is cut off. Or it may appear when the individual is otherwise denied access to alcohol. A clinical example of someone with withdrawal syndrome is presented in Box 2.7.

BOX 2.4

EXAMPLE OF DIAGNOSIS OF ALCOHOL ABUSE

Margie is a 26-year-old single woman who lives at home with her parents. She works as a secretary in a medical office. She drinks only on weekends when she goes to singles' bars. She will have up to eight drinks in an evening. She drives to and from the bar, often leaving the bar quite intoxicated.

Margie meets criterion 2 of substance abuse with her use of alcohol and is diagnosed with alcohol abuse.

BOX 2.5

DIAGNOSTIC CRITERIA FOR SUBSTANCE DEPENDENCE

A maladaptive pattern of substance use leading to clinically significant impairment or distress, as manifested by three (or more) of the following, occurring at anytime in the same 12-month period.

(1) Tolerance, as defined by either of the following:
   (a) A need for markedly increased amounts of the substance to achieve intoxication or desired effect.
   (b) Markedly diminished effect with continued use of the same amount of the substance.
(2) Withdrawal, as manifested by either of the following:
   (a) The characteristic withdrawal syndrome for the substance (refer to criteria A and B of the criteria sets for withdrawal from the specific substances) [See Box 2.6].
   (b) The same (or closely related) substance is taken to relieve or avoid withdrawal symptoms.

(3) The substance is often taken in larger amounts or over a longer period than was intended.
(4) There is a persistent desire or unsuccessful efforts to cut down or control substance use.
(5) A great deal of time is spent in activities necessary to obtain the substance (e.g., visiting multiple doctors or driving long distances), to use the substance (e.g., chain smoking), or recover from its effects.
(6) Important social, occupational, or recreational activities are given up or reduced because of substance use.
(7) The substance use is continued despite knowledge of having a persistent or recurrent physical or psychological problem that is likely to have been caused or exacerbated by the substance (e.g., current cocaine use despite recognition of cocaine-induced depression, or continued drinking despite recognition that an ulcer was made worse by alcohol consumption).

Source: Diagnostic and Statistical Manual of Mental Disorders, Fourth Edition, Text Revision. Washington, DC, American Psychiatric Association, 2000. Reprinted with permission from the *Diagnostic and Statistical Manual of Mental Disorders,* Fourth Edition, Text Revision. Copyright 2000 American Psychiatric Association.

BOX 2.6

ALCOHOL WITHDRAWAL

A. Cessation of (or reduction in) alcohol use that has been heavy and prolonged.
B. Two (or more) of the following, developing with several hours to a few days after criterion A:
   (1) Autonomic hyperactivity (e.g., sweating or pulse rate greater than 100)
   (2) Increased hand tremor
   (3) Insomnia
   (4) Nausea or vomiting
   (5) Transient visual, tactile, or auditory hallucinations or illusions

   (6) Psychomotor agitation
   (7) Anxiety
   (8) Grand mal seizures
C. The symptoms in criterion B cause clinically significant distress or impairment in social, occupational, or other important areas of functioning.
D. The symptoms are not due to a general medical condition and are not better accounted for by another mental disorder.

Source: Diagnostic and Statistical Manual of Mental Disorders, Fourth Edition, Text Revision. Washington, DC, American Psychiatric Association, 2000. Reprinted with permission from the *Diagnostic and Statistical Manual of Mental Disorders,* Fourth Edition, Text Revision. Copyright 2000 American Psychiatric Association.

BOX 2.7
ALCOHOL WITHDRAWAL: THE REPORTER

Michael Dodge, a 29-year-old newspaper reporter, had been a heavy drinker for 10 years. One evening after work, having finished a feature article, he started drinking with friends and continued to drink through the evening. He fell asleep in the early morning hours. Upon awakening, he had a strong desire to drink again and decided not to go to work. Food did not appeal to him, and instead he had several Bloody Marys. Later he went to a local tavern and drank beer throughout the afternoon. He met some friends and continued drinking into the evening.

The pattern of drinking throughout the day persisted for the next 7 days. On the eighth morning, Michael tried to drink a cup of coffee and found his hands were shaking so violently he could not get the cup to his mouth. He managed to pour some whiskey into a glass and drank as much as he could. His hands became less shaky but now he was nauseated and began having "dry heaves." He tried repeatedly to drink, but could not keep alcohol down. He felt ill and intensely anxious and decided to call a doctor friend. The doctor recommended hospitalization.

When evaluated on admission, Michael is alert; he has a marked resting and intention tremor of the hands, and his tongue and eyelids are tremulous. He has feelings of "internal" tremulousness. Lying in the hospital bed, he finds the noises outside his window unbearably loud and begins seeing "visions" of animals, and on one occasion, a dead relative. He is terrified and calls a nurse, who gives him a tranquilizer. He becomes quieter, and his tremor becomes less pronounced. At all times he realizes that the visual phenomena are "imaginary." He always knows where he is and is otherwise oriented. He has no memory impairment. After a few days the tremor disappears, and Michael no longer hallucinates. He still has trouble sleeping, but otherwise feels normal. He vows never to drink again.

When questioned further about his history of drinking, Michael claims that although during the last 10 years he has developed the habit of drinking several scotches each day, his drinking has never interfered with his work or relations with colleagues or friends. He denies having aftereffects of drinking other than occasional mild hangovers, ever going on binges before this one, and needing to drink every day in order to function adequately. He admits, however, that he has never tried to reduce or stop drinking.

Source: Spitzer, R. L., Gibbon, M., Skodol, A. E., Williams, J. B., and First, M. B. (1994). *DSM-IV casebook.* Washington, DC: American Psychiatric Association. Reprinted by permission of American Psychiatric Publishing.

Criteria 3 and 4. These criteria refer to the traditional concept of loss of control. That is, the drinker cannot control his consumption once he has started (3); and (4) despite efforts or intentions, he cannot reduce his drinking or abstain. For example, a drinker may have the intention of having two or three drinks at a local bar, but end up staying until closing, having consumed several drinks. Or the individual may have made several commitments to "cut down" or "go on the wagon," only to resume heavy drinking.

Criterion 5. This criterion indicates that the person's autonomy is seriously compromised by alcohol use. She spends a large percentage of her time drinking, recovering from drinking, and getting the money to purchase alcohol. Many functional aspects of her life are curtailed. An example is a person who spends several hours every day at the local tavern.

Criterion 6. This criterion is similar to criterion 1 for alcohol abuse and a corollary of criterion 5 of alcohol dependence. The criterion is met if, for example, work promotions are given up, hobbies, socializing, or parenting responsibilities are compromised due to alcohol consumption.

Criterion 7. This criterion is met if the individual knows that drinking worsens an existing medical condition such as an ulcer or exacerbates a psychiatric symptom such as depression and yet continues to drink.

It should be noted that the criteria of (1) tolerance, (2) withdrawal, or (3 and 4) loss of control are not required to make the diagnosis of alcohol dependence. Alcohol dependence is similar to what used to be called alcoholism. A clinical example of alcohol dependence is given in Box 2.8.

Sustained full remission is noted when none of the criteria for substance abuse or dependence has been met for the past 12 months.

Alcohol Abuse versus Alcohol Dependence.   Alcohol abuse is less severe than alcohol dependence. Most alcohol research includes either alcohol abuse or dependence diagnoses or both. The reader should be alert to differences in results between alcohol abuse and dependence groups. Results reported in Chapters 6 and 11 suggest that those with alcohol abuse may be able to control their drinking, while those with alcohol dependence cannot.

Multiple Substances

If the client meets the criteria for dependence for more than one substance, the diagnosis should be made for both substances. The diagnosis of polysubstance dependence is reserved for patterns of dependence in which three or more substances are used, when no substance alone meets the criteria of dependence, but taken together they do (American Psychiatric Association, 2000, p. 293).

BOX 2.8

EXAMPLE OF DIAGNOSIS OF ALCOHOL DEPENDENCE

Richard is a married 30-year-old postal clerk. He often becomes depressed when he drinks, which is typically three to four times a week. He drinks with male friends watching sports events, with whom he can begin to argue and threaten when drinking. He promises his wife he will be gone only for an hour, but often spends the entire day drinking with his buddies. He has tried to stop drinking on several occasions, with little success. He has often tried to limit the amounts he drinks, to no avail. His wife is concerned about his drinking.

Richard meets criteria 3, 4, and 7 of substance dependence with his use of alcohol and is diagnosed with alcohol dependence.

Applying the Diagnostic Criteria

In order for the criteria to be met for either disorder, there must be a *pattern of use* within the last 12-month period, in which the criteria are repeatedly fulfilled. A single episode of driving while intoxicated or drinking when it worsens a medical condition are instances where criteria are not met. Just how many instances must occur to meet the criteria is not precise and depends on the clinical judgment of the professional making the diagnosis.

The criteria for the two disorders are separate. Meeting one criterion of dependence does not necessarily warrant a diagnosis of abuse. At least one of the criteria must be met in the abuse category. Similarly, someone meeting one criterion of alcohol abuse and two of alcohol dependence cannot be diagnosed as alcohol-dependent; the correct diagnosis is alcohol abuse.

In order to make the diagnosis, accurate information about alcohol consumption and its consequences is required. There are several methods for gaining the information: structured interview questions, self-administered tests, and clinical interview techniques. Such methods are discussed in most introductory substance abuse texts, such as those by Perkinson (1997) and Lewis et al. (2002). Researchers have developed structured interview techniques to measure diagnoses, such as the Diagnostic Interview Schedule (DIS) (Miller et al., 1995). The areas examined by the DIS are listed in Table 2.6.

Many people are forced into treatment and can be expected to minimize their drinking problems, which puts into question the **validity** of their responses. Hence we cannot be sure of making an accurate diagnosis. Clinical skills are important to gain the trust of the client so that he or she will disclose the accurate information we need. A clinician can defer (put off) making a diagnosis until she is fairly confident the information obtained is accurate. The skills in developing rapport with the client so that this information is obtained are discussed in any introductory counseling text. A particularly useful approach is outlined in *Motivational Interviewing* (Miller & Rollnick, 1991).

Substance-Induced Disorders

It has been known for a long time that excessive use of alcohol and other drugs affects perception, thinking, emotions, and coordination. Alcohol and other drugs can induce depression and other symptoms that mimic other mental disorders. Some of these effects occur in the intoxication phase and some occur in the withdrawal phase. DSM-IV-TR has taken this into account with the category of substance-induced disorders (American Psychiatric Association, 2000, pp. 199–214).

OUTCOME CRITERIA

An important key to determining if intervention is helpful in arresting alcohol use disorders is deciding on appropriate criteria of improvement. One way to think of outcome is to think in terms of remission as discussed in DSM-IV-TR. Remission implies that the disorder is arrested, not cured. It is reasonable to expect that a successful treatment will restore a person to his or her previous level of functioning, before the illness took hold. Epidemiologic studies make estimates of remission, which is discussed in Chapter 5. Outcome studies rarely use remission as the way to measure outcome. Rather, indices of drinking, adaptive functioning, and mood state have been used. Remission is categorical, whereas the other measures are quantitative and permit more powerful statistical tests. Outcomes should be measured at least 6 months after the treatment, in order to be sure the improvements have some stability.

Measurements of Reduced Drinking

An obvious index of improvement in alcohol problems is the degree to which drinking is curtailed.

Total Abstinence.   The best outcome for drinkers who cannot drink safely is total abstinence. Those who fail to abstain, **relapse.** The rate of relapse in a sample is the inverse of the abstinence rate. The way relapse is measured and reported affects the way the results look. In a classic paper, Hunt et al. (1971), summarizing several studies, showed that most people trying to arrest an addictive behavior relapse within 90 days. This sounds terrible. On the other hand, many outcome studies show that most treated drinkers are abstinent at any given point in time, and the number of relapses are few for each drinker in any 3-month time period. Since there is no uniform way in which researchers measure abstinence or relapse, the reader must consider carefully how the researchers have measured it in specific studies. (Relapse is discussed further in Chapter 11.)

Fewer Drinking Days, Fewer Instances of Excessive Drinking, Reduced Average Number of Drinks.   These criteria are used to compare the drinker's former drinking pattern with his or her drinking pattern after treatment or to compare the drinking patterns of a treated group with a control group. The advantage of these measures is that they have a quantitative value. Thus we can measure relative improvement rather than categorical success or failure. Additionally, more powerful statistical tests can be used with quantitative data.

Fewer Negative Consequences of Drinking.   Researchers compare the drinker's alcohol-related problems before treatment and after treatment and/or the treated group with the control group after treatment. This measure is also quantitative.

Measurement of Improvement in Functioning

Many outcome studies measure treated drinkers' adjustment or adaptation to life tasks before and after treatment. Each of the measures below is operationalized and can thus be expressed as a quantitative value in a given time period. Researchers can compare these measures before and after treatment and between the treated and control group.

1. *Work:* days employed, earned income in a standard time period
2. *Family:* family members' ratings of research participant
3. *Health:* number of visits to hospital in a standard time period; life-span comparisons

4. *Legal:* number of problems with the police or courts in a standard time period
5. *Accidents:* number of accidents in a standard time period

Validity and Reliability of Self-Reported Data

Most outcome studies rely on self-reported data. That is, the researcher asks the subject in the study directly about his or her drinking patterns, the consequences of the drinking, and other relevant information. How accurate and truthful are the answers? It is commonly believed that problem drinkers minimize their drinking and negative consequences. Extensive research by matching subject response to collaterals' (family members') independent responses and publicly available data on the individual, and random urinalysis and Breathalyzer tests, indicate that there is reasonable agreement between subject reports and the data from other sources (Dufour, 1999, pp. 111–112). Babor et al. (2000) conducted a large-scale study that supports these conclusions. Additionally, Babor et al. (2000) found that inaccurate reporting of heavy drinkers was not due to deception but to cognitive impairment caused by excessive alcohol consumption. Midanik (1988) reviewed a number of studies and found a wide variability in the validity of self-reported measures, however.

RECOMMENDATIONS

Policy

It was noted in the chapter that beer containers do not indicate the amount of alcohol in each container. Since beer varies from 3 to 9 percent alcohol, it would be wise for producers to label the alcohol content of beer. That way drinkers could estimate the number of standard drinks they were imbibing more accurately.

Treatment

Obtaining an accurate drinking history is obviously important. Since people report greater drinking with more detailed questions, those conducting interviews should learn to ask these detailed questions. When clients are vague about their drinking, the use of a self-monitoring diary may help clients produce a more accurate picture of their drinking.

SUMMARY

In this chapter, the basic measurements used in alcohol research have been defined: the standard drink, BAC, alcohol problem scales, diagnoses of alcohol use disorders, and outcome criteria for alcohol treatment. Special attention has been given to the process of making diagnoses of alcohol abuse and dependence. The chapter has outlined the typical effects of selected BAC levels, how alcohol consumption patterns are surveyed, the range of drinking patterns, and the validity of self-reports.

READINGS

Hunt, W., Barnett, L., and Branch, L. (1971). Relapse rates in addiction programs. *Journal of Clinical Psychology* 27, 455–456.
This is a classic paper that underscores the high rate of relapse in addiction.

Miller, W. R., Heather, N., and Hall, W. (1991). Calculating standard drink units: International comparisons. *British Journal of Addiction* 86, 43–47.
This article provides information on comparing different ways of measuring doses of alcohol used in different studies.

Perkinson, R. R. (1997). *Chemical dependency counseling. A practical guide.* Thousand Oaks, CA: Sage.
A standard text for alcohol and drug abuse counseling.

Spitzer, R. L., Gibbon, M., Skodol, A. E., Williams, J. W., and First, M. B. (1994). *DSM-IV Casebook.* Washington, DC: American Psychiatric Association.
This books provides actual case examples of individuals with many common psychiatric diagnoses.

REFERENCES

American Psychiatric Association (1980). *Diagnostic and statistical manual of mental disorders* (3rd ed.) Washington, DC: American Psychiatric Association.

American Psychiatric Association (1987). *Diagnostic and statistical manual of mental disorders* (3rd ed., Revised). Washington, DC: American Psychiatric Association.

American Psychiatric Association (1994). *Diagnostic and statistical manual of mental disorders* (4th ed.) Washington, DC: American Psychiatric Association.

American Psychiatric Association (2000). *Diagnostic and statistical manual of mental disorders* (4th ed., Text Revision). Washington, DC: American Psychiatric Association.

Babor, T. F., Stenberg, K., Anton, R., & Del Boca, F. (2000). Talk is cheap: Measuring drinking outcomes in clinical trials. *Journal of Studies on Alcohol* 61, 55–63.

Beresford, T. P. (1991). Nosology of alcoholism research. *Alcohol, Health, and Research World* 15, 260–265.

Cahalan, D. (1970). *Problem drinkers: A national survey.* San Francisco: Jossey-Bass.

Charness, M. E., Simon, R. P., & Greenberg, M. D. (1989). Ethanol and the nervous system. *New England Journal of Medicine* 321, 442–450.

Cohen, S. (1983). *The alcoholism problems.* New York: Haworth.

Dufour, M. C. (1999). What is moderate drinking? *Alcohol, Health, and Research World* 23, 5–14.

Hunt, W., Barnett, L., & Branch, L. (1971). Relapse rates in addiction programs. *Journal of Clinical Psychology* 27, 455–456.

Kinney, J. (2000). *Loosening the grip: A handbook of alcohol information.* Boston: McGraw-Hill.

Lewis, J. A., Dana, R. Q., & Blevins, G. A. (2002). *Substance abuse counseling: An individualized approach* (3rd ed.) Pacific Grove, CA: Brooks/Cole.

Midanik, L. T. (1988). Validity of self-reported alcohol use: A literature review and assessment. *British Journal of Addiction* 83, 1019–1029.

Miller, W. R., Heather, N., & Hall, W. (1991). Calculating standard drink units: international comparisons, *British Journal of Addiction* 86, 43–47.

Miller, W. R., & Rollnick, S. (1991). *Motivational interviewing.* New York: Guilford Press.

Miller, W. R., Westerbery, V. S., & Waldron, H. B. (1995). Evaluating alcohol problems in adults and adolescents. In R. K. Hester and W. R. Miller (Eds.), *Handbook of alcoholism treatment approaches: Effective alternatives* (2nd ed.) (pp. 61–88). Boston: Allyn & Bacon.

Nathan, P. E. (1991). Substance use disorders in the DSM-IV. *Journal of Abnormal Psychology* 100, 356–361.

NCADI. Alcohol and BAC Facts. www.clearinghouse.com/factsheets/AlcoholBACTFacts.htm.

Perkinson, R. R. (1997). *Chemical dependency counseling. A practical guide.* Thousand Oaks, CA: Sage.

Pickens, R. W., Swikis, D. S., McGue, M., Lykken, D. T., Heston, L. L., & Clayton, P. J. (1991). Heterogeneity in the inheritance of alcoholism. *Archives of General Psychiatry* 48, 19–28.

Robbins, L. N., Helzer, J. E., Croughan, J., Williams, J. B., & Spitzer, R. L. (1981). *The NIMH Diagnostic Interview Schedule: Version III.* Washington, DC: U.S. Public Health Service Publication ADM-T-42-3.

Schuckit, M. A., Hesselbrock, V., Tipp, J., Anthenelli, R., Bucholz, K., & Radziminski, S. (1994). A comparison of DSM-III-R, DSM-IV, and ICD-10 substance use disorders diagnosis in 1922 men and women subjects in the COGA study. *Addiction* 89, 1629–1638.

Sobell, M. B., Maisto, S. A., Sobell, L. C., Cooper, A. M., Cooper, T. C., Sanders, B., et al. (1980). Developing a prototype for evaluating alcohol treatment effectiveness. In L. C. Sobell, M. B. Sobell, & E. Ward (Eds.), *Evaluating alcohol and drug abuse treatment effectiveness: Recent advances* (pp. 129–150). New York: Pergamon Press.

Spitzer, R. L., Gibbon, M., Skodol, A. E., Williams, J. B., & First, M. B. (1994). *DSM-IV casebook.* Washington, DC: American Psychiatric Association.

Widiger, T. A., Frances, A. J., Pincus, H. A., First, M. B., Ross, R., & Davis, W. (1994). *DSM-IV sourcebook,* Vol. 1. Washington, DC: American Psychiatric Association.

CHAPTER THREE

ALCOHOL AND ITS EFFECTS ON THE BODY

In this chapter, we will look at the nature of the substance alcohol and its effects on the body. A major theme in the research literature is that small doses of alcohol have some positive impact on health, whereas large amounts are harmful to virtually every organ system of the body. Another important research finding is that the combination of cigarette smoking and alcohol consumption is especially harmful to health. In this chapter, the following topics will be discussed:

1. The substance alcohol and how it is produced
2. A short history of alcohol and people
3. How alcohol affects the brain to induce intoxication
4. How alcohol affects the organ systems of the body
5. Safe drinking practices
6. Physical conditions that are made worse by alcohol consumption

ALCOHOL THE SUBSTANCE

There are a variety of alcohols in nature. The alcohol drunk as a beverage is called ethyl alcohol, ethanol, or beverage alcohol. Ethyl alcohol is a psychoactive drug, a food, an irritant, and a depressant. It is an organic compound whose chemical composition is C_2H_5OH, which means that each molecule of alcohol contains two carbon atoms, five hydrogen atoms, and an oxygen-hydrogen radical. Other common types of alcohol are methyl alcohol (wood alcohol) and isopropyl alcohol (rubbing alcohol) (U.S. Department of Health and Human Services, 1993, p. 147). Neither of these alcohols can be safely drunk. Isopropyl alcohol rarely causes problems because its strong taste and odor warns the potential user. Methyl alcohol, on the other hand, is odorless, tasteless, and colorless. Ingesting it can cause blindness and death. The commonly held view that "moonshine" (unregulated, home-made distilled spirits) can cause blindness may be related to the blending of methyl alcohol with ethyl alcohol by some "moonshine" producers.

Alcohol can be classified as a food because it contains calories. A standard drink contains from 100 to 150 calories (U.S. Department of Agriculture, 2000). Alcohol can supply up to 70 percent of the body's caloric needs, though it has no nutrients or protein.

Alcohol is an irritant. It irritates the linings of the body it comes in contact with. This contributes to many of the side effects of excessive alcohol use.

Alcohol is a **psychoactive** drug, which means that it alters our consciousness. It falls into the class of drugs that are **depressants.** That is, it depresses the functioning of the central nervous system (CNS). Increasing doses of alcohol depress more and more of the CNS and brain functioning, affecting the activity rate of different parts of the brain selectively (see Table 2.4). Lower doses, inducing mild intoxication, affect mood, coordination, and cognitive processes but do not compromise essential brain functions. However, with large doses, the brain centers controlling vital functions of the body are sufficiently depressed so that the normal signals controlling breathing and heart function are impaired (Royce, 1981, p. 78). Untreated, this can be fatal (U.S. Department of Health and Human Services, 1993, p. 181). Such is the fate of a few college students each year who "chug-a-lug" large amounts of alcohol quickly (see Box 3.1).

HISTORY OF ALCOHOL AND HUMANS, SHORT VERSION

Alcohol rarely occurs in nature. By chance, yeast sometimes combines with ripe fruit and alcohol is created. Early humans, birds, bees, and bears probably had some episodes of alcohol intoxication, chancing upon and eating this fruit. There is no record of their experiences. Because alcohol was not readily available in nature, these instances were isolated. Early humans probably experimented with crushed fruit and gradually learned to make wine and beer.

The process that creates beer and wine is called **fermentation** (see Figure 3.1). Fruit juice containing sugar is placed in a container with yeast. Yeast is a living organism, which metabolizes sugar and converts it into carbon dioxide and alcohol. Eventually the levels of alcohol rise to about 12 or 13 percent, at which time the yeast is killed (alcohol claims its first victims). Thus, wine and beer, which are produced in this manner, cannot have an alcohol content above 13 percent unless blended with a more concentrated alcoholic beverage. The bubbles in beer and champagne are simply carbon dioxide that has been left in the beverage.

References to alcohol begin with recorded history. The Bible makes many references to wine and intoxication (see Box 3.2).

Roman civilization cultivated vineyards for making wine. Since the Roman era, alcohol has been consumed regularly by people.

Around 1500, a process called **distillation** was used to produce more potent alcoholic substances. Distillation takes advantage of the difference between the boiling points of water and alcohol. Alcohol, having a lower boiling point than water, evaporates at a lower temperature than water. Hence if wine is boiled, the alcohol boils off faster and much of the water remains in the original container. When the resulting gas product is cooled, it liquefies and

BOX 3.1

MIT FRATERNITY PLEDGE IN COMA AFTER DRINKING

A first-year student and fraternity pledge at the Massachusetts Institute of Technology lay in a coma yesterday, apparently after collapsing from alcohol poisoning.

Scott Krueger, 18, of Orchard Park, N.Y., was in the intensive care unit of Beth Israel Deaconess Medical Center last night. Paramedics revived his stopped heart shortly after midnight at the Phi Gamma Delta fraternity house at 28 The Fenway, according to police and officials.

The incident comes exactly one month after a Louisiana college student and member of another fraternity died from alcohol poisoning. And it is the latest in a series of episodes for Phi Gamma Delta nationally—resulting in sanction, suspension, or shutdown of chapters of the fraternity whose members call themselves the "Phi Gams."

Boston police, fire and emergency medical technicians went to the fraternity house at 12:12 A.M., police said. According to an MIT spokesman, fraternity members called campus police at 11:56 P.M. Friday night, saying a student had collapsed.

The MIT spokesman said "it appears that alcohol may have been involved in the incident," which may have occurred during an initiation ritual. Police said vomit and empty liquor bottles were found in Krueger's basement room at the fraternity. In the wake of the incident, the MIT Spokesman said that the fraternity had been suspended pending further investigation, meaning that all social activity at the fraternity was barred.

In the intensive care unit of the medical center, Krueger's parents, Robert and Darlene, said their son's blood alcohol level had soared to .410 percent—about five times the legal limit for drivers—when he collapsed.

Darlene Krueger said that doctors were forced to pump charcoal into the stomach through a tube to soak up the near-lethal amounts of alcohol in his system, a procedure hospital officials said is common in drug overdose cases.

Krueger said she was asleep in her home in Orchard Park, a Buffalo suburb, when she was noti-fied by a nurse that her son had recovered from cardiac arrest and was breathing again.

"They told me it was a party where little fraternity brothers were paired off with big brothers. The freshman had to drink a certain amount of alcohol collectively," said Darlene Krueger, who added that fraternity members told here that her son had passed out on a couch after the party and started to turn blue.

Krueger said her son "never drank" before attending college. Classes at MIT began on Sept. 3. She said, "Someone had to practically force alcohol down his throat, for him to have drunk that much alcohol."

Only weeks into the start of the college year for most students, the kind of drinking Krueger fears her son participated in has taken the life a pledge from another fraternity.

Louisiana State University student Benjamin Wynne, 20, of Covington, La., had about six times that state's legal limit of alcohol when he died of acute alcohol poisoning on August 27. Wynne was pledging to join Sigma Alpha Epsilon, and was drinking heavily at an off-campus "bid night" party when he passed out, police there said.

Alcohol- and hazing-related incidents, including a deadly fire, have plagued Phi Gamma Delta since 1993.

On May 12, 1996, five students died in a fire at the Phi Gamma Delta house at the University of North Carolina at Chapel Hill. The state medical examiner in the case said that four of the five victims were intoxicated, seriously impairing their ability to escape.

In a 1993 incident that showed the complicity of many pledges in keeping pledging rituals secret, a student at the University of Wisconsin-Madison denied being hazed after police found him bound with tape, shackled to a bench and covered with shaving cream.

The student, who refused to complain about the incident, said, "It was just a game." The victim had never drunk alcohol before attending college.

Source: The Boston Globe, September 28, 1997, p. B1.

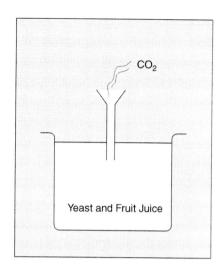

FIGURE 3.1   Fermentation: How Wine and Beer Are Produced. Valve permits CO_2 gas to escape but prevents bacteria from entering.

BOX 3.2

ALCOHOL IN THE BIBLE

Proverbs 23:29–35 discusses the properties and dangers of intoxication as well as some of the addictive properties of alcohol.

For those who linger over wine too long,
    ever on the look-out for the blended
    liquors.
Do not gaze at wine, how red it is,
    how it sparkles in the cup!
    How smoothly it slips down the throat!

In the end its bite is like a serpent's,
    its sting as sharp as an adder's.
Your eyes will see peculiar things,
    you will talk nonsense from your heart.
You will be like someone sleeping in mid-ocean,
    like one asleep at the mast-head.
'Struck me, have they? But I'm not hurt.
    Beaten me? I don't feel anything.
When shall I wake up?...
    I'll ask for more of it!'

has a higher concentration of alcohol, because a percentage of the water has been left behind. Distilled wine is called brandy (see Figure 3.2). The other distilled spirits are created in the same manner but with different food derivatives: vodka is made from potatoes, whiskeys are made from various grains such as rye and corn. The colloquial "still," the device used to distill moonshine, probably owes its derivation from the word "distill."

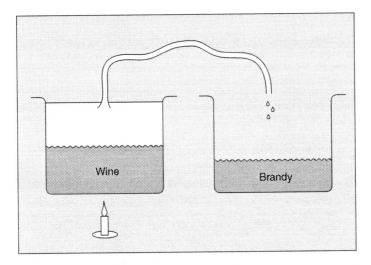

FIGURE 3.2   Distillation of Wine to Brandy. Wine is a mixture of water and alcohol. When heated, the alcohol becomes a gas at a lower temperature, flows through the cooling tube, and condenses into brandy in the other container.

It took the methods of the Industrial Revolution to provide the means to create and distribute alcoholic beverages widely. By the time America was settled, alcohol was a popular and widely available beverage (Lender & Martin, 1987). Americans now spend about $99 billion per year on alcohol (Cook & Moore, 1999).

ALCOHOL AND THE BODY

We will trace alcohol's path as it enters the body and circulates through it.

Absorption of Alcohol into the Bloodstream

Obviously, alcohol begins its journey when it enters the mouth. It begins to be absorbed into the bloodstream even before it reaches the stomach. However, most enters the stomach and goes to the intestine, where the bulk is absorbed directly into the bloodstream, not requiring digestion. The rate of absorption is determined by the type of alcoholic beverage and the amount and type of food in the stomach. The more concentrated the alcohol, the more quickly it is absorbed. Carbonation facilitates absorption. Thus beer and champagne are absorbed faster than other alcoholic beverages of similar alcohol concentration. Food intake before alcohol consumption dramatically slows down absorption (Gentry, 2000). Food that coats the stomach further slows down alcohol absorption into the bloodstream.

Metabolism

Once in the bloodstream, the body works to break down alcohol into its components and eliminate the waste products. The alcohol in the blood circulates through the liver, where most of the metabolic breakdown of alcohol occurs. The basic process is illustrated in Table 3.1. First, alcohol is broken down into acetaldehyde. Acetaldehyde in turn is broken down into acetic acid and then metabolized into carbon dioxide and water, which are excreted.

Acetaldehyde is a highly toxic substance. If the metabolic process is arrested at the point where acetaldehyde is manufactured, high acetaldehyde levels build up and cause facial flushing, palpitations, dizziness, and nausea. Approximately 50 percent of Asians have inherited a faulty enzyme responsible for acetaldehyde metabolism. Consequently, when such Asians drink alcohol, they are not able to metabolize acetaldehyde as efficiently as others. They have been found to have as much as 20 times more acetaldehyde than the average drinker; this excessive acetaldehyde is responsible for what is called the alcohol-flush reaction that is common in Asian drinkers (U.S. Department of Health and Human Services, 1993, p. 152). **Antabuse,** a drug used to help alcoholics abstain, blocks the metabolism of acetaldehyde, causing higher than normal concentrations, resulting in symptoms similar to those of the alcohol-flush reaction in Asians.

There is evidence that some alcohol is metabolized in the stomach as well as the liver (Bode & Bode, 1997). Stomach metabolism is less efficient in women than men, one of the factors that accounts for higher blood alcohol concentrations (BACs) in women ingesting similar amounts of alcohol. Metabolism of alcohol in the stomach lowers the amount entering the bloodstream (Bode & Bode, 1997). *First-pass metabolism of alcohol* refers to this stomach metabolism and the amount of alcohol that is processed in the liver before it circulates throughout the body. Alcohol metabolized in first-pass metabolism does not have psychoactive effects because it is removed from the body before it gets to the brain. It is estimated that no more than 10 percent of alcohol is metabolized this way (U.S. Department of Health and Human Services, 1993, pp. 150–151).

Acute Effects of Alcohol on the Brain

Alcohol, once in the bloodstream, gets to the brain rapidly and affects it considerably, because the brain has many vessels supplying it with blood. The brain is composed of bil-

TABLE 3.1   Basic Metabolism of Alcohol

Alcohol
to
Acetaldehyde
to
Acetic acid
to
Carbon dioxide and water

Source: Adapted from U.S. Department of Health and Human Services, 1993, p. 148.

lions of neurons (nerve cells), which communicate via electric impulses. These impulses travel along the neurons. However, the electric charge cannot go directly to the next neuron, because there is a space between nerve cells. The impulse is carried across this gap by a special chemical called a neurotransmitter. The neuron sending the signal releases a neurotransmitter, which travels across the gap and binds to a receptor on the surface of the receiving neuron (Roberts & Koob, 1997, p. 107). This activates the electrical impulse in this neuron, which travels along its body and is passed on to the next appropriate neuron by its neurotransmitter (see Figure 3.3). Because neurotransmitters help in the transmission of all brain signals, they play a key role in regulating brain activity. Approximately 100 different neurotransmitters have been identified (Roberts & Koob, 1997, p. 107). Research suggests that specific neurotransmitters help regulate specific functions of the brain. For example, the endogenous opioid system helps regulate the brain's response to pain.

Most **psychoactive** drugs obtain their effects by disrupting specific neurotransmitters. For example, heroin primarily affects the endogenous opioid system (Roberts & Koob, 1997, p. 104) and cocaine primarily affects the dopamine system. Alcohol does not have such a precise effect on one specific neurotransmitter; it affects several. Alcohol affects the brain by slowing down the transmission of impulses within nerve cells and between them. Alcohol interferes with glutamate, a neurotransmitter that facilitates the action of other neurotransmitters (Oscar-Berman et al., 1997 p. 70). One part of the glutamate system includes *N*-methyl-D-aspartate (NMDA) receptors, which facilitate excitatory signaling throughout the nervous system (Gonzales and Jaworski, 1997, p. 122). There is evidence that alcohol inhibits NMDA receptors. At the same time alcohol potentiates gamma-aminobutyric acid (GABA), the major inhibitory neurotransmitter (Oscar-Berman et al., 1997, p. 70). Both of these effects are consistent with the depressant properties of alcohol.

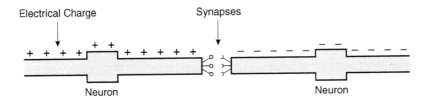

Electrical Charge   Synapses

Neuron   Neuron

Enlargement of Synapse Area

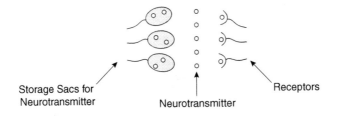

Storage Sacs for
Neurotransmitter   Neurotransmitter   Receptors

FIGURE 3.3   Neurons, Synapses, and Neurotransmitters

Alcohol also stimulates the release of serotonin. Serotonin helps regulate functions such as food and water intake, sexual response, and aggression (Oscar-Berman et al., 1997, p. 70). Serotonin is associated with the pleasure center in the brain and may explain some of alcohol's reinforcing properties. Some research findings suggest that alcoholics have a lower than normal amount of serotonin (Lovinger, 1997, p. 117).

The Effect of Excessive Drinking on Alcohol Metabolism

The body adapts to continuous heavy drinking with a process called **acquired tolerance.** Heavy drinkers can tolerate doses of alcohol that are potentially fatal to light drinkers or abstainers (Charness et al., 1989). Some heavy drinkers have survived BACs of 1.27 percent. This adaptation involves metabolic, nervous system, and behavioral adjustment (Schuckit, 1989, p. 63):

1. The metabolic adjustment causes the rate of metabolizing alcohol to be slightly accelerated in heavy drinkers.
2. The CNS adjustment is mediated by the neurotransmitters, which respond to oppose alcohol's acute depressant effects, and thereby neutralize the depressant effect to some degree (Saitz, 1998, p. 5). One such possible adjustment in the neurotransmitter system is the increase in NMDA receptor sites found in heavy drinkers, which may be an effort to compensate for the inhibition of NMDA receptors caused by heavy alcohol consumption (Gonzales & Jaworski, 1997, p. 125).
3. Behavioral adjustment refers to research findings indicating that heavy drinkers learn to compensate for the impairments induced by alcohol consumption, which results in an improvement in performance of various tasks while intoxicated (Vogel-Sprott, 1997, p. 166).

Alcohol withdrawal is a clinical syndrome that affects people accustomed to regular heavy alcohol intake who either decrease their alcohol consumption or stop drinking completely (see the diagnostic criteria in Box 2.6 and the clinical example in Box 2.7) (Saitz, 1998, p. 5). When a person terminates a prolonged drinking session, the adaptations that developed to offset alcohol's initial inhibitory actions (i.e., CNS acquired tolerance) are unopposed, resulting in a rebound hyperexcitability or withdrawal syndrome (Finn & Crabbe, 1997, p. 149). Consequently, when the alcohol level is suddenly lowered, the CNS cannot immediately adjust but still acts to oppose alcohol's depressant effects for several days, which results in a hyperexcited brain state, explaining most of the symptoms of withdrawal (Saitz, 1998, p. 5), including seizure activity, agitation, and insomnia. A current theory suggests that heightened NMDA receptor activity after cessation of heavy drinking accounts for many of the symptoms of withdrawal (Gonzales & Jaworski, 1997, p. 125).

EFFECTS OF CHRONIC EXCESSIVE CONSUMPTION OF ALCOHOL ON HEALTH

Prolonged heavy use of alcohol can result in serious medical problems. It is estimated that alcohol-dependent individuals have their lifespan shortened by 15 years as a result of medical complications and accidents (Schuckit, 1989, p. 66). Alcoholic patients have many more medical complications than other drug abusers (McLellan, 1986). Medical science has generally not determined exactly how alcohol causes the problems, but it is clear that alcohol can affect virtually every organ system in the body.

Understanding the functioning of the various components of the body is enormously complex. This presentation necessarily simplifies and condenses accepted medical research in describing the effects of alcohol on the various organ systems of the body. A full discourse on this topic would take several volumes.

The Digestive System

Alcohol comes in contact with the surface of the digestive organs and irritates them (Swift & Davidson, 1998, p. 56). This can be a factor in the formation of ulcers, gastritis, and esophagitis. Alcohol also weakens the sphincter muscle separating the stomach from the esophagus, which allows the stomach content to flow back into the esophagus. This process, which is called *reflux* (Klag, 1999, p. 969), can lead to heartburn, inflammation of the esophagus (esophagitis), and ulcers (Bode & Bode, 1997, p. 77). The internal surface of the entire gastrointestinal tract can be damaged by alcohol consumption of more than four drinks per day (Bode & Bode, 1997, p. 77). Heavy drinkers have an increased rate of cancer in the gastrointestinal system. Those who consume more than 21 drinks per week have a tenfold higher rate of esophageal cancer than those that consume less than 7 (U.S. Department of Health and Human Services, 1997, p. 139). Smoking 20 cigarettes or more a day and drinking increase the risk of developing this cancer 45 times more than those who neither smoke nor drink excessively.

Dental Disease. Chronic alcohol abuse increases the incidence of tooth decay, gum disease, and loss of teeth (Bode & Bode, 1997, p. 77).

Pancreas. Pancreatitis is the inflammation of the pancreas, an organ that produces insulin and digestive enzymes (Apte et al., 1997, p. 13). Excessive alcohol intake can cause this condition, though what proportion of cases is not clear (Apte et al., 1997, p. 14). The symptoms of pancreatitis include nausea, vomiting, and severe pain, and it can be fatal. Abstinence from alcohol slows down the disease process and decreases the pain associated with the disorder (Apte et al., 1997, p. 14).

Liver. The liver is the organ most associated with heavy alcohol use. In fact, the rate of cirrhosis, a form of liver disease, has been used to estimate the number of alcoholics in populations. One of the functions of the liver is to metabolize toxic substances in the blood, including alcohol and other drugs. Heavy alcohol consumption progressively affects the liver with continued use:

1. Heavy alcohol consumption first causes "fatty liver," a buildup of fatty tissue around the liver (Maher, 1997, p. 6). The liver returns to normal if the alcohol intake is stopped.
2. If drinking continues, alcoholic hepatitis can result. This means that the liver becomes inflamed. Liver cells are damaged and the liver does not function properly.

With abstinence from alcohol, the hepatitis often will remit. Alcoholic hepatitis occurs in up to 50 percent of heavy drinkers (Maher, 1997, p. 6).

3. If drinking continues, scarring of the liver, called cirrhosis, can occur. This is not reversible and often fatal. Between 40 and 90 percent of the 26,000 annual deaths from cirrhosis are alcohol-related (Maher, 1997, p. 6).

There are many complications of liver disease. Jaundice, evidenced by the yellowing of the skin in Caucasians (and whites of the eyes for all groups), is caused by excessive bile circulating in the blood. Bile is a liver agent that dissolves fat (Klag, 1999, p. 1036).

Ascites is another disorder that is a complication of alcohol liver disease. Because alcohol liver disease causes salt retention, a progressive accumulation of excess fluid results, which is retained primarily in the abdominal region, where it manifests as marked swelling. In some cases vast amounts of fluid can collect, as much as 7 gal (Epstein, 1997, p. 89). This is a serious medical condition. Often the affected person will be quite underweight and will have a protruding abdomen. If the affected individual is a woman, she may look pregnant. This condition is sometimes called "beer belly."

Liver disorders create problems for the brain and reproductive system by the failure to metabolize hormones and toxins properly. These conditions are discussed in their respective sections.

Research indicates that the **threshold** dose of alcohol generally needed to induce liver disease for males is the total amount comprising 6 drinks a day for 20 years or 12 drinks a day for 10 years; females require only a quarter to half that amount (U.S. Department of Health and Human Services, 1997, p. 137). Alcoholics who smoke have a threefold increased risk of contracting cirrhosis (U.S. Department of Health and Human Services, 1997, p. 138).

The Cardiovascular System

The Heart.   The heart is the organ that pumps blood throughout the body. One source of damage that alcohol can impose on the heart is weakening of the heart muscle, called cardiomyopathy (U.S. Department of Health and Human Services, 1997, p. 140). A common symptom of this disorder is an enlarged heart (Zakhari, 1997, p. 25). For men, this typically occurs after 10–20 years of imbibing 8 or more drinks daily (Klatsky, 1999, p. 16). Research indicates that excessive alcohol use is implicated in 20 to 50 percent of all cardiomyopathy cases (Zakhari, 1997, p. 25). It may be reversible with abstinence from alcohol. More men have cardiomyopathy because more men drink heavily, but women are more susceptible to it, needing to consume only 60 percent of the amount that men drink to contract this disorder (Zakhari, 1997, p. 26).

Alcohol can also adversely affect the heart by interfering with its rhythmic coordination (U.S. Department of Health and Human Services, 1997, p. 144). Efficient heart pumping activity requires the muscles of the heart to be well coordinated (rhythmic). When the heart muscle becomes poorly coordinated, the result is **arrhythmia** (absence of rhythm). Both acute alcohol intoxication and chronic alcohol consumption are associated with arrhythmias (U.S. Department of Health and Human Services, 1997, p. 144). "Holiday heart syndrome" is an example of acute alcohol intoxication causing arrhythmia (Zakhari, 1997, p. 26). Heavy consumption of alcohol, which typically occurs during holiday periods, can induce irregular heartbeat. Normal functioning comes with abstinence. Arrhythmia is considered one of the major factors in sudden death of alcoholics.

Coronary Artery Disease.   Coronary artery disease (CAD) occurs when blood vessels that supply blood to the heart are blocked or partially blocked. This is treated with heart bypass surgery, which has become routine in the past 20 years (Klag, 1999, p. 810). One or two drinks a day is associated with reduced risk of CAD. Table 3.2 lists three ways that moderate drinking contributes to reduction in CAD. Alcohol acts to reduce the harmful type of cholesterol, low-density lipoproteins, which is associated with hardening of the arteries and CAD (Zakhari, 1997, p. 22). Additionally, alcohol reduces blood clotting, which decreases the risk of clot formation in the coronary arteries (Zakhari, 1997, p. 23). And third, alcohol helps promote blood clot dissolution (Klatsky, 1999, p. 19).

Stroke.   A stroke is a disorder caused by reduced blood flow to the brain (Klag, 1999, p. 429). Stroke may cause paralysis and/or loss of mental function, depending on the damage caused by the deprivation of blood supply to the brain. There is a clear association between heavy alcohol consumption and an increased incidence of stroke. Five or more drinks per day increases risk 250 to 450 percent (U.S. Department of Health and Human Services, 1997, p. 147). There are two types of strokes. *Hemorrhagic stroke* occurs when blood flow to the brain is impaired due to a ruptured blood vessel that results in bleeding in the brain. Even with relatively low levels of alcohol consumption, women appear to be at increased risk for hemorrhagic stroke (Zakhari, 1997, p. 28). *Ischemic stroke* occurs when blood flow is blocked by a blood clot (Ballard, 1997, pp. 49–52). Moderate drinking reduces the risk of ischemic stroke by as much as 50 percent (U.S. Department of Health and Human Services, 1997, p. 147; Zakhari, 1997, p. 27), probably because of effects similar to those that alcohol has for CAD.

TABLE 3.2   Effects of Alcohol Consumption on Cardiovascular System

BENEFICIAL EFFECTS OF MODERATE DRINKING	HARMFUL EFFECTS OF HEAVY DRINKING
Reduction of plaque deposits in arteries (i.e., arteriosclerosis)	Increased risk for heart muscle disease (i.e., alcoholic cardiomyopathy)
Protection against blood clot formation, which protects against heart attack and atherosclerotic ischemic stroke	Increased risk for disturbed heart rhythm (i.e., arrhythmia)
Promotion of blood clot dissolution, which protects against heart attack and atherosclerotic ischemic stroke	Increased risk for high blood pressure Increased risk for hemorrhagic stroke

Source: Zakhari, 1997.

Hypertension.   Hypertension or high blood pressure increases the risk for stroke as well as heart attack (U.S. Department of Health and Human Services, 1993, p. 173). Alcohol consumption increases the risk of hypertension in men of all age and racial groups. Hypertension reverses within 2 to 3 weeks of reducing alcohol intake.

The Blood System

Heavy drinking is associated with anemia, a condition caused by a lower than normal number of functional red blood cells. Red blood cells carry oxygen to and remove carbon dioxide from cells throughout the body (Klag, 1999, p. 912). Disruption of this process, anemia, causes fatigue, shortness of breath, lightheadedness, reduced mental capacity, and abnormal heartbeats (Klag, 1999, p. 920). Alcohol consumption can cause anemia by reducing the production of red blood cells and interfering with their proper development. More than 25 percent of alcoholics exhibit increases in malformed red blood cells (Ballard, 1997, p. 45). Abstinence from alcohol usually reverses this condition (Ballard, 1997, p. 42).

Certain types of white blood cells are also reduced by heavy alcohol consumption and compromise the body's ability to fight infection. Platelets are cells in the blood that promote clotting. Research has found that heavy drinkers have significantly reduced platelet function and, as a result, their blood takes longer than normal to form clots (Zakhari, 1997, p. 25). This is one reason that alcoholics often suffer from bleeding disorders. Because alcohol reduces clotting factors, drinkers must be careful when taking medications that have the same effect, such as aspirin. Four drinks or more taken daily with aspirin or similar medication may cause gastrointestinal bleeding (Ballard, 1997, p. 47).

The Immune System

Exposure to alcohol disrupts the normal development and maturation of the immune system. Alcohol abuse is associated with a generalized immunosuppressions and dysregulation of immune responses (U.S. Department of Health and Human Services, 1997, p. 164). The association between alcohol misuse and increased frequency and severity of bacterial infections, such as pneumonia and tuberculosis, has been established through extensive research (U.S. Department of Health and Human Services, 1997, p. 166). Excessive alcohol use leads to an increased risk for hepatitis B and C. It is estimated that between 18 and 25 percent of alcoholics have hepatitis C infection (Maher, 1997, p. 10).

The Brain and CNS

A part of alcohol folklore is the term "wet brain," an alcoholic whose brain is severely and irretrievably impaired. It probably refers to what is now known as Korsakoff syndrome, which will be discussed later. While relatively few chronic drinkers suffer such dramatic, irreversible brain disease as "wet brain," chronic alcohol ingestion can cause long-lasting cognitive impairment.

With excessive alcohol consumption, the brain shows physical changes. There is brain shrinkage (Oscar-Berman et al., 1997, p. 65), enlargement of the ventricles (the fluid-filled cavities deep inside the brain) (Oscar-Berman et al., 1997, p. 68), widening of the fissures and sulci (grooves) on the brain's surface, and reductions in cerebral cortex volume (U.S. Department of Health and Human Services, 1993, p. 152). How this physical damage to the brain translates to cognitive impairments is not yet clear. However, it is clear that prolonged use of alcohol leads to neurocognitive deficits in the areas of problem solving, forming visual association, spatial memory, tactual learning, and abstraction ability (U.S. Department of Health and Human Services, 1993, p. 183). Between 50 and 85 percent of non-Korsakoff alcoholics exhibit signs of cognitive decline (U.S. Department of Health and Human Services, 1997, p. 154). Although there is significant recovery following abstinence (U.S. Department of Health and Human Services, 1993, p. 183), the course of recovery of functions is variable. The evidence is now strong that considerable functional recovery occurs during the first 2 to 3 weeks of abstinence (Goldman, 1987, p. 294). Some functions appear to recover fully within months, others within years; even after 4 or 5 years, however, some deficits are present in some heavy drinkers (Parsons, 1987a, p. 288). Older alcoholics recover cognitive functions less fully and take considerably longer to do so (Goldman, 1995, p. 150). Alcoholics are aware of their deficits and seem able to acknowledge them (Parsons, 1987b, p. 172). Evidence has been accumulating that neuropsychologic status has a significant but modest relationship to treatment outcome (Goldman, 1987, p. 314); research indicates that cognitively impaired alcoholics are more likely to relapse (Donovan et al., 1987, p. 345). Figure 3.4 shows the hypothetical curve of recovery of cognitive function in heavy drinkers after abstinence.

In addition to cognitive deficits, chronic excessive alcohol intake has been linked to impaired perception and changes in emotions and personality (Oscar-Berman et al., 1997, p. 65).

Alcohol also interferes with sleep. While alcohol has an immediate effect of sedating the individual, it has a delayed agitating effect, which causes the person to wake up and have difficulty falling back asleep. Alcohol also causes a reduction in REM sleep, the stage of sleep in which dreaming occurs. REM-deprived individuals show a number of symptoms

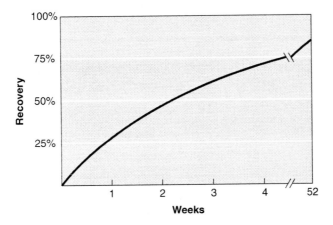

**FIGURE 3.4   Hypothetical Curve of Recovery of Cognitive
Function of an Abstinent Heavy Drinker**

of distress, indicating that REM sleep is an essential aspect of healthy sleep patterns (Oscar-Berman et al., 1997, p. 66). Research shows that abstinent alcoholics often retain sleep abnormalities for up to 2 years (Brower, 2001).

Alcohol interferes with the brain processes that regulate body temperature. Moderate doses of alcohol cause the brain to lower body temperature. This is counterintuitive to drinkers, because alcohol creates a burning or warming sensation, which leads to the impression that alcohol is a warming agent. In cold weather, serious problems can ensue when heavily intoxicated individuals drink more, thinking it will warm them; instead, the alcohol can cause life-threatening declines in temperature (Oscar-Berman et al., 1997, p. 66).

Alcohol harms the cerebellum, resulting in the impairment of muscular coordination. Acutely intoxicated individuals stagger, have balance problems, and have lessened coordination caused by a temporary depressant effect on the cerebellum. Chronic consumption of alcohol can make this impairment irreversible (Oscar-Berman et al., 1997, pp. 7, 66).

Prolonged Withdrawal Syndrome.   Although the terms are no longer in common usage, the combination of cognitive deficits, impaired perception, changes in emotion, and insomnia common in the early abstinent period for heavy drinkers has been called **post acute** or **prolonged withdrawal syndrome** (Trevisan et al., 1998, p. 64). This is a convenient concept that can explain the common symptoms of early abstinence to patients who have just stopped drinking. The therapeutic use of this concept will be discussed in the recommendations section of the chapter.

Wernicke Encephalopathy.   Wernicke encephalopathy is a disorder long associated with alcohol dependence. Its symptoms are confusion, uncoordinated gait, and abnormal eye movements. It is thought to be caused by thiamine deficiency (Oscar-Berman et al., 1997, p. 67). These symptoms remit with thiamine, but residual memory impairments sometimes remain, known as Korsakoff syndrome (U.S. Department of Health and Human Services, 1993, p. 182). Inpatient treatment of alcoholics typically includes large doses of thiamine.

Korsakoff Syndrome.   Korsakoff syndrome is a devastating memory disorder that results in an inability to recall incidents of daily life right after they occur. Sufferers of this condition virtually live in the past (Oscar-Berman et al., 1997, p. 67). Other cognitive deficits (Butters & Granholm, 1987), emotional apathy, personality changes, loss of inhibitions, and **perseveration** often accompany this disorder (Oscar-Berman et al., 1997, p. 69). While relatively rare in excessive drinkers, signs of it were found in 12.5 percent of a sample of postmortem examinations of alcoholics' brains (Langlais, 1995, p. 113). Thiamine deficiency is also implicated in this disorder. There may be some recovery of function, but many of these individuals require custodial care for the remainder of their lives (Goldstein, 1987, p. 365). A dramatic case study of a man suffering from Korsakoff syndrome is given in Box 3.3.

While alcohol ingestion is responsible for much of the insult to the brain that leads to impairment, it is also thought that multiple instances of medically unsupervised alcohol withdrawal may injure the brain and cause impairments, including susceptibility of alcohol withdrawal seizures (U.S. Department of Health and Human Services, 1997, p. 157).

BOX 3.3

EXCERPT FROM A CASE STUDY OF A PATIENT SUFFERING FROM KORSAKOFF SYNDROME

Jimmie was a fine-looking man, with a curly bush of gray hair, a healthy and handsome 49 year old. He was cheerful, friendly, and warm. "Hiya, Doc!," he said, "Nice morning! Do I take this chair here?" He was a genial soul, very ready to talk and to answer any questions I asked him. He told me his name and birth date, and the name of the little town in Connecticut where he was born. He described it in affectionate detail, even drew me a map. He spoke of the houses where his family had lived—he remembered their phone numbers still. He spoke of school and school days, the friends he'd had, and his special fondness for mathematics and science. He talked with enthusiasm of his days in the navy—he was 17, had just graduated from high school when he was drafted in 1943. With his good engineering mind he was a "natural" for radio and electronics, and after a crash course in Texas found himself assistant radio operator on a submarine. He remembered the names of various submarines on which he had served, their missions, where they were stationed, the names of his shipmates. He remembered Morse code, and was still fluent in Morse tapping and touch-typing.

A full and interesting early life, remembered vividly, in detail, with affection. But there, for some reason, his reminiscences stopped. He recalled, and almost relived, his war days and service, the end of the war and his thoughts for the future. He had come to love the navy, thought he might stay in it. But with the GI Bill, and support, he felt he might do best to go to college. His older brother was in accountancy school and engaged to a girl, a "real beauty," from Oregon.

With recalling, reliving, Jimmie was full of animation; he did not seem to be speaking of the past but of the present, and I was very struck by the change of tense in his recollections as he passed from his school days to his days in the navy. He had been using the past tense, but now used the present—and (it seemed to me) not just the formal or fictitious present tense of recall, but the actual present tense of immediate experience. A sudden, improbable suspicion seized me.

"What year is this, Mr. G.?" I asked, concealing my perplexity under a casual manner.

"Forty-five, man. What do you mean?" He went on, "We've won the war, FDR's dead, Truman's at the helm. There are great times ahead."

"And you, Jimmy, how old would you be?"

Oddly, uncertainly, he hesitated a moment, as if engaged in calculation. "Why I guess I'm 19, Doc. I'll be twenty next birthday."

Looking at the grey-haired man before me, I had an impulse for which I have never forgiven myself—it was, or would have been, the height of cruelty had there been any possibility of Jimmie's remembering it.

"Here," I said, and thrust a mirror toward him. "Look in the mirror and tell me what you see. Is that a 19 year old looking out from the mirror?"

He suddenly turned ashen and gripped the sides of the chair. "Jesus Christ," he whispered. "Christ, what's going on? What's happened to me? Is this a nightmare? Am I crazy? Is this a joke?"— and he became frantic, panicked.

"It's okay, Jimmie," I said soothingly. "It's just a mistake. Nothing to worry about. Hey!" I took him to the window. "Isn't this a lovely spring day. See the kids there playing baseball?" He regained his color and started to smile, and I stole away taking the hateful mirror with me.

Two minutes later I reentered the room. Jimmie was still standing by the window, gazing with pleasure at the kids playing baseball below. He wheeled around as I opened the door, and his face assumed a cheery expression.

"Hiya, Doc!" he said, "Nice morning! You want to talk to me—Do I take this chair here?" There was no sign of recognition on his frank, open face.

Note: Patient is in a psychiatric hospital.

Alcoholic liver disease can also contribute to neurologic problems in alcohol-dependent individuals (Oscar-Berman et al., 1997, p. 71). For example, a complication of cirrhosis, called portal-systemic encephalopathy, can cause a blockage that prevents blood flow through the liver. Thus toxins which are usually processed by the liver remain in the blood and circulate to the brain and damage it. Symptoms include muscle incoordination, personality changes, memory loss, confusion, stupor, and muscle rigidity (Butterworth, 1995, p. 123).

Alcoholic Neuropathy.   Alcoholic neuropathy is diagnosed in 5 to 15 percent of alcoholics (Schuckit, 1989, p. 59). It is a deterioration of the peripheral nerves of the hands and feet. Symptoms include tingling and numbness of the hands and feet (Klag, 1999, p. 469).

The Skeletal System

Chronic alcohol consumption has harmful effects on bone development and maintenance at all ages (Sampson, 1998, p. 192). Alcohol inhibits the action of bone-forming cells. For male heavy drinkers, reduced testosterone levels also contribute to loss of bone mass. A reduction in bone mass of 50 percent has been reported in chronic alcoholics (Emanuele & Emanuele, 1997, p. 62).

The Reproductive System

Men.   Studies have found that heavy alcohol consumption results in reduced testosterone levels and increased female sexual hormones (U.S. Department of Health and Human Services, 1997, p. 160). Alcohol consumption causes this condition by directly lowering testosterone levels (Emanuele & Emanuele, 1998, pp. 197–198). Additionally, faulty liver metabolism, caused by alcoholic hepatitis, transforms testosterone into female hormonal equivalents. Hormonal changes induced by excessive alcohol intake are implicated in diminished libido (sexual desire), impotence, testicular atrophy, decreased fertility, and gynecomastia (Emanuele & Emanuele, 1998, p. 197). Gynecomastia is a feminization of the male body, which occurs when there is not sufficient testosterone to block the effects of normally occurring estrogen in men. This condition is most evident by enlarged breasts (Emanuele & Emanuele, 1998, p. 198).

Heavy alcohol consumption has been shown to negatively affect sperm production (Emanuele & Emanuele, 1998, p. 199). Testicular atrophy appears to be common among chronic heavy drinkers, occurring in up to 75 percent of men with advanced alcoholic cirrhosis (Emanuele & Emanuele, 1998, p. 197).

Women.   Even moderate drinking in healthy women can lead to significant reproductive problems (Emanuele & Emanuele, 1997, p. 58). Excessive alcohol intake is associated with menstrual disturbance, spontaneous abortions, miscarriages, fertility, and sexual dysfunction (U.S. Department of Health and Human Services, 1997, p. 160). Alcohol consumption during early adolescence may delay the onset of female puberty (Dees et al., 1998, p. 165).

Pregnancy

Alcohol consumption by a woman while pregnant carries a risk of damage to the fetus. These negative effects have been designated either **fetal alcohol syndrome** (FAS), the more severe disorder, or **alcohol-related neurodevelopmental disorder** (ARND). The diagnostic criteria for FAS are:

1. Prenatal or postnatal growth deficiency or both (weight or length or both below the 10th percentile when corrected for gestational age).
2. Central nervous system disorders, including neurologic abnormality, developmental delay, intellectual impairment, and structural abnormalities (smaller brains and abnormal brain structure) (U.S. Department of Health and Human Services, 1997, p. 199).
3. A distinctive pattern of facial anomalies, including short palpebral fissures (eye openings); a thin upper lip; an elongated, flattened midface; and an indistinct philtrum (the zone between the nose and the mouth) (see Figure 3.5) (U.S. Department of Health and Human Services, 1997, p. 194).

Deficits in functioning associated with FAS are long-lasting and pervasive. There is a persistence of cognitive deficits. A group of closely followed individuals diagnosed with FAS ranging in age from 12 to 40 had a mean IQ of 68, which indicates mental retardation (U.S. Department of Health and Human Services, 1997, p. 198). This FAS sample had reading, spelling, and arithmetic achievement at the second- to fourth-grade level. They had great difficulty with abstractions such as time and space, understanding cause and effect, and generalizing from one situation to another. In some cases they gave bizarre answers, estimating the cost of an airplane to be $3, or the length of a man's spine to be 5 ft.

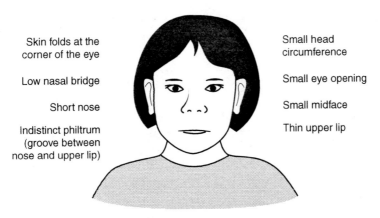

Skin folds at the corner of the eye

Low nasal bridge

Short nose

Indistinct philtrum (groove between nose and upper lip)

Small head circumference

Small eye opening

Small midface

Thin upper lip

FIGURE 3.5   Children with Fetal Alcohol Syndrome Have Characteristic Facial Features

Source: U.S. Department of Health and Human Services, 1993.

FAS children are often described as being hyperactive, impulsive (Jacobson & Jacobson, 1999, p. 29), and having short attention spans (U.S. Department of Health and Human Services, 1997, p. 198). They are socially maladroit and display increased aggression (Jacobson & Jacobson, 1999, pp. 27, 29). These children also suffer from a high rate of mental disorders (U.S. Department of Health and Human Services, 2000, p. 294).

A constellation of less severe effects of alcohol on the fetus is called alcohol-related neurodevelopmental disorder (ARND); such children have intellectual and behavioral deficits that resemble those of FAS but are less severe. ARND children have been found to have:

1. Growth retardation
2. Poor school performance (in reading, spelling, arithmetic)
3. Attention deficits
4. Impassivity
5. Increased aggression
6. Social problems (Jacobson & Jacobson, 1999, p. 29)

Amount and Timing of Maternal Alcohol Consumption and Consequences for the Fetus.   Over 4 percent of children conceived by heavy-drinking pregnant mothers have FAS (U.S. Department of Health and Human Services, 1997, p. 194). Data on alcohol's effect on the fetus has been obtained by using **longitudinal studies.** Longitudinal studies have followed pregnant women through conception and several years of their offsprings' development. Researchers asked the mothers about their alcohol consumption during pregnancy and then calculated the effects of maternal drinking on the children by measuring their performance on various cognitive tasks during their development. Some of the major findings of these studies are summarized in Table 3.3. The table shows that there can be long-lasting negative consequences for children whose mothers drank even less than one drink per day during pregnancy. This research suggests that mothers who have 7 to 14 drinks per week during pregnancy are at risk for having children with ARND (Jacobson & Jacobson, 1999, p. 25). Drinking mothers over 30 years old have an increased risk of having FAS or ARND children (Jacobson & Jacobson, 1999, p. 28).

The guidelines for safe drinking in Box 3.4 indicate no safe level for pregnant women, while Jacobson and Jacobson (1999) calculated that a conservative measure of safe drinking for pregnant women is 0.7 drink per week, or a little less than one drink per week.

There are not much data regarding the effect of the father's alcohol consumption on the fetus during the time of conception. Because of practical difficulties, there are no data for human males on this question. Tests on male laboratory animals, however, show that chronic or acute paternal alcohol consumption may affect behavior, fertility, and reproductive development of offspring (U.S. Department of Health and Human Services, 1997, p. 162).

Prevention of Fetal Alcohol Syndrome and Alcohol-Related Neurodevelopmental Disorder.   Warnings on alcohol products about potential damage to the fetus have been

TABLE 3.3   Effects of Maternal Daily Alcohol Consumption during Pregnancy

OUNCES OF ABSOLUTE ALCOHOL/DAY	NEOBEHAVIORAL OUTCOME	AGE OF CHILDREN AT TESTING
Seattle Study		
Prior to pregnancy recognition		
2.0	Delayed mental development	8 months
	Delayed gross motor development	8 months
	Greater impassivity	7 years
1.5	Lower IQ scores	4 years
	Poorer fine motor coordination	4 years
	Poorer sustained attention	7 years
1.0	Poorer sustained attention	4 years
0.5	Poorer fine motor coordination	4 years
Mid-pregnancy		
2.0	Poorer habituation	1–2 days
1.5	Poorer spatial relations	4 years
1.0	Lower IQ scores	7 years
Any alcohol daily	Slower reaction times	4 and 7 years
	More impulsive behavior	4 years
	Poorer gross motor balance	4 years
Detroit Study		
During pregnancy		
2.0	Delayed gross motor development and	12 months
	Sustained directed activity	12 months
1.0	Slower information-processing speed	6.5 and 12 months
0.5	Delayed mental development—bottom 10%	13 months
	Slower reaction time	6.5 months
	Smaller proportion of fast responses	6.5 months
Any alcohol daily	Delayed mental development	13 months
	Less complex play	12 months

Each ½ oz of alcohol equals one standard drink. Results are from two large-scale longitudinal studies. For references see U.S. Department of Health and Human Services, 1997, p. 208.

Source: Adapted from U.S. Department of Health and Human Services, 1997, p. 208.

shown to decrease consumption in pregnant women, but do not change drinking patterns (U.S. Department of Health and Human Services, 1997, p. 211). Many pregnant women, especially African American women, report not being counseled about FAS during their pregnancies (U.S. Department of Health and Human Services, 1997, p. 212). Supportive counseling, focused on reduction of alcohol consumption, has proved to be an effective preventative measure for heavy-drinking pregnant women (U.S. Department of Health and Human Services, 1997, p. 213).

BOX 3.4

U.S. DEPARTMENT OF AGRICULTURE GUIDELINES FOR DRINKING

Alcoholic beverages supply calories but few nutrients. Alcoholic beverages are harmful when consumed in excess, and some people should not drink at all. Excess alcohol alters judgment and can lead to dependence and a great many other serious health problems. Taking more than one drink per day for women or two drinks per day for men can raise the risk for motor vehicle crashes, other injuries, high blood pressure, stroke, violence, suicide, and certain types of cancer. Even one drink per day can slightly raise the risk for breast cancer. Alcohol consumption during pregnancy increases the risk of birth defects. Too much alcohol may cause social and psychologic problems, cirrhosis of the liver, inflammation of the pancreas, and damage to the brain and heart. Heavy drinkers also are at risk of malnutrition because alcohol contains calories that may substitute for those in nutritious foods. If adults choose to drink alcoholic beverages, they should consume them only in moderation—and with meals to slow alcohol absorption.

WHAT IS DRINKING IN MODERATION?

Moderation is defined as no more than one drink per day for women and no more than two drinks per day for men. This limit is based on differences between the sexes in both weight and metabolism.

> Count as a drink—
> 12 oz of regular beer (150 calories)
> 5 oz of wine (100 calories)
> 1.5 oz of 80-proof distilled spirits (100 calories)

Note: Even moderate drinking provides extra calories.

Drinking in moderation may lower risk for coronary heart disease, mainly among men over age 45 and women over age 55. However, there are other factors that reduce the risk of heart disease, including a healthy diet, physical activity, avoidance of smoking, and maintenance of a healthy weight.

Moderate consumption provides little, if any, health benefit for younger people. Risk of alcohol abuse increases when drinking starts at an early age.

Some studies suggest that older people may become more sensitive to the effects of alcohol as they age.

WHO SHOULD NOT DRINK?

Some people should not drink alcoholic beverages at all. These include:

Children and adolescents.

Individuals of any age who cannot restrict their drinking to moderate levels. This is a special concern for recovering alcoholics, problem drinkers, and people whose family members have alcohol problems.

Women who may become pregnant or who are pregnant. A safe level of alcohol intake has not been established for women at any time during pregnancy, including the first few weeks. Major birth defects, including fetal alcohol syndrome, can be caused by heavy drinking by the pregnant mother. Other fetal alcohol effects may occur at lower levels.

Individuals who plan to drive, operate machinery, or take part in other activities that require attention, skill, or coordination. Most people retain some alcohol in the blood up to 2 to 3 h after a single drink.

Individuals taking prescription or over-the-counter medications that can interact with alcohol. Alcohol alters the effectiveness or toxicity of many medications, and some medications may increase blood alcohol levels. If you take medications, ask your health care provider for advice about alcohol intake, especially if you are an older adult.

ADVICE FOR TODAY

If you choose to drink alcoholic beverages, do so sensibly, and in moderation.

Limit intake to one drink per day for women or two per day for men, and take with meals to slow alcohol absorption.

Avoid drinking before or when driving, or whenever it puts you or others at risk.

Source: U.S. Department of Agriculture, 2000.

60

SAFE DRINKING PRACTICES (FEDERAL GUIDELINES)

Periodically, there are reports on the beneficial effects of moderate drinking on health. The U.S. Department of Agriculture offers guidelines for alcohol consumption (see Box 3.4). Moderate amounts of alcohol have been found to have several health-related benefits, but if alcohol is consumed at greater levels, negative consequences outweigh the potential benefits. For example, Jose et al. (1999), surveying a sample of Dutch adults, found that light and moderate drinkers reported fewer health burdens than either abstainers or heavy drinkers. This common pattern is known as the U-shaped curve, although it conforms more closely to the letter J. That is, abstainers report fewer health problems than heavy drinkers, and low and moderate drinkers report the fewest health problems (see Figure 3.6).

WHO NEEDS TO WATCH THEIR DRINKING?

From research, we know that modest amounts of alcohol are safe and even beneficial for several medical conditions, but excessive drinking can have disastrous consequences. For other medical conditions, some of which are indicated in Box 3.4, no alcohol should be consumed. There has been controversy for some time whether people with alcohol problems can ever drink safely. There will be a full discussion of this issue in Chapter 11. The

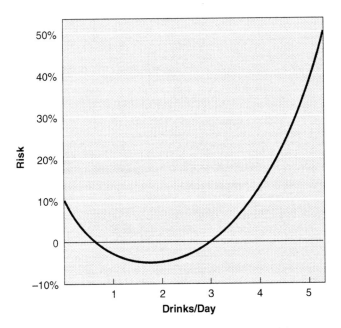

FIGURE 3.6   J-Shaped Curve Illustrating Increased Risk of Health Problems for Abstainers and Heavy Drinkers
Percentages are hypothetical.

following are some of the medical conditions and other circumstances that require careful attention to alcohol consumption.

Hepatitis

Hepatitis is a disorder in which the liver has become inflamed, which impairs its functioning. Since alcohol must be processed by the liver and places additional burdens on it, it is not advisable to drink alcohol while suffering from any type of hepatitis (Klag, 1999, p. 1039).

Hypertension

Alcohol consumption raises blood pressure. If a person already has high blood pressure, called hypertension, alcohol is contraindicated because it could raise the blood pressure further. Furthermore, alcohol interferes with the therapeutic effect of some blood pressure medications (Weathermon & Crabb, 1999, p. 52–53).

Diabetes Mellitus

Diabetes mellitus is a disease that interferes with the body's sugar, fat, and protein metabolism. It is caused most often by a deficiency or lack of the hormone insulin. There is some evidence that *occasional moderate drinking during meals* is helpful to diabetics by lowering blood sugar levels (Emanuele et al., 1998, pp. 213–214). Alcohol has a harmful effect when diabetics eat and drink too much, causing hyperglycemia, increased blood sugar level, and more dangerously, when they drink and do not eat enough (Emanuele et al., 1998, p. 214). This alcohol-induced hypoglycemia, too little sugar in the blood, can cause severe, irreversible neurologic problems, including paralysis, seizures, coma, and even death (Emanuele & Emanuele, 1997, p. 62; Emanuele et al., 1998, p. 215). A diabetic who engages in binge drinking and neglects to eat is putting himself at risk for severe medical complications and perhaps fatal consequences. Diabetics, if they drink at all, should drink only with meals, and then moderately. Regular drinking of more than two drinks per occasion has harmful consequences for diabetics (Emanuele et al., 1998, p. 211).

Gout

Gout is an inflammatory disease of the joints, caused by deposits of uric acid in the joints. Consumption of alcohol increases production of uric acid and therefore should be avoided by people with this disorder (Klag, 1999, pp. 652–653).

Osteoporosis

Osteoporosis causes thinning of the bones, making the person vulnerable to bone fractures. Since bone production is harmed by alcohol consumption, it is recommended that those who have this disorder not drink more than 2 drinks per occasion (Klag, 1999, p. 264).

Gastric and Duodenal Ulcers

Alcohol damages the lining of the gastrointestinal tract, so once ulcers have formed, any alcohol consumption is contraindicated (Klag, 1999, pp. 988, 990).

Sleep Disorders

Alcohol consumption is contraindicated for sleep disorders. Alcohol disrupts normal sleep, as discussed earlier in the chapter. Such disorders include sleep apnea, interrupted breathing during sleep, and bruxism, grinding of teeth (Klag, 1999, pp. 490, 493).

Medication

The effectiveness of some medications is reduced when alcohol is consumed. In other instances, dangerous levels of intoxication can be reached by combining alcohol and **cross-tolerant** medications, such as benzodiazapines (e.g., Valium) (Weathermon & Crabb, 1999). Even commonly used over-the-counter medications, such as antihistamines and aspirin, can have potentially damaging interactions with alcohol. Medication warning labels note the potential danger of known alcohol drug interactions. It is advisable to ask your physician if alcohol can be consumed while taking medication that he or she has prescribed.

CAUSE OF INTERACTION EFFECTS
BETWEEN ALCOHOL AND MEDICATION

Complications in metabolizing both alcohol and medication account for most of the possible interactive effects between alcohol and medication. The interactions are affected by the following conditions.

1. With no alcohol present in a normal drinker or abstainer, the expected rate of metabolism occurs and a therapeutic dose is assured.
2. With moderate alcohol consumption, the liver must metabolize the alcohol as well as the medication, resulting in a slower metabolism of the drug, creating higher medication levels in the body.
3. In chronic heavy drinkers, the liver processes the alcohol before the medication, which may result in slower metabolism of the drug, creating higher medication levels in the body.
4. In chronic heavy drinkers currently abstinent, the activity of the liver has become efficient in eliminating the alcohol and hence may work to metabolize cross-tolerant medication more quickly than normal (i.e., metabolic tolerance), resulting in insufficient levels of pain medication and anesthetics (Weathermon & Crabb, 1999, p. 43). This is one reason newly abstinent alcoholics in treatment are advised to discuss their drinking history with their physician.
5. Because alcohol is a depressant, other drugs that have similar psychoactive effects can intensify the depressant effect. In some instances the combination of alcohol and

another depressant drug creates a depressant effect greater than the sum of the two different doses. This is known as **potentiation.**

RECOMMENDATIONS

Medical Care

Perhaps the most obvious implication of this chapter is the need for good medical care and follow-up for all heavy drinkers. All clients seeking treatment for drinking problems should be advised to get a complete physical examination and urged to follow physician recommendations. Withdrawal from alcohol is a potentially dangerous procedure. Therefore, the need for medically supervised withdrawal should be emphasized to patients and their relatives.

Neurotransmitters and New Medications

One important application of research on neurotransmitters is the development of improved medications to help treat alcohol disorders. Naltrexone, for example, appears to block some of the reinforcing properties of alcohol. Two clinical trials support the efficacy of naltrexone in the treatment of alcoholism (Petrakis & Krystal, 1997). Studies indicate that naltrexone reduces craving for alcohol, loss of control over drinking, and some of alcohol's subjective pleasurable effects. However, more research is needed to confirm these results (Petrakis & Krystal, 1997, p. 158). A drug called acamprosate may block glutamate hyperactivity and reduce withdrawal symptoms (Littleton, 1999). This in turn may allow patients to remain abstinent rather than resume drinking to reduce withdrawal symptoms in early recovery. There are some preliminary studies which indicate that patients taking acamprosate were less likely to drop out of treatment and achieved higher rates of abstinence than those on placebo (Petrakis & Krystal, 1997, p. 160).

The Role of the Physician

Physicians can screen patients for alcohol disorders at several potential important points and provide important interventions.

1. If a person has a disease such as diabetes and drinking should be curtailed (see "Who Needs to Watch Their Drinking?"), physicians must advise the patient about the negative effects of drinking on the health problem. Physicians should be encouraged to offer this advice and receive training on doing so. There is no research indicating how often physicians do this or the approaches they take. Developing intervention models and researching them would be useful.

2. Physicians are in a position to screen for alcohol problems and provide motivation for treatment in a variety of medical settings. It has been shown that brief screenings in medical settings are effective (see Chapter 11), yet physicians do not typically receive training in this area. Such training should become routine.

3. Roche and Evans (1998) point out that alcohol screening has been used traditionally for disease detection. It could also be used to determine if drinking patterns are dangerous, whether or not they qualify for a diagnosis. Dangerous drinking patterns are responsible for many accidents.

4. Physicians are responsible for prescribing appropriate medication. Physicians are now well educated regarding the contraindications of prescribing potentially addicting medications to heavy drinkers. Safer and more effective medications are being developed as part of the treatment of alcoholism, such as naltrexone and acamprosate, discussed earlier in this section. Thus, it is important to encourage patients to be evaluated for appropriate medications to treat the effects of excessive alcohol use.

5. The American Society of Addiction Medicine (ASAM) is the medical society that assures appropriate training for physicians who wish to specialize in this area.

Cognitive Deficits in Heavy Drinkers

The cognitive deficits and other impairments in brain functioning evident after acute withdrawal have been called prolonged withdrawal syndrome (PWS). Consideration of the syndrome suggest several implications for treatment.

1. Because of the high prevalence of cognitive impairment in alcohol abusers, all patients with alcohol use disorders should be screened for cognitive impairment (Donavan et al., 1987, p. 340).

2. Psycho-education about PWS should be routinely offered to alcohol abusers. Newly abstinent patients often experience mental haze ("mocus" feeling), sleep problems, and depression. Reassuring the patient that much of this will often remit simply with time off alcohol will relieve the patient of a great deal of concern about his or her emotional and mental functioning.

3. Treatment tasks should be appropriate for the cognitive capabilities of the patients. In the first week or two following the cessation of drinking, alcoholics' information-processing capabilities are not much better than those of severely brain-damaged individuals. Less demanding content should be presented early. All treatment components should be repeated numerous times over the course of treatment. It makes sense to delay the administration of major treatment components until 1 to 2 weeks after drinking ceases (Goldman, 1987, p. 315).

4. Treatment staff should be educated about cognitive impairment in early phases of abstinence, which may increase an understanding of client behavior and apparent resistance. For example, cognitive impairment may explain some instances of "denial." With limited ability to process information and behavioral inflexibility, affected patients' responses may appear to be a defense mechanism against acknowledging the extent of drinking but instead may be an inability to understand or remember or make the connections that most people take for granted (Goldman, 1995, p. 152). For example, when asked about his last drinking episode, a recently abstinent alcoholic may not recall the amounts or consequences of the drinking. This can be easily misunderstood as denial.

5. Alcoholics Anonymous (AA) can be particularly helpful for clients who have PWS. AA meetings have a simple, regular format, place few demands on participants, offer simple, concrete advice, and use simple slogans, such as "Keep it simple." All of these elements provide structure and "ease of use" for those with impaired cognitive functioning.

6. Studies should be undertaken to see if cognitive remediation in early recovery can improve cognitive functioning and enhance treatment outcome for heavy drinkers (Donavan et al., 1987, p. 356). Another worthwhile investigation would be to develop treatment strategies modeled after approaches used with brain-damaged patients (Parsons, 1987b, p. 173).

Prevention, Education, and Counseling for Women Who Are Planning to Conceive or Are Pregnant

All women who are planning to conceive or are pregnant should be screened for alcohol consumption. There should be provision for special counseling for heavy-drinking pregnant women.

Smoking Cessation and Alcohol Treatment

This chapter highlights the greatly increased risk for many diseases for those who both smoke and drink heavily. Current evidence indicates that it is worthwhile to discuss smoking cessation in conjunction with alcohol treatment. (Chapter 11 summarizes this research.)

SUMMARY

The relationship between alcohol consumption and health generally conforms to a J-shaped curve. Abstinent individuals have slightly more health problems than those who drink moderately. Heavy drinkers have many more health problems than abstainers or moderate drinkers. That is, small amounts of consumption have some positive health effects on CAD, diabetes, and ischemic stroke, while heavy drinking has many harmful effects for virtually every organ in the body. Smoking in combination with heavy drinking creates even greater negative health consequences, as, for example, greatly increasing the risk for several cancers. Women have a greater susceptibility to negative health consequences of alcohol. Heavy-drinking women have greater susceptibility to liver disease, cardiomyopathy, and hemorrhagic stroke than heavy-drinking men.

The chapter discusses the negative consequences of heavy drinking on the various organ systems of the body. Of particular importance is alcohol's multiple effects on the brain. Alcohol consumption affects the brain acutely, in the form of intoxication and withdrawal. The withdrawal symptoms of cognitive impairment, sleep disturbance, and impaired coordination are caused by disruptions in the neurotransmitter system. Some cognitive impairment persists for several weeks or even longer, and has been called prolonged withdrawal syndrome. Chronic conditions include Wernike encephalopathy and Korsakoff syndrome. Alcohol indirectly affects the brain by causing increased risk of stroke and through liver dysfunction, causing portal-systemic encephalopathy.

Moderate safe drinking appears to be in the range of no more than two drinks per occasion for men and no more than one for women. Several medical conditions require very careful attention to alcohol consumption or contraindicate any use.

READINGS

Lender, M. E., & Martin, J. K. (1987). *Drinking in America.* New York: The Free Press, 1987.
A good introduction to the social and political history of alcohol in the United States.

Parsons, O. A., Butters, N., & Nathan, P. E. (1987). *Neuropsychology of alcoholism: Implications for diagnosis and treatment.* New York: Guilford.
An exemplary model of a book in which leading researchers summarize neurocognitive findings on alcoholics and discuss treatment implications.

REFERENCES

Apte, M. V., Wilson, J. S., & Korsten, M. A. (1997). Alcohol-related pancreatic damage. *Alcohol, Health, and Research World* 21, 13–20.

Ballard, H. S. (1997). The hematological complications of alcoholism. *Alcohol, Health, and Research World* 21, 42–52.

Bode, C., & Bode, J. C. (1997). Alcohol's role in gastrointestinal tract disorders. *Alcohol, Health, and Research World* 21, 76–83.

Brower, K. J. (2001). Alcohol's effects on sleep in alcoholics. *Alcohol, Health, and Research World* 25, 110–125.

Butters, N., & Granholm, E. (1987). The continuity hypothesis: Some conclusions and their implications for the etiology and neuropathology of alcoholic Korsakoff's syndrome. In O. A. Parsons, N. Butters, and P. E. Nathan (Eds.), *Neuropsychology of alcoholism: Implications for diagnosis and treatment* (pp. 176–206). New York: Guilford.

Butterworth, R. F. (1995). The role of liver disease in alcohol-induced cognitive deficits. *Alcohol, Health, and Research World* 19, 122–129.

Charness, M. E., Simon, R. P., and Greenberg, M. D. (1989). Ethanol and the nervous system. *New England Journal of Medicine* 321, 442–450.

Cook, P. J., & Moore, M. J. (2000). Alcohol. In J. P. Newhouse and A. Culyer (Eds.), *Handbook of health economics*, Vol. 1B. New York: Elsevier.

Dees, W. L., Hiney, J. K., & Srivastava, V. (1998). Alcohol's effects on female puberty. *Alcohol, Health, and Research World* 22, 165–169.

Donovan, D. M., Walker, R. D., & Kivlahan, D. R. (1987). Recovery and remediation of neuropsychological functions: Implications for alcoholism rehabilitation process and outcome. In O. A. Parsons, N. Butters, & P. E. Nathan (Eds.), *Neuropsychology of alcoholism: Implications for diagnosis and treatment* (pp. 339–360). New York: Guilford.

Emanuele, N., & Emanuele, M. (1997). The endocrine system: Alcohol alters critical hormonal balance. *Alcohol, Health, and Research World* 21, 53–64.

Emanuele, M. A., & Emanuele, N. V. (1998). Alcohol's effects on male reproduction. *Alcohol, Health, and Research World* 22, 195–201.

Emanuele, N. V., Swade, T. F., & Emanuele, M. A. (1998). Consequences of alcohol use in diabetes. *Alcohol, Health, and Research World* 22, 211–219.

Epstein, M. (1997). Alcohol's impact on kidney function. *Alcohol, Health, and Research World* 21, 84–92.

Finn, D. A., & Crabbe, J. C. (1997). Exploring alcohol withdrawal syndrome. *Alcohol, Health, and Research World* 21, 149–156.

Gentry, R. T. (2000). Effect of food on the pharmacokinetics of alcohol absorption. *Alcoholism: Clinical and Experimental Research* 24, 403–404.

Goldman, M. S. (1987). The role of time and practice in recovery of function in alcoholics. In O. A. Parsons, N. Butters, & P. E. Nathan (Eds.), *Neuropsychology of alcoholism: Implications for diagnosis and treatment* (pp. 291–321). New York: Guilford.

Goldman, M. S. (1995). Recovery of cognitive functioning in alcoholics. *Alcohol, Health, and Research World* 19, 148–154.

Goldstein, G. (1987). Recovery, treatment, and rehabilitation in chronic alcoholics. In O. A. Parsons, N. Butters, & P. E. Nathan (Eds.), *Neuropsychology of alcoholism: Implications for diagnosis and treatment* (pp. 361–377). New York: Guilford.

Gonzales, R. A., & Jaworski, J. N. (1997). Alcohol and glutamate. *Alcohol, Health, and Research World* 21, 120–127.

Jacobson, J. L., & Jacobson, S. W. (1999). Drinking moderately and pregnancy: Effects on child development. *Alcohol, Health, and Research World* 23, 25–30.

Jose, S., Van De MHeen, H., Van Oers, J. A., Machenbach, J. P., & Garretsen, H. F. (1999). The U-shaped curve; Various health measures and alcohol drinking patterns. *Journal of Studies on Alcohol* 60, 725–731.

Klag, M. J. (Ed.). (1999). *Johns Hopkins Family Health Book.* New York: HarperCollins.

Klatsky, A. L. (1999). Moderate drinking and reduced risk of heart disease. *Alcohol, Health, and Research World* 23, 15–23.

Langlais, P. J. (1995). Alcohol-related thiamin deficiency: Impact on cognitive and memory functioning. *Alcohol, Health, and Research World* 19, 113–121.

Latour, F., & Pring, J. (1997, September 28). MIT fraternity pledge in coma after drinking. *The Boston Globe,* p. B1.

Lender, M. E., & Martin, J. K. (1987). *Drinking in America.* New York: The Free Press.

Littleton, J. (1998). Neurochemical mechanisms underlying alcohol withdrawal. *Alcohol, Health, and Research World* 22, 13–24.

Lovinger, D. M. (1997). Serotonin's role in alcohol's effects on the brain. *Alcohol, Health, and Research World* 21, 114–120.

Maher, J. J. (1997). Exploring alcohol's effects on liver function. *Alcohol, Health, and Research World* 21, 5–12.

McLellan, A. T. (1986). "Psychiatric severity" as a predictor of outcome from substance abuse treatment. In R. E. Meyer (Ed.), *Psychopathology and addictive disorders* (pp. 97–139). New York: Guilford.

Oscar-Berman, M., Shagrin, B., Evert, D. L., & Epstein, C. (1997). Impairments of brain and behavior: The neurological effects of alcohol. *Alcohol, Health, and Research World* 21, 65–75.

Parsons, O. A. (1987a). Do neuropsychological deficits predict alcoholics' treatment course and posttreatment recovery? In O. A. Parsons, N. Butters, & P. E. Nathan (Eds.), *Neuropsychology of alcoholism: Implications for diagnosis and treatment* (pp. 273–290). New York: Guilford.

Parsons, O. A. (1987b). Neuropsychological consequences of alcohol abuse: Many questions, some answers. In O. A. Parsons, N. Butters, & P. E. Nathan (Eds.), *Neuropsychology of alcoholism: Implications for diagnosis and treatment* (pp. 153–175). New York: Guilford.

Petrakis, I., & Krystal, J. (1997). Neuroscience: Implications for treatment. *Alcohol, Health, and Research World* 21, 157–160.

Roberts, A. J., & Koob, G. F. (1987). The neurobiology of addiction. *Alcohol, Health, and Research World,* 21, #2, p. 101–108.

Roche, A. M., & Evans, K. R. (1998). The implications of drinking patterns for primary prevention, education and screening. In M. Grant and J. Litvak (Eds.), *Drinking patterns and their consequences* (pp. 243–265). Washington, DC: Taylor & Francis.

Royce, J. E. (1981). *Alcohol problems and alcoholism: A comprehensive survey.* New York: The Free Press.

Sacks, O. (1985). *The man who mistook his wife for a hat.* New York: Summit Books.

Saitz, R. (1998). Introduction to alcohol withdrawal. *Alcohol, Health, and Research World* 22, 5–12.

Sampson, H. W. (1998). Alcohol's harmful effects on bone. *Alcohol, Health, and Research World* 22, 190–194.

Schuckit, M. A. (1989). *Drug and alcohol abuse: A clinical guide to diagnosis and treatment.* 3rd ed. New York: Plenum.

Swift, R., & Davidson, D. (1998). Alcohol hangover: Mechanisms and mediators. *Alcohol, Health, and Research World* 22, 54–60.

The New Jerusalem Bible (1985). New York: Doubleday, 23:19.

Trevisan, L. A., Botros, N., Petrakis, I. L., and Krystal, J. H. (1998). Complications of alcohol withdrawal. *Alcohol, Health, and Research World* 22, 61–66.

U.S. Department of Agriculture (2000). Nutrition and your health: Dietary guidelines for Americans, 2000, http://www.health.gov/dietaryguidelines/dga2000/DIETGD.PDF.

U.S. Department of Health and Human Services (1993). *Eighth Special Report to the U.S. Congress on alcohol and health.*

U.S. Department of Health and Human Services (1997). *Ninth Special Report to the U.S. Congress on alcohol and health.*

U.S. Department of Health and Human Services (2000). *Tenth Special Report to the U.S. Congress on alcohol and health.*

Vogel-Sprott, M. (1997). Is behavioral tolerance learned? *Alcohol, Health, and Research World* 21, 161–168.

Weathermon, R., & Crabb, D. W. (1999). Alcohol and medication interactions. *Alcohol, Health, and Research World* 23, 40–54.

Zakhari, S. (1997). Alcohol and the cardiovascular system: Molecular mechanisms for beneficial and harmful action. *Alcohol, Health, and Research World* 21, 21–29.

CHAPTER FOUR

HEREDITY AND ALCOHOL

Is alcoholism inherited? Framed this way, the question implies that there is a categorical yes or no answer. As we have learned so often in research on human behavior, the answer is not that simple. Although research demonstrates that hereditary factors make some individuals more vulnerable to developing alcohol disorders, environmental factors also play an important role in the development of alcoholism. Two types of studies offer support for a genetic transmission of vulnerability to alcoholism. (1) Twin studies compare the shared rates of alcoholism between identical and fraternal twins. Identical twins have the same genetic makeup and fraternal twins share about half of their genes. If identical twins have a higher shared rate of alcoholism than fraternal twins, this is suggestive of a genetic contribution. (2) In adoption studies, adoptees with biologic alcoholic parents can be compared to adoptees whose biologic parents are not alcoholic. If the adoptees with biologic alcoholic parents have a greater rate of alcoholism than those without alcoholic parents, this suggests a genetic contribution.

Researchers are seeking to find out what specific genes are associated with alcoholism and what is being genetically transmitted that makes some individuals vulnerable to alcoholism. In this chapter we will discuss:

1. Basic genetic concepts
2. Twin studies on genetic vulnerability to alcoholism
3. Adoption studies on genetic vulnerability to alcoholism
4. Research on determining what is genetically transmitted
5. Introduction to COGA research: efforts to determine what genes are implicated in alcoholism vulnerability and their function

METHODOLOGY

In genetic research on animals and plants, organisms with known genetic background can be selectively mated with organisms of different genetic makeup; outcomes of these matings can be examined to infer hereditary influences. More recent advances in genetic technology permit the direct manipulation of genetic material of organisms to determine the function of specific genes. Ethical constraints make it impossible to do these types of studies on humans. Instead, more inferential types of research must be conducted such as familial, twin, and adoption studies.

Family studies determine the degree to which alcoholism runs in families. The problem with such studies is the confound of having an alcoholic in the environment, which may contribute to the vulnerability as well as the genetic component.

Twin studies compare the rate of shared alcoholism between identical and fraternal twins. Findings that show a higher rate of shared alcoholism among identical twins than fraternal twins suggest a genetic link to alcoholism vulnerability. These studies have been criticized because of assumptions that have to be made regarding the comparison of shared genetic material of fraternal twins compared to identical twins to calculate heritability (what percentage of alcoholism liability is genetic) (Searles, 1990). Another problem is that twins are a special group of humans, which may make results from these studies not generalizable to other populations.

Adoption studies compare biologic offspring of alcoholics who are adopted out with adopted-out offspring whose biologic parents are not alcoholic. Adopting-out parents, adopting parents, and adoptees all have special characteristics and do not reflect the general population, which also raises the question regarding extrapolation to the population at large (Searles, 1990). For example, because adopting-out parents have a high rate of alcohol problems, adoptees are at higher genetic risk for alcoholism than the general public (Heath, 1995, p. 167).

Making research in this area even more difficult is the concept of genetic heterogeneity. That is, it is believed that several different genes influence the risk of developing alcohol problems. Further, there may be different forms of alcohol problems that have different genetic contributions (Schuckit, 1994).

The methodology of the Human Genome Project relies on recent innovations in replicating DNA material and finding ways to mark it, enabling researchers to construct a map of all human genes. Using techniques and data from this project, the Collaborative Study on the Genetics of Alcoholism (COGA) is seeking to determine the specific genes that add liability to developing alcohol disorders and what these genes control to bring it about.

BASIC HUMAN GENETICS

Humans have 23 chromosome pairs. Each biologic parent provides one chromosome of each pair to its offspring. Within the chromosomes are a total of 60,000–70,000 genes (Merikangas & Avenevoli, 2000), which direct many important activities of the body. We know that gene pairs, separately, or in combination with other gene pairs, direct the formation of enzymes and proteins in the body. Currently scientists know the specific function of only 5,000 gene pairs (Merikangas & Avenevoli, 2000). With the Human Genome Project, the opportunity to determine the function of all gene pairs is feasible. Many diseases have a genetic component. For a few diseases, such as hemophilia, only one gene pair affects outcome. For many diseases, such as diabetes, however, several gene pairs are probably implicated (Collins & Fink, 1995, p. 191). Similarly, it is now believed that the genetic vulnerability to alcoholism is controlled by multiple gene pairs (U.S. Department of Health and Human Services, 2000, p. 160).

Siblings share on average 50 percent of the same genetic makeup. Identical twins share 100 percent of the same genetic makeup because they originate from the same fertilized egg (zygote). Fraternal twins share on average 50 percent of the same genetic makeup, the same as ordinary siblings, because they develop from two separately fertilized eggs. These differences in genetic makeup have provided a means to research genetic factors in alcohol vulnerability.

EVIDENCE OF A GENETIC FACTOR IN VULNERABILITY TO ALCOHOLISM

Family Studies

We have known for a long time that alcohol problems run in families (Schuckit, 1989). For example, one recent study has shown that brothers and sisters of patients in treatment for alcohol dependence have more than twice the frequency of this disorder compared to controls (Bierut et al., 1998). Table 4.1 provides more detailed information about the study's results. The Harvard Study of Adult Development, discussed in Chapter 6, also found heightened risk for alcoholism for those with alcoholic family members.

Twin Studies

In twin studies, researchers compare the rates of shared alcohol use disorders between identical (MZ) and fraternal twins (DZ). The correlation between one twin having the disorder and the other having it is called the *concordance rate*. Thus, if genetic factors are strong, the concordance rate in identical twins should be higher than the rate for fraternal twins. If alcoholism were completely genetically controlled, the concordance rate between identical twins would be 100 percent; that is, if one of the twins had alcoholism, it would be certain the other one did and vice versa.

Kaij (1960, as cited in McGue, 1994) in Sweden identified male fraternal and identical twins who had a public record of alcohol problems. He found a 71 percent concordance rate for alcoholism in MZ males compared to a 32 percent rate in DZ males.

TABLE 4.1   Lifetime Prevalence of Alcohol Dependence for a Sample of Patients in Treatment and Their Siblings Compared with Control Group Subjects and Their Siblings

ALCOHOLICS IN TREATMENT	SIBLINGS OF ALCOHOLICS	CONTROL SUBJECTS	SIBLINGS OF CONTROLS
Men ($n = 916$)	($n = 1,197$)	($n = 111$)	($n = 111$)
100%*	49.7**	16.2	19.8
Women ($n = 296$)	($n = 1,558$)	($n = 106$)	($n = 143$)
100%*	23.8**	3.8	6.0

*$p < 0.001$ versus control subjects.

**$p < 0.001$ versus control siblings.

Source: Bierut et al., 1998. Adapted by permission of the American Medical Association.

In the United States, Veterans Administration (VA) medical records of male identical and fraternal twin veterans were examined for alcoholism. A 26.3 percent concordance rate for alcoholism was found for MZ twins, compared to 11.9 percent for DZ twins (cited in Heath, 1995, p. 168).

Pickens et al. (1991) and McGue et al. (1992) conducted studies of twins of whom one member was treated for alcoholism. Male MZ twins had higher concordance rates for alcohol dependence (0.59) than DZ twins (0.36). For females, MZ twins showed higher concordance rates (0.25) than DZ twins (0.05) for alcohol dependence, but not for alcohol abuse, where the concordance rate was 0.27 for both. Their results suggest that there is a genetic factor for alcohol dependence but not for alcohol abuse.

Heath et al. (1989) found an interaction between genetic and environmental factors in the drinking habits of female twins. The results showed that unmarried identical twins had very similar drinking habits; when one or both of the twins were married, this effect was moderated. The effect of marriage reduced the impact of the genetic contribution by half. The results of this study suggest that marriage may play a protective role for alcohol use disorders in women with a genetic vulnerability to them.

Gabrielli and Plomin (1985) assessed the effect of heredity and environment on drinking practices by noting differences between concordances of identical (MZ), fraternal (DZ) twins, nontwin sibling pairs, and unrelated adoptees raised together. Thus, the effects of genetic contribution and environment could be systematically assessed. The results showed that MZ twins had much greater concordance in their drinking practices than did DZ twins, siblings, or unrelated adoptees. This study showed virtually no effect of shared environment (i.e., unrelated adoptees raised in the same household had very low concordance regarding drinking practices). Should this finding hold up, it suggests that parental impact on their children's drinking behavior is negligible! One criticism of twin studies is that the shared environment and twin status may be confounded. That is, MZ twins may be treated more alike than DZ twins and thus it is not clear whether it is the genetic similarity or the treatment by the parents that is responsible for the similarity in drinking status. However, studies of MZ twins raised separately, which eliminate the confound of shared environment, also show a high concordance rate for alcohol use disorders (U.S. Department of Health and Human Services, 1993, p. 63).

Cadoret (1990), in a review of thirteen twin studies on alcohol problems, concludes that the overall findings support a genetic contribution to alcohol abuse risk. Table 4.2 shows the concordance rates for several of these studies.

Adoption Studies

Several studies have been conducted comparing the rate of alcohol problems of adoptees with biologic alcoholic parents (BAP) with adoptees whose biologic parents were not alcoholic (NBAP). Goodwin's Danish adoption study was the first and most famous. He searched the records of 5,000 nonfamily adoption cases in Denmark in the period 1924–1947, was able to gain the cooperation of 55 male adoptees with BAP, and used as controls 78 adoptees with NBAP (Goodwin, 1976, p. 65). Information on adoptee drinking patterns was obtained by interviews with a psychiatrist who did not know whether the adoptee had an alcoholic parent or not.

TABLE 4.2   Same-Sex Twin Concordance for Alcoholism in Male and Female Samples

STUDY	DIAGNOSIS	CONCORDANCE		MZ/DZ RATIO
		MZ	DZ	
Males				
Kaij (1960)	Chronic alcoholism	0.71	0.32	2.2*
		$n = 14$	$n = 31$	
Hrubec and Omenn (1981)	ICD-8 alcoholism	0.26	0.12	2.2*
		$n = 271$	$n = 444$	
Gurling et al. (1984)	WHO alcohol-dependence syndrome	0.33	0.30	1.1
		$n = 15$	$n = 20$	
Pickens et al. (1991)	DSM-III alcohol dependence	0.59	0.36	1.6*
		$n = 39$	$n = 47$	
Pickens et al. (1991)	DSM-III alcohol abuse and/or dependence	0.76	0.61	1.3*
		$n = 50$	$n = 64$	
McGue et al. (1992)	DSM-III alcohol abuse and/or dependence	0.77	0.54	1.4*
		$n = 85$	$n = 96$	
Caldwell and Gottesman (1991)	DSM-III alcohol dependence	0.40	0.13	3.1*
		$n = 20$	$n = 15$	
Caldwell and Gottesman (1991)	DSM-III alcohol abuse and/or dependence	0.68	0.46	1.5*
		$n = 28$	$n = 26$	
Females				
Gurling et al. (1984)	WHO alcohol-dependence syndrome	0.08	0.13	0.6
		$n = 13$	$n = 8$	
Pickens et al. (1991)	DSM-III alcohol dependence	0.25	0.05	5.0*
		$n = 24$	$n = 20$	
Pickens et al. (1991)	DSM-III alcohol abuse and/or dependence	0.36	0.25	1.4
		$n = 31$	$n = 24$	
McGue et al. (1992)	DSM-III alcohol abuse and/or dependence	0.39	0.42	0.9
		$n = 44$	$n = 43$	
Caldwell and Gottesman (1991)	DSM-III alcohol dependence	0.29	0.25	1.2
		$n = 7$	$n = 12$	
Caldwell and Gottesman (1991)	DSM-III alcohol abuse and/or dependence	0.47	0.42	1.1
		$n = 17$	$n = 24$	
Kendler et al. (1992)	DSMIIIR alcohol dependence	0.32	0.24	1.3*
		$n = 81$	$n = 79$	

*MZ – DZ difference in concordance significant at $p < 0.05$.

Source: Adapted from McGue, 1994.

Table 4.3 summarizes the results, showing that adoptees with alcoholic parents were more likely to suffer from various alcohol problems. Adoptees with BAP averaged 2.05 alcohol problems compared to 1.23 for the controls, a statistically significant result (Goodwin, 1976, p. 70). Using Goodwin's definition of alcoholism (the research was conducted long before DSM-III), 18 percent (10/55) of adoptees with BAP were alcoholic versus

TABLE 4.3   Drinking Problems and Patterns in Adopted Sons with Biologic Alcoholic Parents Compared to Adopted Sons with Nonalcoholic Biologic Parents

SYMPTOM	ADOPTEES WITH BAP n = 55	ADOPTEES WITH NBAP n = 78
Hallucinations*	6%	0%
Lost control*	35%	17%
Amnesia	53%	41%
Tremor	24%	22%
Morning drinking*	29%	11%
Delirium tremens	6%	1%
Rum fits	2%	0%
Social disapproval	6%	8%
Marital trouble	18%	9%
Job trouble	75%	3%
Drunken driving arrests	7%	4%
Police trouble other	15%	8%
Treated for drinking, ever*	16%	1
Hospitalized for drinking	11%	0%
Drinking pattern		
Moderate drinker	51%	45%
Heavy drinker, ever	22%	36%
Problem drinker, ever	9%	14%
Alcoholic, ever*	18%	5%

BAP = biologic alcohol parents. NBAP = nonalcoholic biologic parents. *These differences between the groups are statistically significant, meaning they are unlikley to have occurred by chance.

Source: Goodwin, 1976.

5 percent (4/78) of the controls (Goodwin, 1976, p. 71). Thus, the adoptees with alcoholic biologic parents had almost four times the rate of alcoholism as the controls.

Goodwin also interviewed the siblings of the adoptees with BAP who were not adopted out. The sons who remained with the alcoholic parents actually had fewer signs of alcohol problems than their adopted brothers (p. 75). Goodwin concluded that this was evidence that environmental factors were not an important factor in the development of alcoholism. Goodwin, however, failed to realize that the environmental effect of adoption and other differences between the brothers who were adopted and those who were not are confounds and may have overridden the effect of being raised by an alcoholic parent. Because of these confounds and the small sample size, the result cannot be considered conclusive. The point has also been made that because only 18 percent of the sons with alcoholic parents became alcoholic, environmental factors must also be important in the expression of alcoholism (Fingarette, 1988). Goodwin and colleagues conducted similar studies with female adoptees but did not find elevated rates of alcoholism for female adoptees with alcoholic biologic parents (1977, cited by McGue, 1994).

Another Scandinavian study is the Stockholm adoption study, which identified adoptees in the period 1930–1949 (Cloninger et al., 1981; Cloninger et al., 1985). The researchers had access to records kept by several governmental agencies, which provided them with detailed information on the biologic parents, the adoptive parents, and the adoptees. Both male and female adoptees with biologic alcoholic parents had higher rates of alcoholism than controls, but only the sons had significantly higher rates. Their analysis showed that milder alcohol problems in men and women were found to have a large environmental component, whereas more severe alcohol problems in males were largely genetically determined. These results suggest that there are different types of alcohol disorders, which are differentially responsive to genetic and environmental influences.

Cadoret (1990) investigated the influences of biologic and adoptive parents on Iowa adoptees. He used adoption records to determine if the biologic parents had alcohol problems or antisocial behavior. He interviewed adoptees and adoptive parents to determine if they had an alcohol disorder. This study allowed a comparison of genetic and environmental influences of alcoholic parents on the effect of vulnerability to alcoholism in their offspring. The Iowa data suggest that having biologic alcoholic parents and being raised by an adoptive alcoholic parent both increased the risk for alcoholism. Additionally, those adoptees whose biologic parents were antisocial had elevated rates of alcoholism. In these studies, both male and female adoptees with biologic parents with alcoholism were more likely to develop alcoholism.

A summary of results of adoption studies is given in Table 4.4.

The Extent of Genetic Influence

In a **meta-analysis** of adoption and twin studies, Heath (1995, p. 169) found that genetic contribution is a significant factor in determining susceptibility to alcohol use disorders. According to his analysis of U.S. studies, genetic effects account for approximately 60 percent of the variance in alcoholism risk. The reader must be cautioned not to interpret this figure to mean that a child of an alcoholic has a 60 percent chance of becoming alcoholic. The statistic means that it is estimated that just over half of the risk factors that contribute to alcoholism are genetic (Heath et al., 1997). Heath (1995, p. 170) notes that studies have consistently shown a genetic factor in alcoholism vulnerability despite differences in subject samples, methodologies, and alcoholism diagnoses from the 1920s to the present. In sum, family studies, adoption studies, and twin studies strongly suggest that there is a genetic contribution to alcoholism. At the same time, these studies also imply that there is an important environmental role in the genesis of alcohol disorders. Heath's estimate that 60 percent of the risk factors are genetic implies that the other 40 percent are environmental.

Do Men and Women Differ in Their Genetic Vulnerability to Alcoholism?

Reviewing many adoption and twin studies, McGue (1994) concluded that the genetic contribution to alcoholism is moderate in men but only modest in women. An examination of Tables 4.2 and 4.4 indicates that men more consistently show evidence of a hereditary factor in alcoholism vulnerability than women. Heath et al. (1997) suggest that a reason

TABLE 4.4   Adoptee Risk (%) of Alcoholism as a Function of History of Alcoholism in Biologic Parents

STUDY	HISTORY OF ALCOHOLISM IN BIOLOGIC PARENTS		
	POSITIVE	NEGATIVE	POSITIVE/NEGATIVE RISK RATIO
Males			
Roe (1944)	0.0%	0.0%	1.0
	$n = 21$	$n = 11$	
Goodwin et al. (1973)	18%	5%	3.6*
	$n = 55$	$n = 78$	
Clonninger et al. (1981)	23.3%	14.7%	1.6*
	$n = 291$	$n = 571$	
Cadoret et al. (1985)	61.1%	23.9%	2.6*
	$n = 18$	$n = 109$	
Cadoret et al. (1987)	62.5%	20.4%	3.1*
	$n = 8$	$n = 152$	
Females			
Roe (1944)	0.0%	0.0%	(1.0)
	$n = 11$	$n = 14$	
Goodwin et al. (1977)	2.0%	4.0%	0.5
	$n = 49$	$n = 47$	
Bohman et al. (1981)	4.5%	2.8%	1.6*
	$n = 336$	$n = 577$	
Cadoret et al. (1985)	33.3%	5.3%	6.3*
	$n = 12$	75	

*Rate in positive biologic family history group significantly greater than in negative biologic family history group at $p < 0.05$.

Source: McGue, 1994.

for this finding is the lower rate of alcoholism in women, which makes it more difficult to prove statistically that there is a genetic factor in women's vulnerability to alcoholism. Heath and his colleagues (1997) reanalyzed the data of these studies taking this factor into account and found women were equally affected by genetic factors in susceptibility to alcoholism as men.

WHAT IS GENETICALLY TRANSMITTED?

The twin and adoption studies suggest there is a genetic contribution to creating a vulnerability to alcohol disorders. How could genetic influence cause an increase in vulnerability to alcoholism? Currently, there are three mechanisms under consideration:

1. A genetically transmitted faulty enzyme, which normally has the effect of protecting against alcoholism, impairs the metabolism of alcohol.

2. Alcoholics may have a genetically induced lower response to alcohol, which may make them more susceptible to heavier drinking habits.
3. Some inherited aspects of cognitive functioning may be different in alcoholics. How this would facilitate alcoholism is not clear.

Asian Alcohol-Flush Reaction and Impaired Metabolism of Alcohol

People of Asian descent consistently experience lower levels of alcoholism and higher rates of abstinence than other ethnic groups (Wall & Ehlers, 1995, p. 184). About half have the alcohol-flush reaction (see Chapter 3). The alcohol-flush reaction is caused by a faulty enzyme that is involved in the metabolism of alcohol; the production of this enzyme is controlled by gene transmission. There are three possible genetic variations in transmission:

1. The offspring receives the normal gene from both parents; thus the normal enzyme can be synthesized.
2. The offspring receives one defective gene from one parent and one normal one from the other parent; the enzyme created is only partially effective, giving rise to a reduced capacity to metabolize acetaldehyde and causing a moderate flush reaction.
3. The offspring receives defective genes from both parents and the enzyme created is severely limited in metabolizing alcohol, resulting in a full-blown flush reaction. Figure 4.1 shows the response to alcohol of groups one and two in an experimental study.

The evidence is strong that this inherited trait protects Asians from alcohol use disorders. Asians with the severely impaired enzyme drink very little and rarely become alcoholic. Those with some impairment in acetaldehyde metabolism drink significantly less and are much less likely to be alcoholic than Asians with no impairment (Wall & Ehlers, 1995, p. 186). Only 2 percent of Chinese and Japanese alcoholics have the flushing response, while its overall prevalence is 50 percent in the Chinese and Japanese populations, implying that Chinese and Japanese with the faulty gene rarely become alcoholic (U.S. Department of Health and Human Services, 1997, p. 39).

Thus, this genetic factor influences drinking patterns by providing Asians some protection from alcohol problems, functioning as a built-in negative reinforcer for drinking. Other genes may play a similar role for other genetic groups (Couzigou et al., 1994).

Lowered Response to Alcohol as a Risk Factor

Schuckit (1995, p. 172), investigating differences between sons of alcoholics and control subjects, discovered that sons of alcoholics often had a less intense reaction to alcohol than control subjects. He compared sons of alcoholics ages 18–25 who drank but were not alcoholic with men with no family history of alcoholism. Subjects were given a dose of alcohol based on their weight (ranging from 3 to 5 standard drinks). Their reactions to the alcohol were measured over the next 3 h. Measures included felt intoxication, body sway, and brain activity. Forty percent of the sons of alcoholics but fewer than 10 percent of the control subjects demonstrated low levels or reaction to the alcohol. This suggests that sons

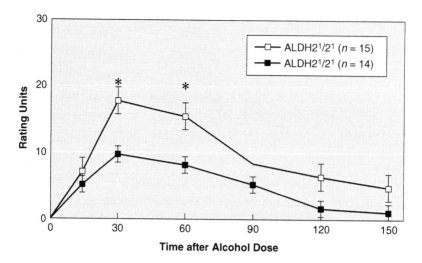

FIGURE 4.1   Subjective Self-Assessment of the "Effects of Alcohol" by Fifteen Men Homozygous for ALDH2[1] (solid squares) [described in text as group 1] and Fourteen Men with ALDH2[1]/ALDH2[2] Genotype (open squares) [described in text as group 2] at Different Times after a Single Dose of Alcohol (0.75 ml/kg body weight). The intensity of reported alcohol effects is presented in arbitrary rating units. Error bars indicate standard error of the mean.
* = significant difference between the groups ($p < 0.05$).
Source: Wall & Ehlers, 1995.

of alcoholics may inherit a high tolerance to alcohol. Feeling less affected by alcohol, these individuals may not get the "warning signs" of intoxication, and thus continue to drink excessively, eventually developing alcoholism. They were followed up when they were about 30 years old. Significantly, 56 percent of the sons of alcoholics with lower levels of alcohol response developed alcoholism, compared with only 14 percent of those with high levels of sensitivity to alcohol. Figure 4.2 shows the differences in response to alcohol between those who later developed alcoholism and those who did not. These findings suggest that low level of response to alcohol may be an important genetic-linked risk factor for alcoholism (Schuckit, 1995, p. 174).

Brain Activity and Alcoholics: Event-Related Potentials

Scientists measure brain wave activity, which provides information about cognitive functioning. One such class of brain waves is called event-related potential (ERP), which appears when a novel stimulus is presented to a subject. Several studies have found that abstinent alcoholics and their offspring have a lowered response in an ERP called P300. Twin studies provide evidence that this response is heritable (Heath, 1994). Polich et al. (1994) conducted a meta-analysis covering thirty studies, which showed that men with family histories of alcoholism had lower P300 responses than those who did not. Thus, the

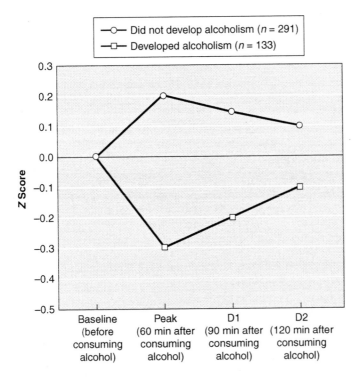

FIGURE 4.2   Responses to Alcohol (Z scores) Compared for 424 Subjects Followed for More than 8 Years to Monitor whether They Developed Alcoholism. Z scores show how far a subject's reaction to alcohol differs from the average response. Levels of reactions were based on subjective reports and changes in body sway and the hormone cortisol. Those who later developed alcoholism had much lower Z scores at their peak blood alcohol concentrations and at subsequent time points, D1 and D2, than those who did not develop alcoholism. (Only subjects for whom all relevant data were available were included.)

Source: Schuckit, 1995.

reduced P300 response may be a **marker** for alcohol use disorders (Porjesz & Begleiter, 1995, p. 233). That is, this lowered brain wave response may reliably predict the development of alcohol problems.

Other Possible Mechanisms

There is some evidence that alcohol reduces stress more in those with a family history of alcoholism than in those without it (Greeley & Oei, 1999), suggesting that there may be some inherited mechanism that makes alcohol a more effective stress reducer, which would make affected individuals more susceptible to excessive drinking. Tarter et al. (1990) found that sons of alcoholics had a higher than average behavioral activity level. This may be an inherited trait and contribute to vulnerability to alcoholism. Schuckit and Crabbe (2000) suggest that another genetically influenced risk factor is an independent psychiatric disorder. That is, certain psychiatric disorders such as antisocial personality disorder have a genetic component. Those with such disorders have a heightened risk for alcohol and other substance use disorders. Thus, the genetic component of risk of developing these psychiatric disorders also may increase the risk of developing alcohol and other substance use disorders.

THE HUMAN GENOME PROJECT

The goal of the Human Genome Project is to decipher the human genetic code (**genome**). All of the 60,000–70,00 human genes can be located and then researched for function. For example, by using genetic maps developed by the project, it has been determined that five different genes appear to play a role in type one diabetes (Collins & Fink, 1995, p. 191). It is believed that alcohol use disorders will also be found to be influenced by several genes (**polygenic**).

The Collaborative Study on the Genetics of Alcoholism (COGA)

Using the results of the Human Genome Project, the Collaborative Study on the Genetics of Alcoholism (COGA) was created to investigate the genetic components of the susceptibility to alcohol abuse and dependency (Beglieter, 1995). Investigators are comparing DNA differences between individuals with a heavy genetic loading for alcohol use disorders (close relatives of alcoholics) with controls, hoping to find the specific genes responsible for the genetic mechanism for increasing risk for alcoholism. For example, investigators are searching for the genes responsible for lowered response to alcohol and those for the lowered P300 brain waves. When these genes are identified, the prevalence of these genes between the group heavily loaded for alcoholism genes and the control group can be compared. If both the genes responsible for P300 and lowered response to alcohol occur at high rates in the group heavily loaded for alcoholism and occur at low rates for those in the control group, it suggests that these genes are implicated in vulnerability to alcoholism. In this way it can be determined whether these specific genes are implicated in a genetic contribution to alcohol problems. If so, these genes could be used as markers of the disorder. Such a finding would provide information about people's vulnerability to alcohol use disorders long before the time they develop the disorder.

RECOMMENDATIONS

Treatment

One of the features of traditional treatment has been to ease the burden of guilt for those with alcohol use disorders. Certainly those with a high genetic loading for these disorders are not responsible for this genetic factor. It could be argued that the sense of responsibility that diabetics have for their disorder applies to alcoholics: they are not responsible for creating the disorder, but once they know the steps they need to take to control it, they have the responsibility to do so. While alcohol use disorders are not as clearly a disease entity, the same logic as treating diabetes makes sense therapeutically. The message to the patient would be: "Many factors contributed to creating your alcohol disorder, including a genetic contribution and environmental factors out of your control. But it's your responsibility now to take appropriate steps to arrest the disorder."

Prevention

Should the COGA project discover markers for alcohol use disorder such as the lowered response to alcohol or lowered P300 brain waves, it would be possible to determine those at risk for the disorder long before it appeared. This would provide an opportunity to provide special prevention measures for these individuals. Employers and insurance companies could use this information to discriminate against those with such markers, however. Safeguards should be developed to protect these individuals.

SUMMARY

Family, twin, and adoption studies indicate that heredity plays a significant role in the risk of acquiring an alcohol use disorder. The current understanding is that a number of different genes contribute to liability and protective factors. This research also indicates that environmental factors play an important role in liability, if only by implication, because heredity factors, though significant, do not reliably account for the occurrence of alcohol use disorders. These genetic components interact with environmental factors. For example, Heath et al. (1989) found that marriage mitigated the genetic expression of heavy drinking in MZ female twins. Current research trends indicate that more severe alcohol use disorders are more under genetic control than less severe alcohol disorders.

For Asians at least, a genetic factor of enzyme production offers protection against alcohol use disorders. Other possible genetic factors include the lowered response to alcohol and the decreased brain wave response found in alcoholics and sons of alcoholics. COGA, using the advances of the Human Genome Project, is investigating whether the latter two mechanisms are reliably associated with specific genes and whether they will reliably be associated with alcohol abusers.

READINGS

Cloninger, C. R., Bohman, M. Sigvardsson, S., & von Knorring, A. L. (1985). Psychopathology in adopted-out children of alcoholics: The Stockholm adoption study. In M. Galanter (Ed.), *Recent developments in alcoholism*, Vol. 3 (pp. 37–51). New York: Plenum.
   This is a good summary of the important adoption study.
Schuckit, M. A. (1994). A clinical model of genetic influences in alcohol dependence. *Journal of Studies on Alcohol* 55, 5–17.
   This article explains the complexity of the genetic contribution to alcoholism vulnerability clearly.

REFERENCES

Beglieter, H. (1995). The collaborative study on the genetics of alcoholism. *Alcohol, Health, and Research World* 19, 228–229.

Bierut, L. J., Dinwiddie, S. H., Begleiter, H., Crowe, R. R., Hesselbrock, V., Nurnberger, J. I., Porjesz, B., Schuckit, M. A., & Reich, T. (1998). Familial transmission of substance dependence: Alcohol, marijuana, cocaine, and habitual smoking. *Archives of General Psychiatry* 55, 982–988.

Bohman, M., Sigvardsson, S., & Cloninger, C. R. (1981). Maternal inheritance of alcohol abuse: Cross-fostering analysis of adopted women. *Archives of General Psychiatry,* 38 965–969.

Cadoret, R. J. (1990). The genetics of alcoholism. In R. L. Collins, K. E. Leonard, & J. S. Searles (Eds.), *Alcohol and the family: Research and clinical perspectives* (pp. 39–78). New York: Guilford.

Cadoret, R. J., O'Gorman, T., Troughton, E., & Heywood, E. (1985). Alcoholism and antisocial personality: Interrelationships, genetic and environmental factors. *Archives of General Psychiatry* 42, 161–167.

Cadoret, R. J., Troughton, E., & O'Gorman, T. W. (1987). Genetic and environmental factors in alcohol abuse and antisocial personality. *Journal of Studies on Alcohol,* 48, 1–8.

Caldwell, C. B., & Gottesman, I. I. (1991). *Sex differences in the risk for alcoholism: A twin study.* Paper presented at the 21st annual meeting of the Behavior Genetic Association, St. Louis, MO.

Cloninger, R., Bohman, M., & Sigvardsson, S. (1981). Inheritance of alcohol abuse: Cross-fostering analysis of adopted men. *Archives of General Psychiatry* 38, 861–868.

Cloninger, C. R., Bohman, M., Sigvardsson, S., & von Knorring, A. L. (1985). Psychopathology in adopted-out children of alcoholics: The Stockholm adoption study. In M. Galanter (Ed.), *Recent developments in alcoholism,* Vol. 3 (pp. 37–51). New York: Plenum.

Collins, F. S., & Fink, L. (1995). The human genome project. *Alcohol, Health, and Research World* 19, 190–194.

Couzigou, P., Coutelle, B., Fleury, B., & Iron, A. (1994). Alcohol and aldehyde genotypes, alcoholism, and alcohol related disorders. *Alcohol and Alcoholism,* Supplement 2, pp. 21–27.

Fingarette, H. (1988) *Heavy drinking: The myth of alcoholism as a disease.* Berkeley, CA: University of California Press.

Gabrielli, W. F., & Plomin, R. (1985). Drinking behavior in the Colorado adoptee and twin sample. *Journal of Studies on Alcohol* 46, 24–31.

Goodwin, D. (1976) *Is alcoholism hereditary?* New York: Oxford University Press.

Goodwin, D. W., Schulsinger, F., Hermansen, I., Guze, S. B., & Winokur, G. (1973). Alcohol problems in adoptees raised apart from alcoholic biological parents. *Archives of General Psychiatry* 28, 238–243.

Goodwin, D. W., Schulsinger, F., Knop, J., Mednick, S., & Guze, S. B. (1977). Psychopathology in adopted and nonadopted sons of alcoholics. *Archives of General Psychiatry* 34, 1005–1009.

Greeley, J., & Oei, T. (1999). Alcohol and tension reduction. In K. E. Leonard and H. T. Blane (Eds.), *Psychological theories of drinking and alcoholism* (2nd ed.) (pp. 14–53). New York: Guilford.

Gurling, H. M., Oppenheim, B. E., & Murray, R. M. (1984). Depression, criminality, and psychopathology associated with alcoholism: Evidence from a twin study. *Acta Genetic Medicine Gemellol* 33, pp. 333–339.

Heath, A. C. (1994). Genetic influences on drinking behavior in humans. *Alcohol and Alcoholism,* Supplement 2, pp. 82–119.

Heath, A. C. (1995). Genetic influences on alcoholism risk. *Alcohol, Health, and Research World* 19, 166–171.

Heath, A. C., Jardine, R., & Martin, N. G. (1989). Interactive effects of genotype and social environment on alcohol consumption in female twins. *Journal of Studies on Alcohol* 50, 38–48.

Heath, A. C., Slutske, W. S., & Madden, P. A. (1997). Gender differences in the genetic contribution to alcoholism risk and to alcohol consumption patterns. In R. W. Wilsnack & S. C. Wilsnack (Eds.), *Gender and alcohol: Individual and social perspectives.* New Brunswick, NJ: Rutgers Center for Alcohol Studies.

Hrubec, Z., & Omenn, G. S. Evidence of genetic predisposition to alcoholic cirrhosis and psychosis: Twin concordances for alcoholism and its biological endpoints by zygosity among male veterans. *Alcoholism: Clinical and Experimental Research* 5, 207–212.

Kaij, L. (1970). *Alcoholism in twins.* Stockholm: Almqvist and Wiksell.

Kendler, K. S., Heath, A. C., Neale, M. C., Kessler, R. C., & Eaves, L. J. (1992). A population based twin study of alcoholism in women. *Journal of the American Psychiatric Association* 268, 1877–1882.

McGue, M. (1994). Genes, environment, and the etiology of alcoholism. In R. Zucker, G. Boyd, & J. Howard (Eds.), *The development of alcohol problems: Exploring the biopsychosocial matrix of risk* (pp. 1–40). Rockville, MD: U.S. Department of Health and Human Services. NIH Publication 94-3495.

McGue, M., Pickens, R. W., & Svikis, D. S. (1992). Sex and age effects on the inheritance of alcohol problems: A twin study. *Journal of Abnormal Psychology* 101, 3–17.

Merikangas, K. R., & Avenevoli, S. (2000). Implications of genetic epidemiology for the prevention of substance use disorders. *Addictive Behaviors* 25, 807–820.

Pickens, R. W., Svikis, D. S., McGue, M., Lykken, D. T., Heston, L. L., & Clayton, P. J. (1991). Heterogeneity in the inheritance of alcoholism. *Archives of General Psychiatry* 48, 19–28.

Polich, J., Pollock, V. E., & Bloom, F. E. (1994). Meta-analysis of P300 amplitude from males at risk for alcoholism. *Psychological Bulletin* 115, 55–73.

Porjesz, B., & Begleiter, H. (1995). Neurophysiological component. *Alcohol, Health, and Research World* 19, 233–234.

Roe, A. (1944). The adult adjustment of children of alcoholic parents raised in foster homes. *Quarterly Journal of Studies on Alcohol* 5, 378–393.

Schuckit, M. A. (1989). *Drug and alcohol abuse: A clinical guide to diagnosis and treatment* (3rd ed.). New York: Plenum.

Schuckit, M. A. (1994). A clinical model of genetic influences in alcohol dependence. *Journal of Studies on Alcohol* 55, 5–17.

Schuckit, M. A. (1995). A long-term study of sons of alcoholics. *Alcohol, Health, and Research World* 19, 172–175.

Schuckit, M. A., & Crabbe, J. (2000). Genetics of alcoholism susceptibility and protection [syllabus material]. http://www.alcoholmedicalscholars.org/gen-out.htm.

Searles, J. S. (1990). The contribution of genetic factors to the development of alcoholism: A critical review. In R. L. Collins, K. E. Leonard, & J. S. Searles (Eds.), *Alcohol and the family: Research and clinical perspectives* (pp. 3–38). New York: Guilford.

Tarter, R. E., Kabene, M., Escalier, E. A., Laird, S. B., & Jacob, T. (1990). Temperament deviation and risk for alcoholism. *Alcoholism: Clinical and Experimental Research* 13, 380–382.

U.S. Department of Health and Human Services (1993). *Eighth Special Report to the U.S. Congress on alcohol and health.*

U.S. Department of Health and Human Services (1997). *Ninth Special Report to the U.S. Congress on alcohol and health.*

U.S. Department of Health and Human Services (2000). *Tenth Special Report to the U.S. Congress on alcohol and health.*

Wall, T. L., & Ehlers, C. L. (1995). Genetic influences affecting alcohol use among Asians. *Alcohol, Health, and Research World* 19, 184–189.

CHAPTER FIVE

STATISTICS ON ALCOHOL USE
Epidemiologic Research on Alcohol

In this chapter, statistical trends of alcohol consumption and its consequences will be explored, using the results of epidemiologic studies. Epidemiologists are researchers who collect data from large populations and determine patterns and trends in disease prevalence. Here we focus on epidemiologic research on alcohol, which explores the patterns of drinking, the extent of alcohol use disorders, problems caused by alcohol use, and variations in consumption among various subpopulations of the United States. Alcohol-related statistics discussed in this chapter include:

1. Annual **per-capita** consumption
2. Drinking patterns in adolescents and adults
3. Percentage of adults with alcohol use disorders
4. Accidents associated with alcohol consumption
5. Cirrhosis deaths
6. Other harmful consequences of alcohol consumption

METHODOLOGY

Epidemiologists collect data from public records and surveys of the population. Researchers must take into account potential reporting problems. For example, physicians underreport alcohol-related illnesses (U.S. Department of Health and Human Services, 1997). Another concern is the accuracy of self-reports about drinking patterns, discussed in Chapter 2. In this chapter the section on high school drinking patterns includes the Monitoring the Future Study's rationale for the accuracy of its self-reported drinking data, which provides some insight into the reasoning process researchers use in arguing for the validity of self-reported survey data.

The studies in this chapter are all observational. Although there may be interesting patterns of occurrences, such as the decline of cirrhosis deaths with the decline of alcohol consumption, these studies cannot prove the direction of causality. It is not proved that the decline in alcohol consumption caused the drop in cirrhosis deaths.

PER-CAPITA CONSUMPTION

The most general statistic about alcohol is the average amount that U.S. citizens consume, per-capita consumption. This statistic is calculated by tabulating the total sales of alcohol per year and dividing by the number of individuals who are 14 years old and older. Figure 5.1 shows the annual per-capita consumption of absolute alcohol for the period 1935–1990. The graph indicates that in 1935, just after repeal of Prohibition, the average American consumed 1.2 gal of alcohol per year. This amount generally increased until 1980–1981, after which it declined gradually to 2.25 gal in 1993. Translated into standard drinks, this means that the average American had 256 drinks per year in 1935 and 576 drinks in 1993, or over a drink and a half a day. This is a lot of alcohol! Why did consumption increase from 1935 until 1980–1981 and decline after that? It makes sense that drinking would increase after Prohibition as alcohol became more available, but the decline since 1981–1982 has no obvious explanation. One thing that happened in this period is that alcohol treatment became widely available. Was treatment responsible for the drop in consumption by helping alcoholics become abstinent? Because so many other things also occurred in this time period such as greater emphasis on health and fitness, use of other drugs such as cocaine and marijuana, changes in the population makeup of the United States, changes in the average age of Americans, all of which may have affected per-capita consumption, we cannot be sure. For comparison, other countries' annual per-capita consumption rates are shown in Table 5.1. The French have the highest rate of consumption, but it has been dropping since 1970. The U.S. rate of consumption is about average.

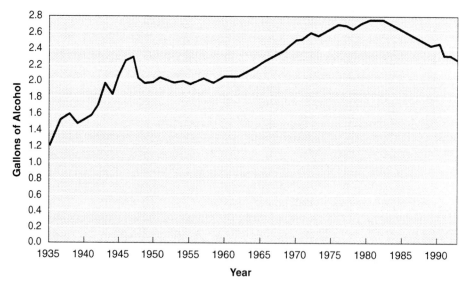

FIGURE 5.1   Total Per-Capita Consumption, United States, 1935–1993

Source: Williams et al., 1995.

TABLE 5.1 Per-Capita Alcohol Consumption (liters of pure alcohol) in Organization for Economic Cooperation and Developmental Countries (1 liter = 1.056 qt)

COUNTRY	1970	1980	1990
Australia	8.1	9.6	8.4
Austria	10.5	11.0	10.4
Belgium	8.9	10.8	9.9
Canada	6.1	8.6	7.5
Denmark	6.8	9.1	9.9
Finland	4.4	6.4	7.7
France	16.2	14.9	12.7
Germany	10.3	11.4	10.6
Great Britain	5.3	7.3	7.6
Iceland	3.2	3.9	3.9
Ireland	5.9	7.3	7.2
Italy	13.7	13.0	8.7
Japan	4.6	5.4	6.5
Luxembourg	10.0	10.9	12.2
Netherlands	5.6	8.8	8.2
New Zealand	7.6	9.6	7.8
Norway	3.6	4.6	4.1
Portugal	9.9	11.0	9.8
Spain	11.6	13.6	10.8
Sweden	5.8	5.7	5.5
Switzerland	10.7	10.8	10.8
Turkey	0.5	0.7	0.6
United States	6.7	8.2	7.5

Source: © Griffith Edwards et al., 1994. Reprinted from *Alcohol Policy and the Public Good* by Griffith Edwards et al. (1994).

Table 5.2 shows the per-capita consumption in U.S. geographic regions. "Wetter" refers to regions that traditionally have high rates of alcohol consumption. "Drier" refers to regions with traditionally low rates of alcohol consumption (Clark & Hilton, 1991, p. 262). Although per-capita consumption is higher in "wetter" regions, per-drinker consumption is higher in "drier" regions. This suggests that there are both more abstainers and more heavy drinkers in "drier" regions.

A shortcoming of the per-capita statistic is that individuals do not necessarily drink their assigned share. After all, alcohol is not rationed or apportioned out. Citizens are free to drink as much or as little as they wish. Because a large percentage of Americans do not drink at all, others are drinking more than their assigned portions! So though the per-capita statistic is useful in seeing overall trends in consumption, it does not really tell us about actual average consumption or typical drinking patterns. For this information, we must employ surveys.

TABLE 5.2   Per-Capita Consumption in Regions of the United States: Gallons of Absolute Alcohol

	APPARENT PER-CAPITA CONSUMPTION				APPARENT PER-DRINKER CONSUMPTION		
	1940	*1964*	*1979*	*1984*	*1964*	*1979*	*1984*
Wetter regions							
New England	1.72	2.48	3.41	3.08	3.14	3.78	4.28
Mid-Atlantic	1.78	2.41	2.67	2.57	2.92	3.53	3.13
East North Central	1.75	2.26	2.67	2.57	3.04	3.75	3.52
West North Central	1.22	1.82	2.45	2.32	2.77	3.95	2.90
Pacific	1.87	2.55	3.38	3.09	3.47	3.99	4.18
Drier regions							
South Atlantic	1.11	1.89	2.81	2.68	3.27	5.44	4.32
East South Central	0.57	1.01	1.95	1.93	2.87	5.48	4.39
West South Central	0.88	1.71	2.62	2.58	2.76	4.21	4.45
Mountain	1.33	2.08	3.29	2.96	3.58	5.31	4.77

ALCOHOL SURVEYS

In surveys, researchers interview a large sample of the population in order to obtain a good estimate of the current drinking practices of the group of interest. Researchers either make special efforts to sample the important subgroups proportionately, or they use statistical procedures to correct the sample of individuals chosen to reflect the population at large. Actual subjects are chosen randomly within certain regions or populations in most of these studies. Three such projects are the National Longitudinal Alcohol Epidemiologic Survey (NLAES), the National Alcohol Surveys (NAS), and the Epidemiologic Catchment Area survey (ECA). Since this type of research generally depends on self-reports, the validity of such self-reports must be assessed. Studies examining self-reports of alcohol consumption for *surveys* have found their reliability good and the validity adequate (Dufour, 1999, p. 12). However, it is important to note that there are shortcomings to alcohol surveys. Researchers who have compared results of surveys with alcohol sales have found that surveys account for only one-third to one-half of what had been sold in the region where the survey was undertaken (Clark & Hilton, 1991, p. 23). This obviously suggests a serious underreporting of consumption. Other research suggests that heavier drinkers underreport consumption more than lighter drinkers. Although these are important limitations, surveys offer the best current picture of drinking practices in the United States.

Drinking Patterns in the United States

Although alcohol is the most commonly used drug, large numbers of Americans abstain. About 28.8 percent of men and 40.6 percent of women are abstainers from alcohol (drank less than once a year) according to the 1984 National Alcohol Survey (NAS) (Midanick & Clark, 1994). Conversely, about 71.9 percent of men and 59.4 percent of women are drinkers. The NLAES survey provides information about drinking patterns in 1992, which is shown in Table 5.3. The higher estimate of abstainers is due in part to the more liberal definition of abstainers than in the 1984 NAS.

Drinking Pattern, Sex, and Age.   Surveys have consistently shown that women drink less frequently than men, drink less when they do drink, and abstain more often (Clark & Hilton, 1991; Greenfield & Rogers, 1999). This pattern is evident in Table 5.3. Surveys also tend to show peak consumption of alcohol in the 18–29 age group, with gradually declining consumption thereafter (Clark & Hilton, 1991; Greenfield & Rogers, 1999). For women, peak drinking occurs in the 30s, later than for men (Fillmore, 1987).

Trends in Recent Drinking Patterns in the United States.   Drinking patterns, like total consumption, vary over the course of time. Midanik and Clark (1994) measured recent changes in drinking patterns by comparing data from NAS surveys conducted in 1984 and 1990. Their analysis indicated that individuals in general consumed less alcohol in 1990 than in 1984. Consistent with this trend:

- A larger percentage of Americans were abstaining from alcohol: 35.0 percent in 1990 versus 30.4 percent in 1980.
- Fewer Americans were drinking weekly: 29.0 percent in 1990 versus 35.9 percent in 1980.
- And fewer Americans were drinking heavily: 3.9 percent in 1990 versus 6.2 percent in 1980.

However, certain subgroups were exceptions to this trend:

- Divorced, Hispanic, and individuals who had less than a high school education reported increases in drinking episodes of 5 drinks or more per occasion.

TABLE 5.3   Percentages of Drinkers with Different Drinking Patterns among Men and Women from the NLAES 1992 Survey

DRINKING PATTERN	FREQUENCY	MEN	WOMEN	TOTAL
Abstainer	<12 drinks/yr	44.24	66.13	55.63
Light drinker	<3 drinks/wk	20.55	18.35	19.41
Moderate drinker	>3 drinks, <14/wk	22.60	11.81	16.99
Heavy drinker	>14 drinks/wk	11.96	03.36	07.48

Source: National Institute on Alcohol Abuse and Alcoholism, 1998.

Who Drinks Most of the Alcohol?   If the per-capita consumption of alcohol is about 1.5 drinks per day, a puzzling question raised is who is drinking the abstainers' and light drinkers' share of alcohol? Greenfield and Rogers (1999) interviewed a large sample of adult drinkers regarding their alcohol consumption over the preceding year. Table 5.4 divides drinkers into percentiles of consumption and shows the consumption levels per occasion and then estimates consumption per year. An interesting feature of the table is that it allows the reader to see if his or her consumption pattern is higher or lower than that of most American drinkers. The table indicates that 50 percent of American drinkers have fewer than 2.3 drinks a week. Thus, if the reader consumes 3 drinks per week, she or he is drinking more than the average American drinker. The estimated yearly consumption rate ranges from 1.47 drinks for the lightest drinkers to 3,309.60 for the heaviest drinkers, the top 2.5 percent. The heaviest drinkers average 9 drinks per day. The top 25 percent of drinkers account for 87 percent of the alcohol drunk in the United States. The mystery is solved: the heavier drinkers consume large amounts of alcohol, compensating for the abstainers' and light drinkers' failure to consume their "assigned" portion.

Are types of alcohol beverage associated with different patterns of drinking? Using data from the NAS survey, Rogers and Greenfield (1999) investigated the type of beverage drunk and style of drinking. They found that beer accounts for 67 percent of all alcohol consumption and that beer accounts for 81 percent of all the alcohol that is reported drunk in hazardous amounts (i.e., 5 drinks or more per occasion) in the United States. These findings contradict the common perception that beer consumption is not as harmful as consumption of spirits.

TABLE 5.4 Means and Cumulative Proportions of Alcohol Consumption for Volume Percentile Subgroups of Drinkers

RANGE IN DRINKS	CUM. % OF DRINKERS	UNWEIGHTED n	WEIGHTED n	MEAN DRINKS/YR	CUM. % CONSUMED	95% CONFIDENCE INTERVALS
<1.5/yr	100	416	400	1.47	100.0	—
1.5–7/yr	90	473	443	3.60	100.0	—
7–12.5/yr	80	544	528	8.26	99.9	99–100
1–2.9/mo	70	538	504	20.53	99.6	99–100
2.9–3.7/mo	60	468	452	37.41	98.8	98–99
0.9–2.3/wk	50	532	538	81.83	97.7	97–98
2.3–3.8/wk	40	448	431	142.02	94.7	94–95
3.8–5.2/wk	30	219	228	244.89	90.4	90–91
0.7–1.2/day	25	253	254	343.86	86.6	86–88
1.2–1.6/day	20	211	221	522.64	80.6	79–82
1.6–2.5/day	15	225	232	723.08	72.6	71–74
2.5–4.2/day	10	215	236	1,165.75	61.1	58–64
4.2–6.1/day	5	101	118	1,883.42	42.2	39–46
>6.1/day	2.5	105	118	3,309.60	26.9	23–31

Cumulative amount of total consumption in 1989–1993 warning label surveys (unweighted n = 4,748 drinkers).

ALCOHOL-RELATED PROBLEMS

Alcohol consumption is implicated in many societal problems. It is estimated that the annual social cost of alcohol abuse is $148 billion (Cook & Moore, 1998). It is estimated that there are 100,000 alcohol-related deaths each year in the United States (U.S. Department of Health and Human Services, 1997, p. 247). Discussed in Chapter 3, for example, are the many medical problems that are either caused or made worse by excessive alcohol consumption. As mentioned in that chapter, cirrhosis deaths have been used as an indicator of the extent of alcohol problems in a specific region. Figure 5.2 shows the **mortality** rates due to cirrhosis from 1910 to 1990. By comparing this figure with Figure 5.1, which shows per-capita alcohol consumption over time, it appears that increases in consumption are related to increases in cirrhosis deaths, and conversely, when consumption drops, so do cirrhosis deaths; note particularly the large drop in cirrhosis deaths during Prohibition, 1920–1933. Although Prohibition has been largely viewed as a failed project, it is clear that the number of cirrhosis deaths dropped dramatically during this period.

Accidents

Alcohol is linked to all types of accidents, most notably automobile accidents. Of the 45,000 deaths caused by automobile accidents each year, alcohol is involved in 43.6 percent. An

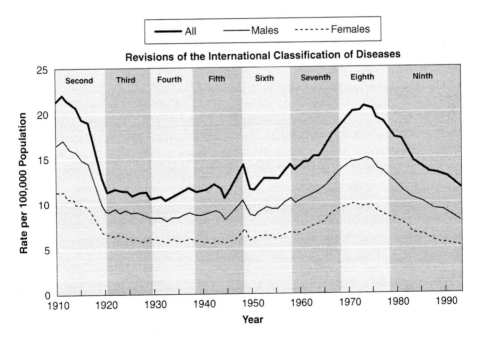

FIGURE 5.2   Age-Adjusted Death Rates from Liver Cirrhosis by Gender: Death Registrations, States, 1910–1932; and United States, 1933–1992

Source: DeBakey et al., 1995.

additional 289,000 individuals are injured in alcohol-related automobile accidents each year. As overall alcohol consumption has declined, so have alcohol-related traffic deaths (U.S. Department of Health and Human Services, 1997, p. 11). Among 16- to 24-year-old drivers, there has been a 30 percent decrease in deaths since 1987; during this same period, however, 25- to 44-year-olds had an increase of 45 percent in alcohol-related traffic deaths.

Alcohol is implicated in a high percentage of all other accidental deaths. An analysis of seven separate studies found that 34 percent of drownings involved alcohol (U.S. Department of Health and Human Services, 1997, p. 254). In a study of accidental boating deaths, it was found that 21 percent of the incidents were shown to be alcohol-related (U.S. Department of Health and Human Services, 1997, p. 255). Approximately one-half of adults who die in house fires (2,500 of the 5,000) have high blood alcohol concentration (BAC) values (U.S. Department of Health and Human Services, p. 254).

Many suicides are associated with alcohol consumption. For example, in one study, nearly 36 percent of suicide victims had a positive BAC (U.S. Department of Health and Human Services, 1997, p. 259). Hawton et al. (1991), in a study of emergency room admissions of suicide attempts, found alcohol had been consumed in the 6-h period before the attempt in 40.8 percent of those attempting suicide.

Dependence Symptoms and Social Problems

Midanik and Clark (1995) examined the NAS alcohol surveys conducted in 1984 and 1990 for changes in alcohol dependence symptoms and negative alcohol-related social consequences. While per-capita consumption has decreased as noted earlier, Midanik and Clark found that neither dependence symptoms nor negative social consequences had. In fact, there was an increase in both in the period 1984–1990.

- 7.6 percent reported three or more dependence symptoms in 1990, versus 6.7 percent in 1984.
- 12.8 percent reported two or more social problems in 1990, versus 10.9 percent in 1984.
- In 1990, three subgroups reported significantly higher rate of two or more social problems than in 1984: ages 18–29, never married, and not employed. The latter group also reported significantly more dependence symptoms.

Binge drinking appears to be a particularly dangerous drinking pattern. Box 5.1 cites supportive research evidence. Box 5.2 summarizes research which implicates binge drinking and drugging in increased death rates at the beginning of the month.

Gender and Age. In almost all surveys, there are significant trends in both gender and age in which:

- Women show fewer dependency symptoms and social problems than men. Women have lower rates of alcohol disorders than men.
- The 18–29 age group reports more problems with alcohol than any other age group (Clark and Hilton, 1991).

BOX 5.1

HARMFUL CONSEQUENCES OF BINGE DRINKING

Several surveys show that binge drinking is a pattern of drinking with harmful consequences. Midanik et al. (1996) analyzed data from the National Health Interview Survey and found that the risk for drunk driving, job problems, and alcohol dependence for those with low or moderate rates of drinking was significantly higher for those who had 5 drinks or more at least once in the past year. Youth who participated in binge drinking were found to have a greater risk for negative consequences than those who did not (see also Table 5.11). Bradley et al. (2001) surveyed female veterans and found that those who had binged in the past year had higher than expected rates of alcohol symptoms, injuries, and multiple sexual partners. Anda et al. (1987; cited in Arria and Gossop, 1998) surveyed convicted drinking drivers and found that 90 percent had reported binge drinking (5 drinks or more, at least once during the month preceding the survey). Bradley et al. (2001), noting the high relationship between binge drinking and problems, suggest that binge drinking could be a useful single-item screening test.

BOX 5.2

DEATH AND TIME OF MONTH

By examining data on death certificates, Phillips et al. (1999) determined that there was an increase in the number of deaths in the United States in the first week of the month compared to the other weeks. When alcohol or drugs were mentioned in the death certificate, even greater differences between the first and last weeks of the month were found. The authors note that government benefits are generally dispensed at the beginning of the month. They reason that this discretionary spending may allow relatively poor individuals to consume large amounts of alcohol and drugs during the first week of the month, with ensuing negative consequences. Examining the death certificates, the researchers found many more alcohol-related deaths than drug-related deaths: alcohol was implicated in 177,736 deaths, while drugs were listed only 21,349 times in the period from 1983 to 1988. Alcohol was implicated eight times more often than a drug reaction as a cause of death.

Table 5.5 shows dependence symptoms and social consequences by gender and age.

PREVALENCE OF ALCOHOL USE DISORDERS

Before the Epidemiologic Catchment Area (ECA) study, information about alcohol abusers had been obtained only from treated patients, which is clearly a nonrandom sample of alcohol abusers. The ECA study provided the first good estimates of alcohol use disorders and the co-occurrence of other mental disorders in the general population. Studies

TABLE 5.5   Dependence Symptoms and Social Consequences by Gender and Age in 1984 and 1990 of Current Drinkers in Percent

| | 3 + DEPENDENCE SYMPTOMS | | | | 2 + SOCIAL CONSEQUENCES | | | |
| | *1984* | | *1990* | | *1984* | | *1990* | |
	%	n	%	n	%	n	%	n
Gender								
Male	8.8	437	9.9	392	15.0	439	16.1	392
Female	4.3	414	5.1	356	6.6	415	9.2	356
Age								
18–29	10.1	282	15.3	223	16.9	283	25.9	223*
30–39	6.8	203	4.7	189	10.0	203	9.6	189
40–49	6.5	121	7.0	124	11.7	122	11.5	124
50–59	2.8	99	3.4	79	5.8	99	3.9	79
60+	2.6	144	2.0	133	3.5	144	1.9	133

Note: Percentages and n's are weighted; n's vary slightly because of missing data. *Difference between 1984 and 1990 significant at 0.05 level by two-tailed test of significance of difference of proportions.

Reprinted with permission from *Journal of Studies on Alcohol*, vol. 56, pp. 395–402, 1995. Copyright by Alcohol Research Documentation, Inc., Rutgers Center of Alcohol Studies, Piscataway, NJ 08854.

on occurrence of disorders such as the ECA typically report yearly prevalence rates and/or lifetime prevalence rates. One-year prevalence shows more accurately what percentage of people have the disorder at a given time. The lifetime prevalence rate of disorders is often reported as well. For the lifetime prevalence rate, subjects are asked if they *ever* had the symptoms of the disorder, while for 1-year prevalence, they are asked if they had these symptoms in the past year.

Epidemiologic Catchment Area Survey

In the ECA study, mental health catchment areas were surveyed in each of five geographic regions across the United States (Robins et al., 1988a). Within each region, 3,000 household residents and 500 institutional residents were randomly sampled and interviewed in person. The Diagnostic Interview Schedule (DIS), based on the DSM-III, was used to diagnose psychiatric disorders, including alcohol use disorders. The procedure for administering this schedule was standardized so that researchers could be confident that the diagnoses were the same when administered by different research groups. The findings reflect the catchment areas but are not representative of the U.S. population. Estimates of the annual prevalence of alcohol use disorders made by the ECA along with the more recent and more representative National Comorbidity Survey and the National Longitudinal Alcohol Epidemiologic Survey are indicated in Table 5.6.

Because many psychiatric diagnoses were examined, this study sheds light on the question of how often people with alcohol disorders also have other psychiatric disorders.

TABLE 5.6   One-Year Prevalence of Alcohol Abuse and Dependence (AAD) Combined and Alcohol Dependence (DEP), Reported by All National Studies, in Percent, by Gender

SURVEY	MEN		WOMEN		TOTAL	
Diagnostic Instrument	*AAD*	*DEP*	*AAD*	*DEP*	*AAD*	*DEP*
Epidemiologic Area Survey (1980)						
DSM-III	11.90	*	4.57	*	6.80	*
National Health Interview Survey (1988)						
DSM-III-R	13.4	9.6	4.4	3.2	8.6	6.3
DSM-IV	9.3	9.2	3.0	3.0	6.0	5.9
National Alcoholism Survey (1990)						
DSM-III-R	*	5.3	*	1.7	*	3.2
DSM-IV	*	5.7	*	2.2	*	3.9
ICD-10	*	7.8	*	3.4	*	5.4
National Comorbidity Survey (1992)						
DSM-III-R	*	*	*	*	9.7	7.2
National Longitudinal Alcohol Epidemiologic Survey (1992)						
DSM-IV	11.0	6.3	4.01	2.6	7.4	4.4

*Data not published.

Source: U.S. Department of Health and Human Services, 1997.

More details regarding this aspect of the study, called **co-morbidity,** will be considered in Chapter 10. To mention some of the important findings:

- Alcohol disorders have a high rate of **remission,** higher than depressive disorders.
- Men with alcohol disorders are 11 times as likely to have antisocial personality as are men without alcohol disorder. This finding extends to populations sampled in Taiwan and Canada (Helzer & Canino, 1988).
- 39 percent of the men suffering from an alcohol disorder had experienced another other psychiatric disorder, whereas 62 percent of women had.
- 21.5 percent of those with alcohol use disorders also had a substance use disorder, while 47.3 percent of those with substance use disorders had an alcohol use disorder.
- For men, the presence of antisocial personality, drug abuse/dependence, major depression, or phobia was associated with active alcohol symptoms. For women, only substance abuse symptoms were associated with active alcohol symptoms.
- Only 7.5 percent of persons with an alcohol use disorder received treatment in outpatient alcohol clinics during the year they were surveyed (Narrow et al., 1993).

The high association of recent drug symptoms with active alcohol problems supports the view that taking drugs makes it more difficult to achieve remission from alcohol disorders or leads to relapse.

What Percentage of Drinkers Develop Alcohol Problems?

The 1-year prevalence rate of alcohol disorders ranges from 6.0 to 9.7 percent, as shown in Table 5.6. Since the surveys shown in Table 5.6 include abstainers, the 1-year prevalence rates of drinkers with alcohol disorders is somewhat higher. Among drinkers, the lifetime prevalence rate for alcohol dependence is 15.4 percent (Anthony et al., 1994).

What Percentage of Drinkers Drink Safely?

Conversely, then, about 90 percent of drinkers do not have an alcohol disorder at any given time, and 84.6 percent of drinkers never develop alcohol dependence. Some of these drinkers, however, are certainly not drinking safely. Clark and Hilton (1991) found in their 1984 survey that 21 percent of drinkers reported at least one dependence problem with drinking. Midanik et al. (1996) found that 17.7 percent of drinkers reported driving while intoxicated. These findings suggest that about 80 percent of drinkers are drinking safely. The ECA survey suggests that the percentages of drinkers who are drinking safely vary from region to region, from 49.1 percent in Durham to 75.3 percent in New Haven (the author calculated the safe drinking percentages by combining the light and heavy drinking categories in Table 5.7).

TABLE 5.7   Lifetime Rates of Various Drinking Categories and Weighted Five-Site ECA Household and Institutional Samples (adjusted to national demographic distribution, 1980 Census)

DRINKING CATEGORY	NEW HAVEN (CT)	BALTIMORE (MD)	ST. LOUIS (MO)	DURHAM (NC)	LOS ANGELES (CA)	ALL SITES
Abs.	5.2	7.5	9.0	28.0	10.7	10.4
Light dr.	72.8	61.9	59.0	47.4	56.9	61.3
Heavy dr.	2.5	3.4	3.7	1.7	2.3	2.9
Prob dr.	8.3	11.9	12.5	11.2	14.8	11.7
Al abuse	4.9	5.1	7.1	4.6	5.7	5.8
Dep.	6.4	10.1	8.8	6.1	9.5	7.9
6 mo. prev.	4.4	6.0	4.7	3.6	5.1	4.7

Abs. = abstinent; Light dr. = nonheavy/nonproblem (social) drinker; Heavy dr. = heavy/nonproblem drinker; Prob dr. = problem drinker (not alcoholic); Al abuse = alcohol abuse only; Dep. = dependence with or without abuse. 6 mo. prev. = six-month prevalence of alcoholism (abuse and/or dependence).

Source: Alcoholism in North America, Europe, and Asia, edited by James E. Helzer, Canino and Chen, Copyright © 1992 by Oxford University Press, Inc. Used by permission of Oxford University Press, Inc.

Alcohol Use Disorder Prevalence among Various Subgroups

Gender Differences.   The U.S. data show that men are much more likely to qualify for an alcohol use disorder than women (see Table 5.6). Data collected so far find the same trend in other countries. Figure 5.3 shows lifetime prevalence for alcohol disorders in cities in four different countries by sex. While the ratio is higher for men in all countries, it is especially marked in Puerto Rico and Taipei. These results suggest that cultural factors interact with gender to affect the rate of alcohol disorders.

Age Differences.   The NLAES survey reports that the 18- to 29-year-old group had the highest rate of alcohol use disorders, 15.94 percent. The rate for the next age group, 30–44, dropped to 7.27 percent, with declines in rate as age increased (44–65, 3.47 percent, and over 65, .64 percent) (U.S. Department of Health and Human Services, 1997, p. 21). These findings are consistent with Midanik and Clark's (1995) findings on age and alcohol-related

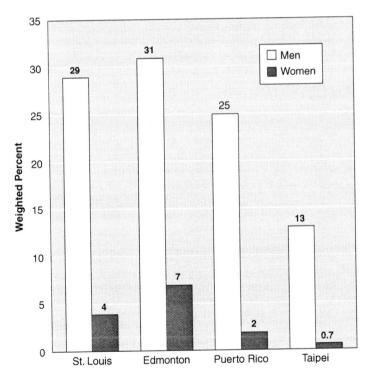

FIGURE 5.3   Lifetime Prevalence of Alcoholism by Sex

Source: Helzer, J. E., Canino, G. J., Hwu, H., Bland, R. C., Newman, S., and Yeh, E. (1998). Alcoholism: Cross-national comparison of population surveys with the Diagnostic Interview Schedule. In R. M. Rose and J. E. Barrett *Alcoholism: Origins and outcome* (pp. 31–47). New York: Raven Press. Reprinted by permission of Lippincott, Williams, and Wilkins.

symptoms as shown in Table 5.5. Surveys have consistently shown that this young age group consumes more alcohol and has more alcohol problems than any other age group (Clark & Hilton, 1991, p. 86).

Geographic Region. The five cities used in the ECA study represent the basic geographic regions of the country. Table 5.7 shows drinking patterns in these five cities. Durham has the highest rate of abstinence, consistent with historical findings that the Southern United States has high rates of abstinence. This has been attributed to Southern Protestant religious groups' practices and beliefs regarding alcohol use. The reader can compare these results with the per-capita findings for region in Table 5.2.

Ethnic Groups. By reputation, Native Americans are said to have a high rate of alcohol use disorders. Some indirect measures seem to support this conception. Native Americans have a higher rate of alcohol-related deaths than the average American. Native Americans have a cirrhosis death rate 4.5 times and an alcohol dependence death rate 3.8 times greater than that of the average American (Manson et al., 1992). In a preliminary study, three reservation communities, one each from the Southwest, the Pacific Northwest, and the Midwest, were surveyed for alcohol use disorders using the DIS (Manson et al., 1992, pp. 117–118). They found that Native Americans had a lifetime prevalence of over 50 percent for alcohol use disorders. Because there is a wide variation in drinking practices among reservation communities, sampling of several additional reservations is needed to confirm these preliminary results.

Compared to other ethnic groups, African Americans (Helzer et al., 1992, p. 85) are less likely to be alcoholic as young men but more likely as age increases, which can be seen in Figure 5.4. This is an interaction effect, where age and drinking patterns change at different rates for African Americans and Caucasians.

A survey of Puerto Ricans (in Puerto Rico) and Mexican Americans in Los Angeles shows that both groups have high rates of problem and heavy drinking, but only the Mexican Americans have an elevated rate of alcohol use disorders (18 percent) (Canino et al., 1992, p. 141). Caetano (1985 and 1988, cited in Clark and Hilton, 1991) found a similar pattern using the results of the 1984 NCS survey. Also notable is the great gender difference in abstention rates. Only 2.7 percent of Mexican American men abstain, compared to 29.5 percent of Mexican American women. The corresponding figures for Puerto Ricans is 7.2 percent versus 31.7 percent. Neff (1991), interviewing residents in San Antonio, found that Mexican Americans drank less frequently than other Americans, but when they drank they consumed larger amounts.

Prevalence of Alcohol Use Disorders in Other Countries

Because standardized instruments have been devised to measure alcohol use disorders (see Box 5.3), we can begin to measure the rates of these disorders among residents of other countries. Table 5.8 shows the lifetime prevalence rates for DSM-III alcohol abuse and or dependence in several foreign cities where the DIS was administered to a random sample of adults. By comparing the results with Table 5.6, the reader can see that U.S. rates of alcohol disorders fall within the range of the foreign cities. The very low rate in Shanghai is

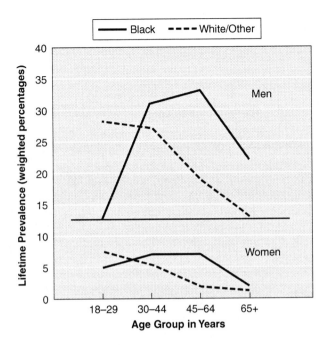

**FIGURE 5.4   Alcohol Abuse and/or Dependence
Prevalence by Age, Sex, and Ethnicity.** Combined five-site
ECA data adjusted to national demographic distribution.

Source: From *Alcoholism in North America, Europe, and Asia,* edited by
James E. Helzer, Canino and Chen, copyright 1992 by Oxford University
Press, Inc. Used by permission of Oxford University Press.

accounted for to some degree by the fact that 77 percent of the sample were abstainers.
Recalculating the rate including drinkers only, the rate remains low at 2 percent. Another
factor suppressing alcohol disorders in Shanghai is the Asian alcohol-flush reaction.

PREVALENCE OF HIGH SCHOOL DRINKING

The Monitoring the Future study (Johnston et al., 2001) examines drug use in eighth, tenth,
twelfth grades and college each year. The research is carefully conducted to gain information
reflecting the overall trends in use among adolescents. In order to select a representative group
of students, geographic areas are chosen and then schools are chosen within these regions. Students are randomly chosen within the school to fill out a questionnaire on their drug use. It is
reasonable to wonder if their responses are valid. The researchers make the following points:

- Protection of confidentiality is maintained and communicated.
- There is high reliability of scores on students retested.
- Degree of consistency among related questions is high. For example, those who
  report few binges report being drunk rarely, and vice versa.

▓ ▓ ▓ ▓ ▓

BOX 5.3

CROSS-CULTURAL DIAGNOSIS

With the development of operationalized diagnoses for alcohol disorders, it has become possible to compare the rates of alcohol disorders across cultures. The World Health Organization in conjunction with the National Institutes of Health in the United States began the Joint Project on diagnosis and classification in 1979. This project used the *International Classification of Diseases*, Tenth Edition (World Health Organization, 1993) criteria for alcohol dependence. Standardized instruments for measuring alcohol de-

pendence were developed and translated into several languages (Room et al., 1996). These were administered to subjects in 100 areas around the world. The tests were found to be appropriate and reliable for use across cultures. Other investigators have used the DSM-III diagnostic criteria for cross-cultural comparisons (Helzer & Canino, 1992). Room et al. (1996), however, document some linguistic and cultural differences that affect comparisons of the alcohol dependence diagnosis across cultures.

TABLE 5.8   Lifetime Prevalence of Alcohol Abuse and/or Dependence in Several Cities, Measured by the DIS

CITY, COUNTRY	PERCENTAGE ALCOHOL ABUSE/DEPENDENCE
Christchurch, New Zealand	18.9
Edmonton, Canada	18.0
Munich, Germany	12.6
Puerto Rico (San Juan not available)	12.6
Taipei, Taiwan	4.9
Seoul, Korea	21.7
Shanghai, China	0.04*

(U.S. estimate, 13.5%, ECA study Robins et al., 1988a). *77% of the interviewed residents reported being abstainers.

Source: Data from Helzer & Canino, 1992.

- The authors state that if there is any bias, it is toward underreporting.
- General trends should be accurate in any event, because the same procedures are used each year (Johnston et al., 1998).

Table 5.9 shows the annual trends in youth 30-day prevalence of having been drunk and binge drinking in the past 2 weeks. Binge drinking is defined as 5 drinks or more per occasion for males and 4 drinks or more for females. Almost 15 percent of eighth graders report binge drinking every 2 weeks. As grade increases, so does the percentage of binge drinking, to 31.3 percent for high school seniors. The large percentage of students who report being drunk at least once a month and report binge drinking every 2 weeks indicate areas of concern, because such drinking is considered hazardous.

TABLE 5.9   **Problematic Drinking Patterns among U.S. Youth**

	1991	1992	1993	1994	1995	1996	1997
Been drunk in last 30 days (%)							
8th grade	7.6	7.5	7.8	8.7	8.3	9.6	8.2
10th grade	20.5	18.1	19.8	20.3	20.8	21.3	22.4
12th grade	31.6	29.9	28.9	30.8	33.2	31.3	34.2
5+ drinks per occasion in last 2 weeks (%)							
8th grade	12.9	13.4	13.5	14.5	14.5	15.6	14.5
10th grade	22.9	21.1	23.0	23.6	24.0	24.8	25.1
12th grade	29.8	27.9	27.5	28.2	29.8	30.2	31.3
College	42.8	41.4	40.2	40.2	38.6	38.3	40.7
Y.A.	34.7	34.2	34.4	33.7	32.6	33.6	34.4

Y.A. = young adult.

Source: Adapted from Johnston et al., 1998.

PREVALENCE OF COLLEGE DRINKING

Individuals tend to drink most heavily between the ages of 18 and 21 (U.S. Department of Health and Human Services, 1997, p. 305). Hence there is concern about drinking in this developmental period. The Harvard School of Public Health College Alcohol Study has provided good data on college drinking since 1993. Each year the researchers randomly select colleges to participate. In 1999, 128 schools in 39 states and the District of Columbia were chosen. A random sample of 225 undergraduates from each college was mailed questionnaires, of whom 60 percent responded. Table 5.10 shows the patterns of use in 1993, 1997, and 1999. Generally, as the table indicates, drinking decreased during this period, except in the category of frequent binge drinking. Table 5.11 shows problems associated with drinking style. It shows that binge drinkers are much more likely to have various difficulties than students who do not. Frequent binge drinkers are 21.11 times more likely to have five such problems than those who do not drink in binges.

The range of reported binge drinking among colleges varied from 1 percent to 76 percent. Particularly high rates of binge drinking were found in fraternity or sorority houses: two out of three drinkers who lived in fraternity or sorority houses indicated they were binge drinkers.

At least 50 percent of the frequent binge drinkers and 30 percent of occasional binge drinkers in this survey could be diagnosed with an alcohol disorder (Knight et al., 2001, cited in Wechsler and Nelson, 2001). However, many of these students "mature out" of this phase of heavy drinking and become normal drinkers. (A full discussion of this issue can be found in Chapter 6.) It has been suggested that interventions for this population need to be different from those for older adults, who have more entrenched patterns of problem drinking.

TABLE 5.10   College Student Patterns of Alcohol Use, 1993, 1997, 1999, in percentages

	PREVALENCE			Change (%)		
	1993	*1997*	*1999*			
Category	*n* = 14,995	*n* = 14,520	*n* = 13,819	'93 v '99	'93 v '97	'97 v '99
Abstainer (past year)	15.4	18.9	19.2	24.7***	22.6***	1.7
Nonbinge drinker[a]	40.1	38.2	36.6	−8.6***	−4.7***	−4.1**
Occasional binge drinker[b]	24.7	22.0	21.4	−13.1***	−11.0***	−2.4
Frequent binge drinker (3 or more × in 2 wk)	19.8	20.9	22.7	14.5***	5.6*	8.5***

[a]Students who consumed alcohol in the past year but did not binge.

[b]Students who binged one or two times in a 2-week period.

*$p < 0.05$; **$p < 0.01$; ***$p < .001$.

Source: Journal of American College Health, vol. 48, March, pp. 199–210, 2000. Reprinted with permission of the Helen Dwight Reid Educational Foundation. Published by Heldref Publications, 1319 Eighteenth St., NW, Washington, DC 20036-1802. Copyright © 2000.

RECOMMENDATIONS

Policy Implications

- Only 7.5 percent of persons with an alcohol use disorder received treatment in outpatient alcohol clinics, according the the ECA study (Narrow et al., 1993, p. 98), giving ample justification for an increase in treatment services.
- Epidemiologic trends show that specific groups need to be targeted for intervention. For example, divorced, never married, not employed, individuals who had less than a high school education, the age group 18–29, and Hispanics report increases in potentially negative drinking patterns. The 25- to 44-year-old age group has shown an increased rate of fatal alcohol-related automobile accidents.
- A study of death rates and time of month found elevated rates at the beginning of the month (see Box 5.1). The researchers suggest that the high rates at the beginning of the month may be due to increased alcohol and drug consumption at that time, facilitated by benefit payments dispersed at the beginning of the month. The implication is that if alcoholic and drug-abusing clients did not receive this money in a lump sum, there would be a decrease in alcohol- and drug-related deaths. Of course it would be challenging to devise a policy that protects against these deaths while ensuring the rights and autonomy of the benefit recipients.

TABLE 5.11   Risk of Alcohol-Related Problems among Students in Different Binge Drinking Categories, 1999

PROBLEM	NON-BINGE $n = 5,063$ %	OCCASIONAL BINGE DRINKERS			FREQUENT BINGE DRINKERS		
		$n = 2,962$ %	*Adjusted* OR	95% CI	$n = 3,135$ %	*Adjusted* OR	95% CI
Miss a class	8.8	30.9	4.70	4.01, 5.51	62.5	16.86	14.40, 19.80
Get behind in schoolwork	9.8	26.0	3.17	2.70, 3.72	46.3	7.94	6.81, 9.28
Do something you regret	18.0	39.6	2.85	2.50, 3.25	62.0	6.94	6.08, 7.93
Forget where you were or what you did	10.0	27.2	2.82	2.41, 3.29	54.0	8.36	7.22, 9.71
Argue with friends	9.7	23.0	2.68	2.28, 3.14	42.6	6.24	5.37, 7.26
Engage in unplanned sexual activities	7.8	22.3	3.17	2.68, 3.76	41.5	7.04	6.00, 8.28
Not use protection when you had sex	3.7	9.8	2.88	2.29, 3.64	20.4	6.13	4.95, 7.63
Damage property	2.3	8.9	2.92	2.20, 3.90	22.7	9.75	7.57, 12.72
Get into trouble with campus or local police	1.4	5.2	3.00	2.08, 4.39	12.7	8.07	5.84, 11.40
Get hurt or injured	3.9	10.9	2.67	2.10, 3.39	26.6	8.16	6.60, 10.16
Require medical treatment for an alcohol overdose	0.3	0.8	2.73	1.17, 6.73	0.9	3.40	1.42, 8.72
Drove after drinking alcohol	18.6	39.7	2.87	2.53, 3.27	56.7	7.64	6.75, 8.66
5 or more alcohol-related problems	3.5	16.6	4.59	3.69, 5.74	48.0	21.11	17.25, 26.04

Note: Only students who drank alcohol in the past year are included. Problems did not occur at all or occurred one or more times. (Percentages represent the students who indicated one or more instances of the problem.) Sample sizes vary slightly for each category because of missing values. OR = odds ratio; CI = confidence interval. Adjusted ORs of occasional binge drinkers versus non-binge drinkers are significant at $p < 0.001$ (OR adjusted for age, sex, marital status, race/ethnicity, and parental college education).

Source: Journal of American College Health, vol. 48, March, pp. 199–210, 2000. Reprinted with permission of the Helen Dwight Reid Educational Foundation. Published by Heldref Publications, 1319 Eighteenth St., NW, Washington, DC 20036-1802. Copyright © 2000.

Reporting of Alcohol-Related Problems. Efforts to gain more accurate estimates of alcohol-related medical problems should be researched. It was noted in the chapter that alcohol-related diagnoses appear to be significantly underreported. Physician reporting of alcohol diagnoses could be improved by employing special diagnostic tools. Johnson et al. (1995) developed such an instrument and reported that its use led to an increase of 71 percent in detecting alcohol use disorders in one hospital study.

Treatment

The evidence of the ECA study suggests that there is a high probability of relapse to alcohol use disorders associated with engaging in drug use. This finding can be relayed to clients who are considering a resumption of drug use while attempting to remain abstinent from alcohol.

SUMMARY

In this chapter, statistics on alcohol consumption and its consequences have been reviewed. The Epidemiologic Catchment Area surveyed was highlighted because it was the first study to explore alcohol and other psychiatric disorders in the general population systematically. Statistics indicate that overall consumption of alcohol has dropped in recent years, but that the number of problems caused by alcohol has generally not diminished. Some important statistics include the following:

- The U.S. per-capita consumption of alcohol per year is 2.25 gal or 576 drinks.
- U.S. consumption of alcohol is about average compared to that of other industrialized countries.
- Since 1981–1982, annual alcohol consumption has decreased in the United States.
- Beer accounts for 67 percent of all alcohol consumption, and it accounts for 81 percent of all the alcohol that is reported drunk in hazardous amounts.
- The heaviest 25 percent of drinkers account for 87 percent of the alcohol drunk in the United States.
- More individuals reported problems with alcohol in 1990 compared to 1984.
- There are 100,000 alcohol-related deaths each year in the United States.
- Of the 45,000 deaths caused by automobile accidents each year, alcohol is involved in 43.6 percent.
- 7.4 to 9.7 percent of Americans could be diagnosed with alcohol dependence and/or alcohol abuse in 1992.
- The rate of alcohol use disorders in the United States is about average compared to that of other industrialized countries.
- Only 7.5 percent of persons with an alcohol use disorder received treatment in outpatient alcohol clinics.
- Women abstain more often than men; when they do drink, they drink less often, less frequently, and have lower rates of alcohol problems and disorders than men. These findings extend to several countries.

- 15 percent of eighth graders, 25 percent of tenth graders, and 31 percent of twelfth graders report binge drinking.
- 40 percent of college students report binge drinking.

READINGS

Helzer, J. E., Burnam, A., and McEvoy, L. T. (1991). Alcohol abuse and dependence. In L. N. Robbins and D. A. Regier (Eds.), *Psychiatric disorders in America* (pp. 81–115). New York: The Free Press.
This chapter presents a good overview of the of the ECA study.

U.S. Department of Health and Human Services (2000). *Tenth Special Report to the U.S. Congress on alcohol and health.*
Every 3 years, statistics and research on alcohol are summarized in this volume by the National Institute on Alcohol Abuse and Alcoholism.

REFERENCES

Anthony, J. C., Warner, L. A., & Kessler, R. C. (1994). Comparative epidemiology of dependence on tobacco, alcohol, controlled substances, and inhalants: Basic findings from the National Comorbidity Survey. *Experimental and Clinical Psychopharmacology* 2, 244–268.

Arria, A. M., & Gossop, M. (1998). Health issues and drinking patterns. In M. Grant and J. Litvak (Eds.), *Drinking patterns and their consequences* (pp. 63–87). Washington, DC: Taylor & Francis.

Bradley, K. A., Bush, K. R., Davis, T. M., Dobie, D. J., Burman, M. L., & Rutter, C. M. (2001). Binge drinking among female Veterans Affairs patients: Prevalence and associated risks. *Psychology of Addictive Behaviors* 15, 297–305.

Canino, G. J., Burnam, A., & Caetano, R. (1992). The prevalence of alcohol abuse and/or dependence in two Hispanic communities. In J. E. Helzer & G. J. Canino (Eds.), *Alcoholism in North America, Europe, and Asia* (pp. 131–155). New York: Oxford University Press.

Clark, W. B., & Hilton, M. E. (1991). *Alcohol in America: Drinking practices and problems.* Albany: State University of New York Press.

Cook, P. J., and Moore, M. J. (2000). Alcohol. In J. P. Newhouse and A. Culyer (Eds.), *Handbook of health economics,* Vol. 1B. New York: Elsevier.

DeBakey, S. F., Stinson, F. S., Grant, B. F., & Dufour, M. C. (1995). Liver cirrhosis mortality in the United States, 1990–1992. Surveillance Report No. 37. Rockville, MD: National Institute on Alcohol Abuse and Alcoholism, Division of Biometry and Epidemiology, Alcohol Epidemiologic Data System.

Dufour, M. C. (1999). What is moderate drinking? *Alcohol, Health, and Research World* 23, 5–14.

Edwards, G. (1994). *Alcohol policy and the public good.* New York: Oxford University Press.

Fillmore, K. M. (1987). Women's drinking across the adult life course as compared to men's. *British Journal of Addiction* 82, 801–811.

Greenfield, T. K., & Rogers, J. D. (1999). Who drinks most of the alcohol in the U.S.? The policy implications. *Journal of Studies on Alcohol* 60, 78–89.

Hawton, K., Fag, J., and McKeown, S. P. (1991). Alcoholism, alcohol and attempted suicide. In D. J. Pittman and H. R. White (Eds.), *Society, culture, and drinking patterns reexamined* (pp. 661–672). New Brunswick, NJ: Rutgers Center on Alcohol Studies.

Helzer, J. E., Bucholz, K., & Robins, L. N. (1992). Five communities in the US: Results of the Epidemiologic Catchment Area survey. In J. E. Helzer & G. J. Canino (Eds.), *Alcoholism in North America, Europe, and Asia* (pp. 71–95). New York: Oxford University Press.

Helzer, J. E., & Canino, G. J. (Eds.) (1992). *Alcoholism in North America, Europe, and Asia.* New York: Oxford University Press.

Helzer, J. E., Canino, G. J., Gwu, H., Bland, R. C., Newman, S., and Yeh, E. (1988). Alcoholism: A cross-national comparison of population surveys with the diagnostic interview schedule. In R. M. Rose and J. E. Barrett (Eds.), *Alcoholism: Origins and outcome* (pp. 31–47). New York: Raven.

Johnston, J. G., Spitzer, R. L., Williams, J. B., Kroenke, K., Linzer, M., Brody, D., De Gruy, F., & Hahn, S. (1995). Psychiatric comorbidity, health status, and functional impairment associated with alcohol abuse and dependence in primary care patients: Findings of the prime MD-1000 study. *Journal of Consulting and Clinical Psychology* 63, 133–140.

Johnston, L. D., O'Malley, P. M., & Bachman, J. G. (1998). *National survey results on drug use from the Monitoring the Future study, 1975–1997* (NIH Publication 144921). Bethesda, MD: National Institute on Drug Abuse.

Johnston, L. D., O'Malley, P. M., & Bachman, J. G. (2001). *Monitoring the Future national survey results on drug use, 1975–2000, Vol. 1: Secondary school students* (NIH Publication 01-4924). Bethesda, MD: National Institute on Drug Abuse.

Manson, S. M., Shore, J. H., Baron, A. E., Ackerson, L., & Neligh, G. (1992). Alcohol abuse and dependence among American Indians. In J. E. Helzer & G. J. Canino (Eds.), *Alcoholism in North America, Europe, and Asia* (pp. 113–130). New York: Oxford University Press.

Midanik, L. T., & Clark, W. B. (1995). Drinking related problems in the US: Description and trends, 1984–90. *Journal of Studies on Alcohol* 56, 395–402.

Midanik, L. T., Tam, T. W., Greenfield, T. K., & Caetano, R. (1996). Risk functions for alcohol-related problems in a 1988 US national sample. *Addiction* 91, 1427–1437.

Midanik, L. T., & Clark, W. B. (1994). The demographic distribution of US drinking patterns in 1990: Description of trends from 1984. *American Journal of Public Heath* 84, 1218–1222.

Narrow, W. E., Regier, D. A., Rae, D. S., Manderscheid, R. W., & Locke, B. Z. (1993). Use of services by persons with mental and addictive disorders: Findings from the National Institute of Mental Health Epidemiologic Catchment Area Program. *Archives of General Psychiatry* 50, 95–107.

National Institute on Alcohol Abuse and Alcoholism (1998). Drinking in the United States: Main findings from the 1992 National Longitudinal Alcohol Epidemiologic Survey. *U.S. Alcohol Epidemiologic Data Reference Manual*, Vol. 6 (First Edition). Bethesda, MD: National Institutes of Health.

Neff, J. A. (1991). Race, ethnicity, and drinking patterns: The role of demographic factors, drinking motives, and expectancies. In D. J. Pittman & H. R. White (Eds.), *Society, culture, and drinking patterns reexamined* (pp. 339–356). New Brunswick, NJ: Rutgers Center on Alcohol Studies.

Phillips, D. P., Christenfeld, N., & Ryan, N. M. (1999). An increase in the number of deaths in the United States in the first week of the month. *New England Journal of Medicine* 341, 93–98.

Robins, L. N., Helzer, J. E., Przybeck, T. R., and Regier, D. A. (1988a). Alcohol disorders in the community: A report from the Epidemiologic Catchment Area. In R. M. Rose & J. E. Barrett (Eds.), *Alcoholism: Origins and outcome* (pp. 15–29). New York: Raven.

Robins, L. N., Helzer, J. E., Przybeck, T. R., and Regier, D. A. (1988b). Alcoholism: Cross-national comparison of population surveys with the Diagnostic Interview Schedule. In R. M. Rose and J. E. Barrett (Eds.), *Alcoholism: Origins and outcome* (pp. 31–47). New York: Raven.

Rogers, J. D., & Greenfield, T. K. (1999). Beer drinking accounts for most of the hazardous alcohol consumption reported in the United States. *Journal of Studies on Alcohol* 60, 732–739.

Room, R., Janca, A., Bennett, L. A., Schmidt, L., & Sartorius, N. (1996). WHO cross-cultural applicability research on diagnosis and assessment of substance use disorders: An overview of methods and selected results. *Addiction* 91, 199–220.

U.S. Department of Health and Human Services (1997). *Ninth Special Report to the U.S. Congress on alcohol and health.*

Wechsler, H. (2000). College binge drinking in the 1990's: A continuing problem. Results of the Harvard School of Public Health 1999 College Alcohol Study. *Journal of American College Health* 48, 199–210.

Wechsler, H., & Nelson, T. F. (2001). Binge drinking and the American college student. *Psychology of Addictive Behaviors* 15, 287–291.

Williams, G. D., Stinson, F. S., Stewart, S. L., & Dufour, M. C. (1995). Apparent per capita alcohol consumption: National, state, and regional trends, 1977–92. Surveillance Report No. 35. Rockville, MD: National Institute on Alcohol Abuse and Alcoholism, Division of Biometry and Epidemiology, Alcohol Epidemiologic Data System.

World Health Organization (1993). *The ICD-10 classification of mental and behavioral disorders: Diagnostic criteria for research.* Geneva: WHO.

CHAPTER SIX

LONGITUDINAL STUDIES ON ALCOHOL
Alcohol and the Life Span

In this chapter we examine how drinking patterns change from early adolescence to old age. We will use the results of longitudinal studies, which follow the changes in drinking behavior of specific individuals over time. Three longitudinal studies merit special attention and are described in some detail. The McCords' (1960) study traced alcoholism in adults who had been intensively studied in childhood. This provides a unique opportunity to see which childhood variables were associated with adult alcoholism. Shedler and Block (1990) closely followed young children through young adulthood and measured drug use in late adolescence. Although they do not report alcohol use, the study is an important one because the impact of childhood variables on drug use patterns in late adolescence was assessed. Vaillant's (1995) study of men followed adolescents from Cambridge, Massachusetts, and college students from Harvard University for 50 years. He traced the changes in drinking patterns over a significant portion of the human life span.

The chapter will trace the development of alcohol initiation, use, abuse, and remission through the life course by splicing together the findings from several longitudinal research studies.

The following questions will be addressed:

1. When do adolescents initiate alcohol use?
2. What are the characteristics of adolescent problem drinkers?
3. Is there a relationship between adolescent alcohol abuse and later adult alcohol abuse?
4. What characteristics distinguish alcohol abusers from normal drinkers before they become abusers?
5. How stable are problem drinking patterns?
6. What is the typical sequence of symptom development in alcohol abusers?
7. Are there some individuals whose alcohol problems remit without treatment?

METHODOLOGY

Longitudinal researchers study a specific group of individuals over a significant time span. The subjects are surveyed periodically during the course of the study, thus tracing the actual changes each of the individuals makes over the time period covered. For example, Schulenberg et al. (1996) surveyed the same group of young adults about their alcohol use patterns every other year from ages 18 to 28. Figure 6.1 shows the time periods covered for several longitudinal studies discussed in this chapter. These studies can determine how stable alcohol use patterns are, how long it takes for alcohol problems to develop, and see if there is a typical course of the disorder. Information can be collected on subjects at young ages, before any develop alcoholism; information can then be collected in adulthood, when some have developed alcoholism. Antecedent differences between those who develop alcohol problems and those who do not can be compared to determine if there are characteristics that are associated with the later development of alcoholism. The McCords' study, discussed later in the chapter, is of this type.

Age differences are reported in both longitudinal and survey studies. In survey data, the age differences are comparisons among groups of different individuals with different ages, thus confounding age differences with individual differences. In longitudinal data, the same individuals are interviewed at successive ages, which eliminates this confound.

Historical Time Period Confound

In both survey and longitudinal studies, a historical confound exists. When researchers measure a group of people in any time period, it may have an unintended significance. To make an obvious case, drinking habits surveyed during Prohibition in the United States give a distorted view of U.S. drinking habits in general. Thus, there may be some occurrence at

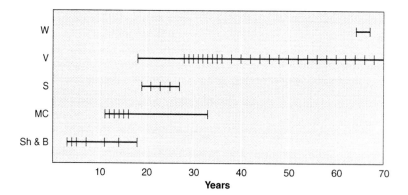

FIGURE 6.1   Time Periods Followed in Longitudinal Studies. W = Walton et al., 2000; V = Vaillant, 1995, Harvard sample; S = Schulenberg et al., 1996; McCord & McCord, 1960; Shedler & Block, 1990.

Note: Vertical lines indicate data collection points.

any given time period that may affect the results of a study, which may limit the ability to generalize the findings to different historical periods.

Other Methodological Concerns

Longitudinal researchers have used several different measures of alcohol problems, which do not typically conform to the alcohol use disorders laid out in Chapter 2. Similarly, criteria for remission vary across studies. These factors make it difficult to make comparisons among longitudinal studies. An additional problem is that some individuals drop out of a study before its conclusion. This process is known as *attrition*. Significant attrition compromises the representativeness of the sample, as dropouts may have characteristics different from those who finish the study.

ALCOHOL IN THE LIFE COURSE

Knowledge of Alcohol before Drinking

Children are aware of alcohol before they begin drinking. They realize it is a special substance and develop expectations about it (Zucker, 1994) that are similar to those of adults (U.S. Department of Health and Human Services, 2000, p. 33). By fourth grade there is an increase in positive expectations about alcohol, and many youths associate alcohol with sexuality and aggression (Miller et al., 1990). It is not yet clear how these expectancies affect later consumption patterns.

Age of Initiation, Use, and Heavy Use of Alcohol

Studies consistently show that alcohol initiation, regular use, and heavy use increase rapidly in mid- to late adolescence and peak in very early adulthood. As part of the Monitoring the Future study (Johnston et al., 2001), seniors were asked to indicate when they had their first drink and when they got drunk for the first time. The results are shown in Table 6.1. Table 5.9 showed that the rate of binge drinking increases during high school. Almost 15 percent of eighth graders report binge drinking, every 2 weeks and 31.3 percent of high school seniors do.

Continuity of Drinking Patterns from Adolescence to Adulthood

Several researchers report a lack of continuity between drinking patterns in adolescence and those in adulthood. D'Amico et al. (2002) report a great variability in binge drinking in adolescents even in the course of 1 year. Donovan et al. (1983) found that most adolescents who were problem drinkers were no longer so 4 years later. Temple and Fillmore (1985–1986) reported that only half of those who reported drinking to get drunk at 18 were doing so at 31. Schulenberg et al. (1996) evaluated changes in drinking with subjects starting in their senior

TABLE 6.1 Incidence of First Use of Alcohol and First Intoxication with Alcohol

GRADE	FIRST USE OF ALCOHOL	FIRST DRUNK
6th or below	7.8%	2.9%
7th–8th	21.7%	13.3%
9th	19.2%	16.5%
10th	14.5%	12.9%
11th	11.6%	11.3%
12th	5.5%	5.4%

Based on retrospective reports of twelfth-grade students in the Monitoring the Future Study, University of Michigan.

Source: Adapted from Johnston et al., 2001.

year in high school with three subsequent biennial assessments. Only 6.7 percent of the frequent binge drinkers maintained a consistent pattern in the time interval following.

On the other hand, several researchers have found more stability in drinking patterns as adolescents move into adulthood. White (1987) reports that for a sample of adolescents followed from ages 15–21, problem drinking remained relatively stable. Grant et al. (1988), following a group of adolescents ranging in age from 17 to 24 for 2 years, also found continuity of drinking behavior over this period. Ghodsion and Power (1987) measured alcohol consumption of British adolescents at ages 16 and 23. They found that those who drank the greatest amounts of alcohol at 16 were the most likely to drink heavily at 23. Galaif et al. (2001) found stability in problem alcohol use from adolescence through young adulthood. O'Neill et al. (2001) found that heavy drinking in college was predictive of alcohol problems 10 years later.

Thus, there appears to be disagreement among studies whether the drinking behavior in adolescence carries over into young adulthood. One way to understand this apparent discrepancy is that there may be several different drinking trajectories between adolescence and young adulthood. Schulenberg et al. (1996), for example, found six patterns of change in binge drinking between adolescence and adulthood. One subgroup remained the same, while another subgroup matured out of binge drinking, and yet another group initiated binge drinking at the end of the measured time interval, as shown in Figure 6.2. Note also that the average of the different patterns would give the mistaken impression that the drinking pattern remained stable. O'Neill et al. (2001), while finding a relationship between college heavy drinking and problems 10 years later, indicate that their findings also support different drinking trajectories.

Developmental Factors Implicated in Alcohol Problems

A number of relevant studies measure the effect of personality, behavioral, and family characteristics in childhood and adolescence on drinking practices in adolescence and adulthood. Table 6.2 indicates the four types of studies.

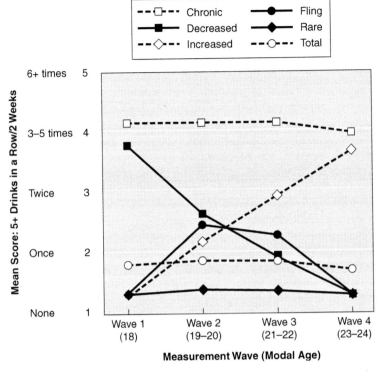

FIGURE 6.2   Mean Scores for 5 Drinks in a Row or More in the Past 2 Weeks by Binge Drinking Trajectory

Source: Reprinted with permission from *Journal of Studies on Alcohol,* vol. 57, pp. 289–304, 1996. Copyright by Alcohol Research Documentation, Inc., Rutgers Center of Alcohol Studies, Piscataway, NJ 08854.

TABLE 6.2   Four Types of Studies That Research the Impact of Childhood and Adolescent Variables on Adolescent and Adult Drinking Patterns

I	Adolescent factors	Impact	Adult drinking
II	Adolescent factors	Impact	Adolescent drinking
III	Childhood factors	Impact	Adolescent drinking
IV	Childhood factors	Impact	Adult drinking

Impact of Childhood Variables on Adult Drinking.   Vicary and Learner (1983) conducted a longitudinal study of children followed through age 19. They report that poor adjustment and coping problems at home and in school at age 5 were associated with heavy alcohol use in early adulthood. Amudsen (1982, cited by Fillmore, 1988) followed all of the 19-year-old Norwegian men screened for military service in 1951 (*n* = 15,810), reviewing institutional records. He found that men who became alcoholics were more likely as children to be of low intelligence, urban, lower social class, have divorced parents, be maladjusted at school, be short in stature, and use drinking to get away from problems. A Finnish longitudinal study (Pulkkinen & Pitkanen, 1994) found that aggressive boys were more likely to become alcoholics than nonaggressive boys. Caspi et al. (1996) conducted an important longitudinal study that included behavioral observations of 1,037 New Zealand boys and girls at age 3 and DSM-III-R diagnoses at age 21. Those boys who were rated under-controlled at 3 were 2.7 times more likely to develop alcohol dependence as adults. Zucker (1994), reviewing longitudinal studies, found childhood antisocial behavior implicated in adult alcoholism. Other childhood factors cited by Zucker included hyperactivity, and inadequate parenting. Galaif et al. (2001) found that childhood sexual abuse led to a greater likelihood of adult drinking problems.

Adolescent Variables and Adolescent Drinking.   Kandel (1978, p. 93), using results of an adolescent longitudinal study, found that "overall, for initiation into hard liquor, the most important class of predictors is involvement in minor forms of deviant behavior." Barnes et al. (2000) found that parental support and monitoring led to fewer instances of alcohol misuse in adolescence. Reifman et al. (1998) found that low parental modeling predicted heavier drinking in later adolescence. Sadava (1987, p. 115) summarizes research on family characteristics of adolescent heavy drinkers: "[T]he family environments of adolescent problem drinkers tend to be relatively harsher and more negative in affect. . . . [F]amilies with problem drinking adolescents have: (1) parental deviant or antisocial behavior, including alcohol abuse, (2) parental disinterest and lack of involvement with their child, (3) lack of affectionate supportive interaction between parents and children."

Adolescent Traits and Adult Drinking.   Donovan et al. (1983, p. 119) found that adolescents who engaged in deviant behavior were more likely to become problems drinkers in young adulthood. Similarly, Harford and Muthen (2000) found that delinquency in adolescence was a predictor of alcohol abuse or dependence in adulthood. Pulkkinen and Pitkanen (1994) found that conduct problems and poor school success at the age of 14 were predictive of male and female problem drinking in their longitudinal study of Finnish youth. Galaif et al. (2001) found that more family support and bonding in adolescence led to fewer adult drinking problems. Newcomb et al. (1986) found that the more risk factors adolescents had, the more likely they would use alcohol with greater frequency 4 years later. Risk factors included poor school performance, social deviance, and poor relationship with parents. On the other hand, Temple and Fillmore (1985–1986) did not find any behavioral or social attribute in high school students related to drinking outcome at 31.

Shedler and Block: Variables Associated with Adolescent Drug Use.   Shedler and Block (1990) closely followed a group of children from ages 3 to 18 and traced the impact of various childhood variables on adolescent drug use. They thoroughly assessed 101 urban, racially diverse children at several points. Parenting was assessed when the children were 5. Drug use information was collected in interviews at age 18.

Shedler and Block found that by age 18, 68 percent of the adolescents had tried marijuana, 39 percent used it once a month, and 21 percent used it more often than weekly. Adolescents were divided into three categories in relation to their drug use:

1. Abstainers, consisting of 29 subjects. This group reported no drug use.
2. Experimenters, 36 subjects, reported using marijuana occasionally to once a month.
3. Frequent users consisted of 20 subjects who reported using marijuana once a week or more.

(Sixteen subjects did not fit into any of these categories for various reasons.)

Frequent users were troubled adolescents, interpersonally alienated, emotionally withdrawn, manifestly unhappy, and expressed their maladjustment through undercontrolled, overtly antisocial behavior. As children, long before the onset of drug use, future frequent drug users were maladjusted, unable to form good relationships, insecure, and showed numerous signs of emotional distress. Mothers of frequent users and abstainers were relatively cold, unresponsive, and underprotective. They gave children little encouragement, were overly pressuring, and were interested in performance. Fathers of frequent users were not different from fathers of the other groups. The researchers conclude: "The traits that characterize the frequent [drug] user can be seen to form a theoretically coherent syndrome, characterized by the psychological triad of alienation, impassivity and subjective distress, predating adolescence and drug use" (p. 626).

Abstainers were tense, overcontrolled, emotionally constricted individuals who were somewhat socially isolated and lacking in interpersonal skills. As children, abstainers were overcontrolled, timid, fearful, and morose.

The "experimenters," by contrast, were the best adjusted of the groups in childhood and adolescence. This finding is controversial because it flies in the face of conventional wisdom, which regards any drug use as harmful. The authors point out that at the time of the study it was normative for adolescents to experiment with marijuana.

Marriage and Drinking

The empirical research suggests that the transition to marriage in early adulthood is associated with declines in alcohol consumption and alcohol-related problems (Leonard & Roberts, 1996). For example, Miller-Tutzauer et al. (1991) surveyed adolescents through young adulthood to discern relationships between marriage and alcohol consumption. Those who married had lower consumption and lower frequencies of heavy drinking than those who remained single. Individuals who married during the course of the study tended to reduce consumption and instances of heavy drinking 1 year before they got married and continued this pattern after marriage. Similar results were found by Chilcoat and Breslau (1996) in a longitudinal study of young adults. These findings suggest that marriage may act as a protection against alcohol problems. Alternatively, alcohol abuse may impede marriage prospects.

The Stability of Drinking Patterns in Adulthood

Using a time interval of 20 years, Temple and Leino (1989) found continuity in drinking patterns for two general population samples of men ages 21 to 59 as measured by mean levels of alcohol consumption per month.

In contrast, findings regarding patterns of problem drinking suggest less continuity. Fillmore (1987a) found that the incidence of heavy drinking and alcohol problems in men decreases with age; chronicity (stability) of alcohol problems is highest in the middle years, decreasing after that time. Both Fillmore and Midanik (1984) and Amudsen (1982, reported by Fillmore, 1988) found that young men are more likely to report sporadic alcohol problems, while middle-aged men are more likely to report chronic problems (Fillmore & Midanik, 1984, p. 29).

Fillmore (1987b) found a very different pattern for women: "Not only do fewer women engage in the behaviors putting individuals at risk for serious alcohol problems, but, compared to the ages of onset for men, onset for women is later, the duration is shorter, and the remission is earlier" (p. 806).

Drinking Patterns of Older Adults

Adults over 50 years of age drink less alcohol, drink less frequently, have fewer alcohol-related problems (Fillmore 1987a,b), engage in less binge drinking (Jackson, 1998; cited in U.S. Department of Health and Human Services, 2000), and have lower rates of alcohol abuse and dependence than younger groups (Grant, 1997). Mirand and Welte (1996) found that older adults in a general population survey had a 6 percent (13 percent for males and 2 percent for females) rate of heavy drinking. Grant (1997) reports that a 12-month prevalence rate of 1.45 percent of alcohol dependence for adults over 55. A survey by Akers and La Greca (1991) found that the elderly rarely developed new alcohol problems in old age. Fillmore et al. (1991) suggest that tolerance decreases with age and may be responsible for the decreased consumption in older adults.

Retirement may increase the rate of alcohol disorders in men. Ekerdt et al. (1989) found that a group of retired men had a 9.0 percent rate of alcoholism, compared to 2.8 percent for a group of men who continued to work. Alcohol consumption was found to be higher in older adults in retirement communities than in age-integrated ones (Akers & La Greca, 1991).

LONGITUDINAL STUDIES ENCOMPASSING
CHILDHOOD AND ADULTHOOD

Cambride-Somerville Project

One of the first longitudinal studies on alcoholism was conducted by McCord and McCord (1960). The subjects of this study were originally chosen for a study on delinquency prevention. Half were provided counseling services and another group was given none. Because the group given the counseling had detailed records, and they did not differ from the control group in childhood measures of adjustment or rates of alcoholism in adulthood, this group was used for the study (p. 14). Records included extensive notes on bimonthly family visits for over 5 years, typically from ages 11 to 16 (p. 12).

To determine who developed alcoholism as adults, subjects of this study were followed up via public records. McCord and McCord found that 10 percent had become alcoholic (p. 11). Subsequently, McCord (1988) interviewed a large percentage of the sample at ages 45 to 53 and found that 32 percent were alcoholic. Comparisons below are based on the original 10 percent that were identified as alcoholic.

Childhood Factors Implicated in Adult Alcoholism.   Subjects who had alcoholic parents had a greater probability of becoming alcoholic themselves, a consistent finding in alcohol research. Subjects of Irish descent had a high rate of alcoholism, while Italian subjects had a low rate of alcoholism (p. 38). Thirty-three percent (5 out of 15) of children who showed evidence of neurologic disorder developed alcoholism, compared to 13 percent with normal neurologic findings (p. 49). Boys who were more aggressive (p. 137) and more hyperactive (p. 139) in childhood were more likely to become alcoholics than those who were not.

Family Factors Implicated in Adult Alcoholism.   Intense conflict in the home was associated with later alcoholism (p. 48). Families that alternately frustrated and indulged dependency needs had higher rates of alcoholism in their sons (p. 89). Mothers who alternated between affection and rejection had more alcoholic sons (p. 57). Fathers who showed little esteem for their wives (p. 63) and were highly rejecting of their sons (p. 74) were more likely to have sons who became alcoholic. Because the researchers do not indicate if there was any correlation among these familial and parental traits, it could be that a small number of families that share these variables account for most of the findings.

The St. Louis Guidance Clinic Study

Robins et al. (1962), in a study similar to the McCords', had access to records of patients at a St. Louis child guidance clinic. They interviewed the patients 30 years later and examined social records for evidence of alcoholism. A group of children who did not attend a child guidance clinic was used as a comparison group. There was a higher incidence of alcoholism among the patient group (15 percent versus 2 percent). In the patient group, Irish Americans had a high rate of alcoholism; those with childhood antisocial problems but not neurotic behavior were more likely to develop alcoholism. Inadequate parenting and lower socioeconomic status were also associated with later alcoholism. The researchers report that 26 percent of the problem drinkers had resumed drinking without apparent problems.

The Study of Adult Development at Harvard

The Study of Adult Development conducted at Harvard University followed 724 normal men for 50 years regarding their alcohol use patterns and general adjustment. It is the longest, most detailed study of alcohol use and problems in a nonclinical sample. Vaillant reported the results of the study first in *The Natural History of Alcoholism* (1983) and subsequently in *The Natural History of Alcoholism Revisited* (1995). Wherever possible, results are taken from the more recent report.

Description of the Study.   The Study of Adult Development began in the late 1930s as two separate studies: one on delinquency and the other on healthy college sophomores at Harvard University. The college sample consisted of 268 male Harvard College sophomores (Vaillant, 1995, p. 308) drawn from the classes of 1939–1941 and 1942–1944. They were a carefully selected group and therefore decidedly not random. Forty percent of the potential subjects were excluded because of mediocre academics, and 30 percent more were excluded because of medical or psychologic difficulties. The delinquency study sample, called Core City subjects, consisted of 456 junior high school Cambridge, Massachusetts, males, followed from 1940 to 1990 (Vaillant, 1995, p. 311). These subjects were used as a control group for the delinquents in the original study but were not delinquent themselves, although the subjects came from severely disadvantaged home environments. Two-thirds of the families were on welfare. The average IQ of the group was below normal (Vaillant, 1995, pp. 314–315).

For both samples, information was obtained by interview and mailed survey. Each Harvard student had eight psychiatric interviews while in college; subsequently, annual questionnaires were mailed to the Harvard men until 1955, at which time the questionnaires were mailed biannually. All subjects were interviewed in 1951. Fifty percent of the subjects and all who were suspected of problem drinking were again interviewed in the period 1971–1976.

The Core City subjects had several interviews during their adolescence. Subjects were reinterviewed at ages 25, 31, and 47. Biennial questionnaires were sent after age 47 (Vaillant, 1995, pp. 308–310). Over the course of the lengthy study, attrition was small; only 6 of the 241 subjects of the Harvard sample and 27 of 456 of the Core City sample were lost to the study (Vaillant, 1995, p. 316).

The Course of Alcohol Problems.   One key finding of the study is that the two samples had very different patterns of alcohol problems. One hundred fifty of 456 (36 percent) Core City men were diagnosed with alcohol abuse by age 60 (Vaillant, 1995, p. 127), while only 52 of 241 (22 percent) of the Harvard sample had abused alcohol by age 70 (Vaillant, 1995, p. 131). The Epidemiologic Catchment Area Survey (ECA) estimate of 23 percent lifetime prevalence for alcohol abuse for males (Robins et al., 1988) suggests that the Core City men had a higher than average rate of alcohol problems, while the Harvard sample had a slightly lower than average rate.

There were other differences between the two samples of alcohol abusers. The Core City alcohol abusers were over three times more likely to have an alcohol-related arrest than the Harvard alcohol abusers (73 percent vs 19 percent) (Vaillant, 1995, p. 29). Age of onset was much earlier for the Core City sample than for the college sample. These differences are readily apparent by examining the graphs showing the age of onset of alcohol abuse in the two samples shown in Figures 6.3 and 6.4. In Core City subjects alcohol abuse or dependence developed over the course of 3 to 15 years on average, while the future alcohol abusers in the college sample drank for as long as 20 years before developing abuse or dependence (Vaillant, 1996).

Figures 6.5 and 6.6 trace the life course of abuse in the two samples. Each time period shows the percentage of those actively abusing alcohol, those who have not yet begun to abuse, and those who have stopped abusing alcohol. Men who abused alcohol had

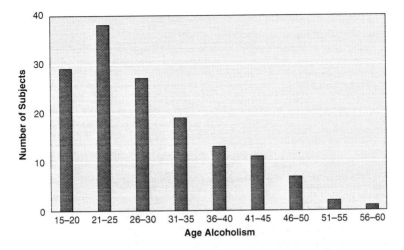

FIGURE 6.3   Age of Onset for Core City Alcohol Abusers. Approximate age at which the 150 Core City men first met the DSM-III criteria for alcohol abuse. Age of onset before age 45 based in part on retrospective data.

Source: Reprinted by permission of the publisher from *The Natural History of Alcoholism Revisited,* by George E. Vaillant, Cambridge, Mass.: Harvard University Press, Copyright © 1983, 1995 by the President and Fellows of Harvard College.

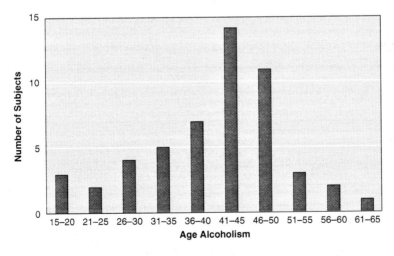

FIGURE 6.4   Age of Onset for College Alcohol Abusers. Approximate age at which the 52 college men first met the DSM-III criteria for alcohol abuse. Age of onset before age 45 based in part on retrospective data.

Source: Reprinted by permission of the publisher from *The Natural History of Alcoholism Revisited,* by George E. Vaillant, Cambridge, Mass.: Harvard University Press, Copyright © 1983, 1995 by the President and Fellows of Harvard College.

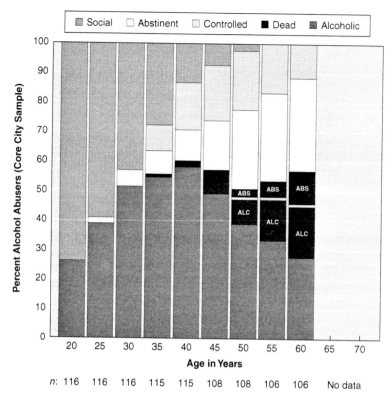

FIGURE 6.5   Life Course of Alcohol Abuse by Core City Alcohol Abusers. This figure reflects the quinquennial alcohol use status of the 116 Core City men who remained active in the study and met the DSM-III criteria for alcohol abuse. The eight men who because of brief duration of alcohol abuse and minimal systems were classified as "social drinkers" have been excluded. The proportions of deaths among men classified as alcohol abused is indicated by the label ALC; the proportion among those classified as stably abstinent, by ABS.

Source: Reprinted by permission of the publisher from *The Natural History of Alcoholism Revisited,* by George E. Vaillant, Cambridge, Mass.: Harvard University Press, Copyright © 1983, 1995 by the President and Fellows of Harvard College.

one of four patterns of abusive drinking over the course of the follow-up (Vaillant, 1995, p. 167):

1. Some men drank with the same pattern of abuse over the course of their drinking.
2. Some men showed a progressively worsening drinking pattern, with drastic consequences until abstinence or death.
3. Sociopathic men who became alcoholic had an early and rapid progression into abuse.

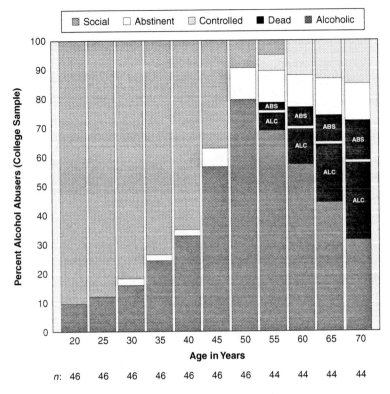

FIGURE 6.6   Life Course of Alcohol Abuse by College Alcohol Abusers.
This figure reflects the quinquennial alcohol use status of the 46 college men
who met the DSM-III criteria for alcohol abuse. The six alcohol abusers
reclassified as "social drinkers" were excluded. The proportions of deaths
among men classified as alcohol abused is indicated by the label ALC; the
proportion among those classified as stably abstinent, by ABS.

Source: Reprinted by permission of the publisher from *The Natural History of Alcoholism
Revisited,* by George E. Vaillant, Cambridge, Mass.: Harvard University Press, Copyright
© 1983, 1995 by the President and Fellows of Harvard College.

4. Some swung into and out of problematic drinking over many years (Vaillant, 1995,
pp. 180–181).

The Core City abusers tended to have one of the first three patterns while the college
abusers more often were of the fourth type. Within type 1, attesting to the stability of this pattern, were 59 Core City men who were abusers at age 47, none of whom developed alcohol
dependence by age 60 (Vaillant, 1996). Twenty of the 22 college abusers had problems with
alcohol off and on from ages 47 to 72 (Vaillant, 1995, p. 181), showing neither a steady pattern of abuse nor a gradual decline in functioning. Thus, at least in these samples of abusive
drinkers, there is great variability in patterns of abusive drinking over the years, with a severe,

declining progression of symptoms occurring only in a minority of the problem drinkers. Of particular interest is the significant number of differences between the two groups of men, suggesting that social and cultural factors heavily influence the course of drinking problems.

Childhood and Adolescent Differences between Those Who Became Alcohol-Dependent and Those Who Did Not. Table 6.3 shows that normal drinkers in the Core City sample were more likely to have closer relationship with their fathers and more childhood environmental strengths compared to future alcoholics. Future alcoholics were more likely to have school behavior problems, truancy, and sociopathic traits. They were more likely to have alcoholic relatives and more likely to be of Irish descent.

Childhood environment did not contribute to alcohol use disorders in college students, as measured by retrospective reports (Vaillant, 1995, p. 76). While those men who became alcohol abusers as adults were rated in college as less shy, inhibited, and self-conscious than those who drank normally, they were also more likely to be seen as erratic, unreliable, show-

TABLE 6.3   Childhood Differences and Similarities between Men Who Never Abused Alcohol and Those Who Became Dependent

	ASYMPTOMATIC DRINKERS (%) ($n = 254 \pm 6$)	ALCOHOL-DEPENDENT (%) ($n = 69 \pm 2$)
Differences		
Irish ethnicity	17	30
Italian ethnicity	35	6
Alcoholism in 2+ ancestors	9	21
Alcoholism in a parent	18	34
School behavior problem and truancy	2	13
Sociopath (5+ on Robins scale)	0.4	30
2+ in jail	4	16
<10th-grade education	28	42
Childhood environmental strengths ("warm")	26	13
Lack of cohesive family	40	51
Close relationship with father	30	13
Similarities		
IQ < 90	28	30
Parents in social class V	32	30
Multiproblem family	11	14
Warm relationship with mother	30	27
Inadequate maternal supervision	36	34
Childhood emotional problems	32	30
Boyhood competence (top quartile)	28	21

Source: Reprinted by permission of the publisher from *The Natural History of Alcoholism Revisited,* by George E. Vaillant, Cambridge, Mass.: Harvard University Press, Copyright © 1983, 1995 by the President and Fellows of Harvard College.

ing poor judgment, and lacking in purpose and values than the adult normal drinkers (Vaillant, 1995, p. 94).

Abstinence and Return to Safe Drinking.   At age 45, twenty-one former alcohol-abusing men in the Core City sample were abstinent. By age 60, there were 47 (Vaillant, 1995, p. 233). The relapse rate for those with 2 years of abstinence was 41 percent, but decreased significantly with longer periods of abstinence (Vaillant & Hiller-Sturmhefel, 1996). Thirty men had 10 or more years of abstinence.

Remission was much less stable for those abusers who attempted to control their drinking. While 27 men reported drinking in a controlled manner at age 45, by age 60, nine had relapsed, six had become abstinent, and only six of the original 27 had maintained a pattern of controlled drinking. An additional 12 alcohol abusers were drinking in a controlled manner at this latter period.

To summarize, of the 150 men who suffered from alcohol abuse in the Core City sample, 47 became abstinent (31 percent) and 18 were drinking in a controlled manner (12 percent) (Vaillant, 1995, pp. 277 and 284) at the age of 60. Formal treatment was not especially helpful for remitted alcohol abusers. Only 20 percent of the securely abstinent group in the Core City sample reported that alcoholism treatment had been important in their recoveries (Vaillant, 1995, p. 237). Among the college sample, 10 alcoholic men received at least 100 hours of psychotherapy. Only two of these men reported any benefit of the therapy regarding remission of alcohol problems (Vaillant, 1995, p. 237). Those who became abstinent in both samples were helped by Alcoholics Anonymous (AA) more often than by treatment (Vaillant, 1995, p. 388).

Life-Long Abstainers.   An interesting finding is that life-long abstainers were rated as having more emotional difficulties than normal drinkers (Vaillant, 1995, pp. 134, 135).

The Lundby Sweden Community Cohort

A longitudinal study conducted in Sweden replicates some of the findings of the Harvard study. In this study, all of the community residents of a town in Sweden were surveyed in 1947, reinterviewed in 1957, and resurveyed in 1972 (Ojesjo, 1984). Additional information was obtained through public records. Because there was a very low rate of alcohol problems among the women, only male rates were reported. Using DSM-III diagnostic criteria, Ojesjo determined that males had a 19.3 percent lifetime probability of any alcohol use disorder and 8.6 percent for alcohol dependence. The highest rate of alcohol disorders occurred when the cohort was 20 to 29 years old. Working-class residents had higher rates of alcohol disorders and had an earlier onset than middle-class residents. Those with less education had higher rates of alcoholism than those with more education.

LONGITUDINAL STUDIES FOLLOWING ALCOHOLICS: THE COURSE OF ALCOHOLISM

Table 6.4 summarizes results of some representative longitudinal studies of alcoholics. Although these studies rely primarily on alcoholics' self-reports, Nordstrom and Berglund

(1987) found that the self-reports of alcoholic subjects in their longitudinal study were generally accurate by comparing them to data from collaterals, medical tests, and public records. The reader can see that there is a large variation in outcome among studies. This can be attributed largely to differences in the samples of alcoholics chosen for study. From 18 to 76 percent were abstinent at the end of the follow-up period. Most who improved were abstinent, but 6 to 30 percent were drinking asymptomatically at the end of the follow-up period.

Stability of Alcoholics' Drinking Patterns

Table 6.4 indicates only the outcome at the end of the follow-up period, so there is no way of knowing the stability of the alcoholics' drinking patterns within the interval studied. By using several interviewing points, research conducted by Skog and Duckert (1993), Taylor et al. (1985), and Vaillant (1995) were able to determine that a large percentage of the alcoholics had unstable patterns of drinking. That is, about 50 percent of the alcoholics followed had periods of abstinence, controlled drinking, heavy drinking, and/or binge drinking over the course of 10 to 20 years. Newcomb et al. (2001) assessed alcohol disorders in a community sample of young adults when they were in their early twenties and again 4 years later. They also report a pattern of great variability in the course of alcohol disorders: 62 percent of those who were alcohol abusers in the first assessment were in remission 4 years later; 25 percent remained abusers, and 13 percent had become alcohol-dependent. Among those who were alcohol dependent at time one, almost half were in remission 4 years later; 30 percent remained dependent; and 22 percent were alcohol abusers. Walton et al. (2000) found a similar pattern of unstable patterns with older adult alcoholics.

Mortality of Alcoholics

Table 6.4 indicates that a large percentage of alcoholics died during the course of the studies. Marshall et al. (1994) found that married alcoholic men had a 3.64 times higher death rate than nonalcoholic married men. The more heavily the alcoholics drank and the earlier problem drinking began, the more years of life were lost. Finney and Moos (1991) found that alcoholics were 9.5 times more likely to die than a matched community sample. On a more optimistic note, Bullock et al. (1992, cited in Marshall et al., 1994) report that alcoholic men who achieve abstinence reduced the risk of mortality to that of a comparable control group of nonalcoholics.

The Typical Course of Alcohol-Related Symptoms

Burke et al. (1990) found that most alcoholics report that their first problem with alcohol occurred between the ages of 15 and 19, based on retrospective reports drawn from the Epidemiologic Catchment Area study.

Schuckit et al. (1995) interviewed alcoholics to determine the average ages at which they experienced alcohol-related symptoms. Table 6.5 summarizes these findings. Drinking in hazardous situations on average first appeared at 21.2 years of age; arguments while drinking at 21.6; blackouts at 23.3; and interference in role obligation at 24 years. An average of

TABLE 6.4 Ten Recent Long-Term Follow-Up Studies of Alcohol Abuse

STUDY AND NATURE OF SAMPLE	NATURE OF TREATMENT	TYPE AND LENGTH OF FOLLOW-UP	SIZE OF ORIGINAL SAMPLE	ATTRITION % Lost or Refused	ATTRITION % Dead	Number of Survivors Followed	OUTCOME FOR SURVIVORS (%) Abstinent	OUTCOME FOR SURVIVORS (%) Asymptomatic Drinkers	OUTCOME FOR SURVIVORS (%) Still Alcoholic
Edwards et al. (1983): Married, alcohol-dependent males age ca. 41	Outpatient treatment or advice	Interview at 10 years	99	13	18	68	28	12	60 ($n = 59$)
Marshall, Edwards, & Taylor (1994): Same sample as above	Same as above	Interview at 20 years	99	2	43	54	44	30	26 ($n = 14$)
Nordstrom & Berglund (1987): Alcohol-dependent males age ca. 32; 70% excellent posthospital adjustment	Inpatient treatment	Interview 21 +/-4 years	105	21	NA	84	18	26	56 ($n = 47$)
O'Connor & Daly (1985): Male voluntary first admission age ca. 48	Inpatient treatment	Questionnaire 20 years	133	30	40	40	67	15	18 ($n = 7$)
McCabe (1986): Married, alcohol-dependent men and women age ca. 40	Inpatient treatment	Interview 16 years	57	4	42	31	26	35	39 ($n = 12$)
Pendry et al. (1982): Alcohol-dependent male inpatients age ca. 40	Behavioral treatment for controlled drinking	Interview/chart 10 years	20	0	20	16	38	6	56 ($n = 9$)
Finney & Moos (1991): High-social-stability men and women age ca. 40	Inpatient treatment	Questionnaire 10 years	113 of 157	10 (35)	17	83	54	24	22 ($n = 18$)
Smith et al. (1983): Alcohol-dependent women age ca. 44	Inpatient treatment	Interview 11 years	103	11[a]	31	61	41[a]		59[a] ($n = 36$)
Westermeyer & Peake (1983): Native Americans, severe dependence, men and women	Inpatient treatment	Interview 10 years	45	7	20	33	21		79 ($n = 26$)
Langle et al. (1993): Alcohol-dependent men and women, age ca. 38	Inpatient treatment	Interview 10 years	96	5	22	70	70		30 ($n = 21$)
Cross et al. (1990): Men and women age, ca. 48	Inpatient treatment and AA	Questionnaire 10 years	200	21	22	114	76		24 ($n = 27$)

[a]Estimate—text not clear.

Source: Reprinted by permission of the publisher from The Natural History of Alcoholism Revisited, by George E. Vaillant, Cambridge. Mass.: Harvard University Press. Copyright © 1983, 1995 by the President and Fellows of Harvard College.

TABLE 6.5 The Sequence of Alcohol-Related Life Experiences for 317 Alcohol-Dependent Men and 161 Alcohol-Dependent Women ($n = 478$)

LIFE EXPERIENCE	NO. (%) WITH SYMPTOM	FIRST OCCURRENCE (AGE +/– SD)
Physical fights while intoxicated	208 (44)	19.72 (4.69)
Drinking/drunk while in hazardous situations	431 (90)	21.21 (7.72)
Hitting others without fighting while intoxicated	92 (19)	21.37 (6.49)
Arguments while drinking	345 (72)	21.61 (7.29)
Started drinking at times not intended	351 (73)	21.84 (7.99)
Drank more or for longer periods than intended	444 (93)	22.26 (8.15)
Problem at work/school related to drinking	221 (46)	22.89 (8.28)
Hit or threw things while drinking	249 (52)	22.94 (8.82)
Lost friends due to drinking	127 (27)	23.28 (8.73)
Blackouts due to drinking	345 (72)	23.30 (8.87)
Drinking interfered with work or other obligations	221 (46)	24.00 (9.43)
Tolerance to alcohol	388 (81)	24.12 (8.86)
Problems with family/friends due to drinking	315 (66)	24.14 (9.13)
Drank mouthwash	43 (9)	24.33 (10.11)
Binge drinking (2+ days of intoxication)	228 (48)	24.56 (8.85)
Used rules to control drinking behavior	189 (40)	24.61 (7.60)
Arrested for alcohol-related behavior (not DWI)	126 (26)	24.84 (10.01)
Periods of little time for nondrinking activities	232 (49)	24.86 (8.85)
Objections about drinking from family/friends/MD	372 (78)	24.87 (9.55)
Decrease important activities to drink	220 (46)	25.00 (9.29)
Accidental self-injury while intoxicated	212 (44)	25.16 (10.42)
Early morning drinking	275 (58)	25.37 (9.66)
Compelling desire for alcohol when unable to drink	171 (36)	25.51 (8.81)
Driving accident due to drinking	87 (18)	25.52 (8.40)
Inability to change drinking behavior	186 (39)	25.61 (9.33)
Hit a family member while drinking	116 (24)	25.84 (95.7)
Wanted to quit or cut down 3 or more times	369 (77)	26.10 (8.92)
Felt guilty about drinking	321 (67)	26.12 (9.59)
Psychological impairment related to drinking	196 (41)	26.34 (9.68)
Considered self an excessive drinker	349 (73)	26.58 (10.06)
Drinking caused problem in love relationship	244 (51)	26.62 (8.67)
Tried, but unable to quit, cut down	217 (45)	27.44 (9.88)
Arrested for drunk driving (DWI)	143 (30)	28.80 (10.71)
Shakes following abstinence	140 (29)	28.94 (10.54)
1st abstinence of 3+ months recorded	335 (70)	29.08 (11.32)
Alcohol withdrawal syndrome (2 or more symptoms)	204 (43)	29.55 (11.02)
Continued use despite knowledge of harm to health	71 (15)	30.34 (12.98)
Initiated help from a health professional	247 (52)	31.03 (10.87)
DTs/hallucinations following abstinence	44 (9)	31.05 (10.16)
2nd abstinence of 3+ months recorded	185 (39)	31.81 (11.63)
Liver problems/ulcer/pancreatitis related to drinking	60 (13)	32.55 (12.62)
3rd abstinence of 3+ months recorded	100 (21)	35.72 (12.49)
Convulsions following abstinence	17 (4)	37.06 (11.32)
4th abstinence of 3+ months recorded	49 (10)	38.84 (11.37)

SD = Standard Deviation

Reprinted with permission from *Journal of Studies on Alcohol*, vol. 56, pp. 218–225, 1995. Copyright by Alcohol Research Documentation, Inc., Rutgers Center of Alcohol Studies, Piscataway, NJ 08854.

11.31 years elapsed between the beginning of alcohol-related problems and seeking help. This more contemporary and more representative study of the sequence of alcoholic symptoms supersedes the historically important Jellinek study that gave birth to the so-called Jellinek curve, which graphically depicted the progression of alcoholic symptoms (Jellinek, 1946).

META-ANALYSES AND REVIEWS OF LONGITUDINAL STUDIES

Fillmore et al. conducted a meta-analysis of twenty-six longitudinal studies on quantity and frequency of alcohol consumption in adults (1991) and reviewed some of the important longitudinal findings regarding alcohol problems (1988). The findings included:

1. Drinking practices in younger age groups do not predict later drinking practices. Young men are more likely to report sporadic alcohol problems, higher incidence, and higher remission of alcohol problems than older men.
2. Older men have a lower prevalence of alcohol problems than younger men, but have higher chronicity of alcohol problems.
3. There is high remission of alcohol problems in old age (Fillmore, 1988).
4. There is greater variation in drinking practices across national boundaries for women in contrast to men (Fillmore et al., 1991).

In another meta-analysis, Johnstone et al. (1996) analyzed twenty-seven longitudinal studies. Their analysis indicates that:

5. During youth and young adulthood, significant and heterogeneous patterns of change in drinking are observed. This result bolsters Schulenberg's findings cited earlier.
6. Drinking patterns during middle and later adulthood display relative stability.
7. National origin is the most significant factor in determining drinking practices.
8. Historical factors are important in determining drinking patterns, suggesting that longitudinal studies conducted in earlier historical periods cannot be extrapolated directly to more current periods.

NATURAL RECOVERY

Another view of the course of alcoholism is presented by research on individuals who overcome drinking problems without treatment, often called "natural recovery." The most interesting finding of these studies is that a large percentage of these remissions consists of controlled drinking. In such studies, subjects are typically recruited by advertisement or **chain referral.** Subjects are interviewed and asked about the duration and seriousness of their alcohol problem, how they were able to change, and their current remission.

For example, Humphreys et al. (1995) conducted a longitudinal study of men and women with alcohol problems who had no professional treatment (AA participation was not considered treatment.). One hundred thirty-five subjects were followed up at 1 and 3 years. Results indicated that 28 became stably abstinent and 29 became moderate drinkers.

Those who became moderate drinkers had originally drunk less, had fewer symptoms of dependence, fewer days intoxicated, fewer drinking-related problems, better social networks, better extended family support, and more education. The abstinent group used AA extensively in the first year of abstinence and had the opposite profile as the moderate drinkers. The authors note that 48.3 percent remitted without professional treatment.

Sobel et al. (2000) reviewed thirty-eight natural recovery studies. The subjects studied had a mean length of recovery of 6.3 years. Forty percent of the subjects reported successful controlled drinking. In general, Sobel et al. felt the studies were methodologically weak. One important problem with these studies is that the participants are not a representative sample of drinkers.

In an effort to address this concern, Rumpf et al. (2000) compared results obtained from a general population survey of drinkers, a representative sample, and subjects recruited by media. Alcohol-dependent subjects in remission for 12 months were selected from both samples. The researchers found that the media-sample alcoholics had greater severity of dependence symptoms. Only 17 percent of the media sample had controlled drinking remission, while the population-based sample had a much higher rate of 81.8 percent. They suggest that media recruitment, which most natural-recovery studies use, may reflect a disproportionate number of severely alcohol-dependent subjects and a smaller proportion of controlled drinking outcomes for problem drinkers than is found in the general population of problem drinkers.

Characteristics of Successful Self-Quitters

Researchers have begun to determine the characteristics of those problem drinkers who can successfully quit on their own. It has been found that self-quitters:

1. Have spousal support (Sobel et al., 1993)
2. Have family and social support (Tuchfield, 1981).
3. Have a relatively stable work situation (Tucker et al., 1994)

Larimer and Kilmer (2000) summarize the findings of natural-recovery literature regarding characteristics of those who were able to resume controlled drinking versus those who abstained:

1. Less severely alcohol-dependent persons were more likely to become controlled drinkers.
2. Those with high levels of education, high self-esteem, and supportive relationships were more likely to resume controlled drinking successfully.
3. Those who had abstinence as a goal had less education, had more severe alcohol-dependence symptoms, and were more likely to use AA.

RECOMMENDATIONS

Prevention

Poor coping skills in children and adolescents and insufficient parenting are risk factors for development of alcohol abuse. Children with these risk factors can be targeted for prevention programs. Two current strategies of prevention work address these deficits. One approach attempts to modify the parenting behaviors that seem to negatively impact the child and adolescent (Dishion & Kavanagh, 2000; Sanders, 2000). The second approach focuses on helping children develop capacities that allow them to be rewarded in conventional goals and behaviors so they do not have to resort to deviant behavior including problem drinking. This approach, called *competence enhancement,* created and researched by Botvin, has been shown to be effective in reducing drug taking (Botvin, 2000) and binge drinking (Botvin et al., 2001) in youth.

At the other end of the age spectrum, retirement and living in homes dedicated for older people appear to increase the risk for developing alcohol problems. Physicians and mental health professionals should screen the newly retired and those who have moved to these communities for alcohol disorders.

Treatment

Detailed Drinking History. Although it is essential for counselors to obtain enough information about drinking and substance use to determine proper diagnoses, it is valuable to go deeper into the drinking history. Findings from this chapter consistently show that most problem drinkers have an unstable pattern of drinking, with periods of abstinence, loss of control, and controlled drinking. There is also a group of problem drinkers whose pattern of abuse remains stable over many years. Only a minority of problem drinkers show evidence of a progressive deteriorating pattern of drinking, suggesting that the AA conviction that all alcoholics have this latter pattern appears to be inaccurate for the majority of problem drinkers. Without a detailed drinking history, the counselor may assume that the client has a progressive deteriorating pattern of drinking. If the counselor insists that the client has such a pattern when the client has a different pattern of drinking, it contradicts the client's personal experience and may lead the client to "deny" that this is relevant to him. If the counselor then cites this as an example of alcoholic denial, a vicious cycle can occur, compromising the rapport between the client and counselor.

Those patients who have an unstable course of periods of controlled drinking, abstinence, and abusive drinking may believe that they can learn to drink safely if only they try harder or some external factor is dealt with. The counselor can appreciate this reasoning while suggesting that a more detailed look at the client's drinking pattern might be helpful. Clients can be asked to chart the periods of sober time, safe drinking time, negative consequences, time spent in trying to control the drinking, and the periods of loss of control. This may help the client see the specific negative consequences of his or her specific drinking pattern. For those patients who have a long history of stable abuse of alcohol, the weighing of the costs and benefits of drinking can be considered. Clients can chart the positive and negative effects it has had over the course of their drinking history. Again, this may help clients see the specific negative consequences of their specific drinking pattern and provide motivation to change.

Addressing Childhood Issues in Alcohol Treatment. It has long been standard practice in alcohol treatment to avoid exploration of childhood issues. Although such intervention is probably not useful in early phases of treatment, the finding that childhood characteristics and parenting practices are correlated with later alcoholism suggests that such exploration may be important for many clients. This is most obvious for those alcoholics who suffered childhood sexual abuse. Counselors who do not feel comfortable exploring childhood issues with clients should encourage those who seem to be troubled by childhood experiences to seek psychotherapy to resolve these issues. Ideally, this should occur after the client is stably abstinent.

Recovery Without Formal Help. The section on natural recovery suggests that many problem drinkers resolve their drinking problem without formal help. Thus it is inaccurate for a counselor to assert that a person with a drinking problem can never resolve it on his or her own. It would be better to inform the client what characteristics are associated with such recoveries and compare them with the client's. Characteristics associated with successful self-quitting are spousal or other family and social support and having a relatively stable work situation. Clients who have these characteristics can be told they might be good candidates for self-quitting. They can be directed to self-help materials and advised to keep in touch about their progress, and if there is difficulty, they can opt for treatment. By maintaining a collaborative relationship, it is more likely that problem drinkers who do not succeed in self-quitting will be willing to contact the counselor for additional help. Those who do not have these characteristics can be told that they have less likelihood of being successful and advised to engage in treatment.

Adolescent and Young Adult Intervention. The finding that adolescent and young adult drinking patterns are less stable than those of older groups suggests that interventions for adolescents with drinking problems should be different from adult treatments. Fillmore and Midanik (1984) found that most adolescent excessive drinkers mature out of heavy drinking. This suggests that it might be better to focus on changing the negative drinking patterns rather than assume that these problematic drinkers have a long-term disease process. The goal of abstinence may not be necessary for most of these drinkers.

Controlled Drinking Versus Abstinence. Results summarized in this chapter indicate that about 10 percent of alcoholics safely return to controlled drinking (though Vaillant's results suggest that abstinence is a more stable remission state). Results from these studies suggest which problem drinkers are likely to be successful in controlling their drinking. This issue is taken up again in Chapter 11, where specific recommendations will be made.

SUMMARY: SPLICING THE LONGITUDINAL STUDIES—ALCOHOL AND THE LIFE COURSE

Knowledge about alcohol is absorbed by children long before they drink. Initiation of alcohol use typically begins in the early teens. By late adolescence, drinking is often frequent and heavy. In the early twenties, alcohol consumption and problems peak in frequency. With increasing age, consumption decreases; however, alcohol disorders occurring in middle age are more chronic. By age 50, consumption of alcohol and alcohol disorders decrease to low levels. The elderly more often abstain, drink less, and have a very low rate of alcohol problems. However, for those who have them, their pattern is unstable, as is the case for most problem drinkers.

Although the average consumption of an age group may be high or low, the longitudinal data show that there is great variability in the stability of drinking patterns. Hence, while drinking increases in early adolescence and peaks in the early twenties, a significant portion of those who are heavy drinkers as teens are moderate drinkers by early adulthood.

Those who develop alcohol problems as adults show a varied course. Many, especially in the early twenties, "mature out" of the problem. Others may drink socially for many years before developing problems. Others have drinking problems early in their drinking careers and continue to have problems for many years. Once a person has developed alcohol dependence, the sequence of symptoms is fairly typical. On average it takes about 11 years for the individual to seek help from the onset of the first symptoms. Age of onset peaks in early adulthood to middle age.

Certain childhood factors appear implicated in higher risk for developing an alcohol problem. Problem behavior, poor adjustment and coping, and aggressive behavior in childhood and adolescence are linked to later alcohol problems. Children raised in families with conflict and poor parenting have an increased risk for developing alcohol problems later on. Children with a history of sexual abuse have an increased risk for developing alcohol disorders.

Studies of natural recovery indicate that many individuals with alcohol problems are able to overcome their difficulties without treatment. Results of Newcomb et al.'s (2001) longitudinal study described above and epidemiologic findings discussed in Chapter 5 also support the conclusion that high rates of remission of alcohol disorders occur without professional treatment. A percentage of those with alcohol problems are able to resume controlled drinking without negative consequences. Those tend to be individuals who are younger, more educated, have more support, and have fewer symptoms of dependence.

Many of the findings of this chapter are consistent with the idea that alcohol disorders are heterogeneous.

READINGS

Fillmore, K. M. (1988). *Alcohol use across the life course.* Toronto: Addiction Research Foundation.
   This volume provides a good summary of longitudinal research on alcohol use.

Shedler, J., and Block, J. (1990). Adolescent drug use and psychological health: A longitudinal inquiry. *American Psychologist* 45, 612–632.
   This methodologically sound study shows the effects of childhood traits on adolescent drug use.

Vaillant, G. E. (1995). *The natural history of alcoholism revisited.* Cambridge, MA: Harvard University Press.
   Vaillant reports the findings of the most comprehensive longitudinal study on drinking patterns in men. The organization is difficult to follow, however.

Zucker, R. A., & Gomberg, E. S. (1986). Etiology of alcoholism reconsidered: The case for a biopsychosocial process. *American Psychologist* 41, 783–793.
   This article critiques some of Vaillant's conclusions in *The Natural History of Alcoholism.*

REFERENCES

Akers, R. L., & La Greca, A. J. (1991). Alcohol use among the elderly: Social learning, community context, and life events. In D. J. Pittman and H. R. White (Eds.), *Society, culture, and drinking patterns reexamined* (pp. 242–262). New Brunswick, NJ: Rutgers Center for Alcohol Studies.

Barnes, G. M., Reifman, A. S., Farrell, M. P., & Dintcheff, B. A. (2000). The effects of parenting on the development of adolescent alcohol misuse: A six-wave latent growth model. *Journal of Marriage and the Family* 62, 175–186.

Botvin, G. J. (2000). Preventing drug abuse in schools: Competence enhancement approaches targeting individual-level etiologic factors. *Addictive Behaviors* 25, 887–897.

Botvin, G. J., Griffin, K. W., Diaz, T., & Ifill-Williams, M. (2001). Preventing binge drinking during early adolescence: One- and two-year follow-up of a school-based preventive intervention. *Psychology of Addictive Behaviors* 15, 360–365.

Burke, K. C., Burke, J. D., Regier, D. A., & Rae, D. S. (1990). Age at onset of selected mental disorders in five community populations. *Archives of General Psychiatry* 47, 511–518.

Caspi, A., Moffitt, T. E., Newman, D. L., & Silva, P. A. (1996). Behavioral observations at age 3 years predict adult psychiatric disorders. *Archives of General Psychiatry* 53, 1033–1039.

Chilcoat, H. D., & Breslau, N. (1996). Alcohol disorders in young adulthood: Effects of transitions into adult roles. *Journal of Health and Social Behavior* 37, 339–349.

Cross, G. M., Morgan, C. W., Mooney, A. J., III, Martin, C. A., & Rafter, J. A. (1990). Alcoholism treatment: A ten year follow-up study. *Alcoholism: Clinical and Experimental Research* 14, 169–173.

D'Amico, E. J., Metrik, J., McCarthy, D. M., Rissell, K. C., Appelbaum, M., & Brown, S. A. (2002). Progression into and out of binge drinking among high school students. *Psychology of Addictive Behaviors* 15, 341–349.

Dishion, T. J., & Kavanagh, K. (2000). A multi-level approach to family-centered prevention in schools: Process and outcome. *Addictive Behaviors* 25, 899–911.

Donovan, J. E., Jessor, R., & Jessor, L. (1983). Problem drinking in adolescence and young adulthood: A follow-up study. *Journal of Studies on Alcohol* 44, 109–137.

Edwards, G., Kyle, E., & Nicholls, P. (1983). What happens to alcoholics? *Lancet* 2, 269–271.

Ekerdt, D. J., DeLabry, L. O., Glynn, R. J., & Davis, R. W. (1989). Change in drinking behaviors with retirement: Findings from the Normative Aging Study. *Journal of Studies on Alcohol* 50, 374–353.

Fillmore, K. M. (1987a). Prevalence, incidence and chronicity of drinking patterns and problems among men as a function of age: A longitudinal and cohort analysis. *British Journal of Addiction* 82, 77–83.

Fillmore, K. M. (1987b). Women's drinking across the adult life course as compared to men's. *British Journal of Addiction* 82, 801–811.

Fillmore, K. M. (1988). *Alcohol use across the life course.* Toronto: Addiction Research Foundation.

Fillmore, K. M., Hartka, E., Johnstone, B. M., Leino, E. V., Motoyoshi, M., & Temple, M. T. (1991). A meta-analysis of life course variation in drinking. *Journal of Addiction* 86, 1221–1268.

Fillmore, K. M., & Midanik, L. (1984). Chronicity of drinking problems among men: A longitudinal study. *Journal of Studies on Alcohol* 45, 228–236.

Finney, J. W., & Moos, R. H. (1991). The long-term course of treated alcoholism: I. Mortality, relapse and remission rates and comparisons with community controls. *Journal of Studies on Alcohol* 52, 44–54.

Galaif, E. R., Stein, J., Newcomb, M. D., & Bernstein, D. (2001). Gender differences in the prediction of problem alcohol use in adulthood: Exploring the influence of family factors and childhood maltreatment. *Journal of Studies on Alcohol* 62, 486–493.

Ghodsian, M., & Power, C. (1987). Alcohol consumption between the ages of 16 and 23 in Britain: A longitudinal study. *British Journal of Addiction* 82, 175–180.

Grant, B. F. (1997). Prevalence and correlates of alcohol use and DSM-IV alcohol dependence in the United States: Results of the National Longitudinal Alcohol Epidemiologic Survey. *Journal of Studies on Alcohol* 58, 464–473.

Grant, B. F., Harford, T. C., & Brigson, M. B. (1988). Stability of alcohol consumption among youth: A national longitudinal survey. *Journal of Studies on Alcohol* 49, 253–260.

Harford, T. C., & Muthen, B. O. (2000). Adolescent and young adult antisocial behavior and adult alcohol use disorders: A fourteen-year prospective follow-up in a national survey. *Journal of Studies on Alcohol* 61, 524–528.

Humphreys, K., Moos, R. H., & Finney, J. W. (1995). Two pathways out of drinking problems without professional treatment. *Addictive Behaviors* 20, 427–441.

Jellinek, E. M. (1946). Phases in the drinking history of alcoholics. Analysis of a survey conducted by the official organ of Alcoholics Anonymous. *Journal of Studies on Alcohol* 7, 1–88.

Johnston, L. D., O'Malley, P. M., & Bachman, J. G. (2001). *Monitoring the future national survey results on drug use, 1975–2000. Volume 1: Secondary school students* (NIH Publication No. 01-4924). Bethesda, MD: National Institute on Drug Abuse.

Johnstone, B. M., Leino, I. V., Ager, C., Ferrer, H., & Fillmore, K. M. (1996). Determinants of life-course variation in the frequency of alcohol consumption: Meta-analysis of studies from the Collaborative Alcohol-Related Longitudinal Project. *Journal of Studies on Alcohol* 57, 494–506.

Kandel, D. B. (1978) *Longitudinal research in drug use.* Washington, DC: Hemisphere-Wiley.

Langle, G., Mann, K., Mundle, G., & Schied, H. W. (1993). Ten years after—The post treatment course of alcoholism. *European Psychiatry* 8, 95–100.

Larimer, M. E., & Kilmer, J. R. (2000). Natural history. In G. Zernig (Ed.), *Handbook of alcoholism* (pp. 13–28). Boca Raton, FL: CRC Press.

Leonard, K. E., & Roberts, L. J. (1996). Alcohol in the early years of marriage. *Alcohol, Health, and Research World* 20, 192–196.

Marshall, E. J., Edwards, G., & Taylor, C. (1994). Mortality in men with drinking problems: A 20-year follow-up. *Addiction* 89, 1293–1298.

McCabe, R. J. (1986). Alcohol-dependent individuals sixteen years on. *Alcohol and Alcoholism* 21, 85–91.

McCord, J. (1988). Identifying developmental paradigms leading to alcoholism. *Journal of Studies on Alcohol* 49, 357–362.

McCord, W., & McCord, J. (1960). *Origins of alcoholism.* Stanford, CA: Stanford University Press.

Miller, P. M., Smith, G. T., & Goldman, M. S. (1990). Emergence of alcohol expectancies in childhood: A possible critical period. *Journal of Studies on Alcohol* 51, 343–349.

Miller-Tutzauer, C., Leonard, K. E., & Windle, M. (1991). Marriage and alcohol use: A longitudinal study of "maturing out." *Journal of Studies on Alcohol* 52, 434–440.

Mirand, A. L., & Welte, J. W. (1996). Alcohol consumption among the elderly in a general population, Erie County, NY. *American Journal of Public Health* 86, 978–984.

Newcomb, M. D., Galaif, E. R., & Locke, T. F. (2001). Substance use diagnoses within a community sample of adults: Distinction, comorbidity, and progression over time. *Professional Psychology: Research and Practice* 32, 239–247.

Newcomb, M. D., Maddahian, E., & Bentler, P. M. (1986). Risk factors for drug use among adolescents: concurrent and longitudinal analyses. *American Journal of Public Health* 76, 525–531.

Nordstrom, G., & Berglund, M. (1987). A prospective study of successful long-term adjustment in alcohol dependence: Social drinking versus abstinence. *Journal of Studies on Alcohol* 48, 95–103.

O'Connor, A., & Daly, J. (1985). Alcoholics: A twenty year follow-up study. *British Journal of Psychiatry* 146, 645–647.

Ojesjo, L. (1981). Long-term outcome in alcohol abuse and alcoholism among males in the Lundby general population. *British Journal of Addiction* 76, 391–400.

Ojesjo, L. (1984). Risks for alcoholism by age and class among males. The Lundby community cohort, Sweden. In D. W. Goodwin, K. T. Van Dusen, & S. A. Mednick (Eds.), *Longitudinal research in alcoholism* (pp. 9–25). Boston: Kluwer.

O'Neill, S. E., Parra, G. R., & Sher, K. J. (2001). Clinical relevance of heavy drinking during the college years: Cross-sectional and prospective perspectives. *Psychology of Addictive Behaviors* 15, 350–359.

Pendry, M. L., Maltzman, I. M., & West, L. J. (1982). Controlled drinking by alcoholics? New findings and a reevaluation of a major affirmative study. *Science* 217, 169–175.

Pulkkinen, L., & Pitkanen, T. (1994). A prospective study of the precursors to problem drinking in young adulthood. *Journal of Studies on Alcohol* 55, 578–587.

Reifman, A., Barnes, B. M., Dintcheff, B. A., Farrell, M. P., & Uhteg, L. (1998). Parental and peer influences on the onset of heavier drinking among adolescents. *Journal of Studies on Alcohol* 59, 311–317.

Robins, L., Bates, W. M., & O'Neil, P. (1962). Adult drinking patterns of former problem children. In D. J. Pittman and C. R. Snider (Eds.), *Society, culture, and drinking patterns* (pp. 395–412). New York: Wiley.

Robins, L. N., Helzer, J. E., Przybeck, T. R., & Regier, D. A. (1988). Alcohol disorders in the community: A report from the epidemiological catchment area. In R. M. Rose and J. E. Barrett (Eds.), *Alcoholism: Origins and outcome* (pp. 15–29). New York: Raven.

Rumpf, H.-J., Bischof, G., Hake, U., Meter, C., & John, U. (2000). Studies on natural recovery from alcohol dependence: Sample selection bias by media solicitation? *Addiction* 95, 765–775.

Sadava, S. O. (1987). Interactional theory. In H. T. Blane and K. E. Leonard (Eds.), *Psychological theories of drinking and alcoholism* (pp. 90–130). New York: Guilford.

Sanders, M. R. (2000). Community-based parenting and family support interventions and the prevention of drug abuse. *Addictive Behaviors* 25, 929–942.

Schuckit, M. A., Anthenelli, R. M., Bucholz, K. K., Hesselbrock, V., & Tipp, J. (1995). The time course of development of alcohol-related problems in men and women. *Journal of Studies on Alcohol* 56, 218–225.

Schulenberg, J., O'Malley, P. M., Bachman, J. G., Wadsworth, K. N., & Johnston, L. D. (1996). Getting drunk and growing up: Trajectories of frequent binge drinking during transition to young adulthood. *Journal of Studies on Alcohol* 57, 289–304.

Shedler, J., & Block, J. (1990). Adolescent drug use and psychological health: A longitudinal inquiry. *American Psychologist* 45, 612–632.

Skog, O. J., & Duckert, F. (1993). The development of alcoholics' and heavy drinkers' consumption: A longitudinal study. *Journal of Studies on Alcohol* 54, 178–188.

Smith, E. M., Cloninger, C. R., & Bradford, S. (1983). Predictors of mortality in alcoholic women: A prospective follow-up study. *Alcoholism: Clinical and Experimental Research* 7, 237–243.

Sobell, L. C., Ellingstad, T. P., & Sobell, M. B. (2000). Natural recovery from alcohol and drug problems: Methodological review of the research with suggestions for future directions. *Addiction* 95, 749–764.

Sobell, L. C., Sobell, M. B., Toneatto, T., & Leo, G. I. (1993). What triggers the resolution of alcohol problems without treatment? *Alcoholism: Clinical and Experimental Research* 17, 217–224.

Taylor, C., Brown, D., Duckitt, A., Edwards, G., Oppenheimer, E., & Sheehan, M. (1985). Patterns of outcome: Drinking histories over ten years among a group of alcoholics. *British Journal of Addiction* 80, 45–50.

Temple, M. T., & Fillmore, K. M. (1985–1986). The variability of drinking patterns and problems among young men, age 16–31: A longitudinal study. *International Journal of the Addictions* 20, 1595–1620.

Temple, M. T., & Leino, E. V. (1989). Long-term outcomes of drinking: A 20-year longitudinal study of men. *British Journal of Addiction* 84, 889–899.

Tuchfield, B. S. (1981). Spontaneous remission in alcoholics: Empirical observations and theoretical implications. *Journal of Studies on Alcohol* 42, 626–640.

Tucker, J. A., Vuchinich, R. E., & Gladsjo, J. A. (1994). Environmental events surrounding natural recovery from alcohol-related problems. *Journal of Studies on Alcohol* 55, 401–411.

U.S. Department of Health and Human Services (2000). *Tenth Special Report to the U.S. Congress on alcohol and health.*

Vaillant, G. E. (1983) *The natural history of alcoholism.* Cambridge, MA: Harvard University Press.

Vaillant, G. E. (1995). *The natural history of alcoholism revisited.* Cambridge, MA: Harvard University Press.

Vaillant, G. E., & Hiller-Sturmhefel, S. (1996). The natural history of alcoholism. *Alcohol, Health, and Research World* 20, 152–161.

Vicary, J. R., & Lerner, J. N. (1983). Longitudinal perspectives on drug use: Analyses the New York Longitudinal Study. *Journal of Drug Education* 13, 275–285.

Walton, M. A., Mudd, S. A., Blowk, F. C., Chermack, S. T., & Gomberg, E. S. (2000), Stability in the drinking habits of older problem-drinkers recruited from nontreatment settings. *Journal of Substance Abuse Treatment* 18, 169–177.

Westermeyer, J., & Peake, E. (1983). A ten-year follow-up of alcoholic Native Americans in Minnesota. *American Journal of Psychiatry* 140, 189–194.

White, H. R. (1987). Longitudinal stability and dimensional structure of problem-drinking in adolescence. *Journal of Studies on Alcohol* 48, 541–550.

Zucker, R. A. (1994). Pathways to alcohol problems and alcoholism: A developmental account of the evidence for multiple alcoholisms and for contextual contributions to risk. In R. A. Zucker, G. Boyd, & J. Howard (Eds.), *The development of alcohol problems: Exploring the biopsychosocial matrix of risk* (National Institute on Alcohol and Alcoholism Research Monograph Research Monograph 26, pp. 255–289). Rockville, MD: U.S. Department of Health and Human Services.

Zucker, R. A., & Gomberg, E. S. (1986). Etiology of alcoholism reconsidered: The case for a biopsychosocial process. *American Psychologist* 41, 783–793.

CHAPTER SEVEN

ENVIRONMENTAL FACTORS AFFECTING ALCOHOL USE
Cultural and Social Research Findings

Alcohol is widely used by diverse populations throughout the world. This chapter explores the use patterns of alcohol among different cultures, countries, and ethnic groups in the United States. The effectiveness of government regulation of alcohol use will also be reviewed. The influence of social factors on alcohol use was evident in findings discussed in the chapters on epidemiology and longitudinal studies. It was noted that:

1. There are large fluctuations in per-capita consumption in the United States over time (Figure 5.1).
2. Countries vary in their per-capita consumption of alcohol (Table 5.1) and rate of alcohol problems (Figure 5.3, Table 5.8).
3. There are regional differences in drinking patterns in the United States (Table 5.2 and Table 5.7).
4. Meta-analysis of longitudinal studies indicates that national origin is the most significant factor in determining drinking practices. Women have greater variability in their drinking patterns among different countries than men, suggesting that women are subjected to and/or respond to more social pressure regarding drinking practices (Chapter 6).
5. African American men have different patterns of consumption as a function of age than do other U.S. ethnic groups (Figure 5.4).
6. Lower-class Americans appear to be more prone to alcohol use disorders than the middle-class Americans (Chapter 6).

Thus, it is clear that social factors have a great impact on drinking practices.
In this chapter, the following questions will be addressed:

1. What are the variations in drinking practices among cultures?
2. How do cultures regulate alcohol use?
3. Is alcoholism universal where alcohol is consumed?
4. What are the variations in drinking practices among U.S. ethnic groups?

5. Does alcohol facilitate aggression and sexual behavior in all cultures?
6. Do regulations on alcohol affect alcohol consumption and alcohol problems?

METHODOLOGY

Traditional anthropologic studies rely on field observations of relatively homogeneous communities conducted by one researcher or a small team of researchers. One problem with such research is that it is not practical or sometimes possible to verify their reports, because many of these groups are difficult to access and few outsiders speak their languages; further, their cultures may be subject to rapid change by impingement of globalization.

In sociologic studies, statistics collected by various government agencies and surveys are used to research the effects of social forces on alcohol consumption. A problem with this area of research is that so many factors operate on the social level, it is hard to be sure that the specific factors being studied are responsible for the outcome. One approach to deal with this problem is to use statistical analysis to partial out extraneous factors. For example, if we are seeking to measure the effect of a state law that lowered the minimum legal drinking age (MLDA) but another law was passed at the same time also affected alcohol consumption, researchers can estimate the impact of the other law and remove that portion statistically to determine the effect of the MLDA law. Researchers can estimate the effects of the other law by comparing its effects in other states where both laws were not enacted simultaneously. There is always the chance that some fortuitous event such as an economic downturn may confound the results of this type of study, however. From this example, it can be seen that social researchers often use many inferential steps to reach their conclusions.

ANTHROPOLOGIC STUDIES
OF CULTURE AND ALCOHOL

Anthropologists historically have studied small groups isolated from modern society to study the diversity of cultural expression of human societies. Heath (1962), for example, studied the Camba, a relatively isolated community of mixed Indian Spanish in Bolivia. Heath observed a twice-a-month pattern of heavy drinking that occurred in social groups. The alcohol the Cambans drank was 89 percent pure alcohol, twice the concentration of hard liquor typically drunk in the United States. During this frequent intoxication, Cambans did not manifest the aggressive or sexual behavior that has been typically associated with it in U.S. culture. Nor did he see any evidence of alcoholism despite their frequent intoxication. In follow-up visits over the course of 10 years, he continued to observe none of the typical harmful effects of heavy drinking that are typical of heavy drinking in the United States. Mac Andrew and Edgerton (1969) cite additional cultures in which intoxication does not lead to aggressive or sexual behavior.

Horton (1991) observed harm-reduction practices long before they were introduced in Western civilization. See Box 7.1 for a discussion of harm reduction and Horton's observations.

Lindman et al. (2000) explored cross-cultural differences among nine countries for beliefs of alcohol-induced positive affect. They found differences in these expectancies

BOX 7.1

HARM REDUCTION

Harm reduction as a prevention and treatment goal has become a popular idea recently. The basic philosophy is that when individuals cannot or will not abstain or curtail their heavy alcohol use, it makes sense to have the goal of reducing the potential harm caused by the dangerous use. The following is an anthropological account of harm reduction used in African cultures:

[I]n some . . . tribes in South Africa, . . . women, who are forbidden to drink at all or permitted to drink very little, are given the role of

policing the drinking bout; and if a man gets aggressive, the women just sit on him, tie him up, put him in a hammock, and leave him there until he sobers up. In other instances the women go around the day preceding the [drinking] party and make sure that all the spears and bow and arrows are gathered up and hidden in a place known only to them, so that nobody can get his hands on a dangerous weapon. Then, when the drinking begins, if anybody gets obstreperous he can fight it out with his fists [limiting the harm that can be inflicted].

Source: Reprinted with permission from *Society, Culture, and Drinking Patterns Reexamined,* by D. J. Pittman and H. R. White. Copyright 1991, Alcohol Research Documentation, Inc., Rutgers Center of Alcohol Studies, Piscataway, NJ 08854.

among countries, but high expectancy of positive affect was not correlated with increased drinking.

Cross-Cultural Comparisons of Child Rearing and Its Effect on Alcohol Consumption Patterns

Different child-rearing practices in different cultures can be compared to see if such factors are associated with drinking patterns or problems. Field (1962), for example, found that sober tribes control aggression severely in their children, whereas tribes that indulge in frequent intoxication are relatively indulgent with their children and permit disobedience and self-assertion. It is not easy to interpret this finding: it may be that indulgence in childhood affects the propensity for heavy drinking and/or it may be that intoxication affects parenting. There is a potential mutual interaction of both factors. Barry (1976) also conducted a cross-cultural analysis of alcohol and child-rearing practices. He concluded that child-rearing practices that fostered dependency conflict were associated with cultures with high frequencies of intoxication. He found that in these cultures, parents had less body contact with children and provided less nurturing to their infants, among other factors; alternatively, his results could be seen to suggest that child neglect is associated with high frequency of adult intoxication.

NATIONAL DRINKING CUSTOMS

There is great variation in customs and regulations regarding alcohol among countries. Per-capita consumption of several countries is shown in Table 5.1. France has the highest rate of consumption and Turkey the lowest of the countries listed.

Much has been made of the differences in drinking practices between Southern European Mediterranean countries and Northern European countries. The Southern European countries include France, Italy, Spain, Portugal, Greece, and the former Yugoslavia. In these countries, wine is viewed as an integral part of daily living, mostly drunk with meals during the day, and is viewed in a positive light. While there are high rates of consumption, there are low rates of intoxication and most kinds of alcohol problems, presumably because drinking is so functionally integrated with the cultures (Heath, 1998; Single & Leino, 1998). These countries tend to have integrated, permissive drinking customs and laws. Northern European drinking practices focus on drinking itself rather than an accompaniment to other activities. These cultures commonly have less concern for moderation: drunkenness is often actively sought and used as an excuse for antisocial or asocial behavior (Heath, 1998, p. 118). These countries tend to have high rates of intoxication with low overall rates of consumption. The Northern European countries employ a more restrictive and controlled approach to alcohol availability. This includes a state monopoly on liquor distribution and sales, restrictions to access alcohol, high alcohol taxes, and severe penalties for alcohol regulation infractions.

Italy

Italy is a Southern European country where wine is viewed as an integral aspect of family life. In a classic if not methodologically sophisticated study, Lolli et al. (1958) conducted a survey of Italians regarding their drinking habits and attitudes. They found that 90 percent of the men and 64 percent of the women were drinkers. Men's average consumption was 4.9 standard drinks per day. Italians surveyed stated the upper limit of safe drinking was, on average, 11.18 drinks per day. Only 1 of the 1,453 surveyed felt that drinking wine could lead to alcoholism.

Italians begin drinking alcohol as children in the context of the family. Sixty-one percent of Italian men and 58 percent of the women tasted an alcoholic beverage before age 11. Eighty-three percent of Italians said their first exposure to alcohol was part of their regular family life. More than half of the men and one-third of the women reported beginning the regular use of wine before age 15.

Since the Italians have traditionally had low rates of alcoholism (Lolli, 1958; Simboli, 1985), many have viewed its drinking customs and attitudes as something to emulate (Heath & Rosovsky, 1998). While Italy has few alcohol-related problems related to intoxication, it does have a high rate of cirrhosis (Simboli, 1985), which is an indicator of medical problems related to alcohol use.

France

Sadoun et al. (1965) conducted a similar survey with the French. Like Italy, France has a high rate of per-capita alcohol consumption, but unlike Italy, France has a high rate of alcoholism. Sadoun et al.'s large survey indicated that 70 percent of the French are daily drinkers. Consumers averaged 4.9 standard drinks per day, the same as the Italians. French men often drink distilled spirits and drink alcohol outside of meals. The French expressed a tolerant view of intoxication as humorous, fashionable, and an expression of virility. The French tended to learn how to drink outside the family.

The authors of the study suggest that French attitudes and practices promote intoxication and alcoholism, while the Italian attitudes and practices protect against harmful drinking patterns. They pointed out that:

1. Italians drink mostly at mealtimes, while the French do not.
2. Italians view intoxication as disgraceful, while the French are tolerant of it.
3. Italians learn to drink as children in the context of family life. The French learn to drink outside the family.

At the time of the survey, now almost a half-century ago, France seemed to be in a state of denial about alcohol problems. Those surveyed in France indicated that 14.4 standard drinks was a safe amount of wine to drink per day for heavy laborers. A large percentage of those surveyed (32 percent of men and 25 percent of women) denied there was excessive drinking in France. Almost half believed that alcohol was not seriously implicated in industrial accidents. Of 120 alcoholics interviewed, only 7 had undergone treatment for alcoholism.

French alcoholism has a different symptom picture than typical U.S. alcoholism. A large percentage of French alcoholics are often never really drunk or sober, drinking steadily during the waking hours. Jellinek (1960) labeled this *delta alcoholism*. The distinguishing symptom of this form of alcoholism is that cessation of drinking induces the alcohol withdrawal syndrome, because the individual is physically dependent on alcohol.

Spain

In Spain, another Southern European country, a general food license permits the sale of alcohol (Rooney, 1991). Thus, wine and other alcoholic beverages are readily available.

Caetano (1988) reported that 60 percent of Spanish men surveyed in Madrid drank nearly every day. Martinez et al. (1988) surveyed a sample of adults in Madrid and found that 43 percent of the population had a pattern of frequent low-maximum consumption of alcohol. They report that Madrid has a low overall rate of alcohol-related problems but note that Spanish culture tends to overlook negative consequences of drinking and these may be missed in statistical reports.

Despite the large quantities of alcohol the Spanish consume, drunkenness is infrequent. However, many men become physically dependent on alcohol, like many alcoholics in France. These men, because of high consumption of alcohol, are at risk for the many medical complications of heavy drinking discussed in Chapter 3.

Latin America

Latin America appears to have adopted many of the drinking practices of its cultural forbear, Spain. Government regulations on alcohol are minimal and availability is high (Smart & Mora, 1986). Statistics are not rigorously tabulated on alcohol problems in Latin American countries, but those that are available indicate a greater than average number of alcohol problems. For example, Mexico and Chile have very high rates of cirrhosis, 48.6 per 100,000 in Mexico and 46.2 per 100,000 in Chile (Edwards, 1994). By comparison, the

U.S. rate is 8.1 (U.S. Department of Health and Human Services, 1997, p. 12). Medina-Mora (1988) surveyed a group of Mexican men and found that the typical drinking pattern consisted of low frequency of drinking episodes but with large quantities consumed per drinking occasion, leading to a high frequency of drunkenness. He also found high rates of abstention but high rates of alcohol problems.

Scandinavia

A survey of all the Scandinavian countries found three common practices:

1. Drinking and working are kept strictly separate.
2. Drinking is not integrated with meals.
3. Drinking tends to be done in situations isolated from daily life, where intoxication is accepted (Makela, 1986).

In Iceland, a Northern European country, a common pattern of drinking among seamen has been observed. On days of infrequent breaks from fishing expeditions, the seamen drink excessively to achieve drunkenness and, as a consequence, are often involved in serious accidents and arrested for misbehavior. Yet sobriety soon sets in once they set sail and are required to work (Plange, 1998).

India

India has a history of prohibition, which has gradually been relaxed (Bennett et al., 1998). There are no full-scale representative surveys, but a preliminary survey showed that males were 44.5 percent abstainers, 16.4 percent social drinkers, and 39.1 percent heavy drinkers or alcoholics. If this is accurate, this is a very different distribution of drinking practices than in most countries. The high level of abstainers is due to religious practices and the recent history of prohibition.

Ireland

Bales (1962) studied a relatively homogeneous group of Irish farming communities of the nineteenth century through examination of literary sources and public records and gained a picture of the effect of culture on alcohol patterns. In this classic paper, Bales found that Irish cultural practices in the use of alcohol, child rearing, and the role status of young Irish men all contributed to the high rate of excessive alcohol consumption.

Social Customs.   In nineteenth-century Ireland, alcohol was emphasized over food in providing hospitality for guests. He notes that the historical problem of famine and an unpredictable food supply led to conflicts and shame about eating. There were no such conflicts about drinking, which may explain some of the resulting social customs that emphasize alcohol over food. Unlike many communities that apply sanctions against intoxication, drunkenness was accepted and tolerated in these communities. The obligatory practice of "treating" promoted intoxication. Treating is a custom in which a man in a pub, joined by friends, must "stand" or "treat" his friends, that is, pay for a round of drinks for all. Each friend in turn is expected to "stand" the rest, until all have done so. It is not difficult to see how this promotes excessive alcohol consumption.

Child-Rearing Practices.　　Although children were made to feel guilty about eating, they were often given alcohol as a reward. There were no ritual practices socializing moderate use of alcohol for children. These factors led children to view alcohol and alcohol intoxication as a less conflicted pleasure than food.

Role Status of Young Men.　　In nineteenth-century rural Ireland, farming was the primary livelihood. Small farms were run by the father. A son did not achieve adult status until the father signed over the farm to him; he was called a "boy" until this happened. He had to obey his father in many trivial details, nor could he marry. Since Ireland at this time had a strong religious conviction that sexual relationships must be deferred until marriage, this set the stage for unresolved rebellious and sexual tension in these "boys." Bales suggests that these tensions were relieved by heavy drinking.

Bales argued that these cultural practices promoted heavy drinking and intoxication and were responsible for the higher rates of alcoholism in nineteenth-century Ireland. In a more recent investigation, Scheper-Hughes (1979) continued to find high rates of alcoholism among Irish men. Some Irish cultural practices had remained the same, such as child-rearing practices. Some were modified: Irish men often remain unmarried for many years, but this had more to do with the emigration of young women to America than with the lengthy status of "boy." These cultural aspects may have contributed to the high rate of alcoholism more recently in Ireland.

ETHNIC CULTURAL INFLUENCES ON DRINKING IN THE UNITED STATES

The United States is composed of diverse immigrant groups from countries all over the world. These groups bring with them many different cultural practices, including their drinking practices. It was noted in longitudinal studies discussed in Chapter 6 (McCord & McCord, 1960; Valiant, 1995) that men of Italian descent had low rates of alcoholism, whereas men of Irish descent had high rates, reflecting the drinking practices of their country of origin. In this section, we will see that the culture of origin still exerts some influence on drinking practices for most immigrant groups. The factor mitigating this effect is *acculturation*, the process of immigrant groups becoming more American and giving up cultural aspects of their countries of origin. Generally, with each succeeding generation, immigrant groups' drinking patterns become more like typical American drinking practices.

Italian Americans

Surveys show that some Italian drinking customs have been retained by Italian Americans but others have changed. Lolli et al. (1958) conducted a survey of Italian Americans. He found that 32 to 53 percent of Italian Americans abstained from wine, a higher percentage than Italians. Compared with Italians, a much smaller percentage of Italian Americans drank exclusively with meals, 7 percent versus 16 percent. Like Italians, Italian Americans had an early introduction to alcohol in childhood. Italians drank more but reported less intoxication than Italian Americans.

Simboli (1985) surveyed and interviewed a sample of Italian Americans living in San Francisco. His overall finding was that Italian Americans' drinking practices became more discrepant from Italian drinking practices with each successive generation. First-generation Italian Americans reported moderate drinking, whereas second and third generations reported more heavy drinking. Wine was the preferred beverage in the first generation, whereas beer and hard liquor were preferred in the second and third generations. The first and second generation of Italian Americans had a relaxed attitude about alcohol, but the third generation did not. Hence the beliefs and practices of Italian Americans about alcohol have undergone considerable modification from those held originally. Each successive generation lost some of the Italian beliefs and practices and moved in the direction of American ones. This is a typical example of acculturation. Still, rates of problem drinking remained low among all generations.

Irish Americans

Clearly, social customs are different for Irish Americans than for the nineteenth-century Irish, yet three longitudinal studies noted in the previous chapter have identified Irish ethnicity as a risk factor for alcoholism. To what extent this risk is cultural and/or hereditary is unclear.

Stivers (1978) traced historical Irish American practices that contributed to their high rates of alcoholism from the nineteenth century until the 1960s. He identifies customs brought over from Ireland as well as factors in the United States that may have contributed to the high rate of alcoholism. The Irish pattern of few and late marriages and the emphasis on chastity was sustained in this country. Bales (1962) had noted that this combination in Ireland may have led to pressures that may have been released by heavy drinking. Stivers also identifies U.S. cultural elements that facilitated excessive drinking. He notes that employment practices of giving alcohol as wages was common in the early twentieth century. There was a good deal of discrimination against immigrants, which may have contributed to escape drinking. He suggests that drinking was symbolic of Irish American identity.

African Americans

Jones-Webb (1998), summarizing several surveys, reports that African Americans drink less and greater percentages abstain from alcohol than whites. But African Americans report similar levels of heavy drinking and have more drinking consequences and alcohol-related mortality than whites. Caetano et al. (1998) notes that African American women have higher abstention rates (55 percent) than white women (39 percent). African Americans acquire drinking later in life, and thus tend to drink less as youth, but they tend to drink more in middle age, when whites begin to decrease consumption (see Figure 5.4).

Hispanic Americans

There is great variation in drinking patterns among different Hispanic groups. Randolph et al. (1998), drawing on survey research, notes that Mexican Americans have high abstention rates, but also the highest rates of binge drinking, patterns similar to Mexican men discussed earlier. Among Hispanic groups, 54 percent of Mexican American men were heavy drinkers, whereas 28 percent of Puerto Rican and only 8 percent of Cuban males were heavy drinkers. (See Chapter 5 for a summary of another survey of Puerto Rican and Mexican American drinking patterns.)

Native Americans

By reputation, Native Americans are said to have a high rate of alcohol use disorders. Some indirect measures seem to support this conception. Native Americans have a higher rate of alcohol-related deaths than the average American. Native Americans have a cirrhosis death rate 4.5 times and an alcohol dependence death rate 3.8 times greater than that of the average American (Manson et al., 1992). In a preliminary study, three reservation communities, one each from the Southwest, the Pacific Northwest, and the Midwest, were surveyed for alcohol use disorders (Manson et al., 1992, pp. 117–118). Manson et al. found that Native Americans had a 50 percent lifetime prevalence rate of alcohol use disorders. There is a wide variation in drinking practices among reservation communities, so sampling of several additional reservations is needed to determine whether these preliminary results reflect the overall rate of Native American drinking problems.

Asian Americans

Makimoto (1998) summarizes the existing surveys of Asian American drinking practices. Asian American adolescents and college students report the lowest percentage of alcohol use of any ethnic group. Chapters 3 and 4 discuss the Asian flush reaction, which acts as a deterrent to drinking, and explains to some degree Asians' lower consumption of alcohol. However, she notes that there are important differences among Asian American subgroups. For example, one survey indicated great differences among different Asian groups in those who reported 10 drinks or more in their lifetime: for Japanese Americans it was 69 percent; for Korean Americans it was 49 percent; for Filipino Americans it was 38 percent; for Vietnamese Americans it was 36 percent; and for Chinese Americans it was 25 percent.

Japanese, Chinese, and Korean Americans were surveyed in Los Angeles by Kitano et al. (1985) and compared with other Californians. Japanese American men had a greater percentage of abstainers (36.4 percent versus 11.6 percent) and more heavy drinkers (26.3 percent versus 15.8 percent) than the comparison community group. Japanese American women were more likely to be abstainers (63.3 percent versus 13.6 percent). Japanese-born men were more likely to be heavier drinkers than Japanese Americans born in the United States (51.8 percent versus 17.3 percent). Chinese Americans had high rates of abstention (males, 47.7 percent; females, 73.8 percent) and low rates of heavy drinking (males, 11.5 percent; females, 0 percent). Korean Americans were intermediate between the Japanese and Chinese Americans: Korean American males were 55.5 percent abstainers and females were 80.8 percent abstainers. Almost 24 percent of Korean American males reported heavy drinking, whereas less than 1 percent of Korean American women did.

Although all immigrant groups have special stresses that may affect rates of alcohol disorders, Vietnamese and Cambodian immigrants appear to be an especially high-risk group for alcohol problems because of cultural differences, wartime suffering, and social disadvantages (Makimoto, 1998).

GOVERNMENT REGULATIONS AND THEIR EFFECT ON DRINKING PRACTICES

So far in this chapter we have focused on the effects of cultural sanctions on drinking practices. Nations such as the United States, consisting of large and complex social organizations, require more formal sanctions to control social interaction than smaller and more homogeneous cultures. Laws, regulations, and their formal administration have become important government functions. With regard to alcohol, governments can regulate its manufacture, sale, and distribution, and can levy taxes on its sale. Governments can limit its use to certain groups and provide sanctions for drinking in an unsafe manner, such as driving while intoxicated.

Prohibition

The most dramatic approach to regulating alcohol is to forbid its use. Several countries have prohibited the use of alcohol for periods of time. In the United States, the Eighteenth Amendment to the Constitution, the Volstead Act, took effect in January 1920 and prohibited the manufacture and sale of alcoholic beverages except for medical purposes (Lender & Martin, 1987). Prohibition succeeded in reducing consumption and alcohol-related problems, but drinking was not eliminated. As the Prohibition era wore on, enforcement became increasingly difficult. Illegal production and distribution of alcohol became relatively common, especially in big cities. Popular sentiment turned against Prohibition and it was repealed in 1933 with the Twenty-First Amendment to the Constitution. Prohibition has also been tried in the Polynesian Islands, Iceland, Finland, Norway, Sweden, Russia, Canada (Lemert, 1991), India (Bennett et al., 1998), and Saudi Arabia and Iran (Heath, 1998). For homogeneous religious countries whose beliefs are prohibitionistic, such as Saudi Arabia and Iran, prohibition has been quite successful.

Regulations Regarding Production and Sale of Alcohol

The manufacture and distribution of alcoholic beverages are often regulated by governments. In the United States, states have primary authority over the sale and use of alcohol (Gordis, 1996). States impose taxes on alcohol. They have laws that provide sanctions for driving while intoxicated, sales to minors, and intoxicated persons. The density of alcohol outlets and their hours of operation can be regulated by state and local governments. Research indicates that all of these measures have effects on drinking practices.

The Effect of Cost on Alcohol Consumption.   In the United States, the relative cost of alcoholic beverages has declined since the post–World War II period. A significant factor has been that inflation-adjusted tax rates on alcohol have declined in this period, as illustrated in Figure 7.1.

Although there are exceptions, current research generally supports the idea that increases in the price of alcohol decrease demand, but by modest amounts. A review of studies on the relation between price and demand indicates that every 1 percent increase in price led to a 0.3 percent decrease in demand for beer, a 1 percent decrease in demand for wine, and a 1.5 percent decrease in demand for spirits (U.S. Department of Health and Human Services, 2000). Edwards (1994) reviewed studies on price and consumption and found that heavy drinkers were at least as responsive to price changes as other drinkers, which challenges the notion that heavy drinkers' consumption is not affected by price.

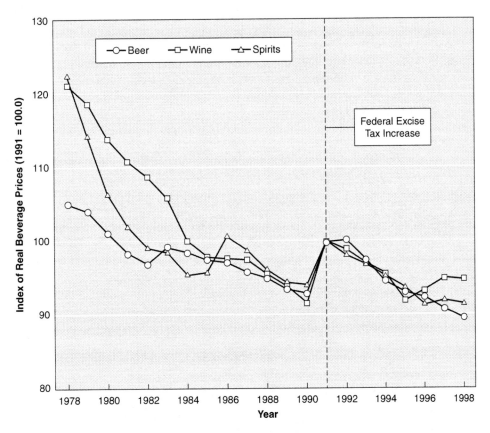

FIGURE 7.1   Inflation-Adjusted Alcoholic Beverage Prices, 1978–1998. Calculated from Consumer Price Index data, not seasonally adjusted for all items: beer, ale, and other malt beverages at home; distilled wine at home; and spirits at home.

Source: Bureau of Labor Statistics, http://stats.bls.gov/sahome.html, December 1999.

Increased Taxes on Alcohol and Their Effect on Alcohol-Related Problems.   Several studies have found that higher alcohol taxes are linked to lower traffic fatality rates. For example, Ruhm (1996, cited in U.S. Department of Health and Human Services, 2000) calculated that every 1 percent increase in the price of beer was associated with a traffic fatality rate decline by nearly the same proportion (0.9%). He also calculated that increasing the federal excise tax on beer in 1988 to the inflation-adjusted equivalent of its value in 1975 would have saved between 3,300 and 3,700 lives annually. Results of a large survey of adults suggest that a modest 10 percent increase in the price of alcoholic beverages would decrease the number of binge drinking episodes per month by approximately 8 percent (U.S. Department of Health and Human Services, 2000). Increased price also reduces other negative alcohol-related events (Yalisove, 1998). Generally, results from diverse research studies suggest that increasing the price of alcohol would have beneficial effects in reducing alcohol-related problems.

Alcohol Outlet Density.   The more alcohol sales outlets there are in an area, the more fatal traffic crashes there are (U.S. Department of Health and Human Services, 2000). Other alcohol-related problems also show a direct relationship between availability of alcohol and an increase in several alcohol-related problems, including homicide and assaultive violence (Scribner et al., 1999; Yalisove, 1998). The implication is that if local or state governments limited the number of outlets that sell alcoholic beverages, there would be reductions in alcohol-related problems.

Sanctions to Reduce Alcohol-Related Problems

Driving while Intoxicated (DWI).   Accidents caused by drinking drivers is a leading cause of death in the United States. Alcohol affects driving performance with blood alcohol concentration (BAC) as low as 0.02% (Hingson, 1996). Table 7.1 shows the probability of being involved in a fatal car crash at several BAC levels.

In 1997 there were 16,000 deaths and 1 million injuries in alcohol-related crashes. Traffic crashes are the leading cause of death for 1- to 34-year-olds. The cost of alcohol-related crashes is estimated to be $45 billion per year (U.S. Department of Health and Human Services, 2000). In 1995, at least 5,585 pedestrians died in alcohol-related crashes (Hingson, 1996). Of these pedestrians, 37 percent had been drinking. The good news is that alcohol-related traffic deaths have dropped by one-third since the early 1980s. Surveys of drivers stopped on Friday and Saturday nights show that positive BACs declined from 36 percent in 1973 to 17 percent in 1996. In 1995, 1.4 million people were arrested for DWI, nearly 10 percent of all arrests (Hingson, 1996). Despite this major effort on the part of law enforcement, it is estimated that only 1 arrest is made for every 300 to 1,000 drunk driving trips. Thus, while there have been improvements, there remains a substantial risk for alcohol-related driving accidents.

Minimum Legal Drinking Age (MLDA).   The greatest reduction in alcohol-related fatal crashes between 1982 and 1995 has been in the 15- to 20-year-old age group, from 5,380 to 2,209 annual deaths (Hingson, 1996). Much of this decline has been attributed to reinstat-

TABLE 7.1   Increased Driving Risk Associated with Several Blood Alcohol Concentrations Compared to Sober Drivers

IF YOU DRIVE WITH A BAC IN THIS RANGE:	YOUR CHANCES OF BEING KILLED IN A SINGLE-VEHICLE CRASH INCREASE BY:
0.02–0.04%	1.4 times
0.05–0.09%	11 times
0.10–0.14%	48 times
0.15% and above	380 times

Source: U.S. Department of Health and Human Services, 2000, p. 384.

ing a minimum drinking age of 21 in several states (Toomey, 1996). Between 1970 and 1975, twenty-nine states lowered the drinking age to 18, 19, or 20, during an era when 18-year-old men were drafted into the military service. It was felt that those who risked their lives for their country should have the right to vote and to drink. Although the voting privilege was retained for the younger ages, ensured by the passage of the Twenty-Sixth Amendment to the Constitution (Chaloupka et al., 1998), between 1976 and 1983, sixteen states restored the drinking age to 21. By comparing rates of alcohol-related accidents between states that lowered or raised the drinking age with those that did not, the effect of changing the drinking age on automobile accidents could be estimated. Several studies indicate that reducing the minimum drinking age led to increases in traffic accidents, while restoring the MLDA to 21 led to a 10 to 15 percent reduction in alcohol-related traffic deaths (U.S. Department of Health and Human Services, 2000).

Many studies show increased use of alcohol by youth in states that lowered the drinking age and decreased alcohol use in states that raised the drinking age. Among high school seniors in states with raised MLDA, there was reduced frequency of drinking (72 percent drank in the past month before raising the MLDA; reduced to 51 percent after the MLDA was raised) and binge drinking (U.S. Department of Health and Human Services, 2000). The decline in alcohol consumption among youth continued even after they turned 21. Alcohol-related problems also decreased in states that raised the MLDA (Toomey et al., 1996). Cook and Moore (2000) analyzed data from the National Longitudinal Survey of youth and found that youths in states with MLDA of 21 drank and binged less over the 5-year period studied than those with a lower MLDA.

Still, enforcement of MLDA is lax. It is estimated that only 5 of 100,000 incidents of minors drinking result in any sanction. Research has shown that strict enforcement and publicity can reduce the frequency of minors' drinking (Toomey et al., 1996).

Zero-Tolerance Laws.   Zero-tolerance laws provide sanctions for drivers under 21 who have positive Breathalyzer readings as low as 0.01% (Toomey et al., 1996). Research indicates that these laws have led to a 20 percent decline in single-vehicle nighttime fatal crashes in drivers under 21. Still, surveys show that 45 to 50 percent of teens are unaware of these laws.

Reducing Legal Driving Limits of BAC to 0.08 Percent.   States that have lowered the legal BAC level from 0.10% to 0.08% have had a significant decline in alcohol-related fatal crashes (Toomey et al., 1996). A federal law provides incentives for all states to adopt the 0.08% standard (Voas & Fisher, 2001).

Targeting Repeat DWI Offenders.   Special sanctions for repeat offenders of DWI have had good results. Lowering convicted drinking drivers' permissible BAC has reduced fatalities in this group. Treatment combined with sanctions and supervision has reduced recidivism (U.S. Department of Health and Human Services, 2000).

Server Laws and Liability.   Between one-third and one-half of intoxicated drivers consumed their last alcohol at bars or restaurants (U.S. Department of Health and Human Services, 2000). About one-third of these drivers had BACs above the legal limit. After server laws were enacted, and training given, there was a 23 percent drop in nighttime crash rates in Oregon. Research has shown that server liability laws, where servers can be sued for damages as a result of serving a minor or intoxicated person that results in an alcohol-related accident, reduced traffic mortality rates in those states that have adopted them (U.S. Department of Health and Human Services, 2000).

Personal Intervention.   Although it is neither a legal matter, promoted, nor widely researched, an additional means to reduce DWI is through personal intervention on the part of spouses, friends, or colleagues. One recent study indicates that this type of intervention can be highly successful (U.S. Department of Health and Human Services, 2000).

ALCOHOL ADVERTISING
AND ALCOHOL CONSUMPTION

Over $1 billion was spent on alcohol advertising in 1996 (U.S. Department of Health and Human Services, 2000, p. 412). Is there evidence that such advertising promotes drinking? In general, studies suggest that advertising does not increase overall consumption, but may encourage people to switch from one brand of alcohol to another. Thus, at the current time there is no research support that shows any benefit to regulating such advertisements (U.S. Department of Health and Human Services, 2000; Whitehead, 1998).

RECOMMENDATIONS

Prevention

This chapter has contrasted the Northern European restrictive policies toward alcohol and the Southern European permissive approach. Prevention philosophy is marked by these two contrasting views. One approach is to integrate alcohol fully into the culture, as the Italians do. The historical idealized picture of Italian drinking practices has been one model for U.S. alcohol education. It has been argued that by integrating alcohol into the culture, drinking behavior is normalized and few alcohol-related problems ensue (Heath & Rosovsky, 1998). In fact, this model has not been adopted for education or prevention efforts on a large scale in the United States. However, this view highlights an important difference between alcohol and other drugs. For many societies, alcohol plays a constructive role and is viewed primarily as a food. Psychoactive drugs, even where legal, have never been viewed this way.

The other approach to prevention is that of the Northern European countries. Adherents of this view point out that with increased exposure to the substance, more individuals are placed at risk for developing alcohol use disorders. Thus, the contrasting approach is to take serious measures to curtail its use. This chapter has cited considerable evidence that regulation of alcohol use has had a positive impact on reducing alcohol-related problems. One possible negative aspect of this approach is that forbidding or severely restricting the use of alcohol makes it more attractive, especially for the rebellious. If all drinking is forbidden, the development of drinking habits may fall outside normal social channels and lose the protective influence of social norms (Heath & Rosovsky, 1998). When drinking is forbidden by religion, for example, Heath and Rosovsky (1998) note that members of such religious groups who experiment with alcohol move on quickly to full-fledged drinking problems. However, there is no research indicating that prohibiting alcohol has increased its problematic use among any population.

It is naive to think that there is one prevention or education effort that would fit the culturally diverse communities that are now prevalent in the United States. Community efforts at prevention must take such diverse cultural views of a community into consideration. A common ground must be found where all can agree on alcohol policy. Targeting specific problems related to alcohol consumption may provide such a common ground. Decreasing rates of driving while drinking, binge drinking, and providing treatment for alcohol-dependent individuals are goals most could agree on. Another approach suggested by Heath and Rosowky (1998) is to bolster informal community controls to enhance healthy and safe attitudes, values, norms, and other expectations about alcohol that can be agreed on in the community.

There are a number of potential initiatives that local governmental agencies could take which could reduce alcohol-related problems. At the same time, community involvement and acceptance of such initiatives are essential. For example, enforcement of MLDA laws would probably reduce minor-age drinking. For communities with large populations of Northern Europeans there might be good agreement on this enforcement. Obviously, Italian and other Southern European immigrant groups would be less supportive of such a policy. Perhaps a policy regarding publicizing and enforcing zero tolerance might be acceptable to both groups, since it is clear that youth who drink and drive are at great risk for automobile accidents. On the other hand, safe drinking guidelines might be approved by Southern European groups but be less acceptable to Northern European descendants. Thus, in our culture, essential differences in philosophy about alcohol use need to be bridged in prevention efforts.

From this chapter, it should be evident that there are a variety of safe drinking patterns and several dangerous ones. In addition to targeting alcohol dependence and those at risk for it, other drinking patterns could be the target of intervention. In the United States, drinking and driving is clearly a dangerous drinking pattern that has been addressed successfully by several measures. In a similar vein, one of the goals of prevention could be extended to focus on the reduction of problematic patterns of drinking such as binge drinking.

Targeting Binge Drinkers.   Findings in this chapter and Chapter 5 suggest that binge drinking is a pattern of drinking with many harmful consequences. Targeting such drinking practices for prevention could reduce alcohol-related problems significantly (Roche & Evans, 1998). Chapter 5 cited studies that showed that binge drinkers have very high rates of driving while intoxicated. These findings suggest that screening for binge drinking and targeting binge drinkers for education and prevention could reduce DWI offenses.

Alcohol Outlet Density.   While research indicates benefits in restricting the availability of alcohol by limiting the number of alcohol sales outlets, state liquor authorities have rarely taken any initiatives in this area. They should be encouraged to do so, at least on a trial basis.

Alcohol Taxes.   While research indicates that increased price reduces problematic use of alcohol, the cost of alcohol on an inflation-adjusted basis is lower than it was in 1978. Increasing taxes on alcohol would probably lead to a reduction of alcohol-related problems.

Treatment

The cultural diversity of the United States suggests that there could be considerable benefit in considering cultural factors in treatment. This chapter has limited its discussion of culture to alcohol use patterns. Within this narrow scope, it would be relevant to determine if the alcoholic's family and/or community have attitudes that promote intoxication. Other cultural beliefs about alcohol may be relevant to alcoholism treatment. For example, an Italian American family might not be aware of the possibility of problematic use of alcohol as a result of cultural beliefs; the family may believe that it is not possible to become alcoholic by drinking wine. Respectful intervention that explains how any type of alcohol can lead to alcoholism is indicated. Many other cultural factors are also important in treatment of alcoholics, such as, for example, the meaning of seeking help outside the family or community, but these issues are beyond the scope of this book.

The attitudes of various groups about alcohol, notably, *machismo* and drinking among Hispanics, may be important factors in drinking practices, but there has been no research on the prevalence of these attitudes nor its impact on drinking.

SUMMARY

Variations in drinking among cultures range from prohibiting its use, promoting frequent intoxication, or viewing alcohol primarily as a food. Some cultures, such as the Northern European countries, strictly regulate the use of alcohol, whereas others, such as the Southern European countries, are quite permissive. How children are introduced to alcohol also varies among cultures.

Most modern Western civilized countries report about the same frequency of alcohol abuse and dependence, except in cultures where alcohol is not readily available. In such countries, such as Saudi Arabia and Iran, the rates of alcohol disorders are lower. Culture affects the expression of alcohol consumption and problems in a significant manner. There is considerable variation in drinking patterns among countries. Some countries have high rates of abstainers and problem drinkers, such as Mexico. Thus, per-capita consumption is not a good indicator of drinking problems in a country. While cultures with patterns of frequent drinking to intoxication tend to have higher alcoholism rates, Heath's study of the Camba found no alcoholism despite frequent heavy drinking.

There are differences in the expression of alcohol problems among different countries. For example, many French and Spanish heavy drinkers are rarely highly intoxicated, but drink such large quantities of alcohol that they must drink in order to stave off withdrawal. For these countries, the major alcohol-related concern is the health-related problems associated with this type of drinking. For the United States, Northern European countries, and Mexico, the major problem is the negative consequences of repeated intoxication.

Although alcohol consumption has been linked to increased aggression and sexual behavior in the United States, anthropologists have found cultures where this association is not typical.

In the United States, immigrant groups generally adhere to many of the alcohol practices that are typical of their country of origin. These practices are attenuated with each succeeding generation; newer generations develop drinking habits more like their contemporary American neighbors. This process is known as acculturation. Nonetheless, there appear to be significant protective effects on drinking problems from having Italian ancestors and a facilitative effect on drinking problems from having Irish ancestors.

Although outright prohibition of alcohol was not successful in the United States, there is considerable evidence that regulation of alcohol has had beneficial effects in reducing drinking and associated social problems. This is particularly evident in the reduction of drunk driving accidents over the past decade. There appear to be several areas of government intervention that could reduce alcohol-related problems in the United States. These include improved enforcement of existing laws, regulating alcohol outlet density, and increasing taxes on alcoholic beverages.

READINGS

Babor, T. F. (1992). Cross-cultural research on alcohol: A quoi bon? Review of methodology used to study cross-cultural variation in alcohol use. In J. E. Helzer & G. J. Canino (Eds.), *Alcoholism in North America, Europe, and Asia* (pp. 33–52). New York: Oxford University Press.
A review of the types of cross-cultural studies that have been conducted.

Bales, R. F. (1962). Attitudes toward drinking in the Irish culture. In D. J. Pittman & C. R. Snyder (Eds.), *Society, culture, and drinking* (pp. 157–186). New York: Wiley.
This classic essay analyzes social customs of the nineteenth-century Irish culture, which may have promoted alcoholism.

Lender, M. E., & Martin, J. K. (1987). *Drinking in America.* New York: The Free Press.
This book discusses historical social and political trends regarding alcohol in the United States.

Scheper-Hughes, N. (1979). *Saints, scholars, and schizophrenics.* Berkeley, CA: University of California Press.
This book discusses Irish culture and drinking practices in the twentieth century, updating Bales's study. Some cultural forces remain the same, which may account for the continued high rate of alcoholism in Ireland at the time of this study.

R E F E R E N C E S

Bales, R. F. (1962). Attitudes toward drinking in the Irish culture. In D. J. Pittman & C. R. Snyder (Eds.), *Society, culture, and drinking* (pp. 157–186). New York: Wiley.

Barry, H. (1976). Cross cultural evidence that dependency motivates drunkenness. In M. W. Everett, J. O. Waddell, & D. B. Heath (Eds.), *Cross cultural approaches to the study of alcohol: An interdisciplinary perspective* (pp. 249–263). The Hague: Mouton.

Bennett, L. A., Campillo, C., Chandarashekar, C. R., & Gureje, O. (1998). Alcoholic beverage consumption in India, Mexico and Nigeria, *Alcohol, Health, and Research World* 22, 243–252.

Caetano, R. (1988). A comparative analysis of drinking among Hispanics in the U.S., Spaniards in Madrid, and Mexican in Michoacan. In *Cultural influences and drinking patterns—A focus on Hispanic and Japanese populations* (National Institute on Alcohol and Alcoholism Research Monograph Research Monograph 19, pp. 273–311). Rockville, MD: U.S. Department of Human Services.

Caetano, R., Clark, C. L., & Tam, T. (1998). Alcohol consumption among racial/ethnic minorities: Theory and research. *Alcohol, Health, and Research World* 22, 233–238.

Chaloupka, F. J., Grossman, M., & Saffer, H. (1998). The effects of price on the consequences of alcohol use and abuse. In M. Galanter (Ed.), *Recent developments in alcoholism*, Vol. 14 (pp. 331–346). New York: Plenum.

Cook, P. J., & Moore, M. J. (2001). Environmental and persistence in youthful drinking patterns. In J. Gruber (Ed.), *Risky behavior among youths: An economic analysis* (Bureau of Economic Research, pp. 375–437). Chicago: University of Chicago Press.

Edwards, G. (1994). *Alcohol policy and the public good.* New York: Oxford University Press.

Field, P. B. (1962). A new cross-cultural study of drunkenness. In D. J. Pittman & C. R. Snyder (Eds.), *Society, culture, and drinking* (pp. 48–74). New York: Wiley.

Gordis, E. (1996). Alcohol research and social policy: An overview. *Alcohol, Health, and Research World* 20, 208–212.

Heath, D. W. (1962). Drinking patterns of the Bolivian Camba. In D. J. Pittman & C. R. Snyder (Eds.), *Society, culture, and drinking* (pp. 22–36). New York: Wiley.

Heath, D. W. (1998). Cultural variations among drinking patterns. In M. Grant & J. Litvak (Eds.), *Drinking patterns and their consequences* (pp. 103–128). Washington, DC: Taylor & Francis.

Heath, D. W., & Rosovsky, H. (1998). Community reactions to alcohol policies. In M. Grant & J. Litvak (Eds.), *Drinking patterns and their consequences* (pp. 205–218). Washington, DC: Taylor & Francis.

Hingson, R. (1996). Prevention of drinking and driving. *Alcohol, Health, and Research World* 20, 219–226.

Horton, D. (1991). Alcohol use in primitive societies. In D. J. Pittman & H. R. White (Eds.), *Society, culture, and drinking patterns reexamined* (pp. 7–31). New Brunswick, NJ: Rutgers Center for Alcohol Studies.

Jellinek, E. M. (1960). *The disease concept of alcoholism.* New Haven, CT: College and University Press.

Jones-Webb, R. (1998). Drinking patterns and problems among African-Americans: Recent findings. *Alcohol, Health, and Research World* 22, 260–264.

Kitano, H. L., Hatanaka, H., Yeung, W. T., & Sue, S. (1985). Japanese-American drinking patterns. In L. A. Bennett & G. M. Ames (Eds.), *The American experience with alcohol* (pp. 335–357). New York: Plenum.

Lemert, E. M. (1991). Alcohol, values, and social control. In D. J. Pittman & H. R. White (Eds.), *Society, culture, and drinking patterns reexamined* (pp. 681–701). New Brunswick, NJ: Rutgers Center for Alcohol Studies.

Lender, M. E., & Martin, J. K. (1987). *Drinking in America,* New York: The Free Press.

Lindman, R. E., Sjoholm, B. A., & Lang, A. R. (2000). Expectations of alcohol-induced positive affect: A cross-cultural comparison. *Journal of Studies on Alcohol* 61, 681–687.

Lolli, G., Serianni, E., Golder, G. M., & Luzzatto-Fegiz, P. (1958). *Alcohol in Italian culture. Food and wine in relation to sobriety among Italians and Italian Americans.* New Brunswick, NJ: Rutgers Center for Alcohol Studies.

Mac Andrew, C., & Edgerton, R. B. (1969) *Drunken comportment: A social explanation.* Chicago: Aldine.

Makela, K. (1986). Attitudes towards drunkenness in four Scandinavian countries. In T. F. Babor (Ed.), *Alcohol and culture: Comparative perspectives from Europe and America*, Vol. 472 (pp. 21–32). New York: New York Academy of Science.

Makimoto, K. (1998). Drinking patterns and drinking problems among Asian Americans and Pacific Islanders. *Alcohol, Health, and Research World* 22, 270–275.

Manson, S. M., Shore, J. H., Baron, A. E., Ackerson, L., & Neligh, G. (1992). Alcohol abuse and dependence among American Indians. In J. E. Helzer & G. J. Canino (Eds.), *Alcoholism in North America, Europe, and Asia* (pp. 113–130). New York: Oxford.

Martinez, R. M., Sanchez, L. M., & Perez, A. C. (1988). Drinking patterns and problems in Madrid. In *Cultural influences and drinking patterns—A focus on Hispanic and Japanese populations* (National Institute on Alcohol and Alcoholism Research Monograph Research Monograph 19, pp. 223–252). Rockville, MD: U.S. Department of Human Services.

McCord, W., & McCord, J. (1960). *Origins of alcoholism*. Stanford, CA: Stanford University Press.

Medina-Mora, M. E. (1988). Comparative analysis of drinking patterns and problems in Mexico. In *Cultural influences and drinking patterns—A focus on Hispanic and Japanese populations* (National Institute on Alcohol and Alcoholism Research Monograph Research Monograph 19, pp. 253–272). Rockville, MD: U.S. Department of Human Services.

Plange, N. (1998). Social and behavioral issues related to drinking patterns. In M. Grant and J. Litvak (Eds.), *Drinking patterns and their consequences* (pp. 89–102). Washington, DC: Taylor & Francis.

Randolph, W. M., Stroup-Benham, C., Black, S. A., & Markides, K. S. (1998). Alcohol use among Cuban-Americans, Mexican-Americans, and Puerto Ricans. *Alcohol, Health, and Research World* 22, 265–269.

Roche, A. M., & Evans, K. R. (1998). The implications of drinking patterns for primary prevention, education and screening. In M. Grant & J. Litvak (Eds.), *Drinking patterns and their consequences* (pp. 243–266). Washington, DC: Taylor & Francis.

Rooney, J. F. (1991). Patterns of alcohol use in Spanish society. In D. J. Pittman & H. R. White (Eds.), *Society, culture, and drinking patterns reexamined* (pp. 381–402). New Brunswick, NJ: Rutgers Center for Alcohol Studies.

Sadoun, R., Lolli, G., & Silverman, M. (1965). *Drinking in the French culture*. New Brunswick, NJ: Rutgers Center for Alcohol Studies.

Scheper-Hughes, N. (1979). *Saints, scholars, and schizophrenics*. Berkeley, CA: University of California Press.

Scribner, R. Cohen, D., Kaplan, S., & Allen, S. H. (1999). Alcohol availability and homicide in New Orleans: Conceptual considerations for small area analysis of the effect of alcohol outlet density. *Journal of Studies on Alcohol* 60, 310–316.

Simboli, B. J. (1985). Acculturated Italian-American drinking behavior. In L. A. Bennett & G. M. Ames (Eds.), *The American experience with alcohol* (pp. 61–76). New York: Plenum.

Single, E., & Leino, V. E. (1998). The levels, patterns, and consequences of drinking. In M. Grant & J. Litvak (Eds.), *Drinking patterns and their consequences* (pp. 7–24). Washington, DC: Taylor and Francis.

Smart, R. G., & Mora, M. M. (1986). Alcohol control policies in Latin America and other countries. In T. F. Babor (Ed.), *Alcohol and culture: Comparative perspectives from Europe and America*, Vol. 472 (pp. 211–218). New York: New York Academy of Science.

Stivers, R. (1978). Irish ethnicity and alcohol use. *Medical Anthropology* 2, 121–135.

Toomey, T. L., Rosenfeld, C., & Wagenaar, A. C. (1996). The minimum legal drinking age. *Alcohol, Health, and Research World* 20, 213–218.

U.S. Department of Health and Human Services (1997). *Ninth Special Report to the U.S. Congress on alcohol and health.*

U.S. Department of Health and Human Services (2000). *Tenth Special Report to the U.S. Congress on alcohol and health.*

Vaillant, G. E. (1995). *The natural history of alcoholism revisited*. Cambridge, MA: Harvard University Press.

Voas, R. B., & Fisher, D. A. (2001). Court procedures for handling intoxicated drivers. *Alcohol, Health, and Research World* 25, 32–42.

Whitehead, S. (1998). The impact of alcohol control measures on drinking patterns. In M. Grant & J. Litvak (Eds.), *Drinking patterns and their consequences* (pp. 153–167). Washington, DC: Taylor & Francis.

Yalisove, D. L. (1998). A review of the research on the relationship between alcohol consumption and aggressive behavior and its implications for education, prevention, treatment, and criminal justice policy. *Security Journal* 11, 237–241.

CHAPTER EIGHT

ALCOHOL, EMOTION, SEX, AND AGGRESSION

In this chapter we survey experimental research about the effects of alcohol on behavior and emotions. Alcohol has pharmacologic effects on the brain, which influence behavior. Additionally, individuals have expectations or beliefs about the effects of alcohol. These beliefs may affect behavior as well as the pharmacologic effects. For example, the expectation that alcohol increases sexual arousal may actually increase sexual arousal as much as the alcohol itself. Research on alcohol expectations evolved from anthropologic observations that customs about alcohol use vary among cultures and result in different consequences for drinking and intoxication (e.g., the Cambans' bouts of intoxication did not lead to aggressive or sexual behavior; see Chapter 7). The following questions will be addressed in this chapter:

1. How does alcohol affect emotions?
2. What is the relationship between alcohol and stress?
3. Does alcohol facilitate aggression?
4. Does alcohol facilitate sexual arousal and behavior?

METHODOLOGY

Measuring Drug Effects

Research procedures have evolved to measure the pharmacologic effects of drugs and eliminate the potential confound of the subject's expectations. The major experimental designs are called

1. Placebo study
2. Single-blind study
3. Double-blind study
4. Balanced placebo study

The first method researchers used to test the effect of a drug was to compare subjects who received the drug with those who did not. Those who received the drug obviously had greater hope that they would be improved than those who did not. It was felt that the "expected benefit" of those receiving the drug might actually affect the effectiveness of the drug. As a first step to reduce this "expected benefit" difference between the groups, placebos were administered to the control group. A **placebo** is an inert substance that is made to look like the active drug that is being tested. The idea was that the "expected benefit" aspect of any intervention would be reflected by the response of the the placebo group, and the degree to which this expectation provided benefit was called the *placebo effect*. The difference in outcome between the group receiving the placebo and the group receiving the drug was taken to be a measure of the effectiveness of the drug.

It was discovered that without further modification of the design, the placebo was dismissed as worthless by the subjects because they knew it was "just a placebo." The first modification in the design was to create a procedure so that the subject did not know if the pill received was the real drug or placebo. This design became known as the **single-blind** study. This modification did not prove sufficient, because the researcher could communicate to the subject in one way or another whether the subject was receiving the drug or placebo and thereby nullify the placebo effect. In the final design, the person administering the drug is also kept in the dark as to whether the subject is receiving the real drug or placebo. This is known as the **double-blind** study. This type of study is now the accepted method of testing new drugs (Shapiro & Shapiro, 1997). How common is the placebo effect, and how strong is it? Shapiro and Shapiro (1997) summarize a number of studies, which indicate that 21 to 58 percent of subjects experience it and it accounts for 28 to 58 percent of their symptom relief. Placebo responses have been found for relief of pain, seasickness (Shapiro & Shapiro, 1997), asthma, and colitis (Fisher & Greenberg, 1997). Additionally, placebos can even induce negative side effects (Fisher & Greenberg, 1997; Shapiro & Shapiro, 1997). Thus, the placebo effect is a significant one and must be considered in evaluating drug effects.

Measuring Alcohol Expectations

There have been two general methods to research alcohol expectations. In one approach, people are surveyed about their alcohol beliefs. Scales have been developed that measure the strength of these beliefs, such as the Alcohol Expectancy Questionnaire (Brown et al., 1987). Research can then be conducted to determine how much these beliefs affect drinking and resulting behavior. In the second approach, alcohol expectations are manipulated in the laboratory by the use of deception. One group of subjects is told they will receive alcohol but are actually given a placebo. Responses in this group can be attributed to expectancy. In this chapter, the experimental manipulation of expectancy will be referred to as **expectancy set,** following George et al.'s (1989) designation. Expectancies refer to beliefs that people develop in the course of their cultural experience.

The Balanced Placebo Design

A group of psychologists became interested in researching alcohol's pharmacologic and expectancy effects on behavior. Carpenter had observed that the typical placebo study did not measure the effect of the drug separate from expectancy set (Martlatt, 1985). That is, the subject getting the real drug is responding to both expectancy set and real drug effects in the placebo designs discussed above. Thus, there was no measure of the pure pharmacologic effect. He suggested adding an **antiplacebo** group, in which the subjects would expect an inert substance but get the real drug. This evolved into the balanced placebo design, which consists of four conditions or four separate groups of subjects. One group is told they will receive the drug and do receive it (I in Table 8.1). This group shows the combined effects of the pharmacology and expectancy set. A second group is told they will receive the drug but receive a placebo (II in Table 8.1). This group's reaction is the expectancy set or placebo effect. A third group is told they will receive a placebo but actually receive the drug (the antiplacebo group; III in Table 8.1). This condition measures the pharmacologic effect without expectancy set. The fourth group expects a placebo and receives a placebo (IV in Table 8.1), which is a control group. In the placebo and antiplacebo groups, the subjects are given deceptive instructions. The effectiveness of this deception is critical to the validity of this design. In alcohol studies, subjects are typically given tonic water and/or vodka. In the placebo condition, subjects are told they are getting tonic and vodka, but just get tonic water. A trace of vodka may be placed on the rim of the glass to give the aroma of alcohol and add to the deception. In the antiplacebo condition, subjects are told they are getting tonic water but get alcohol with the tonic water. Subjects are asked at the end of the study to estimate their blood alcohol concentration (BAC), which is used to determine the effectiveness of the deception. Because subjects can detect high levels of alcohol because of its intoxicating effects regardless of the deceptive instructions, the design is effective only at relatively low BAC levels (generally ranging from 0.05 to 0.10 percent).

This paradigm has been used in tandem with laboratory manipulation of emotional, sexual, or aggressive responses to test the contribution of expectancy set and pharmacologic effects of alcohol consumption on these behaviors. By comparing the responses of the four groups, it can be determined how much expectancy and/or pharmacology contributes to the result. If, for example, both expectancy groups (I and II in Table 8.1) have the same reaction and it is greater than the "get alcohol and expect placebo" group (III in Table 8.1), it can be concluded that expectancy set effects predominate over the pharmacologic effects for the behavior investigated.

ALCOHOL AND EMOTION

In one of the first experimental investigations of alcohol and emotion, Hartocollis (1962) administered alcohol intravenously to psychiatric patient volunteers without disclosing

TABLE 8.1   Balanced Placebo Design

I. Expect alcohol and receive alcohol	II. Expect alcohol and do not receive alcohol (Placebo condition)
III. Do not expect alcohol and receive alcohol (Antiplacebo condition)	IV. Do not expect alcohol and do not receive alcohol

what was being infused. He reports that the patients responded with expressions of elation. Other early researchers found that alcohol ingestion in a sterile laboratory showed minimal effects on emotion (Smith et al., 1975) or enhanced negative emotion (Warren & Raynes, 1972). Researchers reasoned that more accurate results would be obtained if the environments where the drinking occurred were more naturalistic and made the laboratory settings more social, comfortable, and congenial. Smith et al. (1975) provided such a setting for couples to drink alcohol or a placebo. They taped the interactions and portions were coded for emotional expression. They found that subjects who had a low dose of alcohol (BAC of 0.06%), demonstrated a significant increase of all emotional responses, especially elation, compared to the placebo group. Those individuals who had less drinking experience had greater affective changes. In a similar experimental setting, Robbins and Brotherton (1980) found that men tended to become both more depressed and angrier, whereas women became less depressed and angry as BACs increased. Connors and Sobell (1986) reported that college-age subjects who consumed alcohol in a congenial setting reported themselves more elated, egotistic, friendly, and euphoric than those who drank the placebo beverage.

Researchers have devised procedures that manipulate affect in the laboratory and use the balanced placebo design to determine alcohol's effect on negative emotion. For example, Phil et al. (1980) created a bogus test, in which subjects were given difficult problems and multiple-choice answers where none was correct. Those told they had done poorly were expected to feel more depressed. The results indicated that subjects who did not receive alcohol, including the placebo condition, had an increase in depression. Those who received alcohol did not. Similarly, Sayette et al. (1992) raised anxiety in subjects by having them write and deliver a speech about their physical appearance. Those given alcohol showed less anxiety than a placebo or control group. Both of these studies suggest that alcohol has a pharmacologic effect of reducing negative emotion. In a meta-analysis of fourteen studies, Hull and Bond (1986) found that alcohol consumption enhanced mood for normal drinkers, but the expectancy set did not. Greeley and Oei (1999), summarizing studies on social stress and alcohol, found that alcohol reduced anxiety both by self-report and by physiologic measures. Thus the experimental evidence suggests that at low doses for normal drinkers, alcohol serves to facilitate positive mood and relieve negative affect and that these effects are due primarily to pharmacologic effects rather than expectancy.

Alcoholics' Response to Alcohol in Controlled Settings

Several early investigators examined the effects of high doses of alcohol on alcoholics in hospital settings (Mayfield, 1968; McNamee et al., 1968; Nathan et al., 1970; Tamerin & Mendelson, 1969). They report that when sober, the alcoholics claimed they drank to reduce anxiety and depression. Yet when administered alcohol, they appeared and rated themselves more anxious and depressed. Nathan et al.'s (1970) subjects were permitted to achieve very high BACs, above 0.30%, a procedure unlikely to be permitted today because of potential risks to the subjects. Those reaching these high levels of intoxication became psychotic, delusional, and physically aggressive. McNamee et al. (1968) and Tamerin and Mendelson (1969) report their intoxicated alcoholic subjects often expressed extremely painful affect and showed extreme lability of mood yet continued to drink. Tamerin and Mendelson (1969) noted that these negative emotions all disappeared upon sobriety. Paradoxically, then, alcoholics, unlike normal drinkers, seem to have a negative emotional reaction to drinking even though they expect a positive one.

ALCOHOL AND STRESS

Does stress lead to more frequent drinking or alcoholism? In general, research studies have not supported the hypothesis that tension or stress reduction is a major motivation for drinking in most people (Greeley & Oei, 1999). Recent surveys about stress and alcohol use have shown a minimal relationship between stress and alcohol consumption. For example, San Jose et al. (2000) surveyed a large sample of Dutch adults. They found that while increased stress led some to drink more, others reacted by abstaining from alcohol altogether. Recently divorced men, for example, were likely to report abstaining from alcohol, while recently divorced women were more likely to drink more. Having greater numbers of stressors was not associated with heavier drinking.

Although stress does not appear to be related to increased alcohol use, stress may interact with other factors to increase vulnerability to alcohol problems. McCreary and Sadava (2000) surveyed two cohorts of young adults and failed to find a correlation between stress and alcohol use. However, those who reported more stress were more likely to report alcohol problems. Colder and Chassin (1993) interviewed adolescents and found that stress did not predict drinking but stress and negative affect did. Klein (1991) conducted a survey of drinking practices and found that younger subjects were much more likely to drink as the result of an emotional response than older people. Thus, those who respond to stress with negative affect may have an increased risk for alcohol problems. Some modest support for this idea is found in Carpenter and Hasin's (1999) research. They found that those with a diagnosis of alcohol dependence (DSM-IV) demonstrated a greater level of drinking to cope with negative affect than drinkers with no alcohol disorder.

ALCOHOL AND AGGRESSION

Investigators have developed several game simulations to measure aggression in the laboratory. The *competitive reaction time paradigm* is typical. In it, the subject is led to believe that he will be paired with an opponent to test reaction time. Whoever reacts faster will administer a shock to his opponent. In fact, the subject receives only one shock at the beginning of the game. Before the the trial, he can see the level of shock the opponent has selected to give him on his monitor (see Figure 8.1). The subject then selects the level of shock he will administer. The measure of aggression is the level of shock the subject chooses. In fact, there is no opponent; the opponent is computer-simulated. Degree of provocation can be manipulated by the level of shock the "opponent" selects: the higher the level, the higher the provocation. Other opponent behaviors can be simulated to determine if they facilitate or moderate the aggressive response in the subject (Taylor, 1993). A number of studies indicate that this procedure evokes a valid measure of aggression (Taylor & Chermack, 1993; Gustafson, 1993).

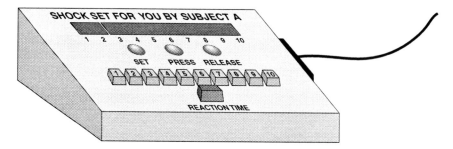

FIGURE 8.1   Task Board Used in the Competitive Reaction Time Paradigm. The buttons numbered 1 to 10 represent progressively higher intensities of shock that can be administered to an opponent. The Set light signals the subject to choose the intensity of shock he or she wishes to administer to the opponent. The Press light signals the subject to depress the Reaction Time key at the bottom, and the Release light signals the subject to release the Reaction Time key as quickly as possible. The digital readout (or feedback light) at the top indicates the intensity of shock set by the opponent for the subject (which is equal to the intensity of the shock received by the subject, if the opponent wins the trial).

Source: Taylor, 1993.

To test for the effect of alcohol intoxication on aggression, a game simulation is combined with a placebo design. That is, before proceeding to the simulated competitive game, subjects receive alcohol or a placebo. For example, Gustafson (1986) used the balanced placebo design with a simulated competition involving potential monetary winnings. Aggression was measured by the subject's deduction of the simulated opponent's winnings. Provocation was simulated by the "opponent's" deductions. The results are shown in Figure 8.2.

Figure 8.2 shows that those who received alcohol, whether they expected it or not, responded with more aggression than those who expected alcohol but did not receive it. These results strongly support the pharmacologic effects of alcohol and not expectancy set effects.

Chermack and Taylor (1995) tested the effect of alcohol expectancies on aggression in the laboratory. They compared the aggressive responses of those with a strong belief in alcohol's disinhibiting effects with a group with low expectations. Even those with low expectancies reacted with higher levels of aggression when intoxicated. These two studies suggest that pharmacologic effects exert a much more powerful effect on aggressive behavior than expectancies. Most experimental studies support a similar conclusion.

Meta-Analytic Studies

Ito et al. (1996) conducted a meta-analysis of forty-nine experimental alcohol and aggression studies. They found that alcohol intoxication increased aggression under conditions of low or high provocation. Additionally, they found that large doses of alcohol increased aggressive behavior more than small doses. In another meta-analytic study of aggression and alcohol experiments, Hull and Bond (1986) also concluded that alcohol, but not expectancy set, increases aggression. Bushman (1990, 1997) conducted two meta-analysis of thirty and sixty experimental studies of alcohol and aggression using the balanced placebo design. He

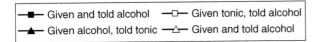

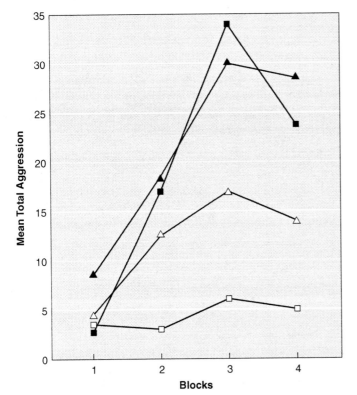

FIGURE 8.2   Mean Total Aggression as a Function of Frustration, Alcohol Dose, and Informational Set. Solid squares denote those given alcohol/told alcohol; solid triangles, given alcohol/told tonic; open squares, given tonic/told alcohol; open triangles, given tonic/told tonic.

Reproduced with permission of author and publisher from: Gustafson, R., Alcohol, frustration and aggression: An experiment using the balanced placebo design. *Psychological Reports*, 1986, 59, 207–218. © Psychological Reports 1986.

found that the antiplacebo condition (III in Table 8.1) was not significantly different from the control condition (IV in Table 8.1). Thus, his analysis suggests that pharmacologic effects do not directly cause aggression. Similarly, the placebo condition (II in Table 8.1) was not significantly different from the control condition, suggesting that expectancy set effects do not increase aggressive behavior. However, the interaction of expectancy and alcohol created a large effect. Figure 8.3 nicely summarizes these findings.

These meta-analytic studies suggest that alcohol facilitates aggression through its pharmacologic properties or a combination of its pharmacologic and expectancy effects.

Facilitating Factors of Aggression in Intoxicated Subjects

Dougherty et al. (1999) found that aggressive responses remained elevated for several hours after alcohol consumption. Gustafson (1993) and Kelly and Cherek (1993) report findings that indicate provocation is important in eliciting aggression from intoxicated subjects. Women as well as men showed increased aggressive responses with alcohol intoxication (Gustafson, 1993; Dougherty et al., 1999). Even those with nonaggressive dispositions

FIGURE 8.3   Psychologic and Pharmacologic Effects of Alcohol on Human Aggression. Capped vertical bars denote 1 standard error. Pharmacology, antiplacebo versus control comparison. Expectancy, placebo versus control comparison. Expectancy and pharmacology confounded, alcohol versus placebo and alcohol versus control comparisons combined.

Source: Bushman, B. (1997). Alcohol and human aggression. In *Recent Developments in Alcoholism.* Vol. 13, *Alcohol and Violence: Epidemiology, Neurobiology, Psychology, and Family Issues,* M. Galanter (Ed.). New York: Plenum. Reprinted by permission of Kluwer Academic/Plenum Publishing and the author.

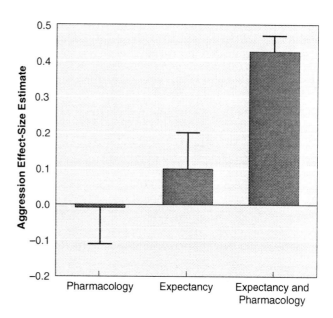

showed higher aggressive responses when intoxicated (Taylor, 1993). Still, those with aggressive tendencies increased their aggression when intoxicated more than those with lower aggressive tendencies (Dougherty et al., 1999).

Intoxicated subjects ignored their opponent's expression of discomfort and kept shocking their opponent, whereas sober clients were responsive by reducing shocks (Taylor, 1993); intoxicated subjects were swayed by social pressure to increase aggression more than those who had had no alcohol (Taylor, 1993). Intoxicated subjects expect more intense shocks from their opponents than sober subjects do (Taylor & Chermack, 1993).

Inhibition of Aggressive Responses in Intoxicated Subjects

Taylor and Chermack (1993) found that once aggression was initiated, it was difficult to suppress the aggressive behavior of intoxicated subjects. Exercises conducted before the competitive task that facilitate reflection about aggressive behavior reduced aggression in intoxicated subjects (Taylor, 1993; Ito et al., 1996). Having a nonaggressive alternative (i.e., giving comfortable vibrations to the opponent's feet) in the situation also moderated the aggressive behavior of intoxicated subjects (Gustafson, 1993).

Other Psychoactive Drugs and Aggression

Benzodiazapines, whose psychoactive effects are similar to alcohol, are the only other drugs that laboratory research has shown to facilitate aggression (Taylor, 1993). In limited experimental research, marijuana (Taylor & Chermack, 1993) and opiate intoxication (Roberts et al., 1998) have been shown to inhibit aggression. Research has not found cocaine intoxication to be associated with increased aggression (Roberts et al., 1998).

Observational Studies

Two observational studies conducted in protected environments provide dramatic support for alcohol's role in facilitating aggression. Boyatzis (1983) conducted observational studies in a simulated bar. Subjects were given beer, distilled spirits, or no alcohol. Boyatzis videotaped subjects and took Breathalyzer readings at three periods. He found that those who had alcohol were more aggressive than those who had none at each time interval, and that as blood alcohol concentration increased, the number of aggressive acts increased. In a study conducted by Maletsky (1976), 80 percent of subjects (18 of 22) with a history of violence and alcohol intoxication, given alcohol intravenously in large doses (over 0.10% BAC), became so violent that they had to be put in restraints.

Graham et al. (2000) conducted an observational study of aggression in bars on weekend evenings. In observations conducted at 12 bars over 93 nights, 105 incidents of aggression were noted. Trained observers coded the behavior of intoxicated patrons who became involved in aggressive incidents. Alcohol intoxication was judged to facilitate aggression by creating a focus on the here and now (see alcohol myopia, later), reducing anxiety about sanctions or danger, and creating heightened emotionality. Factors in the environment judged to facilitate aggression were permissive environments and expectations that aggression would be tolerated.

How Does Alcohol Facilitate Aggression?

Although there is no definitive explanation for alcohol's facilitation of aggression, there are a number of diverse theories, which have in common the basic idea that alcohol impedes mental functioning, limits capacity to reflect, and makes the individual more vulnerable to the demand characteristics of the immediate situation. The most succinct theory is called *alcohol myopia*, and it asserts that alcohol intoxication narrows our perception to the here and now. The individual becomes more vulnerable to provoking cues while at the same time the alcohol intoxication deprives him or her of access to inhibiting cues and meanings (i.e., thinking about the negative consequences of an aggressive response) (Steele & Josephs, 1990). The theories of Pernanan (1993), Parker and Rebhun (1995), and Taylor and Chermack (1993) are similar.

Another contributing factor of alcohol consumption to aggression is the exacerbation or creation of negative affect caused by intoxication (Blum, 1981). This aspect has not been explored experimentally.

Summary of the Research on Alcohol and Aggression

Perhaps the most robust research finding in this book is the evidence that alcohol facilitates aggression. The results show:

1. With provocation, alcohol facilitates aggression in a wide range of different simulated competitive games.
2. With increased doses of alcohol, there is increased aggression.
3. The response occurs in men, women, and individuals who do not have aggressive dispositions.

4. Except for benzodiazapines, which are similar-acting to alcohol, no other psychoactive drugs have been shown to facilitate aggression.
5. Expectancy or expectancy set does not account for the increased aggression.
6. Observational studies show that aggression increases with alcohol intoxication.

In the next chapter, research will be reviewed that finds:

1. Reported and nonreported violence is associated with alcohol intoxication in at least one of the participants 50 percent of the time.
2. Violent crime decreases when alcohol is less available.

SEX AND ALCOHOL

Sex and alcohol have been associated for centuries. Shakespeare made many references to this association. In this respect, the modern world is no different. Murphy et al. (1998) cite several surveys in which the majority of respondents indicate that alcohol and sex go together. By fourth grade, many children have already developed expectancies that associate alcohol with sexuality (Miller et al., 1990). Leigh and Morrison (1991) found that 50 percent of surveyed male and female adolescents had been drinking alcohol at the time of their first sexual experience. In their survey, Cooper and Orcutt (1997) found adolescents and young adults reported having intercourse on the first date 20 percent of the time if one or both partners were drinking, but only 8 percent of the time if neither was drinking.

The combination of alcohol and sex often leads to negative consequences. In a survey of women, 60 percent reported unwanted sexual advances from intoxicated men (Lang, 1985). In another survey of women, half of the women who were sexually assaulted reported that alcohol consumption was involved (Abbey et al., 1999). Kanin (1985, cited in Abbey et al., 1996) interviewed males who had engaged in date rape; 75 percent stated that they purposely got the date intoxicated to have sex with her. Research shows that alcohol consumption is associated with unsafe sex practices.

Research on alcohol and sex has been conducted in five areas:

1. Alcohol and sexual arousal
2. Alcohol and socially disapproved sexual arousal
3. Alcohol's effect on perception of others' sexual attractiveness and intentions
4. Stereotypes of sexual practices of drinking men and women
5. Safe sex practices and alcohol

Normal constraints and ethical principles prevent researchers from investigating the effect of alcohol on explicit sexual behavior in laboratory settings. Instead, various types of erotic materials are used to portray sexual situations. Depending on the focus of of the study, scenarios are created and subjects are asked questions about them. Physiologic arousal is measured with a device that notes circumference changes in penile erection in men and blood flow in the vaginal area for women. Subjective arousal is measured by asking subjects to rate their arousal. These procedures have been combined with the balanced placebo design to measure alcohol's impact on sexual behavior and arousal.

Alcohol and Sexual Arousal

As noted earlier, sexual behavior and alcohol consumption often occur together. Interestingly, research has found that there is an inverse relationship between amount of alcohol consumed and the level of physical arousal for both men and women (Goldman & Roehrich, 1991; George & Norris, 1991; Wilson, 1981). Goldman and Roehrich (1991) have summarized the balanced-placebo design research findings about alcohol and sexual arousal in men and women. They found that alcohol did not increase sexual arousal in men, but expectancy set increased both physiologic and subjective feelings of arousal. Women had almost the opposite reaction. They reported more subjective arousal after consuming alcohol but were not responsive to expectancy set effects.

Alcohol and Socially Disapproved Sexual Arousal and Behavior

Several studies have found that expectancy set has increased men's arousal and viewing time of unconventional erotic materials. For example, it was found that expectancy set significantly increased sexual arousal for men who watched a homosexual film (Wilson & Lawson, 1976) and listened to recordings of rape and violence toward women (Briddell et al., 1978).

Other studies, however, have found that intoxication but not expectancy set decreases the normal discrimination between socially approved sexual behavior and disapproved behavior. Barbaree et al. (1983) found that alcohol-intoxicated subjects responded more similarly to coercive sexual scenarios and mutual scenarios than did sober subjects. Norris et al. (1999) found that intoxicated men showed less empathy for a female sexual victim in a story than sober men. Additionally, they found that hypermasculine men, characterized by having callous sex attitudes toward women, showed less empathy under the intoxicated condition than normal men.

Alcohol's Effect on Perception of Others' Sexual Attractiveness and Intentions

Alcohol intoxication may influence our perceptions of others regarding their sexual availability and sexual attractiveness. Abbey et al. (2000) conducted an experiment in which men and women were paired and given alcohol or a placebo. When alcohol was consumed by the dyad, it enhanced both men's and women's perceptions of their own and their partner's sexuality and disinhibition. Intoxicated male participants ignored cues from the women that indicated a lack of interest. Norris and Kerr (1993) conducted a balanced-placebo design experiment in which men and women were read a sexually explicit story with coercive elements, including forcing the woman to engage in sex acts. Men consuming alcohol created a more negative view of the sexually coerced woman and showed increased willingness to behave like the man depicted in the story. For women, the alcohol led to a more positive appraisal of the man in the story and an increase in likelihood of behaving like the woman in the story. In these studies there were no expectancy set effects.

Stereotypes of Sexual Practices of Drinking Men and Women

Our view of others regarding their sexual availability and related characteristics may be influenced by whether or not we see them drinking alcohol. Participants in laboratory studies consistently view men who consumed alcohol as less responsible than men who did not consume alcohol, for a variety of offenses including rape (Abbey et al., 1996). Abbey et al. (1999), in a survey of college students, found that intoxicated males were expected to be more aggressive and have greater sex drive than were intoxicated females.

George et al. (1988, cited in Crowe & George, 1989; George et al., 2000) found that a drinking woman is perceived by subjects of both genders as less attractive, more sexually available, and more likely to have sex than a nondrinking woman. George (1988, cited in Crowe & George, 1989) also found that male and female college students rated women who had a few drinks of alcohol as being easier and more willing to be seduced, more responsive to a sexual advance, and more willing to engage in foreplay and sexual intercourse. Female victims were rated as more responsible for being raped when appearing intoxicated (Richardson & Campbell, 1982, cited by Abbey et al., 1996). Disturbingly, 40 percent of high school males in one study approved of physically forcing sex on an intoxicated date (Goodchildes & Zellman, 1984, cited by Abbey et al., 1996).

Thus, it seems that the double standard for men and women is very much alive in views about sex and alcohol. Alcohol confers an excuse for men to be more sexually aggressive, while it places blame on women for somehow encouraging sexual advances.

Safe Sex Practices and Alcohol

Does intoxication reduce attention to health and safety considerations relevant to sexual practices? Leigh and Stall (1993) summarize the large body of research that demonstrates that there is an association between alcohol use and unsafe sex. For example, one survey indicates those who frequently drank while having sex were one-seventh as likely to use condoms as occasional drinkers (Bagnall et al., 1990, cited in Murphy et al., 1998).

Several experimental studies suggest that alcohol consumption increases the tendency to engage in risky sex. Fromme et al. (1997) had sober and intoxicated subjects fill out a questionnaire on sexual practices; intoxicated subjects perceived lower risk and fewer negative consequences associated with unsafe sexual practices than sober or placebo subjects.

MacDonald et al. (2000) conducted research with college men to determine the effect of intoxication on their tendency to engage in unsafe sex. After viewing a film clip in which a couple was engaged in foreplay, ending with the discovery that they had no condoms, subjects who had been given alcohol, no alcohol, or a placebo were asked about their reactions to the theme of the film. The results showed that there was an interaction between reported level of sexual arousal and intoxication. Those who were aroused and intoxicated were much more likely to have a favorable attitude toward unprotected sex. When arousal was rated low, intoxicated subjects had no greater favorable attitude toward unprotected sex than sober subjects. There were no expectancy set effects.

Murphy et al. (1998) conducted a laboratory study with college women to see if alcohol and/or alcohol expectancies increased risky sex attitudes. Videotapes of a simulated dating service were shown to the women. Intoxicated women were far more likely to envision a relationship with an attractive man advocating risky sex than were those who had not consumed alcohol. Although there was the same trend for expectancy effects, they did not reach significance.

In summary, alcohol affects sexual arousal and behavior in significant ways, generally through pharmacologic effects, although the expectancy effect does increase sexual arousal in men. Research shows that there are strong stereotypes about drinking men and drinking women in relation to their presumed sexual availability and responsibility for sexual behavior.

RECOMMENDATIONS

Treatment

Psychoeducation about the aggression-facilitating property of alcohol intoxication should be included in all alcoholism treatment programs. This can help reassure abstinent alcoholics that they will be less prone to aggression and hopefully be an incentive to remain abstinent. The facilitative role of alcohol intoxication on aggression should be viewed as a danger for significant others involved with a drinking alcoholic.

Prevention

An important component of any prevention program should be a discussion of the role of alcohol intoxication in facilitating aggressive behavior. Inclusion of the experimental laboratory findings would promote a lively discussion regarding alcohol's facilitating effect on aggression.

Alcohol's facilitating effects on sexual responses should be made known. Hopefully, men will not exploit this knowledge to an extent that exceeds the protective function of informing women. Stereotypes about drinking and sex should be discussed.

Training for Bartenders. Because it has been shown that larger doses of alcohol increase aggression, it would be helpful to stop serving heavily intoxicated bar patrons. Bartenders could be trained to recognize intoxicated patrons and to tactfully refuse to serve any more alcohol to them (Fagan, 1993; Conner & Burns, 1995). Additional training regarding defusing potential violent confrontations among intoxicated patrons would be useful, although the principles have not been developed. The interventions shown to reduce aggression in intoxicated subjects in the laboratory could be used to help develop protocols. Findings that intoxicated individuals become more aggressive when provoked, are vulnerable to social pressure to be aggressive, and have increased risk for aggression that lasts for several hours after drinking might prove useful in developing these protocols. It was also found that offering an intoxicated aggressive person an alternative response reduced aggression. Thus a protocol might include the advice not to provoke intoxicated, angry clients, to separate the client from other people who may be goading him into aggression, to offer the intoxicated person an alternative to the aggression, and to realize that the individual is at risk for aggression for several hours.

SUMMARY

Researchers have devised experimental procedures and designs to test alcohol's effects on emotion, aggression, and sex. Because expectancies about drugs often affect the actual response to the drug, provision has been made for determining the role of expectancies as well as pharmacologic effects though the use of the balanced placebo design. Laboratory studies suggest that alcohol in moderate doses appears to alleviate negative affect and enhance positive emotions for normal drinkers. Paradoxically, alcohol in moderate or large doses administered to alcoholics has been found to enhance negative emotions despite their expectations of improvement in mood.

Several lines of research have shown little relationship between drinking and stress. However, those who react to stress with negative affect may be at risk for developing alcohol problems.

There appears to be a strong relationship between alcohol consumption and aggression, as shown in numerous experimental studies. Men, women, and those with low aggressive tendencies all show increased aggression given moderate doses of alcohol. Results have generally shown that pharmacologic effects and interactions between pharmacologic effects and expectancy set effects increase aggression. Increased doses of alcohol and increased provocation enhance aggressive responding. These effects have been shown to last for several hours after consumption of alcohol.

Intoxicated subjects have been shown to expect more aggression from their opponent, to be less sympathetic to signs of opponent's distress, and to be more susceptible to social influence to increase aggression than nonintoxicated subjects. Once intoxicated subjects become aggressive in the experimental situations, they are difficult to stop. Offering an alternative nonaggressive response during the experiment and self-reflective exercises conducted before the aggression segment, however, did moderate intoxicated subjects' aggression.

Alcohol reduces physiologic sexual arousal in men, while expectancy set enhances it. Alcohol enhances subjective sexual arousal in women, while expectancy set has no effect. Alcohol appears to facilitate men's responsiveness to socially disapproved sexual practices and lessen inhibitions regarding victimizing women sexually, due to both expectancy set and pharmacologic effects. Intoxicated subjects see others as more sexual than when sober. Intoxicated men are more likely to ignore cues that indicate a lack of interest by the potential partner. Men and women are more likely to view sexual coercion more favorably when intoxicated. Women who are drinking are perceived to be more available sexually and responsible for resulting sexual activity than sober women. Intoxicated men are expected to be more sexually aggressive; they are viewed as less responsible for their sexual activity than when sober. There is a correlation between drinking alcohol and unsafe sex practices. Experimental studies indicate that intoxicated subjects are less likely to be responsive to safety concerns when asked to consider a risky sexual scenario.

READINGS

Abbey, A., Ross, L. T., McDuffie, D., & McAuslan, P. (1996). Alcohol, misperception, and sexual assault: How and why they are linked. In D. M. Buss and N. M. Malmuth (Eds.), *Sex, power, conflict; Evolutionary and feminist perspectives* (pp. 138–161). New York: Oxford University Press.
This article summarizes the research on alcohol intoxication and its effect on sexual aggression.

Bushman, B. J. (1997). Effects of alcohol on human aggression: Validity of proposed explanations. In M. Galanter (Ed.), *Recent developments in alcoholism*, Vol. 13, *Alcohol and violence: Epidemiology, neurobiology, psychology, and family issues* (pp. 227–243). New York: Plenum.
This chapter provides a meta-analysis of experimental aggression and alcohol studies.

Fisher, S., & Greenberg, R. P. (Eds.). *From placebo to panacea: Putting psychiatric drugs to the test* (pp. 3–56). New York: Wiley.
This book gives the history of the concept of placebo and the development of research methods to test the effectiveness of drugs.

Steele, C. M., & Josephs, R. A. (1990). Alcohol myopia: Its prized and dangerous effects. *American Psychologist* 45, 921–933.
A classic article which outlines a theory to explain how alcohol intoxication facilitates aggression.

Taylor, S. P. (1993). Experimental investigation of alcohol-induced aggression in humans. *Alcohol, Health and Research World* 17, 108–112.
This article explains the experimental procedure for measuring the effect of alcohol intoxication on aggression.

REFERENCES

Abbey, A., Ross, L. T., McDuffie, D., & McAuslan, P. (1996). Alcohol, misperception, and sexual assault: How and why they are linked. In D. M. Buss and N. M. Malmuth (Eds.), *Sex, power, conflict; Evolutionary and feminist perspectives* (pp. 138–161). New York: Oxford University Press.

Abbey, A., McAuslan, P., Ross, L. T., & Zawacki, T. (1999). Alcohol expectancies regarding sex, aggression, and sexual vulnerability: Reliability and validity assessment. *Psychology of Addictive Behaviors* 13, 174–182.

Abbey, A., Zawacki, T., & McAuslan, P. (2000). Alcohol's effects on sexual perception. *Journal of Studies on Alcohol* 61, 688–697.

Barbaree, H. E., Marshall, W. L., & Yales, E. (1983). Alcohol intoxication and deviant sexual arousal in male social drinkers. *Behavior Research Therapy* 21, 365–373.

Blum, R. H. (1981). Violence, alcohol, and setting: An unexplored nexus. In J. J. Collins & M. E. Wolfgang (Eds.), *Drinking and crime* (pp. 110–142). New York: Guilford.

Boyatzis, R. E. (1983). Who should drink what, when, and where if looking for a fight. In E. Gottheil, K. A. Druley, T. E. Skoloda, & H. M. Waxman (Eds.), *Alcohol, drug abuse, and aggression* (pp. 314–322). Springfield, IL: Thomas.

Briddell, D. W., Rimm, D. C., Caddy, G. R., Krawitz, G., Sholis, D., & Wunderlin, R. J. (1978). Effects of alcohol and cognitive set on sexual arousal to deviant stimuli. *Journal of Abnormal Psychology* 87, 418–430.

Brown, S. A., Christiansen, B. A., & Goldman, M. S. (1987). The Alcohol Expectancy Questionnaire: An instrument for the assessment of adolescent and adult alcohol expectancies. *Journal of Studies on Alcohol* 48, 483–491.

Bushman, B. J., & Cooper, H. M. (1990). Effects of alcohol on human aggression: An integrative research review. *Psychological Bulletin* 107, 341–354.

Bushman, B. J. (1997). Effects of alcohol on human aggression: Validity of proposed explanations. In M. Galanter (Ed.), *Recent developments in alcoholism*, Vol. 13, *Alcohol and violence: Epidemiology, neurobiology, psychology, and family issues* (pp. 227–243). New York: Plenum.

Carpenter, K. M., & Hasin, D. S. (1999). Drinking to cope with negative affect and DSM-IV alcohol use disorders: A test of three alternative explanations. *Journal of Studies on Alcohol* 60, 694–704.

Chermack, S. T., & Taylor, S. P. (1995). Alcohol and human physical aggression: Pharmacological versus expectancy effects. *Journal of Studies on Alcohol* 56, 449–456.

Colder, C. R., & Chassin, L. (1993). The stress and negative affect model of adolescent alcohol use and the moderating effects of behavioral undercontrol. *Journal of Studies on Alcohol* 54, 326–333.

Conner, R. L., & Burns, P. (1995). Law enforcement and regulatory agencies. In R. H. Coombs & D. M. Ziedonic (Eds.), *Handbook on drug abuse prevention: A comprehensive strategy to prevent the abuse of alcohol and other drugs.* Boston: Allyn & Bacon.

Connors, G. J., & Sobell, M. B. (1986). Alcohol and drinking environment: Effects on affect and sensations, person perception, and perceived intoxication. *Cognitive Therapy and Research* 10, 389–402.

Cooper, M. L., & Orcutt, H. K. (1997). Drinking and sexual experience on first dates among adolescents. *Journal of Abnormal Psychology* 106, 191–202.

Crowe, L. C., & George, W. H. (1989). Alcohol and human sexuality: Review and integration. *Psychological Bulletin* 105, 374–386.

Dougherty, D. M., Bjork, J. M., Bennett, R. H., & Moeller, F. G. (1999). The effects of a cumulative alcohol dosing procedure on laboratory aggression in women and men. *Journal of Studies on Alcohol* 60, 322–329.

Fagan, J. (1993). Set and setting revisited: Influences of alcohol and illicit drugs on the social context of violent events. In S. E. Martin (Ed.), *Alcohol and interpersonal violence: Fostering multidisciplinary perspectives* (National Institute on Alcohol and Alcoholism Research Monograph, 24, pp. 161–192). Rockville, MD: U.S. Department of Health and Human Services.

Fisher, S., & Greenberg, R. P. (1997). The curse of the placebo: Fanciful pursuit of a pure biological therapy. In S. Fisher and R. P. Greenberg (Eds.), *From placebo to panacea: Putting psychiatric drugs to the test* (pp. 3–56). New York: Wiley.

Fromme, K., D'Amico, E. J., & Katz, E. C. (1999). Intoxicated sexual risk taking: An expectancy or cognitive impairment explanation? *Journal of Studies on Alcohol* 60, 54–63.

George, W. H., Dermaen, K. H., & Nochajski, T. H. (1989). Expectancy set, self-reported expectancies and predispositional traits: Predicting interest in violence and erotica. *Journal of Studies on Alcohol* 50, 541–551.

George, W. H., & Norris, J. (1991). Alcohol, disinhibiting sexual arousal, and deviant sexual behavior. *Alcohol, Health and Research World* 15, 133–138.

George, W. H., Stoner, S. A., Norris, J., Lopey, P. A., & Lehman, G. L. (2000). Alcohol expectancies and sexuality: A self-fulfilling prophesy analysis of dyadic perceptions and behavior. *Journal of Studies on Alcohol* 61, 168–176.

Goldman, M. S., & Roehrich, L. (1991). Alcohol expectancies and sexuality. *Alcohol, Health and Research World* 15, 126–132.

Graham, K., West, P., & Wells, S. (2000). Evaluating theories of alcohol-related aggression using the observations of young adults in bars. *Addiction* 95, 847–863.

Greeley, J., & Oei, T. (1999). Alcohol and tension reduction. In K. E. Leonard & H. T. Blane (Eds.), *Psychological theories of drinking and alcoholism* (2nd ed.) (pp. 14–53). New York: Guilford.

Gustafson, R. (1986). Alcohol, frustration, and aggression: An experiment using the balanced placebo design. *Psychological Reports* 59, 207–218.

Gustafson, R. (1993). What do experimental paradigms tell us about alcohol-related aggressive responding? *Journal of Studies on Alcohol,* Suppl. 11, 20–29.

Hartocollis, P. (1962). Drunkenness and suggestion: An experiment with intravenous alcohol. *Journal of Studies on Alcohol* 23, 376–389.

Hull, J. G., & Bond, C. F. (1986). Social and behavioral consequences of alcohol consumption and expectancy: A meta-analysis. *Psychological Bulletin* 99, 347–360.

Ito, T. A., Miller, N., & Pollock, V. E. (1996). Alcohol and aggression: A meta-analysis on the moderating effects of inhibitory cues, triggering events, and self-focused attention. *Psychological Bulletin* 120, 60–82.

Kelly, T. H., & Cherek, D. R. (1993). The effects of alcohol on free-operant aggressive behavior. *Journal of Studies on Alcohol,* Suppl. 11, 40–52.

Klein, H. (1991). Cultural determinants of alcohol use in the United States. In D. J. Pittman and H. R. White (Eds.), *Society, culture, and drinking patterns reexamined* (pp. 114–134). New Brunswick, NJ: Rutgers Center on alcohol studies.

Lang, A. R. (1985). The social psychology of drinking and human sexuality. *Journal of Drug Issues* 273–289.

Leigh, B. C., & Morrison, D. M. (1991). Alcohol consumption and sexual risk-taking in adolescents. *Alcohol, Health and Research World* 15, 58–63.

Leigh, B. C., & Stall, R. (1993). Substance use and risky sexual behavior for exposure to HIV: Issues in methodology, interpretation, and prevention. *American Psychologist* 48, 1035–1045.

Mac Donald, T. K., Mac Donald, G., Zanna, M. P., & Fong, G. T. (2000). Alcohol, sexual arousal, and intentions to use condoms in young men: Applying alcohol myopia theory to risky sexual behavior. *Health Psychology* 19, 290–298.

Maletsky, B. M. (1976). The diagnosis of pathological intoxication. *Journal of Studies on Alcohol* 17, 1215–1228.

Martlatt, G. A. (1985). Cognitive factors in the relapse process. In G. A. Martlatt and J. R. Gordon (Eds.), *Relapse prevention: Maintenance strategies in the treatment of addictive behaviors* (pp. 128–200). New York: Guilford.

Mayfield, D. G. (1968). Psychopharmacology of alcohol: II. Affective tolerance in alcohol intoxication. *Journal of Nervous and Mental Disease* 146, 322–327.

McCreary, D. R., & Sadava, S. W. (2000). Stress, alcohol use and alcohol-related problems: The influence of negative and positive affect in two cohorts of young adults. *Journal of Studies on Alcohol* 661, 466–474.

McNamee, H. B., Mello, N. K., & Mendelson, J. H. (1968). Experimental analysis of drinking patterns of alcoholics: Concurrent psychiatric observations. *American Journal of Psychiatry* 124, 1063–1069.

Miller, P. M., Smith, G. T., & Goldman, M. S. (1990). Emergence of alcohol expectancies in childhood: A possible critical period. *Journal of Studies on Alcohol* 51, 343–349.

Murphy, S. T., Monahan, J. L., & Miller, L. C. (1998). Inference under the influence: The impact of alcohol and inhibition conflict on women's sexual decision making. *Personality and Social Psychology Bulletin* 24, 517–528.

Nathan, P. E., Lowenstein, S. M., Solomon, P., & Ross, M. (1970). Behavioral analysis of chronic alcoholism. *Archives of General Psychiatry* 22, 419–430.

Norris, J., George, W. H., Davis, K. C., Martell, J., & Leonesio, R. J. (1999). Alcohol and hypermasculinity as determinants of men's empathic responses to violent pornography. *Journal of Interpersonal Violence* 14, 683–700.

Norris, J., & Kerr, K. L. (1993). Alcohol and violent pornography: Responses to permissive and nonpermissive cues. *Journal of Studies on Alcohol,* Suppl. 11, 118–127.

Parker, R. N., & Rebhun, L. A. (1995). *Alcohol and homicide: A deadly combination of two American traditions.* New York: SUNY Press.

Pernanan, K. (1993). Alcohol-related violence: Conceptual models and methodological issues. In Susan E. Martin (Ed.), *Alcohol and interpersonal violence: Fostering multidisciplinary perspectives.* National Institute on Alcohol and Alcoholism Research Monograph 24 (pp. 37–69). Rockville, MD: U.S. Department of Health and Human Services.

Phil, R. O., Segal, Z., & Yankofsky, L. (1980). The effect of alcohol and placebo on affective reactions of social drinkers to procedure designed to induce depressive affect, anxiety, and hostility. *Journal of Clinical Psychology* 36, 337–342.

Robbins, B. J., & Brotherton, P. L. (1980). Mood changes with alcohol intoxication. *British Journal of Social and Clinial Psychology* 19, 149–155.

Roberts, L. J., Roberts, C. F., & Leonard, K. E. (1998). Alcohol, drugs, and interpersonal violence. In V. B. Van Hasselt & M. Hersen (Eds.), *Handbook of psychological approaches with violent offenders: Contemporary strategies and issues* (pp. 493–519). New York: Kluwer Academic/Plenum.

San Jose, B., Van Oers, H. A., Van De Mheen, H. D., Gararetsen, H. F., & Mackenbach, J. P. (2000). Stressors and alcohol consumption. *Alcohol & Alcoholism* 35, 307–312.

Sayette, M. A., Smith, D. W., Breiner, M. J., and Wilson, G. T. (1992). The effect of alcohol on emotional response to a social stressor. *Journal of Studies on Alcohol* 53, 541–545.

Shapiro, A. K., & Shapiro, E. (1997). *The powerful placebo: From ancient priest to modern physician.* Baltimore: Johns Hopkins University Press.

Smith, R. C., Parker, E. S., & Noble, E. P. (1975). Alcohol and affect in dyadic social interaction. *Psychosomatic Medicine* 37, 25–40.

Steele, C. M., & Josephs, R. A. (1990). Alcohol myopia: its prized and dangerous effects. *American Psychologist* 45, 921–933.

Tamerin, J. S., & Mendelson, J. H. (1969). The psychodynamics of chronic inebriation: Observations of alcoholics during the process of drinking in an experimental group setting. *American Journal of Psychiatry* 125, 886–899.

Taylor, S. P. (1993). Experimental investigation of alcohol-induced aggression in humans. *Alcohol, Health and Research World* 17, 108–112.

Taylor, S. P., & Chermack, S. T. (1993). Alcohol, drugs and human physical aggression. *Journal of Studies on Alcohol* Suppl. 11, 78–88.

Warren, G. H., & Raynes, A. E. (1972). Mood changes during three conditions of alcohol intake. *Journal of Studies on Alcohol* 33, 979–989.

Wilson, G. T. (1981). The effects of alcohol on human sexual behavior. In N. K. Mello (Ed.), *Advances in substance abuse: Behavioral and biological research,* Vol. 2 (pp. 1–40). Greenwich, CT: JAI Press.

Wilson, G. T., & Lawson, D. M. (1976). Expectancies, alcohol, and sexual arousal in male social drinkers. *Journal of Abnormal Psychology* 85, 587–594.

CHAPTER NINE

ALCOHOL, VIOLENT CRIME, CRIMINAL JUSTICE, AND SUBSTANCE ABUSE TREATMENT

Beginning with Wolfgang's classic study on homicide in 1958, many researchers have documented the relationship between alcohol consumption and violent crime. We shall summarize the findings of several studies that document this association. As noted in previous chapters, association is not proof of a causal link between two factors. However, the experimental and observational data from the preceding chapter regarding the influence of alcohol intoxication on aggressive behavior lends support for such a link.

Since the criminal justice system has been more focused on substance abuse than on alcohol abuse, we shall discuss substance abuse as well as alcoholism treatment in this chapter. An important premise of criminal justice substance abuse treatment is that coercion can be used as an effective motivation. We shall review research on its effectiveness. We shall then outline criminal justice approaches to substance abuse treatment. In this chapter, we shall consider:

1. The alcohol–violent crime association
2. The rates of alcohol and substance abuse in criminal justice populations
3. Criminal justice substance abuse treatment
4. The effectiveness of coercion for substance abuse and alcoholism treatment
5. Prison substance abuse treatment
6. Treatment alternatives to prison

METHODOLOGY

For the most part, research discussed in this chapter relies on surveys and government statistics. These data are analyzed using methods similar to those used by sociologists. (See Chapter 7, section on methodology, for a description of these methods.)

This chapter includes a summary of outcome research on criminal justice substance abuse treatment. In these outcome studies, substance-abusing offenders who complete substance abuse programs are compared with a no-treatment group and noncompleters. Such studies have two problems: subjects are not selected randomly for the experimental and control groups, and a large percentage of subjects drop out of treatment. Comparisons between treatment completers, treatment dropouts, and control group subjects suffer from a serious confound: some characteristics of the treatment completers are probably different from those of the other two groups. That is, those who complete substance abuse treatment probably are a special group of substance-abusing offenders that do not represent the average offender. Thus, when those who complete treatment have better outcomes, we cannot say whether it is the treatment or the special characteristics of the treatment completers that account for the better outcomes. For these reasons and others, much of this research lacks methodological rigor (Pearson & Lipton, 1999).

THE ASSOCIATION BETWEEN ALCOHOL CONSUMPTION AND VIOLENT CRIME

Through the use of police records and interviews with victims, perpetrators, and incarcerated individuals, a large body of data consistently links consumption of alcohol with violent crime (murder [Pernanan, 1991; Parker and Rebhun, 1995], rape [Collins and Messerschmidt, 1993], assault [Pernanan, 1991], and domestic violence [Fagan, 1993; Leonard, 1993; Kantor, 1993]). Although there is variation in reported studies, in about 50 percent of recorded violent crimes, the perpetrator has been drinking; alcohol is typically implicated in the victim or perpetrator 60 percent of the time (Roberts et al., 1998). Table 9.1 shows research findings of the percentages of offenders drinking for specific crimes.

Particularly disturbing in this regard is the finding that apparently minor conflicts between intoxicated participants can often lead to severe crimes, including murder (Fagan, 1993; Pernanan, 1991, 1993a). Fagan (1993) suggests that alcohol may fuel these minor conflicts, which may increase the chance of physical violence. Roizen (1993) and Pernanan (1991) have noted that alcohol use is twice as likely in violent incidents with strangers as with acquaintances. It has been found that group violence is more common among men who are intoxicated than when they are abstinent (Pernanan, 1991).

Alcohol intoxication is implicated in violent crime much more often than illicit drug use. For example, a survey of incarcerated offenders found that alcohol was two to four times more likely to be involved in interpersonally violent offenses (homicide, assault, or rape) than illicit drugs (Roberts et al., 1998).

ALCOHOL AND DEGREE OF VIOLENCE

Research has found that heavy alcohol intake is associated with more intense and damaging violence (Pernanan, 1993b) and more frequent injury (Cherpital, 1993). For example, in a survey conducted by Johnson et al. (1978, cited in Roizen, 1993), substantial force was used in rape 37 percent of the time when both offender and victim had been drinking compared to 18 percent when neither had been drinking. In a survey of parolees, it was found that either partner's having an alcohol problem increased the level of violence in domestic violence incidents (Miller et al., 1990).

TABLE 9.1   Percentage of Time at Least One Participant Was Intoxicated at Time of Violent Crime

TYPE OF VIOLENCE	INDIVIDUAL'S DRINKING ALCOHOL (%)	REFERENCES
Rape	50	Shupe, 1954
	53	McCaldon, 1967
	35	Rada, 1975
	57	Rada et al., 1978
	72	Johnson et al., 1978
	65	Barnard et al., 1979
Incest	49	Virkkunen, 1974
	50	Browning & Boatman, 1977
Family violence	40	Gayford, 1979
	15–20	Eberle, 1982
	83	Livingston, 1986
Murder and homicide	36	Wilentz & Brady, 1961
	10	Scott, 1968
	57	Grunberg et al., 1978
	56–83	Bloom, 1980
	56	Lindqvist, 1986
	61	Tinkelberg & Ochberg, 1981
	33	Guze et al., 1968
	57	Mayfield, 1976

Source: Adapted from Miczek et al., 1993.

Research suggests that drinking violent offenders have drunk substantial amounts of alcohol preceding the crime (Pernanan, 1993b). Virkkunen (1974) examined blood alcohol concentrations BACs of murder victims, which averaged 0.241 percent when both participants had been drinking. He argues that it is reasonable to conclude that the perpetrator had a similar level. Shupe (1954) found that 67 percent of those arrested for murder in Columbus, Ohio, from 1951 to 1953 had BACs of 0.10 percent or higher. A recent survey found that the estimated BACs of convicted murderers who were intoxicated at the time of the crime was 0.30 percent (Greenfield, 1998). Table 9.2 indicates the estimated BACs of convicted offenders at the time of offense for several types of crimes.

COMPARISON OF REPORTED AND NONREPORTED VIOLENT ACTS

To determine if alcohol is implicated in less severe violence that is not reported to the police, Pernanan (1991) interviewed a large number of individuals in a small Ontario community about violence. He found that either the victim or the aggressor had been drinking 54 percent of the time. The assailant had been drinking 51 percent of the time. Drinking was implicated in violence between strangers more often than between participants who knew

TABLE 9.2   **Estimated BACs of Offenders Who Were Drinking at the Time of the Offense**

TYPE OF OFFENSE	PROBATIONERS	LOCAL JAIL INMATES	STATE PRISONERS
All offenders	0.16	0.19	0.27
Violent	0.18	0.20	0.28
Homicide	0.22	0.26	0.28
Sexual assault	0.13	0.25	0.28
Robbery	0.32	0.22	0.28
Assault	0.18	0.18	0.30
Property	0.24	0.22	0.30
Burglary	0.26	0.24	0.31
Larceny	0.23	0.23	0.28
Motor vehicle theft	0.34	0.19	0.29
Drugs	0.14	0.15	0.19
Public-order	0.14	0.19	0.23

Source: Adapted from Greenfield, 1998.

each other. By comparing the results of his findings with the police reports of violence in this community, he found that alcohol was implicated in the violent aggressive acts in unreported cases as much as in the reported ones.

Similarly, in a more recent survey of Ontario residents, Wells et al. (2000) found that at least one participant was drinking in 67.9 percent of physical aggression incidents. For those reporting physical aggression, the mean highest number of drinks imbibed per occasion was 8.3, compared to 4.7 for those who did not report any aggression. The researchers conclude that their results suggest alcohol intoxication plays a role in escalation from verbal to physical aggression.

Natural Experiments

Because of alcohol worker strikes, raising or lowering the drinking age, the change in number of alcohol-dispensing outlets, and raising or lowering the excise tax on alcohol, there have been opportunities to examine the effect of availability of alcohol on reported violent crime. Most of these studies indicate that reduced availability of alcohol has lowered the amount of reported violent crime (Cook & Moore, 1993a, b; Fagan, 1993; Lipsey et al., 1997; Parker & Rebhun, 1995). Room (1983) and Edwards (1994) have summarized the considerable research conducted in Scandinavia that shows a positive relationship between availability of alcohol and crime rates.

Comparison of Laboratory Studies on Alcohol and Aggression and Correlational Studies of Alcohol and Violence

As discussed in the previous chapter, the evidence suggests that aggression is facilitated by alcohol in experimental situations and in controlled observational settings. In this chapter we have reviewed research which shows that violence is often associated with alcohol intoxication and that reductions in alcohol availability have lowered crime rates. Both experimental aggression research and violence association studies show that intoxicated individuals are more susceptible to social pressure to be aggressive or violent. Both types of studies show that alcohol intoxication facilitates aggression and violence more than use of other drugs. One important difference between the experimental aggression studies and violence alcohol research is that most experimental studies on aggression and alcohol administer alcohol to subjects to achieve BACs of 0.10% or less, whereas the BACs of reported offenders and victims of violence in reported criminal acts is significantly higher. Still, the consistency of findings across a wide range of different measures of aggression and violence suggests that alcohol is an important contributor to violent behavior.

Drinking Patterns and Violence

Thus far, the findings reviewed have been about the acute effects of intoxication on aggressive behavior. Withdrawal effects as well as intoxication have been associated with increased violence (Badawy, 1986). Additionally, studies show that a pattern of heavy binge drinking is associated with increased risk of violent behavior (Roizen, 1993; Shepherd, 1994). For example, Leonard (1993) reports that heavy drinking patterns in husbands are associated with high rates of marital violence.

Alcohol Use Disorders, Psychiatric Illness, and Violence

Swanson (1993), drawing on the Epidemiological Catchment Area (ECA) data (see Chapter 5 for description of this study), estimates that the general-population 1-year prevalence of violence for those with no alcohol abuse or major mental disorder is 2.28 percent. Those suffering major mental disorders have a violence prevalence rate of 6.98 percent; those with alcohol abuse or dependence and no major mental disorder, 23.62 percent; those with both alcohol and major mental disorder, 23.91 percent.

Figure 9.1 illustrates these findings graphically. While those with a major mental disorder commit a violent act about three times more often than the general population, those with alcohol disorders do so at about ten times the rate of the general population.

Drawing on a large northern Finland community sample of men followed from birth to age 26, Rasanen et al. (1998) found that men with both schizophrenia and alcoholism were 25.2 times more likely to commit a violent act than the average Finnish man. Thirty-six percent of the alcoholic schizophrenics had committed violent crimes, compared to 7.5 percent who were nonalcoholic schizophrenics. That is, alcohol-abusing schizophrenics were five times more likely to commit violent crime than nonalcoholic schizophrenics.

THE CRIMINAL JUSTICE SYSTEM AND ALCOHOL AND SUBSTANCE ABUSE

Rates of Alcohol and/or Substance Abuse Problems in Those with Contact with the Criminal Justice System

The 1997 Annual Report on Adult and Juvenile Arrestees found a range of 51 to 80 percent adults and a range of 41 to 65 percent of juveniles tested positive for illicit drugs in a random

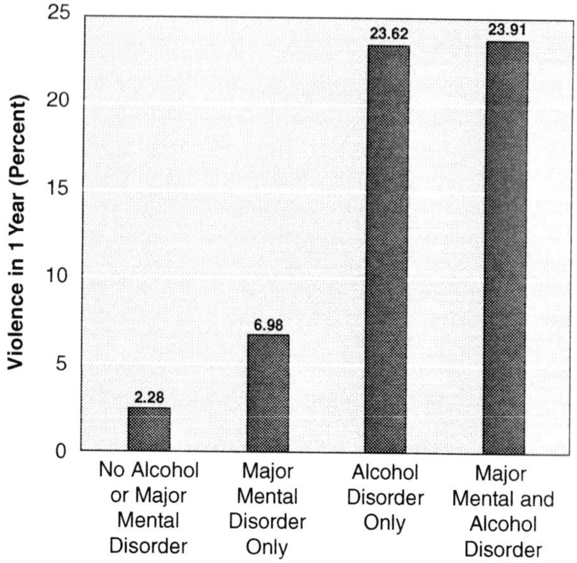

FIGURE 9.1   Estimated One-Year Prevalence of Violence for Those with Alcohol Disorders and/or Major Mental Disorder among Epidemiologic Catchment Area Respondents

Source: Adapted from Swanson, 1993.

sample of those arrested in cities across the country (National Institute of Justice, 1998). A large survey of convicted offenders found that 36 percent were drinking at the time of the offense (Greenfield, 1998, p. 20). In their analysis, CASA (National Center on Addiction and Substance Abuse at Columbia University, 1997) found that 50 percent of state parole and probation violators were using drugs and or alcohol when they committed a new offense, and that alcohol- and drug-abusing offenders were more likely to be reincarcerated than other offenders. More than a third of probationers reported that they had consumed the equivalent of a fifth of liquor in a day (Greenfield, 1998).

Hiller et al. (1999) and CASA (National Center on Addiction and Substance Abuse at Columbia University, 1997) estimate that as many as 80 percent of those in state and federal prisons and local jails might have problems with alcohol or illicit drugs. Regier et al. (1990) estimate that 72 percent of prisoners have a lifetime prevalence of substance abuse and 56.2 percent have alcohol abuse, based on the ECA survey of prisoners. In a detailed study of 69,108 prisoners in New York State in 1997, it was found that 65 percent had substance abuse or alcoholism (New York State Department of Correctional Services, 1997) and almost 50 percent had alcohol problems (New York State Department of Correctional Services, 1996).

Only a small percentage of substance-abusing incarcerated felons receive treatment. A survey of inmates in local jails in 1998 found that only 10 percent of the jailed population had participated in any substance abuse treatment (Wilson, 2000). In New York State, it is estimated that only 13 percent of incarcerated felons receive any substance abuse treatment (New York State Department of Correctional Services, 1997). On the other hand, a larger percentage of offenders reported receiving some type of alcoholism treatment at some time in their lives (Greenfield, 1998). A recent survey (Greenfield, 1998) found that 62 percent of probationers who were drinking at the time of the offense had had some form of alcohol treatment, 65 percent of jailed inmates who were daily drinkers had had some alcohol treatment, and half of state prisoners who were daily drinkers had received some alcohol treatment. These statistics may exaggerate the extent of treatment that offenders received, for two reasons. First, self-help accounted for a significant percentage of the treatment (Greenfield, 1998). Second, data were not collected on treatment duration, which may have been quite minimal. It would be worthwhile to get more detailed information about these prior treatments.

Not suprisingly, a large percentage of clients in substance abuse treatment programs are involved with the criminal justice system. For example, in New York State, over 40 percent of clients in community substance abuse treatment are involved with the criminal justice system (Office of Alcoholism and Substance Abuse Services, 1999).

Co-Morbidity of Substance Use Disorders and Psychiatric Illness in Criminal Justice Populations

Collins (1993) notes that there are high rates of **co-morbidity** in prison populations; that is, there is a significant population of incarcerated individuals with both psychiatric illness and substance abuse. Findings from the ECA survey indicate a prevalence rate of 55.7 percent of mental disorders in prisoners, of whom 81 percent had a co-morbid addictive disorder (Regier et al., 1990). Rates of addictive disorder were especially high for prisoners with antisocial personality disorder (ASPD) (89.9 percent), schizophrenia (92.3 percent), bipolar disorder (89.2 percent), and **dysthymia** (a depressive illness) (93.5 percent).

Co-Morbidity and Rearrest Rates.   Hiller et al. (1996) found that those with both dysthymia and substance abuse were four times more likely to be rearrested than other substance-abusing offenders in a substance-abuse therapeutic community (TC) alternative to incarceration. Lang and Belenko (2000) found that offenders with a psychiatric history were four times more likely to drop out of a substance abuse residential TC alternative to prison than offenders with only substance abuse. Abram et al. (1993), in a study of released prisoners, found that those with ASPD and alcohol use disorders had a higher rearrest rate for violent crime than those with alcohol use disorders or ASPD. Rasanen et al. (1998) found that among the Finnish schizophrenics who had committed crimes, only the alcoholic schizophrenic offenders were recidivists (repeat offenders).

Treatment of Alcoholism and Substance Abuse for Those Involved with the Criminal Justice System

Coercion.   Coercion is a central motivational element in most criminal justice substance abuse treatment; substance-abusing offenders are given choices between treatment or an alternative consequence related to the offense committed, such as incarceration, loss of driver's license, or loss of child custody. Miller and Flaherty (2000) reviewed the research on outcomes of coerced treatment in comparison to voluntary treatment. They found that coerced patients did as well as noncoerced patients or better in retention in treatment, treatment completion, and outcome. Noteworthy is their finding that criminal justice clients did as well or better than other clients in substance abuse programs. In California, Anglin (1988) made use of a natural experiment in which a civil addict program was not adopted uniformly by the courts at its inception. As a consequence, about half of the substance-abusing offenders who were supposed to receive compulsory treatment did not. He compared this group with those who were forced to participate in treatment and found that substance-abusing offenders who were forced to attend treatment did better than the comparison group in reduced drug use and criminal activity. Hubbard et al. (1989), in a very large national study of drug treatment outcome, reported that criminal justice referrals stayed significantly longer in residential and outpatient drug-free programs than referrals from other sources. Criminal activity for those with criminal justice status decreased substantially while they were in treatment. Criminal justice referrals used less drug of choice in the year after treatment than referrals from other sources.

Coercion has also proved to be a successful motivation for alcoholics. For example, Watson et al. (1988) followed coerced and voluntarily treated alcoholics for 18 months and found no differences in outcome for these two groups. These research findings support the efficacy of coercion in criminal substance abuse treatment.

Therapeutic Community.   The therapeutic community (TC) is the most common type of substance abuse treatment utilized by the criminal justice system (Nielsen, 1996). It has a long history of treating such individuals successfully (Wexler, 1995; Wexler & Williams, 1986). The TC view of addiction is that it is a symptom of a disorder of the whole person. The goal of treatment is a global change in lifestyle, including abstinence from alcohol and drugs, elimination of antisocial behavior, employment, and internalization of prosocial values (Nielsen & Scarpitti, 1997). The objectives of treatment are to change negative patterns of behavior, thinking, and feeling that contribute to drug use. The basic agent of change is the community of peers, which confronts and supports members to change in desired ways. TC treatment elements include encounter groups, peer counseling groups, seminars (psychoeducation), rewards and punishments, assigned job functions, and ex-addict and ex-felon staff role models (Wexler, 1986; Nielsen & Scarpitti, 1997). Twelve Step recovery, relapse prevention, and other treatment elements may also be included (Wexler, 1986).

Prison Treatment.   Before describing in-prison substance abuse treatment and its outcome, it is important to recognize that there are many impediments to its successful implementation. Wexler (1986) cites prisoner characteristics that make intervention difficult. He describes them as resentful, viewing efforts to help with mistrust, suspicion, and pervasive cynicism, which results in high resistance to treatment. Additionally, there are differences in goals and philosophies and policies and procedures between general prison personnel and treatment staff, which must be resolved. Treatment programs must take such factors into account. Evaluations of such programs must also consider these factors in assessing the degree of improvement that can be realistically expected. The primary intensive substance abuse treatment in prisons has become the in-prison TC (Hiller et al., 1999; Wexler, 1986, 1999). These programs are based on the TC model described above. Clients are housed separately from general prison population for the 6- to 12-month treatment duration. Wexler has described the Stay 'N Out TC in New York City (1986) and reported the results of an outcome study on this prison TC (Wexler et al., 1992). He compared the outcomes of the TC with others in prison treatments and a no-treatment control group of substance abusers in prison. The measure of outcome was the percentage in each group arrested while on parole of 35 to 41 months. The TC participants had the lowest arrest rate, 26.9 percent. Participants in other substance abuse treatments had 34.6 percent and 39.8 percent arrest rates. Those who had no treatment had the highest rate of arrest, 40.9 percent. Further analysis indicated that the optimal duration of TC treatment was 12 months.

Wexler (1986) suggests that the failure to provide a good transition from prison treatment to release has been the most glaring problem in prison substance abuse treatment. The prison TC is a very different environment from the neighborhoods to which the released prisoners will return. Negative forces that influence drug use and criminal activity will be present. Optimally, treatment should be available to ease and guide the released prisoners back into a productive reengagement with their community. Although many state corrections departments have work release programs that are intended to help soon-to-be released prisoners make the transition back into the community, these programs are not geared to neutralize the special negative influences that may cause substance abusers to relapse (Inciardi et al., 1997). In Delaware, a special work release TC has been created to help this transition. Nielsen et al. (1996) and Nielsen and Scarpitti (1997) describe this TC, known as the Crest program. Crest is a 6-month residential program in which residents are helped to face real-life issues in adjusting to "straight life." Three studies (Inciardi et al., 1997; Martin et al., 1995, 1999) indicate that this TC is more effective than the in-prison TC for outcomes measured at 6 and 18 months and at 3 years. Outcomes were enhanced when clients completed an outpatient program after discharge from the postprison TC.

Subsequently, postprison programs have been opened in California and Texas, with good results. Wexler and colleagues (1998, cited in Hiller et al., 1999; 1999) report improved outcomes at 3 years postdischarge in California's Amity program when prisoners completed both in-prison TC and a community-based TC for transitional aftercare. However, only a small percentage of the Amity prison TC completers in the study elected to enter any treatment after discharge from prison (DeLeon et al., 2000). Hiller et al. (1999) investigated the outcome of the 9-month New Vision in-prison TC in Texas and a 3-month postprison TC. Those who completed both elements were 50 percent less likely to be rearrested in 13–23 months postdischarge. Improvements were maintained by treatment completers at a follow-up of 3 years (Knight et al., 1999). Consistent with the studies reported above, results showed little benefit for completing in-prison TC without completing the postprison TC. Hiller et al. (1999) noted a significant problem was that despite being mandated, 123 of 293 offenders dropped out of the postprison TC. Thus, substance abuse treatment after release from prison shows the most promising results, but procedures must be developed to increase participation and retention rates in these programs.

Pearson and Lipton (1999) conducted a meta-analytic review of corrections-based substance abuse treatment. They concluded that half of the studies were poor-quality research, almost half were of fair quality, and only one was of good quality. Their statistical analysis showed that the TC programs were effective in reducing recidivism. In their analysis, however, Pearson and Lipton (1999) did not distinguish between in-prison TCs and aftercare TCs. They found no evidence that other types of prison substance abuse treatment reduced recidivism, including "boot camp" programs or group counseling programs focused on substance abuse.

Alternatives to Incarceration.   As discussed above, coercion has proved to be an effective motivation for engaging criminal justice substance abusers in treatment. Substance abuse treatment can be mandated as a condition of parole or probation. Those failing to attend or complete treatment can be incarcerated. Drug courts and Treatment Alternatives to Street Crime (TASC) have formal procedures for implementing coerced treatment.

Drug Courts.   Drug courts integrate substance abuse treatment with the justice system process, in which prosecution and defense balance public safety concerns with rehabilitation by offering treatment alternatives to incarceration for appropriate substance-abusing arrestees. These courts began in 1989 in Dade County (Miami), Florida. Elements of these programs include:

1. Early identification and prompt placement of offenders. They are often screened in jail.
2. Access to a continuum of treatment.
3. Frequent drug and alcohol testing.
4. Intensive supervision of the offender with regard to compliance with treatment, abstinence from drugs and alcohol, and criminal activity.
5. Prompt sanction for failure to comply to court provisions (Gebelein, 2000).

Results show that offenders participating in drug courts have 90 percent negative drug screens, retention rate in treatment of over 70 percent, and 5 to 28 percent reductions in crime (Office of Justice Programs, 1998). A study of Delaware Drug Court participants found that drug court clients stayed in treatment longer and completed treatment more often than other clients (Gebelein, 2000). These outcomes appear to be substantially better than stand-alone criminal sanctions, but because of a lack of careful research design, the results cannot be considered definitive. There are now 300 drug courts in 48 states (Office of Justice Programs, 1998).

Treatment Alternatives to Street Crime (TASC).   TASC programs became possible after a U.S. Supreme Court ruling in 1962 that permitted the states to enact laws that could compel addicts into treatment (Weinman, 1992). TASC was created in 1972, modeled after a court program in Washington, D.C. (Leukefeld & Tims, 1990). TASC serves to connect the parole and treatment systems so that treatment needs are met while helping assure community safety. Weinman (1992) summarizes the major functions of these programs:

1. Early identification of drug-involved parolees. Clients can be screened in jail, prior to court appearance or disposition of the case.
2. Assessments match substance abuse treatment with needs of clients.
3. Substantial monitoring of released offenders reinforces compliance with treatment.
4. Unbroken contact with offenders from prerelease through end of parole.

One indicator of the usefulness of these programs is the finding that two-thirds of TASC participants have not had previous drug abuse treatment (Weinman, 1992). Salmon and Salmon (1983) conducted a comparison of outcome for TASC-referred substance abusers to voluntary admissions to New Jersey drug abuse programs. TASC clients in drug-free treatment had lower rates of drug use and arrest than the voluntary clients in the same treatment programs. There were 178 TASC programs in 32 states in 1991.

Treatment Alternatives for Domestic Violence Facilitated by Alcohol Consumption.   Marital violence is the single greatest cause of injury to women, ranking higher than auto accidents, muggings, and rapes combined (Stark & Flitcrat, 1988, cited in Roberts et al., 1998). A large percentage of domestic violence (DV) is committed by men who have been drinking. Surveys conducted by the Office of Justice Programs (Greenfield, 1998, p. v) indicate that three-fourths of the offenders convicted of spousal abuse were drinking at the time of the offense. Roberts (1988) found that 60 percent of battered women who filed charges against their spouse in Marion County (Indianapolis) Indiana, indicated that their spouse was under the influence of alcohol. Recent efforts by DV advocacy groups have highlighted this hidden crime and made the criminal justice system more responsive to the problem. Traditional criminal justice approaches to DV have been legal sanctions including incarceration. Batterer programs and alcoholism treatment are possible alternatives or adjuncts to incarceration.

BATTERER PROGRAMS.   Recently, batterer programs have been developed in lieu of incarceration. These programs typically screen for substance abuse problems as a part of their intervention and either include substance abuse treatment or refer substance-abusing clients for treatment. There is some preliminary evidence that batterer programs are of some help in reducing recidivism (Babcock & Steiner, 1999; Gondolf, 1998). Babcock and Steiner (1999) conducted a study that measured outcomes of Seattle, Washington, court-mandated DV treatment combined with substance abuse treatment when it was detected. Forty-three percent of the offenders mandated to complete substance abuse treatment did so. Only 10 percent of treatment completers committed DV in the 2-year follow-up period, versus 35.6 percent of noncompleters, a significant difference. However, controlling for criminal records and sessions in DV programs, differences between completers and noncompleters were no longer significant. Babcock and Steiner (1999) note that one problem with the Seattle program is that few men suffered any legal consequence for noncompliance with the court mandate.

ALCOHOLISM TREATMENT AND DOMESTIC VIOLENCE.   Three studies have measured the effect of alcoholism treatment on reducing domestic violence. O'Farrell and Murphy (1995) and O'Farrell et al. (1999) researched the effectiveness of behavioral marital therapy for alcoholism. The treatment, averaging twenty-one sessions, consisted of couples sessions and group sessions. The therapy was "designed to teach couples communication behaviors that were alternatives to the hostile and negative interaction patterns that may escalate to violence" (O'Farrell & Murphy, 1995, p. 261). In the study, 44 percent of the participants were in remission from alcohol problems at the end of the first year, and half were in remission after the second year. The percentage of couples reporting violence decreased from 61.3 percent before treatment to 22.7 percent in the first year after treatment and to 18.7 percent in the second year. In the year before treatment, the average number of violent husband-to-wife incidents was 6.6, and wife-to-husband incidents was 10.

In the year after treatment the number of violent incidents decreased significantly, to 1.2 for husband-to-wife and 3.3 for wife-to-husband violence. Unremitted alcoholics continued to have elevated rates of DV, while remitted alcoholics had rates of domestic violence incidents not significantly different from a matched control group. Table 9.3 shows the rates of DV for treated couples compared to the control group.

Maiden (1997) examined the effect of several types of conventional alcoholism treatment on DV by interviewing a sample of treated alcoholics who had domestic partners. Ninety-four percent of the sample indicated they had engaged in some form of verbal or physical domestic violence prior to treatment. Seventy-one percent reported moderate to severe physical violence before treatment, and 56 percent reported at least one instance of severe physical violence before treatment. Over 50 percent said they could not recall a single instance when they had responded to marital conflict in a constructive manner. After treatment, only 1.6 percent of the sample reported severe physical violence; moderate aggression decreased to 20 percent. Successfully treated alcoholics had an improved capacity to respond adaptively to potential disagreements and engaged in less verbal abuse. Inpatient treatment and greater duration of treatment had a greater impact on reducing DV. Although there are a number of methodological shortcomings in this study, the results are encouraging.

TABLE 9.3   Husband-to-Wife Violence: Comparisons of the Alcoholic Sample (n = 88 couples) with Demographically Similar Nonalcoholic Participants (n = 88 men and women) from the National Family Violence Re-Survey (Gelles & Straus, 1985)

VIOLENCE REPORT	NATIONAL SURVEY PARTICIPANTS	ALCOHOLICS BEFORE TREATMENT	p DIFFERENCE	ALCOHOLICS AFTER TREATMENT	p DIFFERENCE
Husband self-report of violence					
Any violence	6.8%	43.2%	0.001	18.2%	0.031
Any severe violence	0%	13.6%	0.001	2.3%	.50 (ns)
Mean of violent behaviors	0.1	3.3	0.001	0.7	0.044
Wife report of husband's violence					
Any violence	12.5%	52.3%	0.001	20.5%	0.17 (ns)
Any severe violence	3.4%	28.4%	0.001	6.8%	0.51 (ns)
Mean of violent behaviors	0.5	4.9	0.001	0.8	.09 (ns)

p = probability. ns = nonsignificant. Note: Total frequency of violent behaviors based on Conflict Tactics Scale items weighted by mean category frequency (Straus, 1990). Details of calculating the statistics and the control group participants are in O'Farrell and Murphy (1995).

Source: Adapted from O'Farrell, T. J., and Murphy, C. M. (1995). Marital violence before and after alcoholism treatment. *Journal of Consulting and Clinical Psychology* 63, 256–262. Copyright © 1995 by the American Psychological Association. Adapted with permission.

CHILD ABUSE FACILITATED BY ALCOHOLISM. Reviews of the research by Widom and Hiller-Strurmhofel (2001) and Miller et al. (1997) have failed to find a strong relationship between parental alcohol abuse and child abuse. There is evidence, however, that alcohol disorders impair good parenting practices. Miller et al. (1997) reviewed a number of studies that show alcoholic parents are more likely to use harsh punishment. Miller et al. (1999) subsequently conducted a study of alcohol-abusing mothers and found that they had significantly higher hostility and punitiveness scores than average mothers. A history of alcohol abuse problems strongly and consistently predicted mothers' verbal aggression toward their children. Current alcohol problems predicted mothers' moderate physical violence toward their children. Even if mothers had a low level of hostility, the presence of current alcohol problems significantly increased levels of mothers' punitiveness. Miller et al. (1999) suggest that alcohol problems interfere with women's abilities to develop effective disciplinary strategies for their children. They recommend that alcoholic mothers in treatment receive special parenting training that includes an understanding of what constitutes excessive levels of punishment and the consequences. There is no accepted model of intervention for alcohol abusers who have committed child abuse, nor research on whether such intervention would be effective.

RECOMMENDATIONS

Treatment Intervention for the Violence–Alcohol Connection

The extensive research linking alcohol to aggression and violence suggests that it would be important to provide education to all alcoholic patients regarding alcohol's association to violence. As a modest start, information should be provided to patients that alcohol facilitates aggression. Discussion of the experimental and controlled observational findings would stimulate interest in the topic.

Typically, there are no special treatment interventions for violent patients in alcoholism treatment (Collins et al., 1997). For example, Gallant (1987), in an eight-page outline of treatment for alcoholics, does not mention violence issues. I am not aware of any protocols for such treatment considerations. Protocols should include screening for violent behavior and co-morbid psychiatric illness with provisions for treatment of both problems when detected. Such protocols need to be developed and tested.

Treatment for the Substance-Abusing
Criminal Justice Offender

Recent outcome research indicates that postprison TC substance abuse treatment provides the best results in reducing crime recidivism. These programs need to be expanded. A significant problem for such programs is the failure of substance-abusing offenders released from prison to attend and complete these programs. It is not clear whether these programs are failing to address certain needs of the clients or that sanctions must be utilized to increase attendance and completion rates. Perhaps attention to co-morbid psychiatric disorders would be helpful, because there are high rates of co-morbid disorders among offenders. Close monitoring of clients with prompt sanctions and rewards may be needed to improve compliance. TASC or drug courts could perform this function. Outpatient aftercare programs should be developed and expanded to provide special interventions for graduates of postprison TCs to help these individuals make a transition from a protected residence to their communities where old temptations abound.

Only nonviolent offenders are eligible for substance abuse treatment in most criminal justice programs. It is understandable that safety issues figure prominently in this decision. Because other treatment contexts are less equipped and even less likely to treat these individuals, it is unlikely that violence-prone alcoholics will receive any treatment. Although safety issues must be taken into account, special programs for violent alcohol-abusing offenders should be developed unless we are content to keep these individuals incarcerated for life.

Another concern is that the focus in criminal justice programs is on drug abuse rather than alcohol abuse. Criminal justice is understandably focused on illicit substances. However, the link between violent crime and alcohol intoxication needs to be heeded. Offenders need to understand that alcohol intoxication is very highly associated with violent crime. Many offenders have either an alcohol problem or a combined alcohol and drug problem. The alcohol part of the equation needs to be addressed. A significant percentage of offenders have substance abuse and a serious mental illness such as schizophrenia. Such individuals typically do not benefit from standard addiction treatment. Programs need to be developed for criminal justice offenders who have combined substance abuse and mental disorders. The next chapter explores these co-morbid disorders and their treatment.

Although TCs show good results in treating criminal justice offenders, and include significant interventions to deal with the special aspects of criminal justice substance abusers, other types of community programs are not geared for these clients. There is a need to develop special provisions for those criminal justice alcohol abusers referred to community treatment programs. Traditional alcohol abuse treatment may not be the most helpful model. We may need to broaden the view of what treatment programs focus on, to go beyond alcohol and substance abuse abstinence. This means, for example, consideration of criminal thinking, criminal activity, violence, and domestic violence issues. These programs should interface with the drug courts and TASC, which can provide close monitoring of client behavior, including criminal behavior during treatment, and facilitate prompt sanctions provided by the courts.

Domestic Violence.   Because of the high percentage of alcohol involvement in family violence, screening should be routine for alcohol problems in settings for DV intervention (Downs et al., 1996). Successful treatment of alcohol problems should be considered an important aspect of DV intervention.

Although alcoholic batterers are often referred for alcoholism treatment (Babcock & Steiner, 1999), there are no protocols for treating battering alcoholic men. At the very least, such men should be provided with an understanding of alcohol's facilitating role in aggression.

Alcohol treatment should include screening for domestic violence and appropriate referral, in light of the high incidence of DV incidents for treated alcoholic men (Maiden, 1997; O'Farrell et al., 1999) and women (Miller et al., 1989).

O'Farrell and Murphy (1995) found that half of the wives of alcoholics had committed some violent behaviors on their husbands. Although further studies need to be conducted to confirm this finding, it appears that a substantial percentage of wives of alcoholics may provoke, instigate, or contribute to DV incidents. Not to blame the victim, or mitigate responsibility for the offender, it could be helpful to include this topic as a part of couples counseling. It is not clear whether battered wives programs take into account the possible contributions of the assaulted spouse to the incidents or whether she is viewed exclusively as a victim. A problem with mandated treatment for DV offenders is that many drop out of treatment and suffer no consequence, as was the case in the Seattle study (Babcock & Steiner, 1999). An agency such as TASC or the drug courts could monitor compliance with treatment, criminal behavior, and drug and alcohol consumption and recommend prompt sanctions when necessary.

Additionally, there should be an effort to reconcile treatment and intervention goals for substance abuse programs and domestic violence programs. The DV program views safety of the victimized spouse as the most important goal, whereas the alcoholism program views the alcoholic's abstinence from alcohol as the most important goal. The ATTC curriculum of New York State on DV is a beginning step in reconciling these goals (Addiction Technology Transfer Center, 1998a).

Marital Discord and Alcohol Consumption.   In addition to being implicated in DV, alcohol apparently plays a significant role in marital discord in general. In a study of Australian couples seeking marital counseling, Halford and Osgarby (1993) found that half of the male spouses had alcohol problems and that over 80 percent of the men and women reported that they disagreed frequently with their spouse about alcohol consumption. An assessment of drinking patterns for both clients should be conducted in all marital counseling (Collins et al., 1997; Kantor, 1993). If one or both of the partners has a drinking problem, they should be referred for alcoholism treatment. More detailed procedures should be developed to deal with alcohol problems in marital therapy.

Child Abuse.   Although researchers have not consistently found that alcoholic parents have an elevated risk of committing child abuse, Miller et al. (1999) found that alcoholic mothers were more hostile and more punitive than nonalcoholic mothers. She recommends that mothers in treatment for alcoholism should receive special parenting training that includes an understanding of what constitutes excessive levels of punishment and its negative consequences.

Government Regulation of Alcohol and Crime Reduction

This chapter cites the evidence that reduced availability of alcohol is associated with decreases in crime. Of course, it would be wrong to think that elimination of alcohol would eliminate crime. However, reducing instances of intoxication would probably reduce levels of some types of crimes. There are additional initiatives that could be developed to reduce the incidence of alcohol-related accidents and crime. Research on alcohol-outlet density and restrictions on alcohol sales indicates that reductions in the availability of alcohol reduces the rate of violent crime. It would be worthwhile to consider limiting the number of alcohol outlets in high-crime areas. Regulating sales of alcohol at street fairs, such as is done in New York City, may be a useful step in reducing alcohol-related assault and sexual violence.

The effectiveness of zero-tolerance laws, minimum legal drinking age (MLDA), and DWI initiatives discussed in Chapter 7 suggest that carefully crafted laws and their enforcement have had positive effects on reductions in crime. Better enforcement of such laws would probably have an even greater effect on crime reduction.

With the advent of new technology, creative measures can be taken to refine drinking laws. For example, selling alcoholic beverages to an intoxicated person is illegal in many states. Breathalyzers could be required in premises selling alcohol to verify BACs, and refusal to serve could be measured objectively. Such devices could also warn patrons when their BAC is over 0.10% and help them decide not to drive.

Coordination between Criminal Justice and Substance Abuse Treatment

An important consideration in this chapter is that the substance-abusing offender is in two domains: the criminal justice system and the treatment system. The two systems have different rules, objectives, tools, desired outcomes, and differing philosophies. Successful outcomes depend on cooperation between them (De Leon, 1988; Leukefeld & Tims, 1990). CASA (National Center on Addiction and Substance Abuse at Columbia University, 1997) recommends that judges, corrections officers, probation and parole officers all be trained to identify and screen for alcohol problems in offenders and be given specific training tailored to their specific responsibilities. Similarly, alcoholism counselors should have specialized training to gain expertise in treating the criminal justice population. The Addiction Technology Transfer Center has developed curricula for training in this area (Addiction Technology Transfer Center, 1997, 1998b). Substance abuse counselors should know the basic procedures of the criminal justice system. When treating a criminal justice client, the counselor should know just where the client stands in the criminal justice system so that he or she can anticipate possible problems and important transitions and discuss them with the client. Criminal justice personnel should understand their role in providing and maintaining motivation for the client to remain treatment compliant.

SUMMARY

An extensive research literature links alcohol and violence. This research does not prove that alcohol is a causal factor in violent incidents, but the extensive corroborating results from controlled observational studies, natural experiments, and laboratory experiments lend strong support for such a link.

A large percentage of criminal justice offenders have substance and/or alcohol use disorders. Substance-abusing offenders often have co-occurring mental diagnoses, which makes treatment more difficult. Outcome research indicates that all types of coercive treatment, including criminal justice coercion, is at least as successful as voluntary substance abuse treatment.

Most criminal justice substance abuse treatment programs, including prison-based programs, are modeled on the therapeutic community (TC). Although some gains have been shown by substance-abusing offenders' completion of in-prison TCs, the most consistent improvements occurs when substance-abusing offenders complete a postprison TC program.

Criminal justice and substance abuse treatment additionally interface in drug courts, TASC, and as a part of probation and parole. Preliminary reports indicate that these coordinated efforts provide good outcomes in reduced criminal activity and drug use.

Domestic violence is highly associated with intoxication and heavy drinking patterns on the part of the male partner. Preliminary outcome research suggests that batterer intervention programs with a substance abuse component are helpful in reducing the incidence of domestic violence. Alcohol treatment has also been shown to reduce the incidence of domestic violence in alcoholics.

READINGS

Pernanan, K. (1991). *Alcohol in human violence.* New York: Guilford.
A classic study on alcohol and violence in a Canadian community.

Rasanen, P., Tuhonen, J., Isohanni, M., Ranakallio, P., Lehtonen, J., & Moring, J. (1998). Schizophrenia, alcohol abuse, and violent behavior: A 6-year followup study of an unselected birth cohort. *Schizophrenia Bulletin* 24, 437–411.
An important study which documents the magnifying effects of alcoholism on recidivism for schizophrenics.

Roberts, L. J., Roberts, C. F., & Leonard, K. E. (1998). Alcohol, drugs, and interpersonal violence. In V. B. Van Hasselt and M. Hersen (Eds.), *Handbook of psychological approaches with violent offenders: Contemporary strategies and issues* (pp. 493–519). New York: Kluwer, Academic/Plenum.
A good summary of the research on alcohol and violence.

REFERENCES

Abram, K. M. Teplin, L. A., & McClelland, G. M. (1993). The effects of co-occurring disorders on the relationship between alcoholism and violent crime: A 3-year follow-up of male jail detainees. In Susan E. Martin (Ed.), *Alcohol and interpersonal violence: Fostering multidisciplinary perspectives* (National Institute on Acohol and Alcoholism Research Monograph 24, pp. 237–251). Rockville, MD: U.S. Department of of Health and Human Services.

Addiction Technology Transfer Center (1997). An introductory curriculum on substance abuse for criminal justice students. New York State, Office of Alcoholism and Substance Abuse. Unpublished paper.

Addiction Technology Transfer Center (1998a). Adult domestic violence: The alcohol/other drug connection. New York State, Office of Alcoholism and Substance Abuse. Unpublished paper.

Addiction Technology Transfer Center (1998b). Training for professionals working with MICA offenders. Cross training for staff in law enforcement, mental health, and substance abuse settings. New York State, Office of Alcoholism and Substance Abuse. Unpublished paper.

Anglin, M. D. (1988). The efficacy of civil commitment in treating narcotics addiction. *Journal of Drug Issues* 18, 527–545.

Babcock, J. C., & Steiner, R. (1999). The relationship between treatment, incarceration, and recidivism of battering: A program evaluation of Seattle's coordinated response to domestic violence. *Journal of Family Psychology* 13, 46–59.

Badawy, A. A. (1986). Alcohol as a psychopharmacological agent. In P. F. Brain (Ed.), *Alcohol and aggression* (pp. 53–83). London: Croom Helm.

Barnard, G. W., Holzer, C., & Vera, H. (1979). A comparison of alcoholics and non-alcoholics charged with rape. *Bulletin of the American Academy of Psychiatry Law* 7, 432–440.

Bloom, J. D. (1980). Forensic psychiatric evaluation of Alaska Native homicide offenders. *International Journal of Law Psychiatry* 3, 163–171.

Browning, D. H., & Boatman, B. (1977). Incest: Children at risk. *American Journal of Psychiatry* 134, 69–72.

Cherpital, C. J. (1993). What emergency room studies reveal about alcohol involvement in violence-related injuries. *Alcohol, Health, and Research World* 17, 162–166.

Collins, J. J. (1993). Drinking and violence: An individual offender focus. In Susan E. Martin (Ed.), *Alcohol and interpersonal violence: Fostering multidisciplinary perspectives* (National Institute on Alcohol and Alcoholism Research Monograph 24, pp. 221–236). Rockville, MD: U.S. Department of Health and Human Services.

Collins, J. J., Kroutil, L. A., Roland, E. J., & Moore-Gurrera, M. (1997). Issues in the linkage of alcohol and domestic violence services. In M. Galanter (Ed.), *Recent developments in alcoholism*, Vol. 13, *Alcohol and violence: Epidemiology, neurobiology, psychology, and family issues* (pp. 387–405). New York: Plenum.

Collins, J. J., & Messerschmidt, P. M. (1993). Epidemiology of alcohol-related violence. *Alcohol Health and Research World* 17, 93–100.

Cook, P. J., & Moore, M. J. (1993a). Economic perspectives on reducing alcohol-related violence. In Susan E. Martin (Ed.), *Alcohol and interpersonal violence: Fostering multidisciplinary perspectives* (National Institute on Alcohol and Alcoholism Research Monograph 24, pp. 193–212). Rockville, MD: U.S. Department of Health and Human Services.

Cook, P. J., & Moore, M. J. (1993b). Violence reduction through restrictions on alcohol availability. *Alcohol Health and Research World* 17, 151–156.

DeLeon, G. (1988). Legal pressure in therapeutic communities. *Journal of Drug Issues* 18, 625–640.

DeLeon, G., Melnick, G., Thomas, G., Kressel, D., & Wexler, D. (2000). Motivation for treatment in a prison-based therapeutic community. *American Journal of Drug and Alcohol Abuse* 26, 33–46.

Downs, W. R., Smyth, N. J., & Miller, B. A. (1996). The relationship between childhood violence and alcohol problems among men who batter: An empirical review and synthesis. *Aggression and Violent Behavior* 1, 327–344.

Eberle, P. A. (1982). Alcohol abusers and non-users: A discriminant analysis of differences between two subgroups of batterers. *Journal of Health and Social Behavior* 23, 260–271.

Edwards, G. (1994). *Alcohol policy and the public good*. New York: Oxford University Press.

Fagan, J. (1993). Set and setting revisited: Influences of alcohol and illicit drugs on the social context of violent events. In Susan E. Martin (Ed.), *Alcohol and interpersonal violence: Fostering multidisciplinary perspectives* (National Institute on Alcohol and Alcoholism Research Monograph 24, pp. 161–192). Rockville, MD: U.S. Department of Health and Human Services.

Gallant, D. M. (1987) Alcoholism: A guide to diagnosis, intervention, and treatment. New York: Norton.

Gayford, J. J. (1979). Battered wives. *British Journal of Hospital Medicine* 22, 496–503.

Gebelein, R. S. (2000). The rebirth of rehabilitation: Promise and perils of drug courts. Papers from the executive session on sentencing and corrections, #6, U.S. Department of Justice, Office of Justice Programs.

Gelles, R. J., & Straus, M. A. (1985). *Physical violence in American families* (2nd release) (computer file). Durham, NH: University of New Hampshire Family Research Laboratory (producer, 1988), Ann Arbor, MI: Inter-University Consortium for Political and Social Research (Distributor, 1991).

Gondolf, E. W. (1998). Multisite evaluation of batterer intervention systems: A 30-month follow-up of court-mandated batterers in four cities. Paper presented at Program Evaluation and Family Violence Research. An International Conference, Durham, NH, July 26–29.

Greenfield, L. A. (1998). Alcohol and crime. Bureau of Justice Statistics, U.S. Department of Justice, Office of Justice Programs, NCJ 168632.

Grunberg, E., Kliner, B. I., & Grumet, B. R. (1978). Homicide and community-based psychiatry. *Journal of Nervous and Mental Disease* 166, 868–874.

Guze, S. B., Wofgram, E. D., McKinney, J. K., & Cantwell, D. P. (1968). Delinquency, social maladjustment, and crime: The role of alcoholism. *Diseases of the Nervous System* 29, 238–243.

Halford, W. K., & Osgarby, S. M. (1993). Alcohol abuse in clients presenting with marital problems. *Journal of Family Psychology* 6, 245–254.

Hiller, M. L., Knight, K., Broome, K. M., & Simpson, D. D. (1996). Compulsory community-based substance abuse treatment and the mentally ill criminal offender. *Prison Journal* 76, 180–191.

Hiller, M. L., Knight, K., & Simpson, D. D. (1999). Prison-based substance abuse treatment, residential aftercare and recidivism. *Addiction* 94, 833–842.

Hubbard, R. L., Marsden, M. E., Rachal, J. V. Harwood, H. J., Cavanaugh, E. R., & Ginzburg, H. M. (1989). *Drug abuse treatment: A national study of effectiveness.* Chapel Hill, NC: University of North Carolina Press.

Inciardi, J. A., Martin, S. S., Butzin, C. A., Hooper, R. M., & Harrison, L. D. (1997). An effective model of prison-based treatment for drug-involved offenders. *Journal of Drug Issues* 27, 161–278.

Johnson, S. D., Gibson, L., & Linden, R. (1978). Alcohol and rape in Winnipeg, 1966–1975. *Journal of Studies on Alcohol* 39, 1887–1894.

Kantor, G. K. (1993). Refining the brushstrokes in portraits of alcohol and wife assaults. In S. E. Martin (Ed.), *Alcohol and interpersonal violence: Fostering multidisciplinary perspectives* (National Institute on Alcohol and Alcoholism Research Monograph 24, pp. 281–290). Rockville, MD: U.S. Department of Health and Human Services.

Knight, K., Simpson, D. D., & Hiller, M. L. (1999). Three-year incarceration outcomes for in-prison therapeutic community treatment in Texas. *Prison Journal* 79, 337–351.

Lang, M. A., & Belenko, S. (2000). Predicting retention in a residential drug treatment alternative to prison program. *Journal of Substance Abuse Treatment* 19, 145–160.

Leonard, K. E. (1993). Drinking patterns and intoxication in marital violence: Review, critique, and future directions for research. In Susan E. Martin (Ed.), *Alcohol and interpersonal violence: Fostering multidisciplinary perspectives* (National Institute on Alcohol and Alcoholism Research Monograph 24, pp. 253–280). Rockville, MD: U.S. Department of Health and Human Services.

Leukefeld, C. G., & Tims, F. M. (1990). Compulsory treatment for drug abuse. *International Journal of the Addictions* 25, 621–640.

Lindqvist, P. (1986). Criminal homicide in northern Sweden 1970–1981: Alcohol intoxication, alcohol abuse and mental disease. *International Journal of Law Psychiatry* 8, 19–37.

Lipsey, M. W., Wilson, D. B., Cohen, M. A., & Derzon, J. H. (1997), Is there a causal relationship between alcohol use and violence? In M. Galanter (Ed.), *Recent developments in alcoholism*, Vol. 13, *Alcohol and violence: Epidemiology, neurobiology, psychology, and family issues* (pp. 245–282). New York: Plenum.

Livingtston, L. R. (1986). Measuring domestic violence in an alcoholic population. *Journal of Social Society Welfare* 13, 934–953.

Maiden, R. P. (1996). The incidence of domestic violence among alcoholic EAP clients before and after treatment. *Employee Assistance Quarterly* 11, 21–46.

Maiden, R. P. (1997). Alcohol dependence and domestic violence: Incidence and treatment implications. *Alcoholism Treatment Quarterly* 15, 31–50.

Martin, S. S., Butzin, C. A., & Inciardi, J. A. (1995). Assessment of a multistage therapeutic community for drug-involved offenders. *Journal of Psychoactive Drugs* 27, 109–116.

Martin, S. S., Butzin, C. A., Saum, C. A., and Inciardi, J. A. (1999). Three-year outcomes of therapeutic community treatment for drug-involved offenders in Delaware: From prison to work release to aftercare. *Prison Journal* 79, 294–320.

Mayfield, D. (1976). Alcoholism, alcohol, intoxication, and assaultive behavior. *Diseases of the Nervous System* 37, 288–291.

McCaldon, R. J. (1967). Rape. *Canadian Journal of Criminal Corrections* 9, 37–59.

Miczek, K. A., Weerts, E. M., & DeBold, J. F. (1993). Alcohol aggression, and violence: Biobehavioral determinants. In Susan E. Martin (Ed.), *Alcohol and interpersonal violence: Fostering multidisciplinary perspectives* (National Institute on Alcohol and Alcoholism Research Monograph 24, pp. 83–119). Rockville, MD: U.S. Department of of Health and Human Services.

Miller, B. A., Downs, W. R., & Gondoli, D. M. (1989). Spousal violence among alcoholic women as compared to a random household sample of women. *Journal of Studies on Alcohol 50*, 533–540.

Miller, B. A., Maguin, E., & Downs, W. R. (1997). Alcohol, drugs, and violence in children's lives. In M. Galanter (Ed.), *Recent developments in alcoholism,* Vol. 13, *Alcohol and violence: Epidemiology, neurobiology, psychology, and family issues* (pp. 357–380). New York: Plenum.

Miller, B. A., Nochajski, T. H., Leonard, K. E., Blance, H. T., Gondoli, D. M., & Bowers, P. M. (1990). Spousal violence and alcohol/drug problems among parolees and their spouses. *Women & Criminal Justice 1*, 55–72.

Miller, B. A., Smyth, N. J., & Mudar, P. J. (1999). Mothers' alcohol and other drug problems and their punitiveness toward their children. *Journal of Studies on Alcohol 60*, 632–642.

Miller, N. S., & Flaherty, J. A. (2000). Effectiveness of coerced addiction treatment (alternative consequences): A review of the clinical research. *Journal of Substance Abuse Treatment 18*, 9–16.

National Center on Addiction and Substance Abuse at Columbia University (1997). Behind bars: Substance abuse and America's prison population. New York: National Center on Addiction and Substance Abuse at Columbia University.

National Institute of Justice (1998). 1997 annual report on adult and juvenile arrestees. Washington, DC: U.S. Department of Justice.

New York State Department of Correctional Services (1996). Profile of 1995 new commitments with suggested alcohol abuse problems based on MAST scores. Albany, NY: New York State Department of Correctional Services.

New York State Department of Correctional Services (1997). Identified substance abusers. Albany, NY: New York State Department of Correctional Services.

Nielsen, A. L. (1996). Integrating the therapeutic community and work release for drug-involved offenders: The CREST program. *Journal of Substance Abuse Treatment 13*, 349–358.

Nielsen, A. L., & Scarpitti, F. R. (1997). Changing the behavior of substance abusers: Factors influencing the effectiveness of therapeutic communities. *Journal of Drug Issues 27*, 279–298.

Nielsen, A. L., Scarpitti, F. R., & Inciardi, J. A. (1996). Integrating the therapeutic community and work release for drug-involved offenders: The Crest program. *Journal of Substance Abuse Treatment 13*, 349–358.

O'Farrell, T. J., & Murphy, C. M. (1995). Marital violence before and after alcoholism treatment. *Journal of Consulting and Clinical Psychology 63*, 256–262.

O'Farrell, T. J., Van Hutton, V., & Murphy, C. M. (1999). Domestic violence before and after alcoholism treatment: A two-year longitudinal study. *Journal of Studies on Alcohol 60*, 317–321.

Office of Alcoholism and Substance Abuse Services (1999). OASAS and the criminal justice system. http://www.oasas.state.ny.us/pio/publications/ms17.htm.

Office of Justice Programs (1998). Looking at a decade of drug courts. http://www.ojp.usdoj.gov/dcpo/decade98.htm.

Parker, R. N., & Rebhun, L. A. (1995). *Alcohol and homicide: A deadly combination of two American traditions.* New York: SUNY Press.

Pearson, F. S., & Lipton, D. S. (1999). A meta-analytic review of the effectiveness of corrections-based treatments for drug abuse. *Prison Journal, 79*, 384–410.

Pernanan, K. (1991). *Alcohol in human violence.* New York: Guilford.

Pernanan, K. (1993a). Alcohol-related violence: Conceptual models and methodological issues. In Susan E. Martin (Ed.), *Alcohol and interpersonal violence: Fostering multidisciplinary perspectives* (National Institute on Alcohol and Alcoholism Research Monograph 24, pp. 37–69). Rockville, MD: U.S. Department of Health and Human Services.

Pernanan, K. (1993b). Research approaches in the study of alcohol-related violence. *Alcohol, Health, and Research World 17*, 101–106.

Rada, R. T., Kellner, R., Laws, D. R., & Winslow, W. W. (1978). Drinking, alcoholism and the mentally disordered sex offender. *Bulletin of the American Academy of Psychiatry Law 6*, 296–300.

Rasanen, P., Tuhonen, J., Isohanni, M., Ranakallio, P., Lehtonen, J., & Moring, J. (1998). Schizophrenia, alcohol abuse, and violent behavior: A 6-year followup study of an unselected birth cohort. *Schizophrenia Bulletin* 24, 437–411.

Regier, D. A., Farmer, M. E., Rae, D. S., Locke, B. Z., Keith, S. J., Judd, L. L., & Goodwin, F. K. (1990). Comorbidity of mental disorders with alcohol and other drug abuse. *Journal of the American Medical Association* 264, 2511–2518.

Roberts, A. R. (1988). Substance abuse among men who batter their mates: The dangerous mix. *Journal of Substance Abuse Treatment* 5, 83–87.

Roberts, L. J., Roberts, C. F., & Leonard, K. E. (1998). Alcohol, drugs, and interpersonal violence. In V. B. Van Hasselt & M. Hersen (Eds.), *Handbook of psychological approaches with violent offenders: Contemporary strategies and issues* (pp. 493–519). New York: Kluwer/Plenum.

Roizen, J. (1993). Issues in the epidemiology of alcohol and violence. In Susan E. Martin (Ed.), *Alcohol and interpersonal violence: Fostering multidisciplinary perspectives* (National Institute on Alcohol and Alcoholism Research Monograph 24, pp. 3–36). Rockville, MD: U.S. Department of Health and Human Services.

Room, R. (1983). Alcohol and crime: Behavioral aspects. In S. H. Kadish (Ed.), *Encyclopedia of crime and justice*, Vol. 1 (pp. 35–44). New York: The Free Press.

Salmon, R. W., & Salmon, R. J. (1983). The role of coercion in rehabilitation of drug abusers. *International Journal of the Addictions* 18, 9–21.

Scott, P. D. (1968). Offenders, drunkenness and murder. *British Journal of Addiction to Alcohol and Other Drugs* 63, 221–226.

Shepherd, J. (1994). Violent crime: The role of alcohol and new approaches to the prevention of injury. *Alcohol and Alcoholism* 29, 5–10.

Shupe, L. M. (1954). Alcohol and crime: A study of the urine alcohol content found in 882 persons arrested during or immediately after the commission of a felony. *Journal of Criminal Law and Criminology* 44, 661–664.

Straus, M. A. (1990). The Conflict Tactics Scale and its critics: An evaluation and new data on validity and reliability. In M. A. Straus and R. J. Gelles (Eds.), *Physical violence in American families* (pp. 49–73). New Brunswick, NJ: Transaction.

Swanson, J. W. (1993). Alcohol abuse, mental disorder, and violent behavior. *Alcohol Health and Research World* 17, 123–132.

Tinklenberg, J. R., & Ochberg, F. M. (1981). Patterns of adolescent violence: A California sample. In D. A. Hamburg and M. B. Trudeau (Eds.), *Biobehavioral aspects of aggression* (pp. 121–140). New York: Alan R. Liss.

Virkkunen, M. (1974). Alcohol as a factor precipitating aggression and conflict behavior leading to homicide. *British Journal of Addiction* 69, 149–154.

Virkkunen, M. (1974). Incest offenders and alcoholism. *Medical Science Law* 14, 124–128.

Watson, C. G., Brown, K., Tilleskjor, C., Jacobs, L., & Pucel, J. (1988). The comparative recidivism rates of voluntary and coerced admission male alcoholics. *Journal of Clinical Psychology* 44, 573–581.

Weinman, B. (1992). A coordinated approach for drug-abusing offenders: TASC and parole (National Institute on Drug Abuse Monograph 118, pp. 232–245). Rockville, MD: U.S. Department of Health and Human Services.

Wells, S., Graham, K., & West, P. (2000). Alcohol-related aggression in the general population. *Journal of Studies on Alcohol* 61, 626–632.

Wexler, H. K. (1986). The Stay 'N Out therapeutic community: Prison treatment for substance abusers. *Journal of Psychoactive Drugs* 18, 221–230.

Wexler, H. K. (1999). Three-year reincarceration outcomes for Amity in-prison therapeutic community and aftercare in California. *Prison Journal* 79, 321–336.

Wexler, H. K., Falkin, G. P., Lipton, D. S., & Rosenblum, A. B. (1992). Outcome evaluation of a prison therapeutic community for substance abuse treatment (National Institute on Drug Abuse Monograph 118, pp. 156–175). Rockville MD: U.S. Department of Health and Human Services.

Wexler, H. K., & Williams, R. (1986). The stay 'n out therapeutic community: Prison treatment for substance abusers. *Journal of Psychoactive Drugs* 18, 221–230.

Widom, C. S., & Hiller-Strurmhofel, S. (2001). Alcohol abuse as a risk factor for and consequence of child abuse. *Alcohol, Health, and Research World* 25, 52–57.

Wilentz, W. C., & Brady, J. P. (1961) The alcohol factor in violent deaths. *American Practicioner's Digest of Treatment* 12, 829–835.

Wilson, D. J. (2000). Drug use, testing, and treatment in jails. Bureau of Justice Statistics Special Report. Washington, DC: U.S. Department of Justice, NCJ 179999.

Wolfgang, M. E. (1958). *Patterns in criminal homicide.* Philadelphia: University of Pennsylvania.

CHAPTER TEN

CO-OCCURRING ALCOHOL USE AND MENTAL DISORDERS

Epidemiology, Treatment, and Treatment Outcome

Research consistently shows that those with alcohol use disorders have high rates of psychiatric disorders. Patients who have both alcohol and psychiatric disorders do not respond well to conventional alcohol treatment (Drake et al., 1993,1998; McLellan, 1986; Rach Beisel et al., 1999; Rounsaville et al., 1987). Developing successful treatment for these patients represents one of the greatest challenges in the substance abuse and mental health systems.

The chapter begins with some basic information about psychiatric diagnosis and additional information about the DSM-IV-TR (DSM-IV-TR is first discussed in Chapter 2). The rate of co-occurrence of alcohol and psychiatric disorders in a large sample of Americans has been measured by two large-scale epidemiological community studies, the Epidemiological Area Catchment Study (ECA) and the National Comorbidity Survey (NCS); their results will be summarized. The possible relationships between co-occurring psychiatric and alcohol disorders will be outlined, avoiding the black-and-white view that one illness causes the other. The most common mental disorders associated with alcohol use disorders will be reviewed. The clinical consensus on special treatment considerations for co-morbid substance use and common co-occurring mental disorders will be outlined. Because alcohol and substance use disorders co-occur with mental disorders at very high rates, treatment programs and outcome research usually include both alcohol and other substance use disorders in their purview; for this reason, substance abuse is also discussed in this chapter.

This chapter includes:

1. Introduction to the DSM-IV-TR
2. Review of epidemiologic data on the co-occurrence of alcohol use disorders and psychiatric illness
3. Outline of the possible relationships between substance use and mental disorders
4. Discussion of commonly co-occurring disorders

5. Clinical consensus treatment recommendations for patients with co-occurring substance abuse and posttraumatic stress disorder (PTSD), sexual abuse, and severe mental illness

6. Summary of current outcome studies bearing on the treatment of co-occurring substance abuse and mental disorders

METHODOLOGY

Epidemiologic methods, used by the ECA and NCA study, are discussed in Chapter 5. Techniques for treating dual diagnosis discussed in this chapter are based on professional knowledge, which is discussed in Chapter 1. Outcome studies in this area suffer from some of the same problems as criminal justice substance abuse treatment outcome research, as discussed in Chapter 9.

ORIENTATION TO THE *DIAGNOSTIC AND STATISTICAL MANUAL,* FOURTH EDITION, TEXT REVISION (DSM-IV-TR)

In Chapter 2, the DSM-IV-TR was briefly discussed in relation to alcohol use disorders. Because it is widely used to diagnose all mental disorders, other aspects of DSM-IV-TR are reviewed here.

The Five Axes of DSM-IV-TR

In addition to a diagnosis, DSM-IV-TR provides a structure to evaluate patients on five dimensions in order to give a fairly complete picture of the person in a condensed and uniform manner. Each of these dimensions is called an *axis.* These are listed in Table 10.1.

Axis I is clinical disorders, which include alcohol abuse and alcohol dependence. Thus, if a diagnosis of alcohol abuse or dependence is made, it is placed on axis I. Axis II is for **personality disorders** and/or mental retardation. Personality disorders are marked by enduring patterns of inner experience and behavior that deviate markedly from normal expectations and are manifested by disturbances in cognition, affect, interpersonal functioning, or impulse control (American Psychiatric Association, 2000, p. 686). The diagnostic criteria for two personality disorders, antisocial personality disorder (ASPD) and borderline personality disorder, are listed in Boxes 10.2 and 10.3. DSM-IV-TR describes mental retardation as a disorder in which significantly subaverage general intellectual functioning causes significant limitation in adaptive functioning (American Psychiatric Association, 2000, p. 49). Axis II disorders are viewed as long-standing disorders, whereas axis I disorders may be temporary and subject to **remission.** An individual can have multiple axis I and II disorders. Axis III is for those medical conditions that may be implicated in the patient's mental disorder. Axis IV is used to take into account the stressors in the person's environment that may be implicated in the mental disorder. Such stressors include death of a family member, divorce, retirement, illiteracy, unemployment, homelessness, extreme

TABLE 10.1   The Five Axes of DSM-IV-TR

Axis I	Clinical disorders; other conditions that may be a focus of clinical attention
Axis II	Personality disorders; mental retardation
Axis III	General medical conditions
Axis IV	Psychosocial and environmental problems
Axis V	Global assessment of functioning

Source: Diagnostic and Statistical Manual of Mental Disorders, Fourth Edition, Text Revision. Washington, DC, American Psychiatric Association, 2000. Reprinted with permission from the *Diagnostic and Statistical Manual of Mental Disorders,* Fourth Edition, Text Revision. Copyright 2000 American Psychiatric Association.

poverty, inadequate health care insurance, and being a victim of a crime (American Psychiatric Association, 2000, pp. 31–32). Axis V, global assessment of functioning (GAF), rates the client's overall adaptive functioning. It is scored on a scale of 0 to 100. The lower the score, the less capable s/he is in caring for him/herself and the more external supportive care s/he will require. For example, someone with suicidal ideation or having any serious impairment in social, occupational, or school functioning, such as having no friends, would be rated between 41 and 50 (American Psychiatric Association, 2000, p. 34).

Psychiatric Diagnoses Co-Occurring with Alcohol Use Disorders

In DSM-IV-TR, diagnoses are grouped into seventeen categories. The categories most commonly researched in relation to alcohol use disorders are **anxiety disorders, mood disorders,** personality disorders, and schizophrenic and other **psychotic disorders.** For purposes of illustration, three diagnoses that commonly co-occur with alcohol use disorders are displayed in Boxes 10.1, 10.2, and 10.3.

A **co-occurring (dual diagnosis** or **co-morbid**) disorder is one in which there is a psychiatric disorder in addition to alcohol and/or other substance abuse or dependence. The mental disorder can be on axis I, such as **dysthymia** or **schizophrenia,** or on axis II, such as a personality disorder. Mental disorders cause a continuum of disruptiveness in adaptive functioning. The GAF score is an indicator of the severity of the disruption. The Addiction Severity Index also provides a measure of the severity of the impairment (McLellan, 1986).

EPIDEMIOLOGY OF CO-MORBID DISORDERS

Measuring the Extent of Association in Co-Occurring Disorders

The degree of co-occurrence between alcohol and mental disorders can be expressed as a percentage or an odds ratio. The *odds ratio* expresses the added risk for having an illness in special populations. In this instance, the odds ratio expresses the increased risk of having a mental disorder for those with an alcohol disorder. Table 10.3 on page 203 shows the association

BOX 10.1

DIAGNOSTIC CRITERIA FOR POSTTRAUMATIC STRESS DISORDER

A. The person has been exposed to a traumatic event in which both of the following were present:
  (1) The person experienced, witnessed, or was confronted with an event or events that involved actual or threatened death or serious injury, or a threat to the physical integrity of self or others.
  (2) The person's response involved intense fear, helplessness, or horror. Note: In children, this may be expressed instead by disorganized or agitated behavior.

B. The traumatic event is persistently reexperienced in one (or more) of the following ways:
  (1) Recurrent and intrusive distressing recollections of the event, including images, thoughts, or perceptions. Note: In young children, repetitive play may occur in which themes or aspects of the trauma are expressed.
  (2) Recurrent distressing dreams of the event. Note: In children, there may be frightening dreams without recognizable content.
  (3) Acting or feeling as if the traumatic event were recurring (includes a sense of reliving the experience, illusions, hallucinations, and dissociative flashback episodes, including those that occur on wakening or when intoxicated). Note: In young children, trauma-specific reenactment may occur.
  (4) Intense psychologic distress at exposure to internal or external cues that symbolize or resemble an aspect of the traumatic event.
  (5) Physiologic reactivity on exposure to internal or external cues that symbolize or resemble an aspect of the traumatic event.

C. Persistent avoidance of stimuli associated with the trauma and numbing of general responsiveness (not present before the trauma), as indicated by three (or more) of the following:
  (1) Efforts to avoid thoughts, feelings, or conversations associated with the trauma.
  (2) Efforts to avoid activities, places, or people that arouse recollections of the trauma.
  (3) Inability to recall an important aspect of the trauma.
  (4) Markedly diminished interest or participation in significant activities.
  (5) Feeling of detachment or estrangement from others.
  (6) Restricted range of affect (e.g., unable to have loving feelings).
  (7) Sense of a foreshortened future (e.g., does not expect to have a career, marriage, children, or a normal life span).

D. Persistent symptoms of increased arousal (not present before the trauma), as indicated by two (or more) of the following:
  (1) Difficulty falling or staying asleep.
  (2) Irritability or outbursts of anger.
  (3) Difficulty concentrating.
  (4) Hypervigilance.
  (5) Exaggerated startle response.

E. Duration of the disturbance (symptoms in Criteria B, C, and D) is more than 1 month.

F. The disturbance causes clinically significant distress or impairment in social, occupational, or other important areas of function.

Source: Diagnostic and Statistical Manual of Mental Disorders. Fourth Edition, Text Revision. Washington, DC, American Psychiatric Association, 2000. Reprinted with permission from the *Diagnostic and Statistical Manual of Mental Disorders,* Fourth Edition, Text Revision. Copyright 2000 American Psychiatric Association.

BOX 10.2

DIAGNOSTIC CRITERIA FOR ANTISOCIAL PERSONALITY DISORDER

A. There is a pervasive pattern of disregard for and violation of the rights of others occurring since age 15 years, as indicated by three (or more) of the following:
  (1) Failure to conform to social norms with respect to lawful behaviors as indicated by repeatedly performing acts that are grounds for arrest.
  (2) Deceitfulness, as indicated by repeatedly lying, using of aliases, conning others for personal profit or pleasure.
  (3) Impulsivity or failure to plan ahead.
  (4) Irritability or aggressiveness, as indicated by repeated physical fights or assaults.

(5) Reckless disregard for safety of self or others.
(6) Consistent irresponsibility, as indicated by repeated failure to sustain consistent work behavior or honor financial obligations.
(7) Lack of remorse, as indicated by being indifferent to or rationalizing having hurt, mistreated, or stolen from another.

B. The individual is at least age 18 years.

C. There is evidence of conduct disorder with onset before 15 years.

D. The occurrence of antisocial behavior is not exclusively during the course of schizophrenia or a manic episode.

Source: Diagnostic and Statistical Manual of Mental Disorders, Fourth Edition, Text Revision. Washington, DC, American Psychiatric Association, 2000. Reprinted with permission from the *Diagnostic and Statistical Manual of Mental Disorders*, Fourth Edition, Text Revision. Copyright 2000 American Psychiatric Association.

between alcohol and mental disorders. For example, 26.2 percent of women with alcohol dependence also have a lifetime occurrence of PTSD; this rate of occurrence (the odds ratio) is 3.60 times more frequent than for women with no alcohol disorder.

Community Surveys

The ECA and NCS are two large-scale epidemiologic studies that measured the degree of co-morbidity of alcohol and mental disorders. The ECA study was larger, but the NCS was more representative of the U.S. population. (The ECA is described in more detail in Chapter 5.) Both studies show a large co-morbidity of alcohol use disorders and mental disorders.

Helzer and Pryzbeck (1988) used data from the ECA study to determine the lifetime prevalence of common psychiatric diagnosis in those with alcohol use disorders. Men with an alcohol use disorder had a co-morbid psychiatric disorder 44 percent of the time, whereas women had a co-morbid disorder 65 percent of the time. Table 10.2 indicates the lifetime co-morbidity odds ratios for alcohol and other disorders. For example, those with alcohol disorders are 4.0 times more likely to have schizophrenia than those in the general population, and are 7.2 times more likely to have drug dependence.

Kessler et al. (1997) report lifetime co-occurrence of alcohol and mental disorders from the NCS. Although the basic trends were the same, the rates of co-morbidity were higher: men with lifetime alcohol abuse had a mental disorder 56.8 percent of the time and

BOX 10.3

DIAGNOSTIC CRITERIA FOR BORDERLINE PERSONALITY DISORDER

A pervasive pattern of instability of interpersonal relationships, self-image, and affects, and marked impulsivity beginning by early adulthood and present in a variety of contexts, as indicated by five (or more) of the following:

(1) Frantic efforts to avoid real or imagined abandonment. Note: Do not include suicidal or self-mutilating behavior covered in Criterion 5.
(2) A pattern of unstable and intense interpersonal relationships characterized by alternating between extremes of idealization and devaluation.
(3) Identity disturbance: markedly and persistently unstable self-image or sense of self.
(4) Impulsivity in at least two areas that are potentially self-damaging (e.g., spending, sex, sub-

stance abuse, reckless driving, binge eating). Note: Do not include suicidal or self-mutilating behavior covered in Criterion 5.
(5) Recurrent suicidal behavior, gestures, or threats, or self-mitigating behavior.
(6) Affective instability due to a marked reactivity of mood (e.g., intense episodic dysphoria, irritability, or anxiety usually lasting a few hours and only rarely more than a few days).
(7) Chronic feelings of emptiness.
(8) Inappropriate, intense anger or difficulty controlling anger (e.g., frequent displays of temper, constant anger, recurrent physical fights).
(9) Transient, stress-related, paranoid ideation or severe dissociative symptoms.

Source: Diagnostic and Statistical Manual of Mental Disorders. Fourth Edition, Text Revision. Washington, DC, American Psychiatric Association, 2000. Reprinted with permission from the *Diagnostic and Statistical Manual of Mental Disorders,* Fourth Edition, Text Revision. Copyright 2000 American Psychiatric Association.

TABLE 10.2   Co-Morbidity with Alcoholism and Other Disorders: Odds Ratios for Alcohol Abuse and/or Dependence and Other Specific Disorders from ECA Data

PSYCHIATRIC DIAGNOSIS	ODDS RATIO
Antisocial personality	21.0
Mania	6.2
Schizophrenia	4.0
Panic disorder	2.4
Obsessive compulsive	2.1
Dysthymia	1.8
Major depression	1.7
Somatization	1.8
Phobic disorders	1.4
Anorexia	1.2
Organic brain syndrome	0.4
Any core diagnosis	2.8
Any drug disorder	7.2

Note: Mania is an old term for bipolar disorder.

Source: Reprinted with permission from *Journal of Studies on Alcohol,* vol. 49, pp. 219–224, 1988. Copyright by Alcohol Research Documentation, Inc., Rutgers Center of Alcohol Studies, Piscataway, NJ 08854.

women with lifetime alcohol abuse had a mental disorder 72.4 percent of the time. Men with alcohol dependence had a 78.3 percent rate of co-morbidity, and women with alcohol dependence had an 86.0 percent rate of co-morbidity. It appears that those with alcohol dependence are at greater risk for having a co-morbid mental disorder than those with alcohol abuse. Substance abuse disorders other than alcohol were most common, followed by **conduct disorders,** ASPD, **anxiety disorders,** and **affective disorders.** Table 10.3 shows the percentages and odds ratios of co-morbid disorders for those with alcohol abuse and dependence from NCS data. In both the ECA and NCS, women have higher rates of co-morbidity.

TABLE 10.3   Lifetime Co-Occurrence of Alcohol Abuse and Alcohol Dependence with Other DSM-III-R Disorders by Sex: National Comorbidity Survey Data

| | ALCOHOL ABUSE | | | | ALCOHOL DEPENDENCE | | | |
| | Men | | Women | | Men | | Women | |
Lifetime disorder	%	O.R.	%	O.R.	%	O.R.	%	O.R.
Anxiety								
GAD	2.6	0.67	8.4	1.31	8.6	3.86*	15.7	3.01*
Panic	1.6	0.79	7.3	1.55	3.6	2.27*	12.0	2.98*
Agor	5.1	1.27	9.3	1.03	6.5	1.82*	18.5	2.53*
Soc p.	10.8	0.97	24.1	1.81*	19.3	2.41*	30.3	2.62*
Sim p.	5.9	0.85	28.2	2.24	13.9	3.11*	30.7	2.63*
PTSD	2.5	0.45*	10.5	1.01	10.3	3.20*	26.2	3.60*
Any	22.7	0.95	48.8	1.78*	35.8	2.22*	60.7	3.08*
Affective								
Depres	9.0	0.65	30.1	1.65*	24.3	2.95*	48.5	4.05*
Dysth	3.6	0.71	10.1	1.33	11.2	3.81*	20.9	3.63*
Mania	0.3	0.15	3.8	2.32	6.2	12.03*	6.8	5.30*
Any	10.2	0.64*	34.5	1.78*	28.1	3.16*	53.5	4.36*
Drug								
Abuse	16.6	5.55*	15.5	6.72	11.1	2.97*	12.4	5.16*
Dep	13.1	1.59	17.8	4.09	29.5	9.81*	34.7	15.75*
Any	29.7	2.96*	33.3	6.00*	40.6	7.73*	47.1	14.12*
Other								
Con dis	25.3	1.45	13.5	2.53	41.6	4.29	22.8	5.83*
AAB	8.8	1.01	8.0	4.20*	24.5	7.10*	18.9	11.98*
ASPD	6.1	1.20	2.1	2.09	16.9	8.34*	7.8	17.01*
Any	27.1	1.24	19.6	3.05*	49.7	5.01*	28.9	6.10*

GAD, generalized anxiety disorder; Panic, panic disorder; Agor, agoraphobia; soc p., social phobia; sim p., simple phobia; PTSD, posttraumatic stress disorder; depres, depression; dysth, dysthymia; dep, dependence; con dis, conduct disorder; AAB, adult antisocial behavior; ASPD, antisocial personality disorder. *The odds ratio is significant at the 0.05 level using a two-tailed test.

Source: Kessler et al., 1997. Reprinted by permission of the American Medical Association.

Table 10.3 also shows that one-third of the men and almost half of the women who have an alcohol disorder also have a substance use disorder. Given the high rate of co-morbid psychiatric disorders and alcohol and/or substance abuse, it is important to evaluate clients in any treatment setting for all three disorders.

Surveys of Clinical (Treated) Populations

Even higher rates of lifetime mental disorders are found in those seeking treatment for alcohol disorders. For example, Hesselbrock et al. (1985) found that 77 percent of hospitalized alcoholics had a lifetime co-morbid mental disorder. Because either or both disorders could be at remission at any point in time, a more accurate estimate of the rates of concurrent co-morbidity is the 6-month prevalence rate. For those with alcohol disorders seeking treatment in the NCS study, 55.0 percent had a 6-month co-morbid mental disorder, compared to 24.4 percent not seeking treatment (Regier et al., 1990). Thus, even using a very conservative measure of co-morbidity, a significant portion of patients have both active alcohol and mental disorders when applying for treatment.

Adolescence and Co-Morbidity

Rohde et al. (1996) found that more than 80 percent of an adolescent sample with an alcohol disorder had another psychiatric disorder. Table 10.4 shows rates of psychiatric disorders with alcohol consumption patterns found in their study.

Depression, **disruptive behavior disorder,** and drug use disorders were associated with alcohol disorders for males and females. Anxiety disorders were associated with alco-

TABLE 10.4   Rates of Psychiatric Disorders in Adolescents According to Alcohol Use

	ABSTAIN (%)	EXPER (%)	SOCIAL (%)	PROBLEM (%)	AB/DEP (%)	χ^2
Depression	16.8	22.8	20.6	39.0	47.9	72.73*
Bipolar disorder	0.8	2.5	0.5	0.8	2.1	7.72
Manic core symptom	4.2	8.1	5.9	5.6	12.8	10.94
Anxiety disorders	7.8	8.6	8.1	9.6	17.0	8.83
Female	9.2	14.5	10.6	10.9	27.1	
Male	6.4	1.1	4.8	8.2	6.5	
Disruptive behavior disorders	2.5	7.1	4.8	8.8	25.5	70.53*
Drug use disorders	0.3	2.0	4.1	15.5	57.4	375.60*
Daily tobacco use	3.4	10.2	21.7	39.4	58.5	211.55*

Abstain = abstainers; Exper = experiments; Social = social drinkers; Problem = problem drinkers; Ab/Dep = abuse/dependence group. (Manic core symptom = distinct period of abnormally and persistently elevated, expansive, or irritable mood.)

Source: Rhode, P., Lewinsohn, P. M., and Seeley, J. R. (1996). Psychiatric comorbidity with problematic alcohol use in high school students. *Journal of the American Academy of Child Adolescent Psychiatry,* 35(1), pp. 101–109. Reprinted by permission of Lippincott, Williams, and Wilkins.

hol disorders in young women. Unlike the findings of Sheldler and Block discussed in Chapter 6, the abstainers do not appear to be a maladjusted group. Greenbaum et al. (1991), drawing on data from the National Adolescent and Child Treatment Study, were able to calculate rates of co-morbidity in a sample of severely emotionally disturbed adolescents. Of those who had **conduct disorders,** 36.1 percent had severe substance abuse. Of those with severe depressive disorder, 48.3 percent had a substance abuse disorder. **Attention deficit disorders** (ADHD) were associated with substance use disorders, but not significantly so.

THE RELATIONSHIP BETWEEN CO-MORBID DISORDERS

In his discussion of co-morbid disorders, Meyer (1986) quotes the familiar saying, "Which came first, the chicken or the egg?" Does the mental disorder cause the substance abuse disorder, or does the substance abuse disorder cause the mental disorder? Meyer (1986) outlines possible relationships, as indicated in Table 10.5. Most important, he expresses the possible relationships in terms of one disorder affecting the other rather than one causing the other. Although it is conceptually more satisfying to expect that one disorder causes the other, the current understanding suggests a more complex interaction between the illnesses (Richards, 1993).

Which Disorder Typically Occurs First?

For those with both disorders, researchers can determine if alcohol disorders typically precede, come at the same time, or come after the mental disorder. In the NCS, for those with alcohol and psychiatric disorders, alcohol disorders most often had a later onset than the mental disorder (Kessler et al., 1997). This trend was stronger for alcohol dependence than for

TABLE 10.5   Possible Relationships between Substance Use Disorders and Psychiatric Disorders

1   Psychiatric disorders may serve as a risk factor for substance use disorders.

2   Psychiatric disorders may modify the course of a substance use disorder in terms of rapidity of course; response to treatment, symptom picture, and long-term outcome.

3   Psychiatric symptoms may develop in the course of chronic intoxication or as an aspect of the withdrawal syndrome.

4   Some psychiatric disorders emerge as a consequence of substance use disorders and persist in remission from the substance disorder.

5   Substance-using behavior and psychiatric symptoms (whether antecedent or consequent) will become meaningfully linked over the course of time.

6   Some psychiatric disorders occur in addicted individuals with no greater frequency than in the general population, suggesting that the psychiatric disorder and the substance use disorder are not specifically related.

Source: Meyer, 1986. Adapted by permission of Guilford Press.

alcohol abuse. Women reported the alcohol disorder occurring after the mental illness more frequently than men. Rohde et al.'s (1996) study of adolescents found that alcohol disorders more often followed the psychiatric disorder. Rohde et al. report that 87.5 percent of the anxiety disorders and 80.0 percent of the disruptive behavior disorders that were co-morbid with alcohol disorders were found to have preceded alcohol use. Although preceding events are not necessarily implicated in causing following events, these studies provide some inferential evidence that psychiatric disorders predispose adolescents and adults to alcohol disorders.

On the other hand, symptoms of anxiety and mood disorders may be caused by excessive alcohol use, as discussed in Chapter 2. Verheul et al. (2000) provide some support for this hypothesis. They interviewed 276 alcohol-abusing patients to determine co-morbid psychiatric diagnoses at treatment entry and 1 year after treatment. Subjects in recovery from alcohol use disorders 1 year after treatment were 16.7 times more likely to have recovered from an original anxiety/mood disorder than those who were not, even though there was no special treatment for these disorders, suggesting that a large percentage of the anxiety/mood disorders measured at baseline were alcohol-related. However, personality disorders did not follow the remission pattern of anxiety/mood disorders. Those in recovery from alcohol disorders retained the symptoms of the personality disorder diagnosed at the beginning of treatment. This suggests that the symptoms of personality disorder measured at the beginning of treatment were not alcohol-induced.

MENTAL DISORDERS FREQUENTLY CO-OCCURRING WITH ALCOHOL DISORDERS

Posttraumatic Stress Disorder

Posttraumatic stress disorder (PTSD) was found in 10.3 percent of alcohol-dependent men and 26.2 percent of alcohol-dependent women in the NCS survey (see Table 10.6.). The diagnostic criteria for this disorder are listed in Box 10.1. The hallmark feature of this disorder is the experience of a **trauma,** which includes being sexually abused, exposed to combat in war, or a victim of a natural disaster or serious crime.

Stewart (1996) has summarized research on the relationship between alcohol use disorders, trauma, and PTSD. She cites evidence that trauma is associated with increased alcohol consumption and disorders:

1. Those surviving natural disasters have increased alcohol consumption.
2. Research indicates that veterans who were in combat have higher rates of alcohol problems than veterans who were not.
3. Sexually assaulted women report higher rates of alcoholism than those who were not.

After reviewing an extensive literature, she concludes, "Evidence suggests that exposure to a wide variety of trauma frequently leads to the development of alcohol abuse" (Stewart, 1996, p. 88).

In reviewing research on disorders co-morbid with PTSD, Stewart found that alcohol abuse was the most prevalent disorder in both clinical and nonclinical samples co-morbid

TABLE 10.6   Personality Disorders in a Clinical Sample of Alcoholics

	MEN (%)	WOMEN (%)	TOTAL (%)
Paranoid	19.7	22.7	20.7
Schizotypal	0.3	3.0	0.8
Schizoid	1.0	1.5	1.1
Histrionic	3.7	7.6	4.4
Narcissistic	6.0	9.1	6.6
Borderline	19.3	36.4	22.4
Antisocial	25.7	9.1	22.7
Avoidant	18.0	18.2	18.0
Dependent	3.7	12.1	5.2
Compulsive	9.7	15.2	10.7
Passive-aggressive	9.7	15.2	10.7
Self-defeating	11.0	22.7	13.1
Any	56.0	66.8	57.9

Source: Morgenstern, J., Langebucher, J., Labouvie, E., Miller, K. T. (1997). The comorbidity of alcoholism and personality disorders in a clinical population: Prevalence rates and relation to alcohol typology variables. *Journal of Abnormal Psychology* 106, 74–84. Copyright © 1997 by the American Psychological Association. Adapted with permission.

with PTSD. For example, she reports that Branchey et al. (1984) found that male veterans suffering from PTSD had very high rates of alcohol disorders (41–85 percent).

Studies report that the onset of PTSD symptoms tends to precede the development of alcohol abuse problems. Stewart (1996) suggests that those with PTSD often drink to alleviate PTSD symptoms of increased arousal, insomnia, exaggerated startle reactions, anxiety, sexual fears, depression, guilt, persistent reexperiencing of the traumatic event, and terrifying nightmares. On the other hand, Stewart (1996) suggests that heavy alcohol use might increase susceptibility to or worsen PTSD. She notes that alcohol withdrawal may be mistaken by those with PTSD as an anxiety symptom of the trauma and thus need special preparation for detoxification.

Ouimette et al. (1998), in reviewing the research on outcome of alcoholism treatment for those with PTSD and an alcohol disorder, found that the literature consistently reports alcoholic patients with PTSD having poorer outcomes than those with alcohol disorders only. Ouimette et al. (2000b) followed a group of patients with both PTSD and substance abuse and found that those who attended PTSD treatment after inpatient substance abuse treatment were more likely to remain in remission from substance abuse than those who had only the substance abuse treatment.

Ouimette et al. (1998), based on their findings and other research, recommend the following treatment guidelines for those with concurrent substance abuse and PTSD:

1. All substance abuse patients should be screened for traumatic stress and PTSD.
2. Substance abuse patients with PTSD should receive concurrent treatment for PTSD.

3. Patients with both disorders should have more intensive substance abuse treatment.
4. Patients with both disorders should have family sessions and self-help involvement where feasible.

Stewart (1996) and Zweben et al. (1994) make some additional recommendations for treating these disorders when they co-occur.

1. Those with both disorders should be provided information on the relationship between the two disorders. They should be warned of the possibility of feeling worse when the individual becomes abstinent, because withdrawal may mimic some PTSD symptoms and symptoms that may have been masked by alcohol use may become evident.
2. Abstinence may not be a realistic goal for these patients at the beginning of treatment.
3. Instead, the therapist should be alert to considerations of safety—for example, contracting with the patient not to drive when intoxicated.
4. Intrusion of PTSD symptoms may induce a relapse and should be anticipated and handled as a learning experience.
5. Clinical skill must be used to determine how much to explore painful feelings of PTSD trauma.
6. Medication should be considered to alleviate symptoms of PTSD.

Najavits (2002) has developed an excellent treatment manual for treating those with these concurrent disorders. Her approach, which combines elements of cognitive behavioral and Twelve Step facilitation techniques, has some preliminary empirical support (Najavits, 2002).

Childhood Sexual Abuse and Alcoholism

Childhood sexual abuse (CSA) is considered a trauma and is often viewed as one of the factors in causing PTSD. However, other mental disorders are prevalent in this group as well (Schulte et al., 1995; Burnam et al., 1988). A substantial literature indicates that adults with alcohol disorders have an elevated rate of childhood sexual abuse experience. Langeland and Hartgers (1998), reviewing studies on sexual abuse, found that five of six population studies provide support for a positive association between CSA and adult alcohol problems. One was Wilsnack et al.'s study (1997), which drew on a representative sample of women. It found that 21.9 percent of women with childhood sexual abuse had symptoms of alcohol dependence, compared to 7.9 percent of those without sexual abuse. These findings suggest that a childhood sexual abuse history may be a risk factor for the development of an alcohol use disorder in adulthood.

It is not surprising, then, that numerous studies of treated alcoholics have found elevated levels of reported childhood sexual abuse. For example, Ouimette et al. (2000a), in a study of 24,959 Veterans Administration patients with substance abuse, found that women reported CSA 49.4 percent of the time and men 8 percent of the time. Rice et al. (2001), drawing on data from the MATCH study (discussed in the next chapter), found that male alcoholic patients reported an 11 percent incidence of CSA and women, 41 percent.

The research consistently finds high rates of childhood sexual abuse for women with an alcohol use disorder. These rates are considerably higher than the 15–30 percent found in community samples of women (Finkelhor, 1979). There is some evidence that men who were sexually abused in childhood have elevated rates of alcohol or substance abuse disorders compared to the general population. Burnam et al. (1988), drawing on Los Angeles ECA data, found that men who were sexually abused in childhood were more likely to develop an alcohol disorder than sexually abused women, and almost half had a substance use disorder. Schulte et al. (1995) found that 60 percent of a group of males in treatment for childhood sexual abuse had alcohol abuse or dependence.

Raising this issue with alcoholic patients is a sensitive one. Both counselor and client may shy away from this topic. It is not surprising that Rohsenow et al. (1988) found that without routine questioning, only 4 percent of men and 20 percent of adult females in a substance abuse program reported childhood sexual abuse. The percentages increased dramatically when routine questioning about sexual abuse was added: the percentages quadrupled for males and tripled for females.

Sexually abused patients generally have more severe symptoms at presentation for alcoholism treatment (Bernstein, 2000; Harvey et al., 1994; Ouimette et al., 2000a) and present unique challenges for achieving a successful outcome. There are no controlled outcome studies for measuring the effectiveness of treatment of sexual abuse and alcohol disorders, but several articles outline a treatment approach to deal with these commonly co-occurring problems, based on clinical experience. Culled from several sources (Stewart, 1996; Sullivan and Evans, 1994; Young, 1990; Zweben et al., 1994), I have found the following guidelines have been stressed:

1. All alcohol abusers should be screened for childhood sex abuse routinely at the beginning of treatment.
2. Sexually abused alcoholics are often in crisis at the beginning of treatment. Crisis management is an essential aspect of treatment. Having staff available for emergency telephone or in-person sessions is important. Inpatient treatment is often helpful as a means to ease the crisis.
3. Education about addiction is suggested, especially for those who are focused on the sexual abuse. Although abstinence from alcohol is a goal, rigid insistence on abstinence is not recommended.
4. Relapse should be anticipated and may reflect an intrusion of sexual abuse issues that can be empathically explored.
5. Safety issues should be reviewed in all aspects of life; relationships should be explored for their trustworthiness and lifestyles explored for safety.
6. Medication should be considered when psychiatric symptoms are severe.
7. After abstinence is stabilized and safety established in the client's life, gradual and sensitive exploration of painful emotions and experiences related to the sexual trauma can begin. Painful memories of sexual abuse trauma may trigger painful emotions and lead to relapse.

Conduct Disorder

A **conduct disorder** is diagnosed when a child has a pattern of consistently breaking the rules of normal social behavior. It is the precursor of antisocial personality disorder (ASPD). Longitudinal research has found that children diagnosed with conduct disorders are more likely to develop alcohol use disorders (Phil & Peterson, 1991). Data from both the NCS survey (see Table 10.6) and Rohde et al.'s data on adolescents (see Table 10.7) also found high rates of alcohol disorders in those who have had conduct disorders. Phil and Peterson (1991) note that children diagnosed with conduct disorders often come from disadvantaged families.

Personality Disorders

The diagnostic criteria for two personality disorders are listed in Boxes 10.2 and 10.3. **Personality disorders** occur in about 44 percent of alcoholics (Verheul, 1995, as cited in Ver-

TABLE 10.7   Integrated Treatment of Co-Occurring Severe Mental Illness and Substance Abuse Disorders

- The patient participates in one program that provides treatment for two disorders—severe mental disorder and substance use disorder.
- The patient's mental disorder and substance use disorder are treated by the same clinicians.
- The clinicians are trained in psychopathology, assessment, and treatment strategies for both mental disorders and for substance use disorders.
- The clinicians offer substance abuse treatment tailored for patients who have severe mental illness. These tailored treatments differ from traditional substance abuse treatment.
    - Focus on preventing increased anxiety *rather than* breaking through denial.
    - Emphasis on trust, understanding, and learning *rather than* on confrontation, criticism, and expression.
    - Emphasis on reduction of harm from substance use *rather than* on immediate abstinence.
    - Slow pace and long-term perspective *rather than* rapid withdrawal and short-term treatment.
    - Provision of stage-wise and motivation counseling (see motivational interviewing, Chapter 11) *rather than* confrontation and front-loaded treatment.
    - Supportive clinicians readily available in familiar settings *rather than* being available only during office hours and at clinics.
    - Twelve Step groups available to those who choose and can benefit *rather than* being mandated for all patients.
    - Neuroleptics (antipsychotic) and other pharmacotherapies indicated according to patients' psychiatric and medical needs *rather than* being contraindicated for all patients in substance abuse treatment.
- Some program components specifically address substance use reduction as a central focus of programming. Components focus especially on integrated treatment.
    - Substance abuse group interventions.
    - Specialized substance abuse assessment.
    - Case management.
    - Individual counseling.
    - Housing supports.
    - Medications and medication management.
    - Family psychoeducation.
    - Psychosocial positive rehabilitation.

Source: Drake et al., 1998.

heul et al., 1998). These disorders are even more common in treated alcohol and substance abusers. Thomas et al. (1999) report that 50 percent of patients in a substance abuse treatment facility had personality disorders, while Morganstern et al. (1997) report a rate of 57.9 percent in a group of treated alcoholics. In their sample of alcoholic patients, Morganstern et al. (1997) report the percentages of different types of personality disorders, which are shown in Table 10.6.

Alcoholics with co-morbid personality disorders have additional problems to address in treatment compared to those without co-morbid disorders, and there are some indications that the former do not respond as well to treatment. For example, Thomas et al. (1999) found that those treated for substance abuse (59 percent of whom were alcoholic) in an inpatient substance abuse program with personality disorders were more likely to relapse during the year following treatment than those without personality disorders.

ASPD is a prevalent personality disorder in alcoholics that has received a great deal of attention. Schubert et al. (1998) conducted a meta-analysis of forty studies on the association between alcohol disorders and ASPD. Their results indicate that the presence of one diagnosis heightens the likelihood of the other. Although more attention has been paid to men with ASPD, the NCS found that alcohol-dependent women had higher odds ratios for ASPD (17.01) than men (8.34) (see Table 10.3). Kranzer et al. (1998), summarizing studies of clinical samples of alcoholics, found ASPD diagnosed in 20 to 51 percent of the patients. Falling within this range, Hesselbrock et al. (1985) found ASPD in 49 percent of the men and 20 percent of the women in a sample of hospitalized alcoholics.

Research indicates that those alcohol abusers with ASPD have more severe alcohol disorders than those who do not. Holdcraft et al. (1998) and Lewis et al. (1996) found that men in two different community-based samples with alcohol disorders and ASPD had earlier age of onset of alcohol disorders and more severe alcoholism. Hesselbrock et al. (1992) found that alcoholic men in a clinical sample who had co-morbid ASPD had earlier onset of alcohol disorders and, in another study (1985), found that alcoholics with ASPD reported earlier first intoxication, earlier regular intoxication, and sought treatment earlier than alcoholics without ASPD. Hesselbrock et al. (1992) found that, when given standard alcohol treatment, alcoholics with ASPD relapsed more rapidly than those without ASPD.

Two types of cognitive behavioral therapies have been advanced as special treatment for alcoholics with ASPD. The modest outcome literature shows mixed results. Kadden et al. (1989) found that alcoholics who had higher sociopathic ratings did better in a type of cognitive behavior therapy, coping skills therapy, than traditional therapy. Loungebaugh et al. (1994) found ASPD patients did better in individually focused cognitive behavioral therapy, which included assertion training, problem solving, and dealing with relapse, than in a relationship focused therapy. However, replication failed to support the better outcomes with this treatment (Kalman et al., 2000).

Severe Mental Illness

Severe mental illnesses include **schizophrenia** and **bipolar disorders.** Those suffering from these disorders have a high rate of co-morbid alcohol disorders: those suffering from bipolar disorder (listed as mania in Table 10.2) are 6.2 times more likely to have an alcohol disorder, those with schizophrenia are four times more likely to have an alcohol disorder.

Rates of substance abuse among these individuals is also high and is often concurrent with alcohol disorders. Treatment programs for those with severe mental illness generally include substance abuse interventions as well as treatment for alcohol abuse.

Patients with severe co-morbid psychiatric disorders do not respond as well to conventional substance abuse or mental health treatments as those with only one of the disorders (Drake et al., 1993, 1998; RachBeisel et al., 1999). McLellan (1986), in an outcome study of several different substance abuse treatment types, found that psychiatric severity was the best predictor of outcome; those patients with greater psychiatric severity had poorer outcomes. Patients with severe psychiatric severity actually got worse in therapeutic community (TC) treatment (see Chapter 9 for a description of this treatment). These results support the need for specialized treatment for individuals with severe co-morbid disorders.

Although treatment for most co-morbid disorders is different in several respects from conventional addiction treatment as discussed for PTSD and childhood sexual abuse, treatment for those with severe mental illness and substance abuse is dramatically different. In conventional therapy, it is generally assumed that the patient can make responsible choices and understand and follow through on commitments. Because severely mentally ill patients often have disorders in thinking (Mueser et al., 1992), these assumptions cannot be taken for granted. When the severity of the illnesses is great, treatment for these patients extends beyond counseling to **intensive case management,** in which patients often need an advocate to help guide them through tasks they cannot negotiate successfully on their own. This includes treatment seeking and compliance, help with housing, health insurance problems, and negotiating entitlement programs. It may require taking on custodial functions such as managing benefits (Ahrens, 1998) if the patient cannot handle money responsibly. For example, Shaner et al. (1995) found that a sample of substance-abusing schizophrenics used almost half of their incomes for illegal drugs. The course of treatment is often prolonged and characterized by relapses in both the mental illness and the substance use disorder. The current clinical consensus is that integrated treatment, treating both disorders in the same facility concurrently, is the preferred approach to treating this group. Table 10.7 is taken from Drake et al. (1998) and indicates the characteristics of integrated treatment. Box 10.4 describes a special self-help group for severely mentally ill substance abusers.

OUTCOME STUDIES FOR SPECIALIZED TREATMENT OF CO-OCCURRING MENTAL ILLNESS AND SUBSTANCE DISORDERS

RachBeisel et al. (1999) and Drake et al. (1998) reviewed four outcome studies that compared integrated treatment with standard substance abuse treatment for severely mentally ill substance abusers. The integrated treatment showed better outcome than control groups in reduced psychiatric hospitalization, decreased drug use, and in two of the studies, reductions in psychiatric symptoms. Although these results are promising, both note that the studies lacked randomization, sufficient controls, and adequate sample sizes.

Moggi et al. (1999) compared the outcome of dually diagnosed patients in several inpatient programs that incorporated many elements of the integrated model with conven-

BOX 10.4

DOUBLE TROUBLE RECOVERY

Just as dual-diagnosis patients require special treatment, they often require special types of self-help. Alcoholics Anonymous (AA) can be helpful to some alcoholics with co-morbid disorders, but others need a place where they can discuss both disorders openly. Vogel et al. (1998) note some limitations of AA for the dually diagnosed, including negative attitudes about prescribed medications and lack of shared experiences in the realm of psychiatric symptoms. One self-help group for dually diagnosed patients is Double Trouble Recovery (DTR), with over 100 chapters. These groups are run by individuals who are recovering from both illnesses and utilize mutual sharing of experiences to support and encourage each other. Laudet et al. (2000) interviewed a number of DTR members and found that the most difficult problems they had to face were

1. Dealing with feelings
2. Work issues
3. Fear of picking up
4. Having money problems
5. Dealing with inner conflicts
6. Not being understood

tional substance abuse programs within the Veterans Administration hospital system. The former incorporated liberal use of medication, supportive approaches, clear structure, and rules, while the standard substance abuse treatment did not. At 1-year follow-up, patients in both types of treatment showed improvement: 38.5 percent of the patients were abstinent, 67.9 percent reported no significant psychiatric symptoms, and 29.3 percent were employed, regardless of treatment type.

Patients in dual-diagnosis programs did better in reduction in psychiatric symptoms (71.4 percent versus 64.5 percent), increased employment (33.8 percent versus 25.1 percent), and time out of hospital (mean of 8.67 months versus 6.13 months) but did not differ in abstinence rates. Less severely mentally ill patients showed greater improvements in the dual-diagnosis programs than the severely mentally ill.

In sum, several studies suggest that an integrated treatment approach is useful in treating those suffering from mental disorders and substance abuse. More methodologically sound studies need to be conducted to substantiate these preliminary studies.

RECOMMENDATIONS

Treatment of Co-Occurring Disorders

Neither the mental health system nor the substance abuse treatment system provides sufficient resources for treatment of co-occurring addictive and mental disorders. On the mental health side, not enough attention is given to treating the addictive disorder. On the substance abuse side, not enough attention is given to the psychiatric disorder. Regrettably, these patients are often treated for their mental disorder in one facility and their addiction in another. This makes it difficult for these patients, who often have limited capacities in concentration, memory, and reasoning, to reconcile the differing demands placed on them

(Drake et al., 1998). Additionally, coordination of treatment is difficult when two separate agencies are providing intervention in similar domains. Integrated treatment eliminates these problems. Although there is preliminary research support for its effectiveness, more attention needs to be given to implementing research that is methodologically more rigorous. For example, none of the outcome studies report on medication compliance (Drake et al., 1998). In the meantime, it makes sense to make more integrated programs available.

In this regard, two positive developments should be noted:

1. The Substance Abuse Mental Services Administration (SAMHSA), a federal agency in the U.S. Department of Health and Human Services, is in the process of devising new guidelines and regulations that will make treatment of co-morbid disorders more available in both substance abuse and mental health programs (Elias, 2002).
2. The American Society of Addiction Medicine's (2001) manual on placement criteria for substance abusers includes detailed provisions for those with co-morbid disorders.

Since personality disorders, PTSD, and sexual abuse are common in patients with alcohol disorders, patients with alcohol disorders should be screened for these disorders. Except for Najavits's (2002) positive preliminary studies on PTSD, there are no empirically supported techniques for treating these dual diagnoses per se. Moggi et al.'s study (1999) provides some support for integrated treatment for these disorders. They found those with less severe psychiatric illnesses did better than the more severely impaired; presumably a significant percentage of these patients had personality disorders, PTSD, and childhood sexual abuse. At this time, integrated treatment appears to be the best choice of treatment for these patients. It includes liberal use of medication, supportive approaches, clear structure, and rules. Referral for adjunctive psychotherapy may be helpful as well, because specialized training in treating these mental disorders is common for mental health professionals.

However, much more attention needs to be paid to alcoholics with co-occurring mental disorders, in terms of both developing treatment principles and empirical validation of these approaches. Personality disorders other than ASPD have been especially neglected.

Training Issues for Mental Health Professionals and Substance Abuse Counselors

Substance abuse counselors typically have no training in understanding or treating mental disorders. Although they cannot be expected to treat mental illness, they should have some understanding of the issues and treatment goals in these areas for the significant population of co-morbid patients. At a minimum, counselor training should include a course in abnormal psychology. Of course, there must be sufficient training and subsequent safeguards to make sure that counselors do not intervene where they lack appropriate expertise. Counselors need to recognize that treatment for co-morbid serious mental illness and substance abuse is very different from typical addiction treatment. Counselors must learn to collaborate with other mental health professionals and recognize the benefit of appropriate medication for these patients.

Counselors should be able to screen for PTSD and sexual abuse and have some orientation to the nature of the disorders to make appropriate referrals (Zweben et al., 1994), because these illnesses are so common in these patients. Unfortunately, many counselors do not have such training. For example, Glover-Graf and Janikowski (2001) surveyed a group of alcoholism counselors and found that 65 percent stated that they had had no formal training in sexual abuse counseling. A majority of the counselors felt that such training would be very important.

Mental health professionals receive minimal training in addictive disorders (Zweben et al., 1994). This training must be augmented, because a very high percentage of patients applying for mental health treatment have addictive disorders. Mental health professionals must learn not only to screen for these disorders, but to develop an integrated treatment approach for treating substance abuse disorders along with the concurrent mental disorder. Drake et al. (1993) recommend the creation of a new mental health specialty, dual-diagnosis specialists.

Adolescent Alcohol Abuse Treatment

The very high rates of co-morbidity of psychiatric disorders in adolescents with alcohol abuse suggest that their treatment should include psychiatric attention more directly and consistently than adult substance abuse treatment (Rohde et al., 1996). Substance use disorders are a major component of the problems of a large number of adolescents with serious emotional disturbances and should be addressed concurrently (Greenbaum et al., 1991). This special population needs much more clinical and research attention.

Prevention

Alcohol use disorders are the most common co-morbid disorders associated with PTSD. Stewart (1996) points out that early identification of trauma and consideration of addiction potential may not only reduce PTSD but may also reduce the incidence of alcohol use disorders. An important aspect of treating trauma such as survivors of natural disasters should be screening for alcohol disorders (Glover-Graf & Janikowski, 2001) and education about the addiction potential inherent in experiencing a traumatic event.

SUMMARY

The DSM-IV-TR is used for determining psychiatric diagnoses. Each individual is rated on five dimensions, called axes, which give a summary of the person's mental functioning.

In addition to many clinical studies that have measured rates of co-occurring disorders, two large-scale population studies, ECA and NCS, have estimated the rates of co-morbidity of alcohol and psychiatric disorders in the general population. All of these studies indicate that there are high rates of co-occurring psychiatric disorders in individuals with alcohol use disorders. Especially prevalent are substance use disorders, personality disorders, PTSD, and mood disorders. Similarly, those suffering from psychiatric disorders often have co-occurring alcohol use disorders. Those with bipolar disorder, schizophrenia, and ASPD have very high rates of alcohol disorders.

There are many ways these disorders can interact. From epidemiolgic data so far, it appears that, in general, psychiatric disorders precede the alcohol disorder. It is likely that some psychiatric disorders increase the risk of developing an alcohol use disorder, as, for example, ASPD and PTSD. On the other hand, it is likely that alcohol use disorders create symptoms that mimic some psychiatric disorders, especially mood and anxiety disorders. At the present time, it is probably best to think of these disorders as interacting with each other rather than one causing the other.

Those having a psychiatric disorder as well as an alcohol disorder have been found to have poorer treatment outcomes. The greater the severity of the psychiatric illness, the less is the likelihood of successful outcome.

PTSD is an anxiety disorder caused by a trauma. Those with PTSD have a heightened risk of developing alcohol disorders. It is hypothesized that these individuals drink in order to mask symptoms of the disorder.

Childhood sexual abuse is common in those with alcohol disorders. Such experiences can cause trauma and induce PTSD. Special treatment considerations are discussed for PTSD and sexually abused patients. There is preliminary support for the effectiveness of combined treatment for co-morbid PTSD and substance abuse disorders.

Alcohol abusers have a high rate of personality disorders. Special treatment for ASPD, one common co-occurring personality disorder, and alcohol disorders has had some modest preliminary support in two studies, but one study failed to show improved outcome.

Those suffering from co-morbid severe mental illness and substance use disorders represent an extremely challenging group of patients to help. Schizophrenia and bipolar disorders co-occurring with substance use disorders demand special treatment considerations, on which there is a general consensus. This approach, often called integrated treatment, has fairly substantial empirical support, although most of the studies lack control groups or randomization of subjects.

READINGS

American Psychiatric Association (2000). *Diagnostic and statistical manual of mental disorders* (Fourth Edition, Text Revision). Washington, DC: American Psychiatric Association.
An essential reference for all mental health professionals.

Najavits, L. M. (2002). *Seeking safety: A treatment manual for PTSD and substance abuse.* New York: Guilford.
This excellent book can be used by alcoholism and substance abuse counselors as well as mental health clinicians to guide the initial phase of treatment for those suffering from PTSD and substance abuse. The book is a model for addressing co-morbid substance abuse and other psychiatric disorders. It combines elements of cognitive behavioral and Twelve Step facilitation approaches.

Richards, J. R. (1993). *Therapy of the substance abuse syndromes.* Northvale, NJ: Jason Aronson.
Richards presents a provocative and creative paradigm for understanding and treating co-morbid disorders.

Spitzer, R. L., Gibbon, M., Skodol, A. E., Williams, J. B., & First, M. B. (1994). *DSM-IV casebook.* Washington, DC: American Psychiatric Association.
Provides examples of how diagnoses are made.

REFERENCES

Ahrens, M. P. (1998). A model for dual disorder treatment in acute psychiatry in a VA population. *Journal of Substance Abuse Treatment* 15, 107–112.

American Psychiatric Association (2000). *Diagnostic and statistical manual of mental disorders* (Fourth Edition, Text Revision). Washington, DC: American Psychiatric Association.

American Society of Addiction Medicine (2001). ASAM PPC-2R: ASAM patient placement criteria for the treatment of substance-related disorders (Second Edition—Revised). Chevy Chase, MD: American Society of Addiction Medicine.

Bernstein, D. P. (2000). Childhood trauma and drug addiction: Assessment, diagnosis, and treatment. *Alcoholism Treatment Quarterly* 18, 19–30.

Branchey, L., Davis, W., & Lieber, C. S. (1984). Alcoholism in Vietnam and Korea veterans: A long-term follow-up. *Alcoholism: Clinical and Experimental Research* 8, 572–575.

Burnam, M. A., Stein, J. A., Golding, J. M., Siegel, J. M., Sorenson, S. B., Forsythe, A. B., & Telles, C. A. (1988). Sexual assault and mental disorders in a community population. *Journal of Consulting and Clinical Psychology* 56, 843–850.

Drake, R. E., Bartels, S. J., Teague, G. B., Noordsy, D. L., & Clark, R. E. (1993). Treatment of substance abuse in severely mentally ill patients. *Journal of Nervous and Mental Disease* 181, 606–611.

Drake, R. E., Mercer-McFadden, C., Mueser, K. T., HcHugo, G. J., & Bond, G. R. (1998). Review of integrated mental health and substance abuse treatment for patients with dual disorders. *Schizophrenia Bulletin* 24, 589–608.

Elias, E. (2002). Personal communication. Special expert, Substance Abuse and Mental Health Services Administration.

Finkelhor, D. (1979). Early and long-term effects of child sexual abuse: An update. *Professional Psychology: Research and Practice* 21, 325–330.

Glover-Graf, N. M., & Janikowski, T. P. (2001). Substance abuse counselors' experiences with victims of incest. *Journal of Substance Abuse Treatment* 20, 9–14.

Greenbaum, P. E., Prange, M. E., Friedman, R. M., & Silver, S. E. (1991). Substance abuse prevalence and comorbidity with other psychiatric disorders among adolescents with severe emotional disturbances. *Journal of the American Academy of Child and Adolescent Psychiatry* 30, 575–583.

Harvey, E. M., Rawson, R. A., & Obert, J. L. (1994). History of sexual assault and the treatment of substance abuse disorders. *Journal of Psychoactive Drugs* 26, 361–367.

Helzer, J. E., & Pryzbeck, T. R. (1988). The co-occurrence of alcoholism with other psychiatric disorders in the general population and its impact on treatment. *Journal of Studies on Alcohol* 49, 219–224.

Hesselbrock, V., Meyer, R., & Hesselbrock, M. (1992). Psychopathology and addictive disorders: The specific case of ASPD. In C. P. O'Brien & J. H. Jaffe (Eds.), *Addictive states* (pp. 179–191). New York: Raven.

Hesselbrock, M. N., Meyer, R. E., & Keener, J. J. (1985). Psychopathology in hospitalized alcoholics. *Archives of General Psychiatry* 42, 1050–1055.

Holdcraft, L. C., Iacono, W. G., & McGue, M. K. (1998). Antisocial personality disorder and depression in relation to alcoholism: A community-based sample. *Journal of Studies on Alcohol* 59, 222–226.

Kadden, R. M., Getter, H., Cooney, N. L., & Litt, M. D. (1989). Matching alcoholics to coping skills or interactional therapies: Post treatment results. *Journal of Consulting and Clinical Psychology* 57, 698–704.

Kalman, D., Longabaugh, R., Clifford, P. R., Beattie, M., & Maisto, S. A. (2000). Matching alcoholics to treatment: Failure to replicate finding of an earlier study. *Journal of Substance Abuse Treatment* 19, 183–187.

Kessler, R. C., Crum, R. M., Warner, L. A., Nelson, C. B., Schulenberg, J., & Anthony, J. C. (1997). Lifetime co-occurrence of DSM-III-R alcohol abuse and dependence with other psychiatric disorders in the National Cormorbidity Survey. *Archives of General Psychiatry* 54, 313–321.

Kranzer, H. R., Mason, B. Modesto-Lowe, V. (1998). Prevalence, diagnosis, and treatment of comorbid mood disorders and alcoholism. In H. R. Kranzler & B. J. Rounsaville (Eds.), *Dual diagnosis* (pp. 107–136). New York: Marcel Dekker.

Langeland, W., & Hartgers, C. (1998). Child sexual and physical abuse and alcoholics: A review. *Journal of Studies on Alcohol* 59, 336–348.

Laudet, A. B., Magura, S., Vogel, H. S., & Knight, E. (2000). Recovery challenges among dually diagnosed individuals. *Journal of Substance Abuse Treatment* 18, 321–329.

Lewis, C. E., Bucholz, K. K., Spitznagel, E., & Shayka, J. J. (1996). Effects of gender and comorbidity on problem drinking in a community sample. *Alcoholism: Clinical and Experimental Research* 20, 466–476.

Loungabaugh, R., Rubin, A., Malloy, P., Beattie, M., Clifford, P. R., & Noel, N. (1994). Drinking outcomes of alcohol abusers diagnosed as antisocial personality disorder. *Alcoholism: Clinical and Experimental Research* 18, 778–785.

McLellan, A. T. (1986). "Psychiatric severity" as a predictor of outcome from substance abuse treatment. In R. E. Meyer (Ed.), *Psychopathology and addictive disorders* (pp. 97–139). New York: Guilford.

Meyer, R. E. (1986). How to understand the relationship between psychopathology and addictive disorders: Another example of the chicken and the egg. In R. E. Meyer (Ed.), *Psychopathology and addictive disorders* (pp. 3–16). New York: Guilford.

Moggi, F. Ouimette, P. C., Finney, J. W., & Moos, R. H. (1999). Effectiveness of treatment for substance abuse and dependence for dual diagnosis patients: A model of treatment factors associated with one-year outcomes. *Journal of Studies on Alcohol* 60, 856–866.

Morgenstern, J., Langenbucher, E. L., & Miller, K. J. (1997). The comorbidity of alcoholism and personality disorders in a clinical population: Prevalence rates and relation to alcohol typology variables. *Journal of Abnormal Psychology* 106, 74–84.

Mueser, K. T., Bellack, A. S., & Blanchard, J. J. (1992). Comorbidity of schizophrenia and substance abuse: Implications for treatment. *Journal of Consulting and Clinical Psychology* 60, 845–856.

Najavits, L. M. (2002). *Seeking safety: A treatment manual for PTSD and substance abuse.* New York: Guilford.

Ouimette, P. C., Brown, P. J., & Najavits, L. M. (1998). Course and treatment of patients with both substance use and posttraumatic stress disorders. *Addictive Behaviors* 23, 785–795.

Ouimette, P. C., Kimerling, R., Shaw, J., & Moos, R. H. (2000a). Physical and sexual abuse among women and men with substance abuse. *Alcoholism Treatment Quarterly* 18, 7–17.

Ouimette, P. C., Moos, R. H., & Finney, J. W. (2000b). Two-year mental health service use and course of remission patients with substance use and posttraumatic stress disorders. *Journal of Studies on Alcohol* 61, 247–253.

Phil, R. O., & Peterson, J. B. (1991). Attention-deficit hyperactivity disorder, childhood conduct disorder, and alcoholism: Is there an association? *Alcohol, Health, and Research World* 15, 25–31.

RachBeisel, J., Scott, J., & Dixon, L. (1999). Co-occurring severe mental illness and substance use disorders: A review of recent research. *Psychiatric Services* 50, 1427–1434.

Regier, D. A., Farmer, M. E., Rae, D. S., Locke, B. Z., Keith, S. J., Judd, L. L., & Goodwin, F. K. (1990). Comorbidity of mental disorders with alcohol and other drug abuse. Results from the Epidemiologic Catchment Area study. *Journal of the American Medical Association* 264, 2511–2518.

Rice, C., Mohr, C. D., Del Boca, F. K., Mattson, M. E., Young, L., Brady, K., & Nickless, C. (2001). Self reports of physical, social and emotional abuse in an alcoholism treatment sample. *Journal of Studies on Alcohol* 62, 114–123.

Richards, J. R. (1993). *Therapy of the substance abuse syndromes.* Northvale, NJ: Jason Aronson.

Rohde, P., Lewinsohn, P. M., & Seeley, J. R. (1996). Psychiatric comorbidity with problematic alcohol use in high school students. *Journal of the American Academy of Child and Adolescent Psychiatry* 35, 101–109.

Rohsenow, D. J., Corbett, R., & Devine, D. (1988). Molested as children. A hidden contribution to substance abuse. *Journal of Substance Abuse Treatment* 5, 13–18.

Rounsaville, B. J., Dolinsky, Z. S., Babor, T. F., & Meyer, R. E. (1987). Psychopathology as a predictor of treatment outcome in alcoholics. *Archives of General Psychiatry* 44, 505–513.

Schubert, D. S., Wolf, A. W., Patterson, M. B., Grande, T. P., & Pendelton, L. (1998). A statistical evaluation of the literature regarding the associations among alcoholism, drug abuse, and antisocial personality disorder. *International Journal of the Addictions* 23, 797–808.

Schulte, J. G., Dinwiddie, S. H., Pribor, E. F., & Yutzy, S. H. (1995). Psychiatric diagnoses of adult male victims of childhood sexual abuse. *Journal of Nervous and Mental Disease* 183, 111–113.

Shaner, A., Eckman, T. A., Roberts, L. J., Wilkins, J. N., Tucker, D. E., Tsuang, J. W., & Mintz, J. (1995). Disability income, cocaine use, and repeated hospitalization among schizophrenic cocaine abusers. *New England Journal of Medicine* 333, 777–783.

Stewart, S. H. (1996). Alcohol abuse in individuals exposed to trauma: A critical review. *Psychological Bulletin* 120, 83–112.

Sullivan, J. M., & Evans, K. (1994). Integrated treatment for the survivor of childhood trauma who is chemically dependent. *Journal of Psychoactive Drugs* 26, 369–378.

Thomas, V. H., Melchert, T. P., & Banken, J. A. (1999). Substance dependence and personality disorders: Comorbidity and treatment outcome in an inpatient treatment population. *Journal of Studies on Alcohol* 60, 271–277.

Verheul, R., Hartgers, C., Van Den Brink, W., & Koeter, M. W. (1998). The effect of sampling, diagnostic criteria, and assessment procedures on the observed prevalence of DSM-III-R personality disorders among treated alcoholics. *Journal of Studies on Alcohol* 59, 227–236.

Verheul, R., Kranzler, H. R., Poling, J., Tennen, H., Ball, S., & Rounsaville, B. J. (2000). Axis I and axis II disorders in alcoholics and drug addicts: Fact or artifact. *Journal of Studies on Alcohol* 61, 101–110.

Vogel, H. S., Knight, E., Laudet, A. B., & Magura, S. (1998). Double trouble in recovery: Self-help for people with dual diagnoses. *Psychiatric Rehabilitation Journal* 21, 356–364.

Wilsnack, S. C., Vogeltanz, N. D., Klassen, A. D., & Harris, T. R. (1997). Childhood sexual abuse and women's substance abuse: National survey findings. *Journal of Studies on Alcohol* 58, 264–271.

Young, E. B. (1990). The role of incest issues in relapse. *Journal of Psychoactive Drugs* 22, 249–258.

Zweben, J. E., Clark, H. W., & Smith, D. (1994). Traumatic experiences and substance abuse: Mapping the territory. *Journal of Psychoactive Drugs* 26, 327–344.

CHAPTER ELEVEN

OUTCOME STUDIES ON ALCOHOL AND DRUG ABUSE TREATMENT
From the Rand Report to the MATCH Study

On a typical day approximately 800,00 clients receive alcohol treatment in the United States (Greenfeld, 1998). Treatment for alcohol disorders costs approximately $7.5 billion per year (U.S. Department of Health and Human Services, 2000). Given the extent of the problems caused by alcohol disorders (discussed in Chapters 3 and 5) and the great cost of treatment, it is important to review research that measures how effective alcoholism treatment is. This chapter will introduce a large number of studies evaluating the outcome of treatments for alcohol disorders and discuss research that seeks to determine if some treatments are more effective than others. Many of the more recent studies examine the outcome of combined alcohol and drug treatment and are included in the chapter. As noted in Chapter 5, a high percentage of individuals who suffer from an alcohol disorder also have a substance use disorder, thus making combined treatment a sensible approach.

One type of outcome research determines the efficacy of treatment as it is actually provided. This gives us a measure of the actual help that alcoholics get in real treatment situations. The Rand report is of this type. A second type of research carefully tests the effects of specific treatment techniques and compares the outcomes with a control condition. This type of research helps determine whether some treatments are more effective than others and provides alcohol programs with potentially innovative treatments to implement.

In this chapter the following questions will be considered:

1. What is alcoholism treatment and what can reasonably be expected from it? Included will be descriptions of the common treatments: Twelve Step facilitation (TSF), cognitive behavioral therapy (CBT), and motivational interviewing.
2. How effective is alcoholism treatment? Included will be consideration of three major outcome studies: the Rand report, the VA Outcome study, and the MATCH study.
3. Are some treatments more effective than others?
4. Are certain types of treatment more effective for certain types of patients (treatment matching)?
5. What causes relapse?
6. Does family treatment help engage the alcoholic?

7. How does the goal of controlled drinking versus abstinence affect outcome?
8. What are the research findings on AA?
9. Is smoking cessation an appropriate goal in conjunction with alcohol treatment?
10. What actually occurs in treatment? Examination of process factors.
11. Are there common factors among all treatments that are responsible for positive outcomes?

METHODOLOGY

As indicated above, there are two types of outcome research. Research that studies treatment as it is actually provided makes use of experimental designs that are typically less rigorous than those testing specific therapies, because the researchers often cannot assign subjects randomly to different conditions, do not specify the treatment provided, and often do not have control groups. The research on specific therapies, called clinical trials, can specify the treatments more precisely and assign patients to treatment and control groups randomly.

There is a problem interpreting results of outcome studies that do not use a control group. If a group of alcoholics is provided treatment and they show great improvement but there is no control group, we cannot be sure that the treatment is responsible for the positive change, because a large percentage of alcohol disorders goes into remission without treatment (see Chapter 5). To account for this, researchers compare the outcomes of a control group, which receive minimal or no treatment, to the outcomes of the treatment group. If the treatment group has done significantly better than the control group, it can be concluded that the treatment is responsible for the difference. Other designs may compare the relative effectiveness of two or more different treatments. Even here it is preferable to have a control group in order to have a comparison between the treated and the not-treated group. Outcome research has some similarities with drug trial research, discussed in Chapter 8.

Generalizability of Results

One premise of the book is that there is a great heterogeneity in those suffering from alcohol disorders. Hence, generalizing from an outcome study to any overall conclusion about alcoholics requires an assessment of the population of subjects used. Some of these factors include gender, age, degree of severity of alcohol disorder, co-morbid pathology and severity of pathology, and criminal justice involvement. For example, it would not be accurate to estimate rates of antisocial personality disorder (ASPD) for all alcoholics from studies of males who have criminal justice involvement. Nor would it be appropriate to generalize from patients with alcohol abuse to those with alcohol dependence. Most of the studies cited in this chapter have large heterogeneous samples of alcoholics.

Specifying the Treatment

In clinical trials of innovative therapies, treatment interventions are often carefully specified. The therapists are given extensive training in specific treatment techniques and they are monitored when providing treatment. This is an effort to ensure treatment integrity. In large-scale outcome research, however, the actual techniques used in alcoholism treatment have been rarely measured, so that what goes on in the sessions has been typically an unknown "black box." In more recent large-scale research, such as the MATCH study, efforts have been made to specify treatment techniques similar to the methods of clinical trial research.

Specifying the Outcome

Outcomes are typically measured in abstinence rates and reductions in negative drinking events. Regrettably, there are no standard outcome measures used by such studies, which makes comparisons difficult. For example, abstinence has been measured in varying intervals, from the preceding month of the interview to continuously abstinent since treatment initiation.

Many outcome studies seek verification of self-reports regarding alcohol consumption and problems with collateral interviews and/or objective blood/breath tests (see Chapter 2 for additional discussion of outcome criteria and self-report verification).

The minimal length of time that must pass before the outcome can be considered meaningful is 6 months, but stability of outcome often does not occur until 3 years of remission (see the Harvard Study of Adult Development in Chapter 6).

Accounting for Dropouts

As discussed in Chapter 9, one difficulty in outcome research is that many clients drop out of treatment or follow-up. Because researchers do not have complete results for those who drop out, the data no longer reflect a random sample of alcoholics. The dropouts make it difficult to generalize to all alcoholics because we cannot typically determine why they drop out and if their absence biases the results. For example, if one treatment has a high dropout rate, but those who remain do well, and another treatment has a low dropout rate but a lower success rate, it would not be fair to say that the former is the better treatment, because a big side effect of this treatment is a failure to engage the large number who drop out. Good research accounts for these dropouts in a number of ways, first, by calculating the outcome rates, which include the dropouts as failures. Additionally, studies compare demographic data between the dropouts and completers. If there are no significant differences, researchers often conclude that the missing dropout data do not affect the results.

Dummy Treatment

Advocates of a specific treatment often devise experiments to test whether their treatment is superior to a competitive one. They may inadvertently slant the procedure to favor their intervention. Thus, there is the danger that the competitive treatment will be delivered in a less than optimal manner. Regrettably, this consideration has been neglected in outcome research.

WHAT IS ALCOHOLISM TREATMENT AND WHAT CAN REASONABLY BE EXPECTED FROM IT?

A key consideration is what alcoholism treatment consists of and what can reasonably be expected from it. To date, the major alcohol treatments are primarily psychosocial in nature. They consist of some combination of education, persuasion, exhortation, confrontation, and dialogue. Counselors have only a limited amount of contact with clients in outpatient treatment, usually 1 or 2 hours a week or 1 or 2 84ths of a person's waking life. Additionally, there are a multitude of external circumstances that clinicians cannot influence. Against this backdrop, counselors must help clients change entrenched habits that have been developing for 10 years or more (Lindstrom, 1992). These considerations suggest that current alcoholism treatments can have, at best, a modest impact on outcome. Thus, although complete cure for all alcoholics is an understandable and desirable goal, at this point, psychosocial treatments for alcohol disorders can be reasonably expected to help a percentage (although perhaps large) of alcoholics for limited time periods (although perhaps relatively long). The author's view of people's expectations of alcoholism treatment is discussed in Box 11.1.

Still, alcoholism treatment outcome research must demonstrate that treatment improves drinking behavior in alcoholics more than no treatment. The purpose of the control group allows a comparison of the treatment to no or minimal treatment. Unfortunately, very few large-scale studies include a control group. I will highlight the two studies with such comparisons, and I will draw on research findings on untreated alcoholics that suggest reasonable benchmarks for treatment outcome comparisons. (See also discussions on remission in Chapters 5 and 6.)

THE COMMON ALCOHOLISM TREATMENTS

Twelve Step Facilitation Model (TSF)

The Twelve Step facilitation model, a professional treatment, has also been called the Minnesota model, the disease concept, and Twelve Step treatment. The treatment is based on the premise that active participation in Alcoholics Anonymous (AA) will help the alcoholic become and remain sober. Thus the primary goal is to promote AA involvement. Techniques include education about alcoholism and helping patients confront the effects of their drinking on their lives. The counselor teaches practical methods of staying sober based on the experiences of AA members. If the counselor is a member of AA, he or she may use self-disclosure by sharing his or her own experiences in recovery. In addition to monitoring attendance and progress in AA, the counselor helps the client understand the processes of AA, such as obtaining an AA sponsor and working the Twelve Steps (shown in Table 1.2), and supports AA premises such as the goals of abstinence and spiritual development. It is important to keep in mind that this model of treatment is separate from AA. Some elements of TSF are not principles of AA, such as the use of confrontation (Miller & Kurtz, 1994). A large percentage of TSF counselors are recovering alcoholics and AA members themselves (Saxe et al., 1983).

▓ ▓ ▓ ▓ ▓ ▓▓

BOX 11.1
TREATMENT OUTCOME EXPECTATION FALLACY

I have found it a common expectation that alcoholism treatment should achieve a very high standard of success, which does not correspond to current reality. This high expectation about alcoholism treatment I have labeled the **treatment outcome expectation fallacy.** Why do people have it? One reason is that we have a tendency to seek simple solutions to complex problems. If this book has had any impact on the reader, it should be clear that alcohol disorders are heterogeneous, caused and maintained by a variety of factors. Because a multitude of factors can operate to contribute to remission and/or relapse, and many are out of the control of the therapist, it seems reasonable to conclude that treatment can improve the probability of a good outcome but not insure it.

Perhaps another reason people have a high expectation for alcohol treatment is derived from the medical model of alcoholism: if alcoholism is a disease, as we commonly hear, professional treatment should succeed in treating it. We assume that in successful medical treatment of diseases such as tuberculosis, most of the cases will be cured or achieve remission. If treatment fails to work in a large number of cases, it is assumed that doctors either do not understand some aspect of the disease process or have not developed the necessary technology to treat it. Alcohol disorders, however, are quite different from typical medical diseases. There is no known specific physical cause. Interventions are more indirect and less specifiable than medical procedures: alcoholism counselors use persuasion, education, confrontation, and empathy to influence an entrenched long-standing habit as compared to, for example, a specified surgical procedure used by physicians.

To take an example from Chapter 9, consider two perspectives from which to view outcome research on alcoholism treatment and domestic violence (DV). Recall that half of the problem drinkers in BCT family treatment achieved remission from alcohol abuse and decreased their DV to levels of a nonalcoholic control group. This is encouraging. On the other hand, alcohol disorders did not go into remission for the other half, and DV did not decrease for this group. Statistically, then, one could argue that a victim of DV lowers her risk for continued DV about 50 percent by supporting or insisting on alcoholism treatment for her spouse. But it is no sure thing. She still has a significant risk of continued DV because only half of the men remitted. Further, the DV in the remitted men is at the same rate as controls, meaning that even when the alcohol disorder is treated successfully, DV is not completely eliminated. If you take the position that any additional DV is unacceptable, the results are disappointing. Thus, our perspective plays an important role in determining whether we can be satisfied with alcohol treatment outcomes that decrease DV but do not eliminate it.

Alcoholics Anonymous (AA)

By contrast, AA itself is a self-help spiritual fellowship for alcoholics helping other alcoholics. It is based on the personal experiences of alcoholics who became sober through a spiritual process. Members share their experiences with newcomers to provide practical, nonprofessional help in becoming sober. New members are encouraged to choose a sponsor to help them learn about AA, obtain practical advice on how to stay sober, and work the Twelve Steps. The sponsor is an AA member who offers help based on his or her personal experiences in AA. AA principles are explained in the book, *Alcoholics Anonymous* (Alcoholics Anonymous World Services, 1976).

TABLE 11.1   Remission Rates for Treated and Untreated Alcoholics, 18-Month Follow-up

| | | REMISSION RATES (%) | | |
| | | Treated Alcoholics | | |
Remission Status	Untreated Alcoholics	Low Amount of Treatment	High Amount of Treatment	All Treated Clients
Abstained 6 months	13	22	26	24
Abstained 1 month	13	16	21	21
Normal drinking	28	20	26	22
Total remission	54	58	73	67
Daily consumption (oz)	3.2	2.9	2.2	2.5
n	241	184	272	596

Source: David J. Armor et al., *Alcoholism and Treatment.* RAND Book 011848, New York: Wiley, 1978. Copyright © RAND 1978. Adapted by permission.

Cognitive Behavioral Treatment (CBT)

Cognitive behavioral treatment for alcohol disorders is based on the view that excessive drinking is a learned habit. The treatment consists of employing methods to unlearn the maladaptive drinking behaviors and teach adaptive skills regarding the drinking behavior and general life skills. There are several types of CBT, of which relapse prevention and behavioral self-control training are discussed later in the chapter. Each type of CBT contains a combination of didactic topics, which may include training in drink refusal skills, coping with alcohol environments, problem solving, interpersonal skills, mood regulation, coping skills for dealing with stress, communication skills, and assertiveness. Specific skills are taught, followed by role-plays in which the client applies the specific new skills. Clients are often given homework such as monitoring their drinking or drink urges and recording them in a diary in the interval between sessions. In CBT, the treatment goal may be abstinence or controlled drinking. If controlled drinking is the goal, there are specific techniques to teach drinking moderation.

Motivational Interviewing (MET)

Motivational interviewing has as its goal to develop motivation for the individual to change the addictive behavior (Miller & Rollnick, 1991). Instead of focusing on drinking behavior, the counselor focuses on the client's ambivalence or lack thereof regarding the drinking. The goal is to create ambivalence when there is none, and when there is, to help the client resolve it on the side of quitting. The techniques are based in part on client-centered therapy such as empathic listening to engage the patient's cooperation. The therapy is also linked to the stages of change model developed by Prochaska et al. (1992), outlined later in the chapter. By determining the client's stage of readiness to change, appropriate goals and techniques can be employed to help the patient become committed to change. Once the client's motivation is sufficiently engaged, he can mobilize his own resources to change or move on to additional types of treatment.

IS ALCOHOLISM TREATMENT EFFECTIVE?

A number of large, methodologically sound studies have been conducted that measure the outcome of alcoholism treatment as it is actually delivered. The first such study was the Rand report, in which a large number of treated alcoholics were followed for 18 months and then at 4 years after treatment. More recently, a Veterans Administration (VA) study followed a large number of substance abusers in VA programs and compared the effectiveness of three types of treatment.

The Rand Report

Armor et al. (1978) conducted the first large study of alcoholism treatment outcome. Researchers followed 1,340 alcoholic patients treated in eight representative programs for 18 months with a completion rate of 62 percent. Four hundred clients who had made contact but were not admitted to treatment served as a control group. About half of this group attended AA or received other treatment during the interval investigated, however.

Although the typical patient's attendance in the treatment program was erratic and sporadic, patients showed a large reduction in drinking after treatment. At intake the patients averaged 8.4 oz of absolute alcohol per day. At 6 months after treatment began only 27 percent were drinking more than 1 oz per day; at 18 months, it was 32 percent.

At 18 months, treated clients had a remission rate of 67 percent, compared to 53 percent for untreated clients. Included in the remission category were 22 percent who were drinking asymptomatically. Another third included as remitted had reported no drinking in the past month but some drinking in the past 6 months. The rest had abstained for 6 months. For those with at least 15 sessions (noted as high amount of treatment in Table 11.1), the remission rate was 73 percent.

Subtracting the remission rate of the control group from the treated group (67 percent – 53 percent), we can estimate that treatment improved outcome by 14 percent. For treatments of longer duration the effect was a 20 percent improvement. Type of treatment, treatment setting, and professional versus paraprofessional therapist were not significant variables. For those subjects who had little or no treatment, regular AA attendance raised remission rates from 55 percent to 71 percent, suggesting that AA attendance is as effective as professional treatment for those who choose to participate in AA.

The researchers continued the study by interviewing 85 percent of the original participants 4 years later (Polich et al., 1981). At 4 years, they found that 28 percent of the treated patients were currently abstaining and 22 percent had been abstinent for 1 year or more. Eight percent were drinking low quantities of alcohol with no problems, averaging fewer than 4 drinks per occasion. Ten percent were drinking larger amounts with no problems, ranging from 4 to 10 drinks per occasion and averaging 6. Almost three-fourths of treated patients and one-half of the control group attended AA during the 4-year period. Only 13 percent of the sample were stable abstainers, and 9 percent were stable nonsymptomatic drinkers in the period from 18 months to the 4-year follow-up. In general, alcohol remission was unstable. Large numbers of the treated and untreated alcoholics shifted back and forth between periods of abstinence and drinking.

Fifty-seven percent of the treatment group had drunk in the past month. Fifty-four percent were having alcohol problems and considered unremitted at the 4-year follow-up. Of those who were drinking, 45 percent were drinking more than 11 drinks per occasion. Those who drank and had any dependence symptoms or adverse consequences were likely to fare poorly in health, remission from alcoholism, and survival. Low-consumption drinkers with any alcohol-related symptoms had a high relapse rate.

The VA Outcome Study

A large outcome study of patients from fifteen substance abuse inpatient treatment programs in the VA has recently been conducted (Moos et al., 1999). The study followed patients treated in VA Substance Abuse Programs, rated as predominately TSF, CBT, or a combination of the two. Of a potential pool of 4,192 patients, 3,698 began the study and 3,084 completed follow-up, an 84 percent rate of completion. The sample was diagnosed with 40 percent alcohol dependency, 17 percent drug dependency, and 43 percent having both dependencies. Thirty-five percent had an additional psychiatric diagnosis.

The results showed that 40 percent were abstinent in the ninth to twelfth month after treatment. Thirty percent had had no substance-related problems in the year after treatment. Arrests had decreased from 34 percent to 22 percent and employment had increased from 24 percent to 38 percent compared to preadmission rates. Fifty-six percent had attended some self-help meetings. Several other reports have been published using data from this study, which will be discussed later in the chapter.

Meta-Analysis of Outcome Research

Miller at al. (2001) conducted a meta-analysis of large alcoholism outcome studies that combines the results of seven multisite studies, including the Rand report, the VA study discussed above, and the MATCH study discussed below. The meta-analysis showed that 24 percent of patients in outpatient treatment maintained abstinence and over 11 percent maintained moderate asymptomatic drinking for 1 year. Drinking days dropped from 63 percent before treatment to 18 percent after treatment. Those who continued drinking had averaged 77 drinks per week before treatment and afterwards were averaging 10 drinks per week, an 87 percent reduction. Compared to pretreatment levels, drinking-related problems were reduced by almost 60 percent. The remaining 66 percent had some periods of heavy drinking, but even this group showed substantial improvement. They drank less often and they consumed less when they did drink.

In summary, there is substantial research which indicates that alcoholics improve after alcoholism treatment. However, only one of these large-scale studies included a control group. Thus it is important to estimate the remission rates for untreated alcoholics to determine the degree to which treatment contributes to positive outcomes.

Comparing Outcomes of Treated and Untreated Alcoholics

Two studies compare untreated samples with treated alcoholics: Timko et al.'s study and the Rand report. Additionally, a study that followed untreated alcoholics and epidemiologic data help establish an estimate of improvement without treatment.

Ojesjo (1981) followed alcoholics who had minimal treatment for 15 years. The rate of remission was 30 percent of the the entire sample and 41 percent for the surviving sample. Ojesjo suggests that these findings may be used as a good estimate of outcome for an untreated sample of alcoholics. Timko et al. (1995, 2000) followed a sample of alcoholics for 8 years, who were screened for treatment and self-chose either no professional treatment, professional treatment, and/or AA. Both treated and untreated alcoholics improved, but the treated group (including AA) improved much more. Figure 11.1 shows the percent abstinent in treated and untreated alcoholics over time. Fifty-four percent of the treated group were abstinent in the past 6 months at 8 years, compared to a 26 percent rate of abstinence for the untreated group.

Table 11.2 shows that remission rates and improvements in drinking behaviors are moderately better in the treated sample.

This study provides us with an estimate of how untreated problem drinkers fare in comparison to those treated. Because subjects were free to choose their treatment condition, the samples are not random and results do not conclusively reflect the effects of treatment.

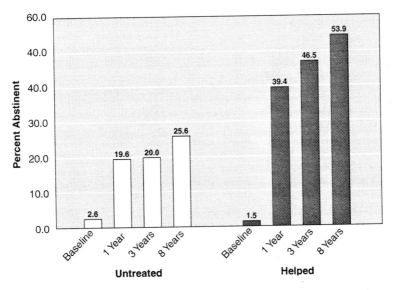

FIGURE 11.1 The Course of Abstinence among Untreated (*n* = 78) and Helped (*n* = 388) Individuals

Source: Reprinted with permission from *Journal of Studies on Alcohol,* vol. 61, pp. 529–540, 2000. Copyright by Alcohol Research Documentation, Inc., Rutgers Center of Alcohol Studies, Piscataway, NJ 08854.

TABLE 11.2   Drinking Patterns of Four Treatment Status Groups at Baseline, 1 Year, 3 Years, and 8 Years (n = 466)

Drinking Variable	No Treatment (n = 78)	AA Only (n = 74)	Treatment Only (n = 74)	Treatment and AA (n = 248)	χ^2
TREATMENT STATUS GROUP					
Abstinent (%)					
Baseline	2.6	1.5	1.4	1.6	0.34
1 Year	19.6	47.5	20.6	42.4	20.50**
3 Years	20.0	50.0	25.9	50.9	26.06**
8 Years	25.6	48.5	45.9	57.7	25.30**
Benign drinking pattern (%)					
Baseline	3.9	1.5	4.1	2.4	0.95
1 Year	38.2	55.9	33.3	50.4	7.67*
3 Years	42.0	63.8	43.1	57.9	8.90*
8 Years	47.4	63.6	54.1	65.3	8.47*
No drinking-related problems (%)					
Baseline	6.4	1.5	10.8	3.2	8.11*
1 Year	53.6	59.3	38.7	51.9	5.69
3 Years	59.2	70.7	42.1	58.8	8.58*
8 Years	53.8	68.2	59.5	68.1	6.30
In remission (%)					
Baseline	2.6	1.6	2.7	2.0	0.24
1 Year	42.6	54.2	35.5	48.3	8.63*
3 Years	47.9	66.7	36.8	57.5	16.25**
8 Years	43.6	62.1	55.4	63.0	9.98*

Baseline analyses control for gender and marital status; 1-, 3-, and 8-year analyses control for gender, marital status, and baseline functioning. *$p < 0.05$, **$p < 0.001$.

Reprinted with permission from *Journal of Studies on Alcohol*, vol. 61, pp. 529–540, 2000. Copyright by Alcohol Research Documentation, Inc., Rutgers Center of Alcohol Studies, Piscataway, NJ 08854.

The Rand report, discussed above, made a comparison between the treated and untreated samples, finding that treatment improved remission by 14 percent. At the 18-month follow-up, the Rand study's control subjects had about 13 percent (author's estimate) rate of abstinence, compared to the 24 percent (author's estimate) rate of abstinence in the treated group.

Both Timko et al. and the Rand study found remission rates of about 50 percent for the untreated samples they followed for intervals of 18 months (Armor et al., 1978) and 3 years (Timko et al., 2000). Remission included a relatively high percentage of asymptomatic drinking, 42 percent in Timko et al.'s sample and 28 percent in the Rand study. Epidemiologic research from the Epidemiological Catchment Area Survey, discussed in Chapter 5, (ECA) suggests that remission rates for an alcohol use disorder is about 50 percent (Helzer et al., 1991). These results taken together suggest that about half of all problem drinkers are in remission at any given time. It should be kept in mind that remission means that the criteria for an alcohol disorder have not been met in the preceding year. A portion of those classified as remitted have sporadic problems with alcohol and/or consume large amounts of alcohol without meeting the criteria for an alcohol disorder. Many remitted alcoholics, especially of the type just discussed, will slip back into an active alcohol disorder, as indicated by longitudinal studies of alcoholics (Vaillant, 1995; Taylor et al., 1985; Skog and Duckert, 1993) and the 4-year follow-up of the Rand report (Polich et al., 1981).

In summary, in the two studies in which there were comparison groups of treated and untreated alcoholics, treated alcoholics had a much higher abstinence rate than the untreated alcoholics. When measured by remission or decreased drinking symptoms, the studies show more modest improvement for treated patients compared to the untreated group. Longitudinal and epidemiologic research suggests remission rates of between 30 and 50 percent for untreated alcoholics, respectively.

Do Effects of Treatment Fade with Time?

Several studies provide information on the duration of treatment effects. One method is to follow a group of treated patients for a long period to see if gains are maintained. A more rigorous method compares the treated group with an untreated group over long periods.

Finney and Moos (1991) followed a sample of treated alcoholics for 10 years. Abstinence rates of about 50 percent and non-problem-drinking rates of 15 percent were consistent in the last 5 years of the 10-year follow-up period, suggesting that treatment effects did not fade.

A few studies give a good estimate of effectiveness of treatment compared to a control group over extended periods, such as Timko et al.'s study described above. Examining Table 11.2 and Figure 11.1, we can see that treatment effects are positive in all outcome measures in all periods of follow-up through 8 years. The most marked benefit of treatment is the increased rate of abstinence.

Vailliant's (1983) study of treated alcoholics found virtually no differences in outcome after 2 years compared to untreated alcoholics. By 8 years, while the remission rate for treated alcoholics was not appreciably different from the controls, about 45 percent, abstinence rates of the treated group had increased from 20 to 38 percent, while abstinence rates remained the same, about 20 percent, for the untreated group (p. 287).

The Rand report yields similar results. In the treated sample, the remission rate decreased from 67 percent at 18 months to only 46 percent at 4 years, indicating a fading of treatment effects. However, abstinence in the treated group had increased from 24 percent (authors' estimate) to 28 percent, while it had only increased from 13 percent (author's estimate) to 16 percent in the untreated group (Polich et al., 1981, p. 37).

Thus the data are fairly consistent. Treatment has an initial and enduring positive effect on rates of abstinence, while it has a more modest effect on overall remission rates.

ARE SOME TREATMENTS MORE EFFECTIVE THAN OTHERS?

A variety of outcome studies have compared the effectiveness of specific treatments with competing treatments or control conditions.

The MATCH Study

The most objective and careful study was the MATCH study (Project MATCH Research Group, 1997), which compared three types of treatment: Twelve Step facilitation (TSF), cognitive behavioral treatment (CBT), and motivational enhancement treatment (MET). The study was conceived to test the usefulness of matching clients to treatments based on patient characteristics. Here the overall results and comparisons among the three treatments are discussed.

Five outpatient and five aftercare sites were drawn on to recruit subjects. Aftercare consisted of outpatient treatment after an inpatient treatment for alcoholism. Of 2,193 potential outpatient clients, 952 became subjects (Ss); of 2,288 aftercare clients, 774 became Ss. Loss of recruitment was due to refusal to participate, while others were screened out for various reasons. Ninety-five percent of the subjects were alcohol-dependent and 5 percent had alcohol abuse. Patients were randomly assigned to one of the three treatment types.

CBT focused on overcoming skills deficits and increasing the ability to cope with situations that precipitate relapse. The TSF treatment goal was to motivate clients to become active in AA and begin to work on the Twelve Steps. MET treatment, similar to motivational interviewing, focused on building motivation to change drinking behavior and mobilizing the person's own resources. More details of the treatments are discussed earlier in the chapter; complete descriptions are available in the respective manuals (Nowinski et al., 1995; Miller et al., 1995; Kadden et al., 1995).

Impressive efforts were made to assure treatment integrity. The three treatments were manual guided; therapists were carefully trained, monitored, and supervised to assure that treatments were delivered according to the treatment manuals.

Treatment duration was 12 weeks. CBT and TSF consisted of weekly sessions, while MET consisted of four sessions over the 12-week period. Over 90 percent of the patients and 75 percent of the collaterals (relatives who could estimate patients' alcohol consumption) were interviewed 1 year after treatment. Blood samples were drawn from over 80 percent of the patients. Comparisons of laboratory findings and collaterals' reports with subjects' reports generally confirmed the verbal reports of subjects regarding their drinking.

Results indicated that 35 percent of aftercare patients and 19 percent of the outpatients were abstinent after 1 year. Additionally, 12.4 percent of the outpatient sample and 7.3 percent of the aftercare patients were drinking safely. There were no significant differences between treatments in percent days abstinent (PDA) and drinks per drinking day (DDD), the primary outcome measures. However, in the outpatient sample, TSF clients had the highest rates of abstinence, 24 percent. By comparison, CBT clients had a 15 percent rate and MET clients had a 14 percent rate.

The lack of a control group prevents any conclusion about whether any of these treatments are more effective than no treatment. The authors conclude that treatments embodying very different treatment philosophies appear to produce comparably good outcomes.

Three-year outcomes were obtained from 84.7 percent of the outpatient sample (Project MATCH Research Group, 1998). Results indicate that 29.4 percent of those followed were abstinent in the 3-month period preceding the interview at 3 years. TSF clients had higher rate of abstinence, 36 percent, compared to CBT clients, 24 percent, and MET clients, 27 percent. TSF treatment outcome was better in PDA and DDD than CBT but not MET. The authors conclude that there were few differences in outcome among the treatments, although TSF continued to show a slight positive advantage.

Similarly, Ouimette et al. (1997a) and Moos et al. (1999) using data from the VA study, report remission rates were similar in CBT and TSF programs, but participants in TSF were significantly more likely to be abstinent, 45 percent, compared to CBT treatment, 36 percent.

The results of the studies discussed above are in line with the conclusion drawn in 1990 by the Institute of Medicine (1990) that no single treatment has been found superior for alcoholics.

OUTCOME RESEARCH ON SPECIALIZED TREATMENTS AND TREATMENT GOALS

Brief Treatments

Brief treatments may consist of as little as a 10-minute intervention, or as many as three sessions with periodic medical follow-up. The client is provided with the results of alcohol screening and any biologic tests, advised to curtail his or her drinking, and may be given some suggestions about stopping. Bien et al. (1993) has summarized the outcome research on brief treatment. Of ten randomized trials of brief treatment in health care settings, they found seven of the studies reported significant improvement in reductions in drinking. In thirteen randomized trials that compared the outcomes of brief intervention with more extensive treatment for problem drinkers, there were no differences between brief treatments and the more extensive treatments in outcome. Edwards and Rollnick (1997) found that there were attrition rates from 44.3 to 83.2 percent, averaging 70.6 percent in brief-intervention outcome studies, which compromise the generalizablity of these findings, however.

Relapse and Relapse Prevention

Relapse, resuming problematic drinking, is a common phenomenon for alcoholics whether or not they have had treatment. Most treated alcoholics relapse within the first year of treatment completion. (The reader can examine any of the outcome studies summarized in this chapter to confirm this.) Researchers have asked alcoholics what factors contributed to their relapses. Table 11.3 shows some of the findings of one such study. McKay (1999) has pointed out that alcoholics may not be able to recall these events accurately and/or may distort them. Two studies measured the differences between retrospective and prospective recall and found that retrospective reports overestimated negative affect prior to relapse. In one of them, Hall et al. (1990) found that stress and negative emotion increased risk of slip only when measured retrospectively and not prospectively. In general, the two measures were not highly related.

Marlatt (1985) reasoned that if alcoholics could develop skills to prevent relapse, they would have improved treatment outcomes. He developed a program of relapse prevention.

TABLE 11.3   Analysis of Relapse Situations with Alcoholics

RELAPSE SITUATION	PERCENT ($n = 70$)
Negative emotional states	38
Negative physical states	2
Positive emotional states alone	—
Testing personal control	9
Urges and temptations	11
Interpersonal conflict	18
Social pressure	18
Positive emotional states with others	3

Source: Marlatt, 1985. Adapted by permission of Guilford Press.

Patients were helped to examine what factors contributed to their relapses and develop skills to avoid, overcome, or resist these threats. Outcome research has not, however, established that the approach has a high degree of effectiveness. Miller et al. (1995) reports that three studies supported its efficacy and four did not. Irvin et al. (1999) conducted a meta-analytic review of relapse prevention, which included 26 studies of 9,504 subjects. He found that relapse prevention had only a very modest impact on reducing substance use.

Family Treatment

There is limited research on the outcome of family treatment of alcoholism. Miller et al.'s (1995) meta-analysis indicates that three studies had positive results for family therapy and two did not. (In the section on domestic violence of Chapter 9, there is a summary of an outcome study on family therapy of alcoholism.) Box 11.2 describes Al-Anon, a self-help group for families of alcoholics.

The family may be used to help engage the alcoholic in treatment. The traditional method has been the Johnson intervention. This approach is confrontational and coercive, using family members' leverage to force the alcoholic into treatment. Results show that

---

BOX 11.2

AL-ANON

Just as AA is a nonprofessional self-help group for alcoholics, Al-Anon, based on the Twelve Steps and traditions of AA, is a nonprofessional self-help group for friends and family members of alcoholics. Al-Anon focuses on improving the family member's spiritual growth rather than on the alcoholic (Al-Anon Family Group Headquarters, 1982). The goal of Al-Anon is to help the "significant other" of the alcoholic have a better adjustment to the reality of having to deal with an alcoholic. Members attend Al-Anon meetings, work the Twelve Steps, and obtain sponsors in a manner similar to AA members.

when families go through with confrontation, the alcoholic often goes into treatment. However, the family often chooses not to go through with the confrontation.

Miller et al. (1999) developed a cognitive behavioral approach to help the family influence drinking behavior and engage the alcoholic in treatment. In one study, they compared the effectiveness of this approach with the Johnson intervention and Al-Anon facilitation, which encouraged Al-Anon participation. One hundred thirty subjects were randomly assigned to Al-Anon facilitation, the Johnson approach, or the cognitive behavioral approach, called community reinforcement and family training (CRAFT). Families treated with Al-Anon facilitation and CRAFT completed more scheduled sessions than those treated with the Johnson intervention. After 6 months, 64 percent of the alcoholics whose families participated in CRAFT therapy had begun treatment, compared to 23 percent whose families were in the Johnson intervention and 13 percent whose family members had attended Al-Anon facilitation, demonstrating a significant advantage for CRAFT. After treatment, family members reported less depression, greater family cohesion, and relationship happiness regardless of type of intervention.

Meta-Analysis of Outcomes of Specific Treatments

Miller et al. (1995) conducted a meta-analysis of 211 treatment-outcome research studies. The selected studies compared a specific form of treatment with a control group or another treatment. To be included, studies had to assign subjects to conditions randomly and have a minimum 6-month follow-up. Studies with stronger methodology were given greater weight. The results of their analysis can be divided into three segments: those treatments with good evidence for effectiveness, those treatments with some evidence for effectiveness, and those with little evidence of effectiveness. The results are shown in Table 11.4.

Most of the treatments are types of CBT, because more research has been conducted on the efficacy of these treatments. Brief descriptions of the treatments are listed in the glossary of therapies at the end of the chapter. More detailed discussion of the specific cognitive behavioral treatments can be found in Hester and Miller (1995).

The results of the study suggest that those treatments in the first group shown in Table 11.4 appear to merit serious consideration. Miller et al.'s finding that traditional TSF treatment had poor outcomes, listed in Table 11.4 as "confrontation" and "general alcoholism counseling," is mitigated by the more recent findings of the MATCH study and VA studies, published after Miller's analysis was done.

Controlled Drinking as a Goal

Most alcohol treatment programs have viewed abstinence as the preferred goal (Rosenberg & Davis, 1994), yet research has consistently shown that a portion of problem drinkers appear to be able to drink safely even when their treatment has been abstinence-oriented.

Controlled Drinking Training. Several studies have investigated whether specific training for controlled drinking enhances this outcome. Sanchez-Craig et al. (1984) conducted a study that randomly assigned early-stage problem drinkers to abstinence or controlled drinking goals. All patients were given cognitive behavioral treatment for their

TABLE 11.4   Summary of Results of Miller et al. Meta-Analysis of Which Types of Treatment Show the Most Empirical Support

I. Treatments that had good evidence for effectiveness
   1. Brief interventions
   2. Social skills training
   3. Motivational enhancement
   4. Community reinforcement approach
   5. Behavior contracting

II. Treatments that had both positive and negative results
   1. Aversion
   2. Client-centered
   3. Relapse prevention
   4. Self-help manual
   5. Cognitive therapy
   6. Covert sensitization
   7. Behavioral marital therapy
   8. Antabuse

III. Treatments that had predominately negative results
   1. Behavioral self-control training
   2. Psychotherapy
   3. Confrontation
   4. General alcoholism counseling

Note: Treatment types are defined in the glossary of therapies at the end of the chapter.

Source: Adapted from Hester & Miller, 1995.

problem drinking. Half were told that the objective was abstinence, the other half, controlled drinking. In the latter condition, specific techniques for reducing alcohol consumption and minimizing negative consequences were taught, called behavioral self-control training (BSCT). Although there was marked reductions in drinking over a 2-year period, from 51 drinks per week before treatment to 13 drinks after treatment, assignment to controlled drinking did not improve outcome. Clients assigned abstinence as a goal developed moderate drinking on their own. Sanchez-Craig et al. (1989) reported similar outcomes when early problem drinkers were given the choice of abstinence or controlled drinking as their goal.

Miller et al. (1992) evaluated BSCT controlled drinking training outcomes in an 8-year follow-up. Results indicated that only 14 percent were able to drink asymptomatically; more were stably abstinent, 23 percent. The results of these studies suggest that little is gained by teaching controlled drinking. Miller et al. (1992) suggest that a trial period of controlled drinking may be a more useful strategy when clients reject abstinence as a goal than to insist on abstinence. In many instances, when such individuals fail at controlled drinking, they are willing to switch to abstinence, as did a majority of the ultimate abstainers in Miller et al.'s (1992) study.

Who Should Abstain and Who Are Candidates for Controlled Drinking? Research has generally supported the idea that some characteristics of drinkers make them good candidates for controlled drinking, while other characteristics suggest abstinence is the safest goal. Results of the Rand report (Polich et al., 1981) found that those who were younger, drank less, and had fewer dependence symptoms at admission were more likely to become stable non-problem drinkers. Lindstrom (1992), analyzing Rand report data, found that younger men with low severity of alcohol dependence were less prone to relapse when non-problem drinking was their goal compared to abstinence. The reverse was true for older men with high severity of alcohol dependence. Table 11.5 shows the analysis of relapse patterns for abstinence and controlled drinking goals with younger and older married and unmarried men in the Rand study.

In other research on controlled drinking, it has been found that feminine gender (Sanchez-Craig et al.,1989; Helzer et al.,1985; Taylor et al., 1986), low incidence of family alcoholism (Sanchez-Craig et al., 1989), less severe drinking problems (Helzer et al.,1985), older age of onset, and fewer lifetime alcohol-related problems (Taylor et al., 1986) were associated with successful controlled drinking. (See also the section on controlled drinking in Chapter 6.)

Stability of Controlled Drinking versus Abstinence. Four important studies show that abstinence is a more stable goal than controlled drinking for those with more severe alcohol disorders, what we now call alcohol dependence. The core city sample from the Study of Adult Development (Vaillant, 1995) (see Chapter 6) included twenty-one men who were

TABLE 11.5 Expected Relapse Rates at 4 Years Predicted from Regression Analysis for 6-Month Abstainers versus Nonsymptomatic Drinkers at 18 months

BACKGROUND CHARACTERISTICS AT ADMISSION	AGE UNDER 40		AGE 40 OR OVER	
	ABSTAINING 6 MONTHS OR MORE AT 18 MONTHS (%)	NON-PROBLEM DRINKING AT 18 MONTHS (%)	ABSTAINING 6 MONTHS OR MORE AT 18 MONTHS (%)	NON-PROBLEM DRINKING AT 18 MONTHS (%)
High severity of dependence[a]				
Married	7	17	4	50
Unmarried	16	7	10	28
Low severity of dependence[b]				
Married	16	7	11	28
Unmarried	32	3	22	13

Relapse rates are based on predictions from a logit regression model fitted using the 200 cases who reported either 6 months of abstention or nonsymptom drinking at 18 months. (The model's coefficients can be found in Polich et al., 1981, p. 179). [a]High severity of dependence represents 11 or more symptom events (blackouts, tremors, missing meals, morning drinking, drinking continuously for 12 hours) during the 30 days preceding admission to treatment. [b]Low severity of dependence represents 1 to 10 such events. Subjects with no dependence symptoms at admission are excluded from the table.

Source: Adapted from Table 7.8, p. 180 from J. M. Polich et al., *The Course of Alcoholism: Four Years after Treatment,* New York: John Wiley & Sons, publishers, 1981. Copyright RAND 1990.

abstinent alcoholics at age 47. At age 60, eighteen had remained continuously sober (86 percent). Twenty-two alcoholic men were in remission by controlling their drinking at age 47. At age 60, only eight (36 percent) remained controlled drinkers. Helzer et al. (1985) interviewed a large number of alcoholics 5 to 7 years after contact with a hospital. Inquiring about the prior 3 years' drinking pattern. He found that 15 percent had sustained abstinence, compared to 6.2 percent with sustained controlled drinking. Welte et al. (1983), in a large-scale study of treated alcoholics, compared 3-month with 8-month outcomes. They found that 12 percent who had been abstinent at 3 months had relapsed at 8 months, while 32 percent of the controlled drinkers at 3 months had relapsed in the same period. The Rand study reported that 13 percent of the followed sample were stable abstainers (Polich et al., 1981) and 9 percent were stable nonsymptomatic drinkers in the period from 18 months to the 4-year follow-up.

There are no good follow-up studies comparing the stability of controlled drinking and abstinence outcomes for those with alcohol abuse. A review of the epidemiologic studies discussed in Chapter 5 suggests that most young drinkers who qualify for alcohol abuse go into remission. It is reasonable to assume that most of these individuals remain in remission. Additionally, Lindstrom (1992) notes that younger and less dependent drinkers in the Rand study (Table 11.5) who were drinking in a controlled manner had lower relapse rates compared to those who had abstinence as a goal. Hence it can be argued that those with alcohol abuse are more likely to be stable controlled drinkers than are those who are alcohol dependent. Longitudinal research on outcomes of alcohol abusers is needed to provide empirical support for this inference.

TREATMENT MATCHING

Lindstrom (1992) suggests the best chance to improve outcome rates is in treatment matching. It may be that specific treatments may bring about superior results for specific subtypes of those suffering from alcohol disorders. Conversely, this same treatment may work poorly for other subtypes, thus masking its superiority in helping a specific subtype. Subtyping can be done on the basis of demographic considerations such as gender and age, or other variables such as severity of alcohol dependence, severity of co-morbid psychiatric illness, and type of psychiatric illness. The most substantial support for treatment matching comes from McLellan's (1986) study matching six types of alcohol treatment with patient characteristics. This group was compared to a group that was not matched. The matched groups showed a 37 percent improvement in outcome over the unmatched group in a 6-month follow-up. (Matching criteria can be found in Lindstrom, 1992, p. 165.)

Matteson et al. (1994) reviewed thirty experimental studies of treatment matching. Because of methodologic limitations of the studies, they suggested that the findings should be considered tentative. Preliminary findings include:

1. Female alcoholics may do better in educational or medically oriented programs, while males may do better in peer group therapy.
2. ASPD and high-psychiatric-severity alcoholics may do better in basic coping skills than interactional-focused treatment (see Chapter 9 for details).

3. Socially unstable alcoholics, alcoholics with high psychiatric severity, and alcoholics who are behaviorally impaired by drinking may benefit from more intense interventions.

In more recent matching studies, however, little improvement in outcome has resulted from matching. Ouimette and colleagues, using VA study data (Ouimette et al.,1999a, b), found that matching patient characteristics to TSF and CBT treatment did not improve outcome. Neither patients with psychiatric illness nor patients forced into treatment differed in outcome among the treatments compared to those without these factors (Ouimette et al., 1997). In the MATCH study cited earlier, several predictions were made regarding the interaction of patient characteristics and kind of treatment patients received. In general, these predictions were not confirmed. There were, however, three matching effects:

1. Low psychiatric severity patients did better in TSF than CBT.
2. MET outcomes were better with low-motivation clients than CBT at the 1-year follow-up.
3. MET proved to be more effective for clients high in anger at the 3-year follow-up than the other treatments.

In sum, Lindstrom's (1992) conclusion remains accurate today: there is little evidence for improved outcomes with treatment matching.

AA AND RESEARCH

Although AA has been a significant element in the U.S. approach to combatting alcoholism for over 60 years, only a modest number of research studies had examined this approach until the last few years. Two meta-analyses of research on AA were conducted on these earlier studies. Tonigan et al.'s (1996) analysis found that outpatients benefited more on drinking outcomes from AA involvement than inpatients. Emrick et al.'s (1993) analysis found that good outcomes in AA were enhanced when participants engaged in activities recommended by AA. They note that participants drop out of AA at rates similar to those in professional treatment. They report dropout rates of 50 percent by the fourth month, and 75 percent by the twelfth month. They also note that 68 percent of AA members had some professional treatment before entering AA but only 30 percent indicated alcohol rehabilitation treatment as a factor in joining AA. Both Tonigan et al. (1996) and Emrick et al. (1993) concluded that the methodology of most of these early studies was poor.

More recent research has overcome many of these methodologic weaknesses. Still, it is important to note that a randomized study comparing the results of AA with professional treatment is not possible because of ethical considerations. Researchers cannot forbid subjects from attending AA during the course of a study. Thus, there will always be potential confounds in studies on AA, including the studies discussed here.

Ouimette et al. (1998), using the subjects from the VA project described above, compared aftercare results of patients who chose aftercare treatment, AA, both aftercare and AA, or no aftercare 1 year after discharge from inpatient treatment. Patients with no aftercare had poorest outcomes, with 30.5 percent remitted. Aftercare treatment resulted in a remission rate of 35.3 percent, AA only, 49 percent, and aftercare treatment with AA, 66.3 percent. Most of the remission was abstinence, with safe drinking a successful goal for only 5 percent of the participants. The results of this study suggest that AA plays an important role in aftercare outcomes.

Humphreys et al. (1999) also drew on the VA study to determine the effect of professional treatment on AA participation. It may be recalled that the VA programs were of three types: CBT, TSF, and a combination of CBT and TSF (Moos et al., 1999). While 56 percent of the total sample attended self-help meetings, patients in TSF programs had significantly more AA involvement after treatment than CBT. Those patients with higher self-help involvement had better outcomes. This suggests that the improved outcome of TSF is due to the effect of the client's engagement and use of self-help. When the effect of AA attendance was statistically partialled out, the difference between TSF and CBT was nonsignificant, suggesting that the most important ingredient of the TSF treatment was the AA involvement. A similar statistical analysis of the MATCH study found AA involvement to be the most important factor in drinking outcome (Tonigan et al., 2000). Hoffmann et al. (1983) and Watson et al. (1997) found that weekly AA attendance after inpatient treatment for alcoholism was associated with better treatment outcomes.

Although AA is a spiritual program, Winzelberg and Humphreys (1999) found that nonreligious patients in the VA study attended AA and benefited from it as much as religious patients. Ouimette et al. (1998) found that those with dual diagnoses also benefited from AA participation.

SMOKING CESSATION AND ALCOHOL TREATMENT

It is common knowledge that smoking is a high health risk (U.S. Department of Health and Human Services, 1988). Smoking prevalence is 75 percent higher among drinkers than among nondrinkers (Shiffman & Balabanis, 1995). Among alcoholic samples, smoking rates have been found as high as 97 percent (Monti et al., 1995); 75 percent of inpatients in a Minnesota county admitted for alcoholism over the course of several years were smokers (Hurt et al., 1996). This suggests that alcoholic smokers are at high risk for tobacco-related illnesses. (Chapter 3 cites evidence that smoking and drinking combine synergistically to increase the risk for contracting certain diseases.) By examining the death certificates of patients treated for alcoholism in the Minnesota sample described above, Hurt et al. (1996) were able to determine that 50.9 percent of the patients died from a tobacco-related cause, while 34.1 percent died from an alcohol-related cause, indicating that smoking is a significant contributor to mortality in over half of patients treated for alcoholism. Certainly efforts should be made to help smoking alcoholics stop smoking as well as drinking.

There are three important considerations in the implementation of smoking cessation for treated alcoholics:

1. Do current techniques of smoking cessation help alcoholics stop smoking?
2. Do such efforts interfere with alcohol treatment?
3. When is the best time period to help alcoholics with smoking cessation?

Neither Campbell et al. (1998) nor Bobo et al. (1998) found smoking cessation in conjunction with alcoholism treatment helpful in reducing smoking. In Bobo's study, which made use of a control group, the results indicated that the smoking cessation did not interfere with alcohol remission; in fact, those receiving tobacco cessation treatment had higher rates of alcohol abstinence than those who had only alcohol treatment. This study and five others cited by Bobo et al. (1998) have shown that smoking cessation did not adversely affect alcohol treatment outcomes. Several studies suggest that the optimal time for tobacco intervention is at least a month after inpatient treatment. Gulliver et al. (2000) followed tobacco use patterns of alcoholics who were treated in three inpatient substance abuse programs. They found that 45 percent of the smokers decreased their smoking at 6-month follow-up, with a mean reduction of 45.4 percent. Monti et al. (1995) found that readiness to change smoking is greater a month after treatment and that smoking cessation was more successful after some sobriety. Sobell et al. (1995), following alcoholics in natural recovery, found that those alcoholics who smoked tended to stop smoking after they had become abstinent from alcohol.

The research to date, then, suggests that smoking cessation does not harm alcohol recovery and that treatment for smoking should begin at least a month after inpatient treatment or when the patient feels he or she is comfortably abstinent from alcohol.

PROCESS FACTORS

There are a large number of outcome studies on alcoholism treatment, but little work has been conducted to determine what is really going on in treatment sessions and what in the sessions is actually helpful. Process factor research examines the therapeutic processes that occur in actual alcoholism treatment sessions. Morgenstern and colleagues have begun to specify these processes and test their usefulness. They began by developing (Morgenstern & McCrady, 1993) a list of TSF processes from researching the literature and surveying disease concept practitioners, shown in Table 11.6.

Morgenstern et al. (1996, 1997) then surveyed patients before and after TSF treatment regarding their acceptance of TSF and/or common therapeutic factors and the degree to which it affected outcome. They found that common factors appeared to operate more than the disease concept elements. Finney et al. (1998) compared factors that are linked to improvement in TSF and those linked to CBT treatment. They found that patients in TSF treatment increased in the TSF factors, such as acceptance of an alcoholic identity. Similarly, the CBT patients increased in CBT factors, such as an increase in **self-efficacy.** However, TSF patients increased in CBT factors to the same degree as CBT patients. Finney et al. (1998) suggest that CBT factors may be common factors that mediate treatment success regardless of treatment type. This preliminary work suggests that there may be more similarities than differences between treatments as they are actually practiced.

Transtheoretical/Nonspecific Factors in Outcome

One explanation for the common finding that different alcoholism treatments produce similar outcomes is that there are common factors in all of the therapies that are the important

TABLE 11.6   Twelve Step Facilitation Treatment Processes

1. Help client accept disease notion of alcoholism.
2. Reduce denial. This includes helping client become aware of the destructive aspects of alcohol use and helping client to acknowledge a loss of control over drinking.
3. Help client understand that recovery is a lifelong process and that s/he will require the help of others in order to remain sober.
4. Facilitates client's identification with people in recovery.
5. Facilitate client's commitment to attend AA meetings, find a sponsor, and work the 12 steps.
6. Reduce co-dependent denial. This includes co-dependent's acknowledgment that their partner has a drinking problem and that their behavior contributes to that problem.
7. Help client accept co-dependent label and make a connection to an appropriate self-help group.
8. Facilitate a spiritual experience in recovery and help client to believe in a Higher Power.
9. Help client understand that recovery is a lifelong process and that s/she will require the help of others to stay sober.

Source: Reprinted with permission from *Research on Alcoholics Anonymous: Opportunities and Alternatives,* by B. S. McCrady and W. R. Miller. Copyright 1993, Alcohol Research Documentation, Inc., Rutgers Center of Alcohol Studies, Piscataway, NJ 08854.

factors in outcome. This view is called the transtheoretical or nonspecific factors approach. For example, the social skills of the therapist may be an important common factor, perhaps more important than techniques derived from the various theories of treatment. Some support for this idea is suggested by Lindstrom's (1992) summary of psychotherapy research, which indicates that therapist factors account for outcome more than specific therapies.

Therapist Effectiveness.   Some support for the importance of common factors comes from studies of the effectiveness of different therapists. Regardless of training, theoretical views, and profession, there is a great range of effectiveness by different therapists (Miller & Rollnick, 1991). Within clinics, some therapists have very good success rates, while others do poorly. McLellan & McKay (1998b) cite four studies of addiction treatment that document between therapist differences. In these studies, therapist traits that facilitated positive outcome included in-session interpersonal functioning, ability to form a helping alliance, and demonstrating accurate empathy, genuineness, concreteness, and respect (McLellan & McKay, 1998b). In a study that supports the importance of therapist factors, Miller et al. (1980) found that the degree of empathy shown by therapists was associated with improvement in drinking behavior. Interestingly, patients who had therapists rated with higher empathy had better outcomes than a control condition, and patients who had therapists rated lower in empathy actually did worse than the control condition.

Professional versus Paraprofessional Therapy.   Several studies have been conducted that compare the outcomes of patients treated by professionals and paraprofessionals. For example, Strupp and Hadley (1979) compared outcomes of patients treated by professional therapists and college professors, finding that the college professors did as well as therapists. They point out there was great variation in outcomes among dyads in both groups, suggesting that this interaction should be investigated further.

Durlak (1979) and Berman and Norton (1985) reviewed studies comparing professional and paraprofessional outcome in conducting therapy. Based on forty-two and thirty-two studies, respectively, neither review showed that professional treatment was superior to the paraprofessionals'. Lindstrom (1992) suggests that this finding supports the importance of nonspecific factors in therapeutic outcomes, because paraprofessionals have little or no education about theory and technique of therapy and still do as well as the professionals.

Stages of Change

A second transtheoretical view is the stages-of-change model. Prochaska et al. (1992) observed that individuals who were trying to change addictive behavior progress through stages of motivation as they succeed in overcoming the addiction. By determining the client's motivational stage, appropriate goals and techniques can be employed to help the individual change. The stages, shown in Figure 11.2, are:

1. Precontemplation. The addicted person is not aware of his problem and has no intention to change.
2. Contemplation. The addicted person is aware of his problem and is considering change but has not made a commitment to do so.
3. Preparation. The addicted person is intending to take action in the near future. He may have made small changes, but has not made sufficient change to alter the addictive behavior.
4. Action. The addicted person takes the necessary actions to overcome the addiction.
5. Maintenance. The addicted person is in remission and must work to prevent relapse and consolidate gains made in the action stage.
6. Relapse. The relapse may take the person back to any of the prior stages (adapted from Prochaska et al., 1992, and Miller & Rollnick, 1991).

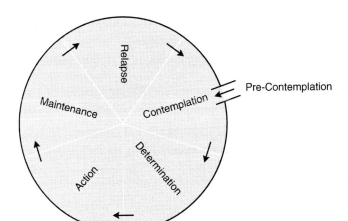

**FIGURE 11.2 Prochaska and
Di Clemente's Six Stages of Change**

Source: Miller and Rollnick, 1991. Adapted by permission of Guilford Press.

There is research evidence that the stage of change is a good predictor of treatment outcome (McLellan & McKay, 1998b).

RECOMMENDATIONS

Research

Most research has examined outcome and neglected what actually happens in therapy. This raises some interesting research questions. What treatment is being provided by the average alcohol counselor? How closely are clinicians adhering to the philosophy and techniques they espouse? How different in practice are theoretically different approaches? For example, it would be expected that self-disclosure would be more common in TSF treatment, yet there is no research indicating how common it is or if it is beneficial. Results of a survey by Ramsdell and Ramsdell (1993) of former patients at a mental health clinic indicated that 60 percent of the patients stated that their therapists had shared personal information and that it had been beneficial. A similar study conducted by Knox et al. (1997) indicated that therapist self-disclosure was basically positive and pointed to specific types of self-disclosure and positive effects. Such research should be replicated for TSF and CBT.

Rarely have patients been asked about what was helpful about treatment, as did Miller et al. (1992) and Ramsdell and Ramsdell (1993) in their research. I think it would be useful to do so routinely. It would also be valuable to interview patients who drop out from treatment to determine why they left.

Matteson et al. (1994) and Strupp and Hadley (1979) suggest that it would be valuable to evaluate matches between counselors and clients in order to gain insight into why some counselors do better with some clients than others.

Clinical Implications of Incidental Research Findings

Bien et al. (1993) summarized research which indicates that practical steps of reminder letters, telephone calls, and making the referral appointments facilitate referral success. The MATCH study made use of such devices, which may account for its high completion rate of treatment and follow-up. These practical devices might improve patient participation, completion, and successful referral in any type of alcohol treatment.

Typically, counselors are concerned when patients become resistant to treatment interventions. Miller et al. (1993) suggest that counselors can use such resistance in a positive way by viewing it as signal to reevaluate the current treatment strategy and change to a more fruitful one.

Counselor Training

Because there is currently no superior alcohol treatment type, enhancing the nonspecific curative factors of therapists might be the most dramatic way to improve treatment effectiveness. Training to develop counselors' social skills and training in fostering the therapeutic relationship may be very productive in enhancing outcome.

Treatment Matching

Although there are no strong findings, the treatment matching studies suggest that angry patients and patients who have low motivation would do best in MET, clients with low psychiatric severity would do best in TSF, clients with high psychiatric severity would do best in special integrated treatment programs (see Chapter 10), and less intact and more severe alcohol dependence would do best in more intensive services. There are two additional treatment matching paradigms that could prove effective.

1. Lindstrom (1992) has proposed matching patients to appropriate treatment goals and types of interventions. Table 11.7 is my effort to devise a paradigm for matching patients to treatment goals and types of interventions. Thus, early-stage alcohol abusers could have the goal of controlled drinking and could be directed to a program that offers BSCT. At the other extreme, some alcoholics with additional disabilities such as severe psychiatric problems and HIV-related illness may require a goal of harm reduction and a sheltered living environment. Thus, there are graded goals from controlled drinking, abstinence, to reduced negative drinking consequences, depending on the intactness of the patient. The goal is then matched to an appropriate therapeutic setting. Table 11.7 can also be viewed as a simplified view of patient placement criteria. Detailed placement criteria have been laid out by the American Society of Addiction Medicine (2001).

2. McLellan and McKay (1998a) have begun to explore the usefulness of providing specialized services to patients. Their idea is to evaluate substance abuse clients to determine special needs they might have in addition to substance abuse treatment. Such needs may

TABLE 11.7   Matching Patients to Goals, Treatment Methods, and Facilities

TYPE OF PATIENT	GOAL	TREATMENT METHOD	FACILITY
Alcohol abuser, early stage	Controlled drinking	Moderate drinking training such as BSCT	Medical or mental health facility
Alcohol-dependent, no psychiatric problems	Abstinence	TSF, MET, or CBT	Outpatient alcoholism facility
Alcohol-dependent, with moderate depression or anxiety	Abstinence	Highly structured treatment, Antabuse	Outpatient alcoholism facility
Alcohol-dependent, moderate psychiatric problems, family or work problems	Abstinence	Structured inpatient treatment	Inpatient alcohol rehabilitation program
Alcohol-dependent with severe chronic mental illness	Harm reduction	MET, provision of psychiatric care, and case management	Sheltered living facility

BSCT = Behavioral self-control training; TSF = Twelve Step facilitation; MET = motivational enhancement therapy; CBT = cognitive behavior therapy.

Source: Derived from Lindstrom, 1992, p. 285, Table 24.1.

include marital counseling, psychiatric care, and vocational counseling. In addition to substance abuse counseling, clients are matched to the additional treatment services they require. Preliminary research provides evidence for better outcomes for patients who are provided these targeted specialized services (McLellan & McKay, 1998a).

Controlled Drinking as a Goal

Alcohol treatment programs rarely consider controlled drinking as a legitimate goal (Rosenberg & Davis, 1994), but research has shown consistently that about 10 percent of those with drinking problems can do so. Research has also shown that there are patient characteristics that are associated with successful controlled drinking. For those clients who match these characteristics, controlled drinking is a reasonable goal, and a trial of controlled drinking training can be implemented. As a first approximation, those with alcohol abuse are possible candidates for controlled drinking, while those with alcohol dependence are generally not.

Controlled Drinking Training. CBT has a number of protocols to assist problem drinkers in the goal of becoming moderate, safe drinkers (Sanchez-Craig,1993; Sobell & Sobell, 1993). The client should be informed that an initial period of abstinence is a favorable sign for the goal of controlled drinking, and that lack of control at the beginning of treatment is predictive of failure of controlled drinking (Miller et al., 1992). Of course, clients, regardless of profile and degree of drinking problem, should not be discouraged from the goal of abstinence if they wish it. If controlled drinking is the goal, it should be carefully monitored, following the protocol of one of the CBT controlled drinking treatments; if the client is not succeeding, the goal should be reevaluated.

Negotiating Treatment Goals. Another group of patients may benefit from an initial trial of controlled drinking training. For those who reject abstinence, a trial period of controlled drinking training makes sense both as a treatment goal and as a strategy. Such patients are more likely to cooperate when they can try a trial of controlled drinking. For example, Sanchez-Craig et al. (1984) found more problem-drinking clients were abstinent for an initial period when their goal was controlled drinking compared to abstinence. Those failing to successfully achieve the controlled drinking goal can then be encouraged to switch to abstinence as a goal. Miller et al. (1992) found that a number of patients who originally chose controlled drinking as a goal switched to an abstinence goal and achieved it.

Alcoholics Anonymous

The research in the chapter shows important benefits for patients who attend AA, including those suffering from co-morbid disorders and those without religious beliefs. Professional treatment, not surprisingly, has been shown to have an impact on patient participation in self-help. Counselors should encourage patient involvement in AA and other self-help, both as an adjunct to treatment and as a possible alternative to it.

Smoking Cessation and Alcohol Treatment

Current research suggests that the best time to intervene with smoking cessation is at least a month after treatment for alcoholism has been initiated. Campbell et al. (1998) suggest that clinical staff should be offered smoking cessation first; those staff who succeed in quitting would be good role models for those smoking patients who wish to quit.

SUMMARY

Large-scale and methodologically sound studies of alcoholism treatment outcome consistently show a significant but modest improvement in remission (decrease in symptoms) compared to untreated alcoholics. Results from the Rand report, for example, showed about 20 percent more patients with at least fifteen treatment sessions were in remission than the untreated group.

Treatment has a more substantial impact on abstinence rates; usually about twice as many treated alcoholics achieve abstinence as untreated samples. Recent research suggests that these treatment effects are maintained for at least 8 years.

No specific treatment appears to be best for a heterogeneous population of problem drinkers. Recent results indicate, however, that TSF has a modest advantage in abstinence outcomes.

Brief treatment interventions, typically conducted in medical settings, have an impressive success rate in reducing drinking and drinking problems.

Although relapse is a common phenomenon in most recovery, relapse prevention therapy has not demonstrated great efficacy.

Family treatments have shown promising preliminary results in engaging the alcoholic into treatment and providing good treatment outcome.

Controlled drinking has been found to be a consistent outcome for 10 percent of problem drinkers. Patient characteristics associated with this outcome are: being younger, female, having fewer alcohol-dependence symptoms, and having social support. Specific training in controlled drinking has not been shown to enhance successful controlled drinking outcomes.

Research indicates that abstinence is a more stable outcome than controlled drinking for those with alcohol dependence. There are no similar longitudinal outcome studies that show the stability of controlled drinking versus abstinence for alcohol abusers.

Despite a large number of studies on matching patients to specific treatments, few matching effects have been found. McLellan's (1986) study provides the strongest support for matching effects. The MATCH study showed that patients with low motivation and high anger did better in MET. TSF was better for low-psychiatric-severity patients. A different approach to matching is to provide specialized services for those who need them, in addition to substance abuse treatment. Preliminary research suggests that this may be a more effective way to enhance substance abuse treatment effectiveness.

Research into AA processes and outcome has advanced considerably in the past several years. AA attendance and involvement is strongly associated with abstinence and other positive outcome measures. Although there are confounding factors, the statistical procedure of partialling out has been employed in some studies, which reduces such factors.

Research findings suggest that smoking cessation for treated alcoholics does not interfere with alcohol treatment but should be delayed until at least 1 month after treatment or the patient is stably in remission.

There has been little research on the actual processes that occur in alcoholism treatment. The limited research to date suggests that common factors in treatment may be the most predictive factors of outcome.

READINGS

Hester, R. K., & Miller, W. R. (1995). *Handbook of alcoholism treatment approaches: Effective alternatives.* Boston: Allyn & Bacon.
A good introduction to cognitive behavioral approaches to treating alcoholism.

Hubble, M. A., Duncan, B. L., & Miller, S. D. (1999). *The heart and soul of change: What works in therapy.* Washington, DC: American Psychological Association.
This book discusses research findings on the common factors that operate in psychotherapy.

Lindstrom, L. (1992). *Managing alcoholism: Matching clients to treatment.* New York: Oxford University Press.
A thoughtful review of alcoholism outcome research.

Miller, W. R., & Rollnick, S. (2002). *Motivational interviewing* (2nd ed.). New York: Guilford.
A concise, sensible approach to engaging clients with addictive disorders.

Yalisove, D. L. (1998). The origins and evolution of the disease concept of treatment. *Journal of Studies on Alcohol 59,* 469–476.
This article describes how TSF developed from AA volunteers in alcoholism facilities.

GLOSSARY OF THERAPIES

Antabuse: Taking of this drug each day serves to protect against drinking, because drinking while on this medication causes a severe painful reaction. (See Chapter 3.)

Aversion treatment: Using classical conditioning techniques, makes the smell and taste of alcohol aversive by pairing it with a nausea-inducing drug. This was one of the first behavioral techniques used for alcohol treatment, but it is no longer in popular use.

Behavioral contracting: Involves setting specific goals and reinforcing behaviors that are consistent with these goals. An example is a patient taking Antabuse for a specified period and receiving a reward for doing so.

Behavioral marital therapy: Behavioral techniques are used to help the problem drinker abstain. Elements include developing communication skills between the couple and developing a relapse plan.

Behavioral self-control training: A cognitive behavioral therapy that can have either controlled drinking or abstinence as a goal. Techniques include goal setting of drinking goals, self-monitoring of drinking behavior, learning alternate coping skills to deal with anxiety, and learning drink-refusal skills. If moderate drinking is the goal, learning to moderate consumption through sipping and timing of drinks is taught.

Brief intervention: May consist of as little as a 10-minute intervention or as many as three sessions with periodic medical follow-up. The client is provided with the results of alcohol screening and any biologic tests, advised to curtail his or her drinking, and may be given some suggestions about stopping.

Client-centered therapy: Developed by Carl Rogers to treat mental health problems. Two key elements of the therapy are appropriate empathy and genuineness on the part of the therapist (Monte, 1999, p. 762).

Cognitive therapy: A variant of cognitive behavioral therapy (CBT), described in this chapter.

Community reinforcement approach: A broad-based behavioral approach, which in addition to standard CBT, attends to reinforcement in the environment by providing marital counseling, job counseling, and provision of alcohol-free leisure-time activities.

Confrontation: An early version of Twelve Step facilitation (TSF).

Coping and social skills training: Develops interpersonal skills, mood regulation, coping skills for dealing with stress, coping with alcohol environments, and communication skills, including drink refusal and assertiveness.

Covert sensitization: Uses guided fantasy to connect alcohol to imagined aversive consequences in order to discourage its use; similar to aversive conditioning.

General alcoholism counseling: An early version of Twelve Step facilitation (TSF).

Motivational enhancement or **motivational interviewing:** A therapy that evaluates the patient's motivation and helps the patient develop a commitment to change by working with the patient's ambivalence about drinking.

Psychotherapy: General psychotherapy, with no special techniques for treatment of alcoholism.

Relapse prevention: Based on the premise that educating the patient about relapse and learning skills to minimize relapses will improve outcome of addiction treatment.

Self-help manual: The patient is given a written guide to provide advice for curtailing or abstaining from alcohol consumption.

REFERENCES

Al-Anon Family Group Headquarters. (1982). *Al-Anon faces alcoholism.* New York: Al-Anon Family Group Headquarters.

Alcoholics Anonymous World Services (1976). *Alcoholics anonymous.* New York: Alcoholics Anonymous World Services.

American Society of Addiction Medicine (2001). ASAM PPC-2R: ASAM patient placement criteria for the treatment of substance-related disorders (Second Edition—Revised). Chevy Chase, MD: American Society of Addiction Medicine.

Armor, D. J., Polich, J. M., & Stambul, H. B. (1978). *Alcoholism and treatment.* New York: Wiley.

Berman, J. S., & Norton, N. C. (1985). Does professional training make a therapist more effective? *Psychological Bulletin* 98, 401–407.

Bien, T. H., Miller, W. R., & Tonigan, J. S. (1993). Brief interventions for alcohol problems: A review. *Addiction* 88, 315–336.

Bobo, J. K., McIlvain, H. E., Lando, H. A., Walker, R. D., & Leed-Kelly, A. (1998). Effect of smoking cessation counseling on recovery from alcoholism: Findings from a randomized community intervention trial. *Addiction* 93, 877–887.

Campbell, B. K., Krumenacker, J., & Stark, M. J. (1998). Smoking cessation for clients in chemical dependence treatment. *Journal of Substance Abuse Treatment* 15, 313–318.

Durlak, J. A. (1979). Comparative effectiveness of paraprofessional and professional helpers. *Psychological Bulletin* 86, 80–92.

Edwards, G. K., & Rollnick, S. (1997). Outcome studies of brief alcohol intervention in general practice: The problem of lost subjects. *Addiction* 92, 1699–1704.

Emrick, C. D., Tonigan, J. S., Montgomery, H., & Little, L. (1993). Alcoholics Anonymous: What is currently known? In B. S. McCrady and W. R. Miller (Eds.), *Research on Alcoholics Anonymous* (pp. 41–76). New Brunswick, NJ: Rutgers.

Finney, J. W., & Moos, R. H. (1991). The long-term course of treated alcoholism: I. Mortality, relapse and remission rates of comparisons with community controls. *Journal of Studies on Alcohol* 52, 44–54.

Finney, J. W., Noyes, C. A., Coutts, A. I., & Moos, R. H. (1998). Evaluating substance abuse treatment process models: I. Changes on proximal outcome variables during 12-step and cognitive-behavioral treatment. *Journal of Studies on Alcohol* 59, 371–380.

Greenfeld, L. A. (1998). *Alcohol and crime.* U.S. Department of Justice, Bureau of Justice Statistics, Office of Justice Programs, Publication NCJ 168632.

Gulliver, S. B., Lalman, D., Rohsenow, D. J., Colby, S. M., Eaton, C. A., & Monti, P. M. (2000). Smoking and drinking among alcoholics in treatment: Cross-sectional and longitudinal relationships. *Journal of Studies on Alcohol* 61, 157–163.

Hall, S. M., Havassy, B. E., & Wasserman, D. A. (1990). Commitment to abstinence and acute stress in relapse to alcohol, opiates, and nicotine. *Journal of Consulting and Clinical Psychology* 58, 175–181.

Helzer, J. E., Robins, L. N., Taylor, J. R., Carey, K., Miller, R. H., Combs-Orme, T., & Farmer, M. B. (1985). The extent of long-term moderate drinking among alcoholics discharged from medical and psychiatric treatment facilities. *New England Journal of Medicine* 312, 1678–1682.

Helzer, J. E., Burnam, A., & McEvoy, L. T. (1991). Alcohol abuse and dependence. In L. N. Robins and D. A. Regier (Eds.), *Psychiatric disorders in America* (pp. 81–115). New York: Freedom.

Hester, R. K., & Miller, W. R. (Eds.) (1995). *Handbook of alcoholism treatment approaches: Effective alternatives.* Boston: Allyn & Bacon.

Hoffmann, N. G., Harrison, P. A., & Belille, C. A. (1983). Alcoholics Anonymous after treatment: Attendance and abstinence. *International Journal of the Addictions* 18, 311–318.

Humphreys, K., Huebsch, P. D., Finney, J. W., & Moos, R. H. (1999). A comparative evaluation of substance abuse treatment: V. Substance abuse treatment can enhance the effectiveness of self-help groups. *Alcoholism: Clinical and Experimental Research* 23, 558–563.

Hurt, R. D., Offord, K. P., Croghan, I. T., Gomez-Dahl, L., Kottke, T. E., Morse, R. M., & Melton, J. (1996). Mortality following inpatient addictions treatment: Role of tobacco use in a community-based cohort. *Journal of the American Medical Association* 275, 1097–1103.

Institute of Medicine (1990). *Broadening the base of treatment for alcohol problems.* Washington, DC: National Academy Press.

Irvin, J. E., Bowers, C. A., Dunn, M. E., & Wang, M. C. (1999). Efficacy of relapse prevention: A meta-analytic review. *Journal of Consulting and Clinical Psychology* 67, 563–570.

Kadden, R., Carroll, K., Donovan, D., Cooney, N., Monti, P., Abrams, D., Litt, M., & Hester, R. (1995). *Cognitive-behavioral coping skills therapy manual.* National Institute on Alcohol Abuse and Alcoholism Project MATCH Monograph Series, Volume 3. Rockville, MD: National Institute of Health Publication 94-3724.

Knox, S., Hess, S. A., Petersen, D. A., & Hill, C. E. (1997). A qualitative analysis of client perceptions of the effects of helpful therapist self-disclosure in long-term therapy. *Journal of Counseling Psychology* 44, 274–283.

Lindstrom, L. (1992). *Managing alcoholism: Matching clients to treatment.* New York: Oxford University Press.

Marlatt, G. A. (1985). Relapse prevention: Theoretical rationale and overview of the model. In G. A. Marlatt and J. R. Gordon (Eds.), *Relapse prevention* (pp. 3–70). New York: Guilford.

Mattson, M. E., Allen, J. P., Longabaugh, D., Nickless, C. J., Connors, G. J., & Kadden, R. M. (1994). A chronological review of empirical studies matching alcoholic clients to treatment. *Journal of Studies on Alcohol,* Suppl. 12, 16–29.

McKay, J. R. (1999). Studies of factors in relapse to alcohol, drug and nicotine use: A critical review of methodologies and findings. *Journal of Studies on Alcohol* 60, 566–576.

McLellan, A. T. (1986). "Psychiatric severity" as a predictor of outcome from substance abuse treatment. In R. E. Meyer (Ed.), *Psychopathology and addictive disorders* (pp. 97–139). New York: Guilford.

McLellan, A. T., & McKay, J. R. (1998a). Components of successful treatment programs: Lessons from the research literature. In A. W. Graham and T. K. Schultz (Eds.), *Principles of addiction medicine* (2nd ed.) (pp. 327–343). Chevy Chase, MD: American Society of Addiction Medicine.

McLellan, A. T., & McKay, J. R. (1998b). The treatment of addiction: What can research offer practice? In S. Lamb, M. R. Greenlick, and D. McCarty (Eds.), *Bridging the gap between practice and research: Forging partnerships with community-based drug and alcohol treatment* (pp. 147–185). Washington, DC: National Academy Press.

Miller, W. R., Brown, J. M., Simpson, T. L., Handmaker, N. S., Bien, T. H., Luckie, L. F., Montgomery, H. A., Hester, R. K., & Tonigan, J. S. (1995). What works: A methodological analysis of the alcohol treatment outcome literature. In R. K. Hester & W. R. Miller (Eds.), *Handbook of alcoholism treatment approaches: Effective alternatives* (pp. 12–44). Boston: Allyn & Bacon.

Miller, W. R., Genefield, G., & Tonigan, J. S. (1993). Enhancing motivation for change in problem drinking: A controlled comparison of two therapist styles. *Journal of Consulting and Clinical Psychology* 61, 455–461.

Miller, W. R., and Kurtz, E. (1994). Models of alcoholism used in treatment: Contrasting AA and other perspectives with which it is often confused. *Journal of Studies on Alcohol* 55, 159–166.

Miller, W. R., Leckman, L., Delaney, H. D., & Tinkcom, M. (1992). Long-term follow-up of behavioral self-control training. *Journal of Studies on Alcohol* 53, 249–261.

Miller, W. R., Meyers, R. J., & Tonigan, J. S. (1999). Engaging the unmotivated in treatment for alcohol problems: A comparison of three strategies for intervention through family members. *Journal of Consulting and Clinical Psychology* 67, 688–697.

Miller, W. R., & Rollnick, S. (1991). *Motivational interviewing.* New York: Guilford.

Miller, W. R., Taylor, C. A., & West, J. C. (1980). Focused versus broad-spectrum behavior therapy for problem drinkers. *Journal of Consulting and Clinical Psychology* 48, 590–601.

Miller, W. R., Walter, S. T., & Bennett, M. E. (2001). How effective is alcoholism treatment in the United States? *Journal of Studies on Alcohol* 62, 211–220.

Miller, W. R., Zweben, A., Di Clemente, C., & Rychtarik, R. G. (1995). *Motivational enhancement therapy manual.* National Institute on Alcohol Abuse and Alcoholism Project MATCH Monograph Series, Volume 2. Rockville, MD: National Institute of Health Publication 94-3723.

Monte, C. F. (1999). *Beneath the mask* (6th ed.). Fort Worth, TX: Harcourt Brace.

Monti, P. M., Rosenow, D. J., Colby, S. M., & Abrams, D. B. (1995). Smoking among alcoholics during and after treatment: Implications for models, treatment strategies, and policy. In J. B. Fertig and J. P. Allen (Eds.), *Alcohol and tobacco: From basic science to clinical practice* (National Institute on Alcohol and Alcoholism Research Monograph 30, pp. 187–206). Bethesda, MD: National Institutes of Health.

Moos, R. H., Finney, J. W., Ouimette, P. C., & Suchinsky, R. T. (1999). A comparative evaluation of substance abuse treatment: I. Treatment orientation, amount of care, and 1-year outcomes. *Alcoholism: Clinical and Experimental Research* 23, 529–536.

Morgenstern, J., Frey, R. M., McCrady, B. S., Labouvie, E., & Neighbors, C. J. (1996). Examining mediators of change in traditional chemical dependency treatment. *Journal of Studies on Alcohol* 57, 53–64.

Morgenstern, J., Labouvie, E., McCrady, B. S., Kahler, C. W., & Frey, R. M. (1997). Affiliation with Alcoholics Anonymous after treatment: A study of its therapeutic effects and mechanisms of action. *Journal of Consulting and Clinical Psychology* 65, 768–777.

Morgenstern, J., & McCrady, B. S. (1993). Cognitive processes and change in disease model treatment. In B. S. McCrady and W. R. Miller (Eds.), *Research on Alcoholics Anonymous* (pp. 153–164). New Brunswick, NJ: Rutgers.

Nowinski, J., Baker, S., & Carroll, K. (1995). *Twelve step facilitation therapy manual.* National Institute on Alcohol Abuse and Alcoholism Project MATCH Monograph Series, Volume 1. Rockville, MD: National Institute of Health Publication 94-3722.

Ojesjo, L. (1981). Long-term outcome in alcohol abuse and alcoholism among males in the Lundby general population, Sweden. *British Journal of Addiction* 76, 391–400.

Ouimette, P. C., Finney, J. W., Gima, K., & Moos, R. H. (1999a). A comparative evaluation of substance abuse treatment III. Examining mechanisms underlying patient-treatment matching hypotheses for 12-step and cognitive-behavioral treatments for substance abuse. *Alcoholism: Clinical and Experimental Research* 23, 545–551.

Ouimette, P. C., Finney, J. W., & Moos, R. H. (1997). Twelve-step and cognitive-behavioral treatment for substance abuse: A comparison of treatment effectiveness. *Journal of Consulting and Clinical Psychology* 65, 230–240.

Ouimette, P. C., Gima, K., Moos, R. H., & Finney, J. W. (1999b). A comparative evaluation of substance abuse treatment IV. The effect of comorbid psychiatric diagnoses on amount of treatment, continuing care, and 1-year outcomes. *Alcoholism: Clinical and Experimental Research* 23, 552–557.

Ouimette, P. C., Moos, R. H., & Finney, J. W. (1998). Influence of outpatient treatment and 12-step group involvement on one-year substance abuse treatment outcomes. *Journal of Studies on Alcohol* 59, 513–522.

Polich, J. M., Armor, D. J., & Braiker, H. B. (1981). *The course of alcoholism: Four years after treatment.* New York: Wiley.

Prochaska, J. O., Di Clemente, C. C., & Norcross, J. C. (1992). In search of how people change: Applications to addictive behaviors. *American Psychologist* 47, 1102–1114.

Project MATCH Research Group (1997). Matching alcoholism treatments to client heterogeneity: Project MATCH Posttreatment drinking outcomes. *Journal of Studies on Alcohol* 58, 7–29.

Project MATCH Research Group (1998). Matching alcoholism treatments to client heterogeneity: Project MATCH three-year drinking outcomes. *Alcoholism: Clinical and Experimental Research* 22, 1300–1311.

Ramsdell, P. S., & Ramsdell, E. R. (1993). Dual relationships: Client perceptions of the effect of client-counselor relationship on the therapeutic process. *Clinical Social Work Journal* 21, 195–212.

Rosenberg, H., & Davis, L. D. (1994). Acceptance of moderate drinking by alcohol treatment services in the United States. *Journal of Studies on Alcohol* 55, 167–172.

Sanchez-Craig, M. (1993). *Saying when: How to quit drinking or cut down.* Toronto: Addiction Research Foundation.

Sanchez-Craig, M., Annis, H. M., Bornet, A. R., & Macdonald, K. R. (1984). Random assignment to abstinence and controlled drinking: Evaluation of a cognitive-behavioral program for problem drinkers. *Journal of Consulting and Clinical Psychology* 52, 390–403.

Sanchez-Craig, M., Leigh, G., Spivak, K., & Lei, H. (1989). Superior outcome of females over males after brief treatment for the reduction of heavy drinking. *British Journal of Addiction* 84, 395–404.

Saxe, L., Dougherty, D., Esty, K., & Fine, M. (1983). The effectiveness and costs of alcoholism treatment. *Health Technology Case Study 22,* Office of Technology Assessment. Washington, DC: U.S. Government Printing Office.

Shiffman, S., & Balabanis, M. (1995). Associations between alcohol and tobacco. In J. B. Fertig and J. P. Allen (Eds.), *Alcohol and tobacco: From basic science to clinical practice* (National Institute on Alcohol and Alcoholism Research Monograph 30, pp. 17–36). Bethesda, MD: National Institutes of Health.

Skog, O., & Duckert, F. (1993). The development of alcoholics' and heavy drinkers' consumption: A longitudinal study. *Journal of Studies on Alcohol* 54, 178–188.

Sobell, M. B., & Sobell, L. C. (1993). *Problem drinkers: Guided self-change treatment.* New York: Guilford.

Sobell, M. B., Sobell, L. C., & Kozlowski, L. T. (1995). Dual recoveries from alcohol and smoking problems. In J. B. Fertig and J. P. Allen (Eds.), *Alcohol and tobacco: From basic science to clinical prac-*

tice (National Institute on Alcohol and Alcoholism Research Monograph 30, pp. 207–224). Bethesda, MD: National Institutes of Health.

Strupp, H. H., & Hadley, S. W. (1979). Specific versus nonspecific factors in psychotherapy: A controlled study of outcome. *Archives of General Psychiatry* 36, 1125–1136.

Taylor, C. T., Brown, D., Duckitt, A., Edwards, G., Oppenheimer, E. & Sheehan, M. (1985). Patterns of outcome: Drinking histories over ten years among a group of alcoholics. *British Journal of Addiction* 80, 45–50.

Taylor, J. R., Helzer, J. E., & Robins, L. N. (1986). Moderate drinking in ex-alcoholics: Recent studies. *Journal of Studies on Alcohol* 47, 115–121.

Timko, C., Finney, J. W., Moos, R. H., & Moos, B. S. (1995). Short-term treatment careers and outcomes of previously untreated alcoholics. *Journal of Studies on Alcohol* 56, 597–610.

Timko, C., Moos, R. H., Finney, J. W., & Lesar, M. D. (2000). Long-term outcomes of alcohol use disorders: Comparing untreated individuals with those in Alcoholics Anonymous and formal treatment. *Journal of Studies on Alcohol* 61, 529–540.

Tonigan, J. S., Miller, J. R., & Connors, G. J. (2000). Project MATCH client impressions about Alcoholics Anonymous: Measurement issues and relationship to treatment outcome. *Alcoholism Treatment Quarterly* 18, 25–41.

Tonigan, J. S., Toscova, R., & Miller, W. R. (1996). Meta-analysis of the literature on Alcoholics Anonymous: Sample and study characteristics moderate findings. *Journal of Studies on Alcohol* 57, 65–72.

U.S. Department of Health and Human Services (1988). *The health consequences of smoking. A report of the surgeon general.* Rockville, MD: U.S. Government Printing Office.

U.S. Department of Health and Human Services (2000). *Tenth Special Report to the U.S. Congress on alcohol and health.*

Vaillant, G. E. (1983). *The natural history of alcoholism.* Cambridge, MA: Harvard University Press.

Vaillant, G. E. (1995). *The natural history of alcoholism revisited.* Cambridge, MA: Harvard University Press.

Watson, C. G., Hancock, M., Gearhart, L. P., Mendey, C. M., Malovrah, P., & Raden, M. (1997). A comparative outcome study of frequent, moderate, occasional and nonattenders of Alcoholics Anonymous. *Journal of Clinical Psychology* 53, 209–214.

Welte, J. W., Lyons, J. P., and Sokolow, L. (1983). Relapse rates for former clients of alcoholism rehabilitation units who are drinking without symptoms. *Drug and Alcohol Dependence* 12, 25–29.

Winzelberg, A., & Humphreys, K. (1999). Should patients' religiosity influence clinicians' referral to 12-step self-help groups? Evidence from a study of 3,018 male substance abuse patients. *Journal of Consulting and Clinical Psychology* 67, 790–794.

CHAPTER TWELVE

SUMMARY AND RECOMMENDATIONS

Now that we have surveyed a large body of alcohol research, it is time to make an effort to put it in perspective. First, I will summarize the findings by chapter. Second, I will indicate content areas that are discussed in more than one chapter and summarize their combined findings. Third, I will make some recommendations for treatment, prevention, policy, and research that flow from the overall findings of the book. Fourth, I will discuss policy initiatives that have attempted to enhance the connection between alcohol research and clinical practice. Fifth, I will try to provide a broad perspective of future directions for alcohol and U.S. society. Finally, I will offer some suggestions to help clinicians and policy makers keep up with important alcohol research findings.

In the chapter, I will discuss:

1. Summary of findings by chapter
2. Linking the chapters that discuss the same content
3. Research implications for treatment, prevention, and policy
4. Efforts to bring research to practice
5. The big picture: Alcohol in U.S. society
6. How to keep up with alcohol research

SUMMARY OF FINDINGS BY CHAPTER

Chapter 1. How Do We Know about Alcohol and Alcoholism? Knowledge about Alcohol, Alcohol Problems, and Alcoholism

This chapter distinguishes between personal, professional, and research knowledge about alcohol. It provides the reader with an introduction to research methods.

Chapter 2. Measurement and Basic Concepts of Alcoholism Research

This chapter introduces basic alcohol concepts and measurement units, including diagnostic criteria for alcohol disorders and ways of measuring alcohol consumption.

Chapter 3. Alcohol and Its Effects on the Body

This chapter discusses the biologic and medical aspects of alcohol use. Current safe-drinking guidelines are detailed, along with the many difficulties that are caused by excessive use. Medical conditions that make even moderate drinking unsafe are discussed.

Chapter 4. Heredity and Alcohol

This chapter summarizes the considerable evidence that heredity plays a role in creating vulnerability to alcohol disorders or offering protection from them. We know that the Asian alcohol-flush reaction offers protection to Asians from alcohol disorders. A similar mechanism may operate for other ethnic groups. Possible underlying genetic mechanisms that may increase vulnerability to alcoholism include a lowered response to alcohol, special cognitive traits, and temperamental disposition. The Collaborative Study on the Genetics of Alcoholism is currently exploring the genetic factors that contribute to alcohol vulnerability, using the findings of the Human Genome Project.

Chapter 5. Statistics on Alcohol Use: Epidemiologic Research on Alcohol

This chapter summarizes a number of findings about drinking patterns and their consequences in large populations. It is estimated that the annual social cost of alcohol abuse is $148 billion and that over 100,000 Americans die of alcohol-related causes. It is estimated that 7.4 to 9.7 percent of adult Americans have alcohol use disorders. According to Epidemiological Catchment Area Survey (ECA) estimates, only 7.5 percent of those with an alcohol disorder receive treatment. Additionally, high percentages of adolescents and young adults habitually drink in dangerous quantities. Such drinking practices may not be indicative of an alcohol disorder but still warrant intervention because of potential alcohol-related problems such as DWI and violence.

Chapter 6. Longitudinal Studies on Alcohol: Alcohol and the Life Span

This chapter summarizes the important longitudinal studies on alcohol consumption patterns, the development of alcohol disorders, and the course of alcohol disorders. Results of these studies indicate that certain childhood factors appear to be implicated in higher risk for developing an alcohol problem. Problem behavior, poor adjustment and coping, aggressive and undercontrolled behavior in childhood and adolescence are linked to later alcohol problems. Children raised in families with conflict and poor parenting have an increased risk for developing alcohol problems later on. Many adolescents and young adults who are heavy drinkers will become moderate drinkers as they mature. Other adolescents who drank little as teens develop alcohol disorders later in life. Of course, a percentage of young heavy drinkers go on to develop alcohol disorders. Those with alcohol disorders often have unstable drinking patterns, having periods of controlled drinking, abstinence, and binges.

Chapter 7. Environmental Factors Affecting Alcohol Use: Cultural and Social Research Findings

This chapter discusses the large differences among countries in drinking practices, patterns, and even types of alcohol problems. Highlighted is the dichotomy between Northern European drinking practices, which are restrictive compared to Southern European drinking practices, which are more permissive. The chapter discusses government regulation of alcohol, which affects consumption, drinking patterns, and alcohol-related problems. In general, there are many effective government controls on alcohol sales and consumption, which have been shown to reduce alcohol-related problems.

Chapter 8. Alcohol, Emotion, Sex, and Aggression

This chapter explores the large body of experimental literature on alcohol's effects on behavior and emotion. At moderate doses for normal drinkers, alcohol has been found to promote positive emotions and suppress negative ones. For alcoholics, alcohol creates negative emotions. Experimental research in laboratory settings has consistently found that alcohol facilitates aggression. Alcohol has a variety of effects on sexual arousal and behavior. It negatively affects safe-sex practices. Additionally, there are strong stereotypes about drinkers' sexual behavior. Intoxicated men are viewed as less responsible and intoxicated women as more responsible for coercive sexual behavior than when abstinent.

Chapter 9. Alcohol, Violent Crime, Criminal Justice, and Substance Abuse Treatment

This chapter focuses on the alcohol–crime link and criminal justice substance abuse treatment programs. In about 50 percent of violent crimes, alcohol has been consumed by the perpetrator. Violence tends to be more severe when the assailant is intoxicated. Results from several surveys indicate that at least half of incarcerated offenders have an alcohol or drug abuse disorder. Only a small percentage of these offenders receive adequate treatment. Outcome research shows that the postprison therapeutic community (TC) is the most promising of the prison-related treatments. However, it is difficult to get offenders to enter these programs and remain until completion.

Drug courts and treatment alternatives to street crime (TASC) both offer treatment as an alternative to prison. Both programs show promise, but no substantial research has been conducted to evaluate them.

Chapter 10. Co-Occurring Alcohol Use and Mental Disorders: Epidemiology, Treatment, and Treatment Outcome

In this chapter, co-occurring mental and alcohol disorders are discussed. The rates of co-occurring disorders is at least 44 percent for men and 65 percent for women. Those with both disorders have poorer outcomes in conventional alcoholism treatment. Integrated treatment of both disorders has shown improved outcome in preliminary studies compared to conventional substance abuse treatment.

Chapter 11. Outcome Studies on Alcohol and Drug Abuse Treatment: From the Rand Report to the MATCH Study

Several large-scale outcome studies indicate that treatment for alcohol disorders is effective. No specific type of alcohol treatment has been found to be superior. Nor have studies found that matching patients to different treatments provides greatly improved outcomes. Participation in AA appears to be as effective as professional treatment for those who attend regularly. Remission rates of treated alcoholics are moderately higher than for those without treatment. The largest benefit of treatment is the increased outcome of stable abstinence, which occurs at about twice the rate as in untreated alcoholics.

OVERLAPPING CONTENT DISCUSSED IN DIFFERENT CHAPTERS

Because the book is organized by type of research, there is overlap in the content covered by some of the chapters. Major linkages between chapters are listed below.

Age Trends and Alcohol Consumption

Chapters 5 and 6 both discuss age trends and alcohol consumption. Initiation into drinking begins in the early teens; most of those who are going to drink do so by age 18. Data from epidemiologic and longitudinal studies show that younger drinkers, ages 18–29, drink more than other age groups, but their heavy drinking patterns tend not to be chronic. Middle-aged drinkers are less often heavy drinkers, but those who are tend to be more chronic. Older people abstain more often, drink less, and have lower rates of alcohol problems than younger age groups.

Difference in Drinking Practices among Ethnic Groups and Geographic Regions

Chapter 5 provides statistical information on the patterns of use of alcohol among groups, and Chapter 7 discusses differences in customs and regulations among groups. There are great differences in amounts of alcohol consumed and consumption patterns among different countries. Women's drinking patterns are more variable than men's as a function of nationality.

Government Policies of Alcohol Regulation

Chapter 7 discusses driving while intoxicated (DWI) regulation, minimum legal drinking age, limiting availability of alcohol, and server laws. Chapter 9 cites evidence that reduced availability of alcohol leads to reductions in crime.

Research on Controlled Drinking as a Goal for Problem Drinkers

Chapters 6 and 11 both include discussions on controlled drinking. Controlled drinking consistently occurs in about 10 percent of remitted alcoholics, whether they are treated or not. Special training in controlled drinking does not enhance this result. Abstinence is a more stable outcome than controlled drinking for alcohol-dependent individuals. There are no data on the stability of controlled drinking for alcohol abusers.

Epidemiologic Data

The methodology of epidemiology is discussed in Chapter 5. The Epidemiological Catchment Area Survey, the first important epidemiologic study on alcohol, is described in detail in Chapter 5. Chapters 9 and 10 draw on these data.

Risk Factors for Vulnerability to Alcohol Use Disorders

Genetic risk factors are detailed in Chapter 4. Childhood patterns, parenting practices, and social class factors that increase the risk of developing alcohol disorders are discussed in Chapter 6. Cultural risk factors are detailed in Chapter 7.

RESEARCH SUGGESTIONS FOR TREATMENT, PREVENTION, AND POLICY

Each of the content chapters makes recommendations for improved practices in treatment, prevention, and/or policy. This section integrates these recommendations.

Alcoholism Treatment Recommendations

Those applying for alcohol disorder treatment should be encouraged to obtain good medical care and follow-up (Chapter 3) and be screened for:

1. Prolonged withdrawal syndrome (cognitive impairment) (Chapter 3)
2. Trauma (Chapter 10)
3. Childhood sexual abuse (Chapter 10)
4. Violence potential (Chapter 9)
5. Domestic violence (Chapter 9)
6. Criminal justice involvement (Chapter 9)
7. Other psychiatric disorder (Chapter 10)
8. Substance abuse (Chapter 10)

Clients should be provided concurrent and modified treatment for:

1. Co-morbid psychiatric disorders (Chapter 10)
2. Posttraumatic stress disorder (Chapter 10)
3. Childhood sexual abuse (Chapter 10)
4. Violence (Chapter 9)

Treatment goals should be tailored to the alcohol diagnosis, other co-occurring disorders, and characteristics of the patient. Treatment goals include:

1. Controlled drinking (Chapters 6 and 11)
2. Abstinence (Chapters 6 and 11)
3. Harm reduction (Chapter 10)

Alcoholics Anonymous attendance is consistently associated with good outcomes. Therapists, regardless of orientation, should recommend that patients become acquainted with AA and encourage participation (Chapter 11).

Adjunct medications such as naltrexone and acamprosate show promise in reducing craving and relapse. Therapists should encourage patients to consider such medications (Chapter 3). Medications to treat co-occurring mental disorders should also be utilized (Chapter 10).

McLellan and McKay (1998) reviewed the research literature on addiction treatment and made recommendations for best practices for the treatment of addiction. Although there are some differences, by and large, their recommendations are similar to those listed here.

Treatment of Adolescent Alcohol Use Disorders

The majority of adolescents and young adults who engage in binge drinking develop safer drinking practices in adulthood. Hence intervention should be geared to attention to negative consequences of binge drinking rather than providing treatment for a chronic alcohol use disorder (Chapter 6).

For those adolescents with alcohol use disorders, research has found high rates of co-occurring psychiatric disorders (Chapter 10). This suggests that treatment for adolescent alcohol abusers should include treatment for the co-occurring disorder, rather than stand-alone alcoholism treatment, which is commonly provided for adults with alcohol disorders.

Recommendations for Mental Health Treatment

Mental health patients should be screened for alcohol and substance abuse disorders and provided treatment for these disorders concurrently (Chapter 10). Couples applying for couples counseling should be screened for alcohol disorders and provided alcoholism treatment if detected (Chapter 9).

Education of Mental Health Professionals
and Alcoholism Counselors

Training of Alcoholism Counselors.   Alcoholism counselors should receive some basic training about psychiatric disorders, because they are so common in addictive illness (Chapter 10). Training in screening for the areas described above should also be provided. Because no specific alcoholism treatment provides best overall results, additional training in common therapeutic factors might be most beneficial. Such skills include nurturing the therapeutic relationship, providing accurate empathy, and increased in-session interpersonal relatedness (Chapter 11).

Training of Mental Health Professionals.   As noted above, there are high rates of co-occurrence of mental disorders and substance abuse. Just as it makes sense for the alcoholism counselor to have some understanding of mental illness, mental health professionals should receive training in treating addictive illness (Chapter 10).

Proposed New Mental Health Professional.   Drake et al. (1993) suggest the creation of a new profession for treating those with co-morbid substance abuse and mental illness (Chapter 10).

Prevention

Research has implicated several childhood risk factors in the later development of alcohol use disorders. They include problem behavior, poor adjustment and coping, aggressive behavior, and attention deficit disorder in childhood and adolescence. Children raised in families with conflict and poor parenting have an increased risk for developing alcohol problems later on. Children with these risk factors can be targeted for prevention programs (Chapter 6). Competence enhancement approaches to alcohol and drug problem prevention show the most promise (Chapter 6). Drug and alcohol education should include discussion of alcohol's facilitating effects on aggression (Chapter 8) and violence (Chapter 9).

To reduce the incidence of birth defects, pregnant women should be provided information about the danger of drinking while pregnant (Chapter 3).

Most medical screening for alcohol problems is oriented toward identifying those with alcohol disorders. It is advisable to screen for dangerous drinking patterns as well (Chapter 3).

Policy

Most alcohol problems are not caused by alcoholics, but by individuals who engage in occasional dangerous drinking practices. Therefore, although treatment of alcohol disorders is important, education, prevention, and law enforcement must also play a role in reducing the negative impact of alcohol misuse. Research indicates that government regulation and enforcement of laws restricting alcohol availability and use have been effective. DWI, minimum legal drinking age, and zero-tolerance laws have reduced alcohol-related problems significantly (Chapter 7). All of these laws can be publicized and enforced more vigorously. Taxation and restrictions on the availability of alcohol have not been fully utilized in this country to reduce consumption. Research suggests that these might have a positive effect on reducing alcohol-related problems (Chapters 7 and 9).

Research Recommendations

This book has reviewed many research findings that have important implications for treatment and prevention. Still, there are many important alcohol-related issues that need to be researched more thoroughly.

Process Research of Alcoholism Treatment.   Great effort has been spent on determining outcome of alcohol treatment, but relatively little work has been done in specifying the processes that occur in treatment. What are the types and frequency of interventions made by counselors? Which types of interventions are the most helpful? How different are the interventions of counselors with different theoretical perspectives? For example, one interesting comparison would be the amount of self-disclosure used by Twelve Step facilitation (TSF) counselors compared to those counselors using cognitive behavioral therapy (CBT).

There are large differences of effectiveness among counselors, yet we know little about why these differences occur. Research to uncover these differences would allow us to determine what specific skills or personal characteristics in counselors enhance the outcome of alcoholism treatment.

Controlled Drinking and Alcohol Abuse.   There is sufficient documentation that alcohol dependence does not lend itself to controlled drinking as a goal, but more rigorous research on such a goal for alcohol abusers (as defined by DSM-IV-TR) would be valuable to help determine whether it is a responsible goal for them.

Research on Specialized Treatment of Alcohol and Substance Abuse.   Little research has been conducted on the outcome of adolescent alcohol and substance abuse treatment. Similarly, little research has been conducted for those suffering from frequently co-occurring alcohol and mental disorders, notably PTSD, childhood sexual abuse, and personality disorders.

Methodologically sound studies need to be conducted for testing the outcomes of alcoholism and substance abuse treatment for the severely mentally ill and those involved with the criminal justice system.

Research to Practice

Recently, attention has been given to the need to develop better sharing of information between researchers and clinicians in the alcoholism and substance abuse field. Sorensen and Midkiff (2000) state that formats need to be developed for efficient dissemination of information between practitioners and researchers. Three such initiatives are listed below.

Researcher in Residence Program.   Sponsored by the National Institute on Alcohol Abuse and Alcoholism and the Center for Substance Abuse Treatment, the Researcher in Residence program arranges brief technical assistance visits by researchers to help programs adopt research-based improvements in clinical practice. A preliminary study has been conducted in New York State, where several researchers spent 2–3 days at cooperating treatment facilities to discuss recent research findings in a specific area and its clinical implementation (Hilton, 2001). As might be expected, alcoholism counselors relied on personal and clinical experience more than on research findings to decide on best practice (see Chapter 1). It was found that existing treatment perspectives were impediments in implementing motivational interviewing but not in accepting naltrexone treatment. This program has the potential of improving the dialogue between researchers and clinicians.

Clinical Trials Network.   The National Institute on Drug Abuse (NIDA) has created the Clinical Trials Network, which will implement relationships between researchers and clinical substance abuse treatment programs to test new methods of treating addictions (Sorensen & Midkiff, 2000). This program will allow researchers to learn about the practical realities to which clinicians must respond, while providing an opportunity for clinicians to develop an understanding of research and its utility. Further information on this program is available at NIDA's web site, http://www.drugabuse.gov.

The Addiction Technology Transfer Center.   The Addiction Technology Transfer Center (ATTC) has been developed to promote the transmission of addiction research knowledge to treatment practitioners. The ATTC has developed several curricula and training manuals, which integrate research findings into substance abuse and alcoholism treatment practice. Three of their papers are referenced in Chapter 9.

Practice to Research

This book has focused on the research-to-practice side of the equation. Equally important is the practice-to-research side. Researchers need to find opportunities to engage in dialogue with practitioners to:

1. Determine treatment issues that need investigation
2. Utilize clinicians' insights, which can lead to important research projects
3. Collaborate with clinicians in conducting research, to help ensure that potential confounds are considered and to ensure that the research has practical utility

In Chapter 2, I suggested that research articles should include a discussion of clinical implications. Additionally, conferences of researchers and clinicians can be held to explore the practice implications for research in a specific area. The outcome of such conferences should lead to a consensus of various treatment practices.

THE BIG PICTURE: ALCOHOL IN U.S. SOCIETY

I offer some brief reflections that I hope will provide the reader with some perspective about the relationship between alcohol and U.S. society. How can we best accommodate to alcohol in our society?

Alcohol Education

If we follow the permissive Southern European model of alcohol consumption, learning to drink safely should be consciously adopted as a part of child rearing. Even if parents do not approve of drinking, they should take an active role in discussing the pros and cons of drinking with their children. Informal surveys of my college students suggests that the first drinking episode of many U.S. youth is conducted with peers and leads to high levels of intoxication. This appears to be an unnecessarily risky way to begin to learn about alcohol.

Prevention

Unsafe drinking is but one group of several behaviors that put people at risk for many potential problems. Other areas include drug abuse, unsafe sexual practices, poor health habits, and unsafe driving practices. It might be better to think of prevention in terms of including all of these problems and could be thought of as health/safety promotion.

Social and Legal Policy

Research suggests that restrictions on alcohol use and enforcement of laws regarding unsafe use curtail drinking-related accidents and crime. Advocacy groups such as Mothers Against Drunk Driving have helped elected officials enact legislation and enforce laws that reduce alcohol problems. Certain segments of the community will always be opposed to such restrictions based on personal convictions regarding alcohol and/or civil liberties. It is not easy for elected officials in a democracy to balance public health and safety issues with civil liberties. It is hoped, however, that the research presented here will at least provide useful information for the debate.

Treatment Integration

Traditionally in the United States, alcohol and substance abuse treatment has been separate from mental health treatment. Would it be better to integrate these treatments? Because of the high degree of co-morbidity in both populations, there is merit to the idea. Such a step would require that mental health professionals develop an understanding of addictive disorders, which is not currently provided in their professional schools.

Alcoholism/Substance Abuse Counselor

Scant attention has been given to the status and function of alcoholism/substance abuse counselors, despite their critical role in alcoholism and substance abuse treatment. When this status was created in the 1970s the ambiguous term *paraprofessional* was coined to describe their status (Staub & Kent, 1973). Is this simply a term for a "second-class" mental health worker? Should alcoholism counselors become professional mental health workers? There needs to be a systematic review to clarify ambiguities in their roles and functions. For example, should the training of alcoholism/substance abuse counselors be upgraded so that they gain an understanding of psychiatric disorders and research? Should these counselors be considered technicians or clinicians? That is, should they be taught to follow standard treatment protocols, or should they be trained to develop clinical skills as other mental health professionals are?

READINGS: KEEPING UP WITH RESEARCH FINDINGS

Books

There are many good books on alcohol research, many of which have been noted in earlier chapters. The following are excellent overviews of current alcohol knowledge and research:

Galanter, M. (Ed.) (Annual). *Recent developments in alcoholism.* New York: Plenum. An annual which reviews research areas in alcoholism.

Graham, A. W., & Schultz, T. K. (1998). *Principles of addiction medicine* (2nd ed.). Chevy Chase, MD: American Society of Addiction Medicine. This large volume is a comprehensive collection of chapters on all aspects of addiction research and treatment principles.

Special Reports to the U.S. Congress on alcohol and health. Every 3 years, the National Institute on Alcoholism and Alcohol Abuse (NIAAA) prepares this volume, which summarizes the current knowledge of the alcohol field. It is available from NIAAA, Publications Distribution Center, P.O. Box 10686, Rockville, MD 20849, for a modest price. It is also available online at the NIAAA web site, http://niaaa. nih.gov/index.htm.

Periodicals

A quick look at the references in this book reveals a broad array of professional journals and books that report research findings on alcoholism. It would be impossible to keep up with all of them. To save the reader from being overwhelmed, I recommend a modest number of resources, which provide a good overview of current alcohol research.

Alcohol Health and Research World. If you subscribe to any journal, I recommend this one. It is published quarterly by the NIAAA. Each issue focuses on a specific research topic. Often glossaries and explanations of basic concepts are included. To order, contact: Superintendent of Documents, P.O. Box 371954, Pittsburgh, PA 15250-7954. Recent issues are also available online at NIAAA's web site, listed below.

Science and Practice Perspectives. A new journal published by the National Institute on Drug Abuse will report new research findings with commentary by clinicians. The publication is free and may be ordered on line at its web site, listed below.

Alcohol Alert. This is an NIAAA quarterly bulletin that provides brief reviews of research findings on specific alcohol-related topics. It is available online at NIAAA's web site.

Counselor, the journal of the association of addiction professionals (NAADAC), devotes a section to abstracts of recent research findings and often highlights research findings in feature articles.

Clinician's Research Digest, published by the American Psychological Association, often abstracts research on addiction.

Databases

If there is a specific topic you wish to investigate, it is worthwhile to learn to use a database. You can select an area of interest and see abstracts of recent research. You can then go to the journal where the article is published. Some journals are now online, but you may have to go to a library to read the actual article. The two most useful databases in alcohol research are ETOH and Psychlit.

ETOH is accessible and free on the Internet at http://etoh.niaaa.nih.gov/.

Psychlit, the database of the American Psychological Association, is available through libraries or on the Internet if you are an APA member.

The Internet

The Internet has a great deal of information on alcohol. Not all of the information is reliable or valid, however. Two reliable government-sponsored sources are

NIAAA web site. The site provides research, clinical guidelines, and other valuable information (http://niaaa.nih.gov/index.htm).

National Institute on Drug Abuse web site. This site provides information about recent substance abuse research advances (http://www.drugabuse.gov).

REFERENCES

Drake, R. E., Bartels, S. J., Teague, G. B., Noordsy, D. L., & Clark, R. E. (1993). Treatment of substance abuse in severely mentally ill patients. *Journal of Nervous and Mental Disease* 181, 606–611.

Hilton, M. E. (2001). Researcher in residence program: Experiences from New York State. National Institute on Alcohol and Alcoholism Research. Unpublished paper.

McLellan, A. T., & McKay, J. R. (1998). The treatment of addiction: What can research offer practice? In S. Lamb, M. R. Greenlick, and D. McCarty (Eds.), *Bridging the gap between practice and research: Forging partnerships with community-based drug and alcohol treatment* (pp. 147–185). Washington, DC: National Academy Press.

Sorensen, J. L., & Midkiff, E. E. (2000). Bridging the gap between research and drug abuse treatment. *Journal of Psychoactive Drugs* 32, 379–382.

Staub, G. E., & Kent, L. M. (Eds.) (1973). *The para-professional in the treatment of alcoholism.* Springfield, IL: Thomas.

GLOSSARY

Acquired tolerance: The body's adaptation to habitual heavy drinking, which minimizes its impact.

Affective or mood disorders: Include depressive and bipolar disorders. See DSM-IV-TR for further details.

Alcohol withdrawal: Occurs with the sudden cessation of alcohol after prolonged heavy use.

Antabuse: A drug that prevents the breakdown of acetaldehyde, the first step in alcohol metabolism. Acetaldehyde is toxic and creates nausea, headache, and increased heart rate if not rapidly metabolized. It has been used for many years as an adjunct to treatment, by providing the alcoholic who takes it with an incentive not to drink.

Antiplacebo: An experimental condition in which the subject expects a placebo but receives the actual drug.

Anxiety disorders: Include panic disorder, phobia, posttraumatic stress disorder, and generalized anxiety disorder. See DSM-IV-TR for further details.

ARND (alcohol-related neurodevelopmental disorder):   A gestational disorder similar to fetal alcohol syndrome (FAS) but with less severe consequences to the offspring.

Attention deficit disorders: Disorders typically diagnosed in childhood or adolescence and characterized by impaired concentration. See DSM-IV-TR for further details.

Arrhythmia: A condition in which the heart has an irregular heartbeat.

Balanced placebo design: An experimental design that separates expectancy effects and pharmacologic effects by including an antiplacebo condition.

Bipolar disorder: A diagnostic category of DSM-IV-TR in which the individual has severe swings in mood, including elation and depression; formerly called manic depressive illness. See DSM-IV-TR for further details.

"Blind" interviews: The interviewer does not know any of the critical variables about the individuals he or she is interviewing.

Chain referral: A research sample obtained by asking the first participants if they know others who have overcome drinking problems on their own, who would participate in the study.

Cohort: The group of subjects followed in a longitudinal study.

Co-morbid disorders, co-occurring disorders, or dual diagnosis: Terms which indicate that an individual is suffering from an addictive disorder and a psychiatric illness.

Co-morbidity: Occurs when an individual is suffering from an addictive disorder and a psychiatric illness.

Concordance rate: The correlation between one twin having the trait under investigation and the other having it.

Conduct disorder: A disorder in children and adolescents relating to violating societal norms. See DSM-IV-TR for further details.

Confounding variable: An underlying factor that may account for the association between two variables.

Control group: A group of subjects who do not receive the hypothetical "cause" of the phenomenon in question. Those, for example, who receive the placebo rather than the active ingredient such as medication.

Correlation coefficient: A statistic that measures the degree to which two variables are linearly related. A positive correlation means that both events increase and decrease together. An inverse or negative correlation means that as one event increases, the other decreases.

Cross-tolerance: Refers to a process in which acquired tolerance is conferred to a drug by taking other drugs with similar effects.

Depressants: Psychoactive drugs that have the property of slowing down the central nervous system.

Disruptive behavior disorders: A category in DSM-IV-TR that includes attention-deficit hyperactivity disorder, conduct disorder, and oppositional defiant disorder. See DSM-IV-TR for further details.

Distillation: The process of separating combined liquids through use of evaporation and cooling.

Double-blind: An experimental design for testing the effectiveness of a treatment, in which neither the subject nor the person administering the treatment knows if the real or placebo treatment is being dispensed.

Dysthymia: A mood disorder that consists of moderate depressive symptoms. (See DSM-IV-TR for further details.)

Effect size: A statistical concept that estimates how much the dependent variable is changed by the independent variable.

Epidemiology: The study of how diseases spread. In alcohol research, the patterns of consumption and alcohol problems in different groups.

Expectancy: Refers to beliefs about the effects of alcohol.

Expectancy set: Refers to a laboratory manipulation (placebo condition) in which the subject expects to receive alcohol but does not. It is a measure of the effect of expecting alcohol on behavior.

Experiential expertise: What we learn to do from our personal experience.

Experiential knowledge: What we know from our personal experience.

Experimental group: The subjects who are exposed to the experimental treatment. For example, the subjects who receive alcohol rather than the placebo in a study testing the effect of alcohol on behavior.

FAS (fetal alcohol syndrome): A gestational disorder caused by maternal drinking during pregnancy. Resulting offspring have symptoms including stunted growth and mental retardation.

Fermentation: A process whereby yeast metabolizes sugar and creates alcohol and carbon dioxide. This is the process that creates beer and wine.

Genome: The entire genetic makeup of a life form.

Hypothesis: A prediction based on a theory.

Impaired control: Some drinkers are not able to confidently limit their alcohol intake. This is called impaired control.

Intensive case management: Necessary when patients cannot take responsibility for day-to-day needs such as hygiene and ensuring safety for themselves. A professional case manager supervises, guides, and ensures that these basic functions are provided.

Lifetime/annual prevalence: The percentage of the population that has a disorder either ever or in the past year.

Longitudinal studies: Follow specific subjects for long periods of time. Chapter 6 is devoted to longitudinal studies.

Markers: Traits that are connected to an underlying genetic process.

Meta-analysis: A statistical method that combines the results of several studies to generate a statistical appraisal of the combined studies.

Mood disorder: A diagnostic category in DSM-IV-TR that includes dysthymia and bipolar disorder. See DSM-IV-TR for further details.

Mortality: Frequency of number of deaths in proportion to a population: death rate (Morris, 1978).

Neurotransmitter: A chemical substance that carries an electrical impulse from one neuron to another.

Null hypothesis: A prediction that the relationship between the independent and dependent variable takes a specific value (usually zero, indicating that only chance is operating).

***p* level:** An abbreviation for probability level. It is a measure of the confidence that we have in rejecting the null hypothesis and accepting the predicted outcome.

Per capita: Per person. From Latin, meaning per head.

Perseveration: A constant repetition of responses, long after they are appropriate.

Personality disorders: A diagnostic category in DSM-IV-TR that includes antisocial personality disorder and borderline personality disorder. These are long-standing disorders marked by an enduring pattern of inner experience and behavior that deviates markedly from the expectations of the individual's culture and is manifested by disturbances in cognition, affectivity, interpersonal functioning, or impulse control. See DSM-IV-TR for further details.

Placebo: An inert substance that is made to resemble the active ingredient being tested for effectiveness in an experiment.

Placebo effect: The degree of relief that can be attributed to the subject's expectation of hope.

Polygenic: More than one gene pair is involved in controlling the trait under investigation.

Potentiation: Occurs when two drugs combine and the psychoactive effect is greater than the sum of the two different doses of the separate drugs.

Prolonged withdrawal syndrome or postacute withdrawal: Refers to symptoms related to alcohol withdrawal after the 5- to 7-day initial period of withdrawal. Symptoms include cognitive impairments, insomnia, and depression. Most of the symptoms remit within several weeks of abstinence.

Psychoactive: Refers to those drugs that affect acute brain activity. Such drugs often make a person "high" or intoxicated.

Psychotic disorder: A severe mental disorder characterized by delusions, hallucinations, and/or disorganized speech. See DSM-IV-TR for further details.

Relapse: A resumption of problematic drinking after a period of remission.

Reliability: Freedom of measurements from random error. For example, the degree to which subjects show the same scores on tests that measure their alcohol use.

Remission: The condition when a disease process is not active. For example, alcohol abuse in remission means the person does not currently meet the criteria for alcohol abuse.

Schizophrenia: A severe mental disorder characterized by a severe thought disorder. See DSM-IV-TR for further details.

Self-efficacy: Refers to the felt ability to overcome a problem. A person with high self-efficacy will have more confidence about succeeding in overcoming his or her drinking problem than a person with low self-efficacy.

Single-blind: An experimental design for testing the effectiveness of a treatment, in which the subject does not know if he or she is receiving the real or placebo treatment.

Standard drink: Equals 0.5 oz of pure alcohol.

Threshold: The level at which a phenomenon occurs. In this book, the threshold means that consumption of alcohol above amounts that are likely to induce disease.

Trauma: An experienced event that is perceived as actually or threatening serious injury to oneself or others. See DSM-IV-TR for further details.

Treatment outcome expectation fallacy: The common belief that alcoholism treatment should be able to provide stable long-term remission for most alcoholics. It is my view that this is currently unrealistic given the modest tools we have to treat this disorder.

Validity: The degree to which the obtained result is accurate. For example, the accuracy of self-reports of alcohol use.

Variables: Measurable components of interest in research. The independent variable is the component that is the hypothetical factor influencing the phenomenon under investigation. For example, alcohol is an independent variable that may influence how much aggression is expressed. The outcome variable, or dependent variable, is the variable that is changed by the independent variable. In the example, it would be how much aggression is expressed.

REFERENCE

Morris, W. (Ed.) (1978). *American heritage dictionary.* Boston: Houghton Mifflin.